2002

THE RUSTED HAUBERK

UNIVERSITY PRESS OF FLORIDA

Gainesville Tallahassee Tampa Boca Raton Pensacola Orlando Miami Jacksonville

The

RUSTED

HAUBERK

Feudal Ideals of Order
and Their Decline

EDITED BY LIAM O. PURDON
AND CINDY L. VITTO

Copyright 1994 by the Board of Regents of the State of Florida
Printed in the United States of America on acid-free paper
All rights reserved

99 98 97 96 95 94 6 5 4 3 2 1

Library of Congress Cataloging-in-Publication Data

The Rusted hauberk: feudal ideals of order and their decline / edited
by Liam O. Purdon and Cindy L. Vitto.
p.   cm.
Includes bibliographical references and index.
ISBN 0-8130-1281-3 (cloth).—ISBN 0-8130-1282-1 (pbk.)
1. Literature, Medieval—History and criticism.   2. Feudalism in
literature.   3. Literature and society.   I. Purdon, Liam O.
II. Vitto, Cindy L.
PN671.R87   1994
809'.02—dc20   93-45369

The University Press of Florida is the scholarly publishing
agency for the State University System of Florida, comprised of
Florida A & M University, Florida Atlantic University, Florida
International University, Florida State University, University of
Central Florida, University of Florida, University of North
Florida, University of South Florida, and University of West
Florida.

University Press of Florida
15 Northwest 15th Street
Gainesville, FL 32611

To Marie, the Rogers, Nancy, and Dianne,
whose Steinway she loves

CONTENTS

ABBREVIATIONS

ABR	*American Benedictine Review*
AHR	*American Historical Review*
ChauR	*Chaucer Review*
EETS	Early English Text Society
ELN	*English Language Notes*
ELH	*English Literary History*
ELR	*English Literary Renaissance*
EC	*Essays in Criticism*
JEGP	*Journal of English and Germanic Philology*
JIH	*Journal of Interdisciplinary History*
MS	*Medieval Studies*
MLR	*Modern Language Review*
NLH	*New Literary History*
PLL	*Papers on Language and Literature*
PMLA	*Publications of the Modern Language Association*
RPol	*Review of Politics*
SAC	*Studies in the Age of Chaucer*
SAQ	*South Atlantic Quarterly*
SMC	*Studies in Medieval Culture*
SP	*Studies in Philology*
STC	Short-Title Catalogue
UTQ	*University of Toronto Quarterly*

ACKNOWLEDGMENTS

IT IS DIFFICULT to know where to begin acknowledging those who have directly or indirectly helped conceive, execute, and complete the following essay collection. We would be remiss if we did not express our gratefulness, first, to the other contributors without whose scholarly work, good humor, and patience the following pages would not have been possible. Nor should we neglect the National Endowment for the Humanities in these opening remarks, for the Endowment's sponsoring of the 1986 Summer Seminar on medieval European feudalism not only brought scholars of literature and history together but also provided the inspiration and direction for this interdisciplinary essay collection. A special debt of gratitude is owed to all the members of that seminar; to the seminar's organizer and leader, Thomas N. Bisson, whose learning, good will, and patience were an inspiration to all; and to Otto Gründler, director of the Medieval Institute, whose inclusion of two special sessions devoted to the subject of feudal ideals and realities in the Twenty-Fourth International Congress on Medieval Studies program provided the opportunity for further interdisciplinary investigation and discussion of the subject matter covered here.

No less deserving of gratitude for their helpfulness in a variety of ways too numerous to enumerate are Jane Chance, Bill Pollard, Donald Ziegler, Michel Arthur, Evelyne Shellard, Alexander Bell Hay Allen, Claude Jones, James Sanderson, Paul Wadkovsky, Alan Webster, Janet Harriman, Brian Olphi, Sandra Kouguell, Dasha Jitkoff, Elizabeth Jergens, Jacqueline Astor, Malcolm King, Kimon Caperneros, Minna Doskow, Nathan Carb, Bob Vitto, Ken and Marion Ferguson, George Romeo, Karen Heiser, Kathy Sand, Kathy Leishman, and Sue Schwenk. A final special thank you is offered to Walda Metcalf for her patience and singular kindness.

INTRODUCTION

WHEN THE KNIGHT of the Middle Ages rode into battle, he protected the central portion of his body by donning a hauberk. Carl Stephenson describes the hauberk as "a shirt of mail that was constructed by sewing metal scales on a leather foundation or—the much more expensive process—by welding iron links to form a continuous fabric." Stephenson goes on to explain that the hauberk reached to the knee, with slashes to allow for horseback riding, and included elbow-length sleeves and a hood.[1]

According to Ramon Lull's influential treatise on knighthood, *The Book on the Order of Chivalry,* the hauberk could be even more important as metaphor than as physical protection:

> The hauberk signifies a castle and fortress against vices and faults. Just as a castle and fortress are closed all about, likewise a hauberk is strong and closed on all sides, signifying to a noble knight that he in his spirit ought not to enter into treason or any other vice.[2]

The hauberk, like the feudal system itself, is here described as a closed system, impermeable provided that the various links in the chain do not give way. The sublunary world being what it is, however, no ideal system can remain intact, if indeed its ideality ever physically existed. Just as the hauberk was susceptible to rust, so the feudal system was inevitably subject to change.

Although both the hauberk and the feudal system have become obsolete, the age they represent, even as it slipped into an irretrievable past, impressed itself indelibly on the Western imagination. The feudal ideal of order—whatever romantic images that phrase may evoke in the modern consciousness—may never have existed, but its perceived passing has been mourned for centuries, beginning in the Middle Ages.

The essays collected in this volume examine various aspects of the rusting of the hauberk, or the decline of that feudal ideal. Traditionally, historians have documented the reality of feudal custom and practice, while literary scholars have concerned themselves with artistic representations of feudal ideals. Recently, though, with the growth of "critical historicism,"[3] a small but increasing number of studies have attempted to bridge the gap—that is, to explore the relations between the expressed ideals of the feudal age and actual custom and practice. One aim of critical historicism is to perceive that history, too, is a cultural construct, another "text." Placing historical data alongside the "literary," we become aware of the ways in which the two complement, influence, and contradict each other. In other words, our approach changes from that of "objectivist scholarship" to an approach that "recognizes the historical consequences of much of our subject."[4]

Realizing that from our vantage point we shall never be able to recapture the past accurately, what we *can* hope to do is to analyze the ways in which a particular culture represented its reality to itself. As Jean E. Howard explains, "Rather than erasing the problem of textuality, one must enlarge it in order to see that *both* social and literary texts are opaque, self-divided, and porous, that is, open to the mutual intertextual influences of one another. . . . In short, instead of a hierarchical relationship in which literature figures as the parasitic reflector of historical fact, one imagines a complex textualized universe in which literature participates in historical processes and in the political management of reality."[5]

Such a perspective is especially important in medieval studies, where the high-minded ideals of the time are too often accepted without question by scholars and romanticized by the general public. For example, scholars of medieval literature and history continue to include and analyze chivalric codes or codes of love propounded by writers like Ramon Lull and Andreas Capellanus without taking into account the fact that these codes were hardly applicable to everyday medieval life.

Collectively, the essays in this volume explore the interactions between literature and social reality, each one focusing upon some aspect of the feudal ideal of order. The result is a rich interplay of insights into the depiction of feudal ideals and discrepancies between expressed ideals and documented evidence. Before proceeding further, however, perhaps a definition is in order. Exactly what is meant by that elusive term *feudalism*, and what do we know about feudal ideals of order? The word *feudal* was first used in the seventeenth century, in a pejorative sense, "applied to almost any privilege or custom that seemed unfair or ridiculous."[6] Philologically, though, the word seems to have derived from a Germanic word for *cattle*, the only important trade commodity at the dawn of the Middle Ages.[7] (Note, by way of comparison, the similarity between the English words *cattle* and *chattel*.) The West Frankish court adopted the word, turning it into *fie* or *fief*, which took on wider meanings: arms, clothing, horses, food, land—in brief, all things necessary to support a warrior.[8] *Fief* then became *feudum* in Latin.[9]

Like the word, the institutions of feudalism originated in Frankish territory. Charles Martel (689?–741), grandfather of Charlemagne, found himself short of cash but in need of a reliable military force. He combined two traditions, the benefice system of the Frankish church, which granted land for a fixed term in return for services, and the old tradition of Frankish kings having a band of chosen men sworn to them by special oaths.[10] (The comitatus had been remarked upon by Tacitus in his *Germania*, as early as the second century.)[11] As the Carolingian system of government declined in the ninth and tenth centuries, the feudal system—the voluntary relationship between lord and vassal—remained strong. In the East Frankish kingdom, strong kings maintained their power over the system; in the West Frankish kingdom, strong lords overpowered the monarch and wrought anarchy by exercising political muscle within their feudal dominions.[12] Yet France never came completely under the sway of the feudal system; some land remained allodial, or independently owned.

By contrast, William the Conqueror's invasion of England and his production of the *Domesday Book* ensured that England would become a complete, closed feudal system. The West Frankish pattern, the struggle for power between monarchs and lords, prevailed in England, with the balance of power largely decided by the leadership abilities of the monarch. We should not forget that Magna Carta is a direct result of the political realities of feudalism.

One difficulty in defining the term is that scholars have tended to use *feudalism* interchangeably with words for related concepts, such as *chivalry* or *manorialism*.[13] Indeed, even our choice of title, *The Rusted Hauberk*, is problematic in this respect; using the hauberk as metaphor risks a false perception that our subject will be restricted to the male-centered chivalric ideal of knighthood. For the purposes of this book, we would distinguish chivalry as a code of honor and ethics applicable primarily to knights and other nobles (almost exclusively male) as they perform on the battlefield or in courtly halls.[14] Chivalry emphasizes individual rather than social behavior. Feudalism, on the other hand, is a social construct that in some way embraces all individuals within its confines. Based in a socioeconomic and political system, feudalism constitutes a pattern for ordering society as a whole and, concomitantly, a pattern for ordering the relationships of individuals within that society. The right actions of individuals (male and female, of all classes) are necessary to maintain the system; however, it is the system itself that commands our attention, for its breakdown would result in social havoc.

Acknowledging the philological and historical origins of feudalism, together with the need to distinguish feudalism from chivalry, we have yet to approach the essence of the term. What we have so far is a stark description, void of power. For at its height (or, at least, at its remembered height), feudalism engaged men and women completely—not just their social status or economic survival, but their political finesse, their ethical sense, their religious obligation. Living within a feudal structure meant knowing where one belonged and where one's duties lay. In addition, the entire system accorded with the concept of universal order decreed by God. As he was master over all, making his claim on each soul and demanding certain obeisances, so feudal lords had the right to regulate their own kingdoms. And as the ceremony of the Mass exercised a sort of mystical power over the beholders, so the ritual of homage and fealty took on a quasi-religious significance. Thus feudalism is a difficult concept to pin down precisely because it infused so many areas of medieval life, often at deep psychological levels.

How can we account for this all-pervasive nature of the feudal concept? The essays collected here help by providing a core definition, one that seems to extend through the various cultures and the various centuries of the Western Middle Ages. Most of our authors agree that the essential characteristic of feudalism and feudal order is loyalty, in the sense of a personal and mutual obligation between inferior and superior, or vassal and lord. If we grasp this concept of loyalty as the basic expression of the feudal ideal of order, we go far toward understanding the power of that ideal as a master trope of the Middle Ages, congruent with at least two other generally acknowledged conceptual frameworks of the time: the notion of hierarchical order and the idea of "word as bond."[15]

All three concepts—loyalty, hierarchy, and the importance of oath keeping—are evident in the public rite of vassalage, so familiar to those who participated in it that they have left us few detailed descriptions of the ritual and no symbolic interpretations of it. The rite of vassalage, the cornerstone of the feudal system, consisted primarily of three ceremonies: the act of homage (including the enclosure of the vassal's hands by those of his lord and the exchange of a kiss), the oath of fealty, and the investiture of the fief. These three rites emphasize, respectively, the symbolic significance of gesture, speech, and object.[16] The account of the ceremony of April 1127, in which Count William Clito received the vassals of his predecessor, includes all three aspects:

First they did homage [*hominium*] in this way. The count asked each one if he wished without reserve to become his man [*homo suus*], and he replied 'I wish it,' and with hands clasped and enclosed by the hands of the count, they were bound together by a kiss. Secondly, he who had done homage pledged his faith [to the count] in these words: 'I promise by my faith that from this time forward I will be faithful to Count William and will maintain my homage to him entirely against every person, in good faith and without deception.' Thirdly he swore this on the relics of saints. Then, with a wand which he held in his hand, the count gave investiture [*investituram*] to all those who in this compact had promised fealty and done homage and taken an oath.[17]

The public nature of these acts, the reciprocal responsibilities entered into, and the general exclusion of women and lower-class males from full participation in the ceremony indicate that, at its highest and most powerful level, feudalism was an aristocratic pact of loyalty designed to promote social order. Simultaneously, the rite contained elements of Christian symbolism, marking the sanctity of the action: the "mingling of hands" (*immixtio manuum*) in the way that became the normal posture for prayer, and the usual practice of sealing the oath of fealty by swearing on a sacred object. At the completion of the ceremony, both lord and vassal were reciprocally bound in love and duty to one another, to the benefit of peace and social order.

Reality, though, rarely matches the ideal. As several of the following essays demonstrate, conflicting loyalties challenged the system, forcing vassals to fight against their lesser lords in order to fulfill their duty to a liege lord. In addition, both lords and vassals were quite capable of treacherous acts that annulled the loyalty they had sworn to, even if the parties involved did not officially renounce their bond.[18]

Another threat to the feudal ideal came from classes not directly involved in the benefits offered by that ideal. In theory, medieval society was composed of three estates—clergy, knights, and peasants—each expected to fulfill its ordained duties in order to maintain the feudal structure. But as monarchs and nobles jostled for power, so too did clergy, peasants, even women, despite the fact that the feudal ideal for these groups consisted of obedience to those above them. Clergy owed obedience to God and were to remember that property and other worldly goods were unimportant; in practice, however, many monasteries possessed great wealth and wielded political power rivaling that of the aristocracy. Peasants were to work the land so that the other estates could carry on their duties. In England, the Peasants' Revolt of 1381 shocked nobles, who saw the rebellion as an unimaginable breach of the social structure. Finally, women were to swear a chaste submission to God or to husband, depending on their vocation as religious or wife. Yet the outcry against corrupt nuns and the literature devoted to instructing wives indicate difficulties in keeping women within the boundaries prescribed for them by the feudal model.

Thus the feudal ideal of order, with its emphasis on loyalty *within a hierarchy*, primarily benefited those at the top, providing them with a rationale for keeping others subordinate. Theoretically, this arrangement allowed all three estates to work together harmoniously and interdependently. In practice, continual struggles for status, wealth, and power challenged the ideal.

Typically, historians have characterized the decline of the feudal ideal as the movement toward cash payments rather than personal service.[19] Thus feudal lords eventually found it more convenient to hire retainers; vassals found it easier to offer payment than military service. (The ceremony of homage was gradually modified as well, with the kiss omitted.)[20] The conventional term for this new system, "bastard feudalism," signals the historians' perception of decline, even moral decay. The present volume investigates this decline of feudal ideals of order from more than the economic perspective, measuring the ways in which the voiced ideals of truth, honor, loyalty, and courage (often summed up in the useful word "worship," ubiquitous in the Arthurian tales) do not measure up to historical realities. This perception is not new; those living in the feudal age were themselves acutely aware of the discrepancy between ideal and real, practically from the inception of the feudal system. Arthur B. Ferguson has observed that "the ability to separate the ideal from the actual is a basic characteristic of the mind of the period, and one that has failed to receive from the student of intellectual history the attention it deserves."[21]

This discrepancy between the ideal and the actual is responsible for the ongoing debate about the validity and vitality of feudalism. As John Schwetman indicates in his contribution to our volume, Johan Huizinga's monumental work *The Waning of the Middle Ages* established the theory that, by the later Middle Ages, chivalric ideals had declined;[22] only recently have scholars disputed this view to suggest that those ideals may always have existed more in theory than in practice. Thomas S. Kuhn's *The Structure of Scientific Revolutions* may help us to understand the difficulty if we remember Kuhn's assertion that initial breakdowns of a system usually result in concerted efforts to validate the traditional paradigm. Only later, after considerable struggle, will a new paradigm take the place of its predecessor.[23]

The purpose of this volume is to reexamine feudal paradigms of order in an effort to perceive and evaluate the gap that always existed between ideal and real, between theory and practice. The attention of contemporary authors to feudal ideals indicates the effort to hold onto the system even as it was perceived to be deteriorating. Rather than concentrating on historical evidence for a decline in feudal ideals of order, we document primarily the decline as perceived by authors of various lands and times under the sway of feudal custom and practice.

The essays that follow indicate the far-reaching power of feudal ideals in another sense as well: far from being restricted to the aristocrats who participated in the rite of vassalage, the paradigm influenced all members of society to some degree.

Although each of the following essays can profitably be read singly, it is our belief that as a whole they make a powerful "textualized" statement about the ambiguous nature, but the undeniable attraction, of feudal ideals of order. In the brief commentary that precedes each section, we endeavor to highlight the special contribution of each essay and its relation to this overall theme. We have, of course, merely teased the surface of this topic, but we hope that our volume will inspire others to continue the work begun here.

Notes

1. Carl Stephenson, *Mediaeval Feudalism* (Ithaca, N.Y.: Cornell University Press, 1942), 62. See also Marc Bloch, *Feudal Society*, 2 vols., trans. L. A. Manyon (Chicago: University of Chicago Press, 1961), 1:291, and Philippe Contamine, *War in the Middle Ages*, trans. Michael Jones (London: Basil Blackwell, 1984), 175–92.

2. This modern translation of Ramon Lull's *The Book on the Order of Chivalry* is taken from *The History of Feudalism*, ed. David Herlihy (New York: Harper & Row, 1970), 330.

3. Howard Horwitz, in "'I Can't Remember': Skepticism, Sympathetic Histories, Critical Action," *SAQ* 87 (1988):790, proposes "critical historicism" as a more inclusive term to replace "New Historicism."

4. For an explanation of Lee Patterson's approach, see *Negotiating the Past: The Historical Understanding of Medieval Literature* (Madison: University of Wisconsin Press, 1987), especially the first two chapters, and the introduction to *Literary Practice and Social Change in Britain, 1380–1530* (Berkeley & Los Angeles: University of California Press, 1990).

5. "The New Historicism in Renaissance Studies," *ELR* 16 (1986):25.

6. *Dictionary of the Middle Ages*, ed. Joseph R. Strayer, 13 vols. (New York: Charles Scribner's Sons, 1982–89), 5:52.

7. For another derivation of the word, see Bloch, *Feudal Society*, 1:xviii–xx, 2:441–42; and F. L. Ganshof, *Feudalism*, trans. Philip Grierson (London: Longmans, 1952), xv–xviii.

8. Bloch, *Feudal Society*, 1:163–75; Ganshof, *Feudalism*, 96–134.

9. Sidney Painter, "Feudalism and Western Civilization," in *Feudalism and Liberty: Articles and Addresses of Sidney Painter*, ed. Fred A. Cazel, Jr. (Baltimore, Md.: Johns Hopkins University Press, 1961), 2.

10. Painter, "Feudalism and Western Civilization," 3.

11. See Stephenson, *Medieval Feudalism*, 2–4, for a discussion of the comitatus.

12. Painter, "Feudalism and Western Civilization," 4–5.

13. See Lois Roney, chapter 11, for a discussion of the distinctions among *feudalism, chivalry,* and *manorialism.* The intellectual construct of *feudalism* itself has also recently been the subject of debate. See Elizabeth A. R. Brown, "The Tyranny of a Construct: Feudalism and Historians of Medieval Europe," *AHR* 79 (1974):1063–88, and Thomas N. Bisson, "The Problem of Feudal Monarchy: Aragon, Catalonia, and France," *Speculum* 53 (1978):1160–78.

14. See Bloch, *Feudal Society,* 2:312–19; Maurice Keen, *Chivalry* (New Haven & London: Yale University Press, 1984), 8–17; and Johan Huizinga, *The Waning of the Middle Ages: A Study of the Forms of Life, Thought, and Art in France and the Netherlands in the XIVth and XVth Centuries* (1924; New York: Doubleday Anchor, 1954), 67–77.

15. See D. W. Robertson, Jr., *A Preface to Chaucer* (Princeton, N.J.: Princeton University Press, 1962), for an explanation of the pervasive influence of the hierarchal model in medieval thought. For other related discussions of order, see Bloch, *Feudal Society,* 1:145–62, 219–30; Ganshof, *Feudalism,* 63–95; and Huizinga, *Waning of the Middle Ages,* 56–67. J. Douglas Canfield's *Word as Bond in English Literature from the Middle Ages to the Restoration* (Philadelphia: University of Pennsylvania Press, 1989) remarks on the importance of fulfilling one's oaths as a trope extending throughout much of Western literature.

16. See Jacques Le Goff, "The Symbolic Ritual of Vassalage," in *Time, Work, and Culture in the Middle Ages,* trans. Arthur Goldhammer (Chicago & London: University of Chicago Press, 1980),237–87. Le Goff speculates that the act of homage established an inequality between the two principals, but that the kiss accompanying the oath of fealty made the participants equal. The investiture then becomes a contract entered into by two equals. Le Goff also contends that women did not ordinarily participate in the kiss because, from a social and religious point of view, they could not be made equals.

17. Galbert of Bruges, *The Murder of Charles the Good,* trans. and ed. James Bruce Ross (Toronto: University of Toronto Press, 1982), 206–7.

18. In chapter 8, Karen S. Nicholas discusses *diffidatio* and *exfestucatio,* or the breaking of the feudal bond. For a technical discussion of the act of renunciation, see also Bloch, *Feudal Society,* 1:211–18, and "Les formes de la rupture de l'hommage dans l'ancien droit féodal," in *Mélanges historiques,* 2 vols. (Paris: S.E.V.P.E.N., 1963), 1:189–209.

19. For further discussion of reasons leading to the decline of the feudal ideal, see Rodney Hilton, *Class Conflict and the Crisis of Feudalism,* 2d rev. ed. (London & New York: Verso, 1990), 166–72.

20. See J. Russell Major, "'Bastard Feudalism' and the Kiss: Changing Social Mores in Late Medieval and Early Modern France," *JIH* 17 (1987):509–35. Major argues that the change in ceremony was due to a change in social mores rather than a decline in expected loyalty.

21. *The Indian Summer of English Chivalry: Studies in the Decline and Transformation of Chivalric Idealism* (New York: AMS Press, 1984), 26–27.

22. 93–107.

23. 2d ed. (Chicago: University of Chicago Press, 1970), 86–87.

PART I

Resisting Dissolution

Validating Feudal Ideals of Order

THE TWO ESSAYS in this part of the collection, studies dealing with late medieval literary works, consider the social, political, and linguistic dimensions of the feudal ideal of order as a system of relationships within a hierarchal society. The system in each case is examined as the only perceived practical means of containing the dissolution of a culture that formerly was stabilized by feudal custom and practice. Accordingly, both essays suggest that the traditional feudal paradigm of order, though now advocated as a radical corrective, was in fact never inviolable.

Cindy L. Vitto's "Feudal Relations and Reason in *Cleanness*" considers the sociopolitical dimensions of the feudal ideal of order, arguing that feudal reciprocity—that is, the mutual obligation between lord and vassal—is presented in the poem as the principal relationship that must be used to order and stabilize society. She arrives at this conclusion by demonstrating that the *Pearl*-Poet combines the concepts of heavenly and earthly order in *Cleanness* through the imagery of feudal custom and practice, with God serving as the head of the hierarchy and providing an ideal for those below to imitate. Ruled by reason, Noah, for example, obeys his Lord instantly and receives, as the result of vassal-like obedience, a promise in "cortays wordez" that no further destruction will follow. Abraham, who deferentially acknowledges God and "Sire," demonstrates his likeness to God by playing the part of courteous host and thus appears as chief servant in a noble hall. Lot's reason enables him to be a worthy vassal who knows how to speak fairly and offer pleasing food. Nebuchadnezzar, who disrupts the notion of a vassal-like obligation by challenging both heavenly and earthly order, eventually acknowledges the need for a kind of vassalic reciprocity and thereby shows that God may allow for the challenge of power but will not tolerate the disregard of feudal relations and the renunciation of feudal obligation through irrationality. Belshazzar, the final exemplar, rejects feudal order based upon reciprocity and governs by caprice.

Complementing these examples of proper or improper vassal-like obligation is the *Pearl*-Poet's image of the household as microcosm of the ideal of social and political order. In the Wedding Feast parable, the household is described as being perfectly ordered in feudal terms. As the focus of attention turns from this feudal ideal to the households of each historical figure in the poem, the deterioration of the feudal principles of order and behavior becomes more apparent and pronounced. This progressive deterioration reaches its culmination in Belshazzar's court, where no feudal rules order society. Indeed, the absence of any order lends an apocalyptic urgency to the description of misrule apparent in Babylon. In this way, the poem's paradigm of feudal obligation functions as a measuring stick for the worsening condition of society and humanity.

Daniel F. Pigg's "Imagining Feudalism in *Piers Plowman*: Attempts to Restore Order" further examines the feudal ideal of relationship based on reciprocity and cooperation as an essential sociopolitical ordering principle. According to Pigg, Langland's imagining of and theorizing about a social model of authority—the ternary model vitalized by feudal custom and practice—is an attempt to reassert stability within a society that has lost its sense of order. As a result, the plowing of the half acre becomes perhaps the most important event in the first part of the poem, not because it is one of the poem's most dramatic events, but rather because it is an attempt by Langland, in his search for truth, to discover a correlate of his quest's objective in the form of an imagined feudal agrarianism.

Two other ways in which Langland pursues this quest in the poem to reassert order include, according to Pigg, the Prologue scene to the B text and the action after the pardon in passus 7. In the former, the vision of the manorial village is presented as a conceptual view of the feudal world, which, though in a state of decay, can be revitalized through a reassertion of feudal custom and practice. The granting of the pardon is similarly connected with the concept of feudal order and practice. This link is established implicitly through the association between a world of feudal custom and practice and living within the concept of truth.

1 Feudal Relations and Reason in *Cleanness*

NE ASPECT of *Cleanness* that sets it apart from other poems in the Cotton Nero manuscript is a simultaneous emphasis on teaching a religious precept and celebrating the comeliness of feudal life, especially the pleasures of a well-ordered hall and the proper relationship between lord and vassal. *Sir Gawain and the Green Knight* portrays the niceties of noble life in castle and hall, but little overt attention is given to religious matters. *Pearl*, *Patience*, and *Saint Erkenwald*, on the other hand, concentrate almost exclusively on religious lessons, although the *Pearl*-maiden does suggest a spiritual mirroring of medieval society in her depiction of the court of heaven, with herself as queen. More explicitly than the other Cotton Nero poems, *Cleanness* combines the concepts of heavenly and earthly order through the imagery of feudalism, with God himself serving as the head of the hierarchy and providing an ideal for those below to imitate.[1] Throughout the poem the paradigm of feudalism provides a measuring stick for the worsening condition of humanity.

It should come as no surprise that the *Cleanness*-Poet would select the feudal relationship as the figure of proper relations between God and humanity. The knight, the symbolic representative of the feudal system, was also a *miles Christi*, with his armor metaphorically outlined in Ephesians 6:13–17. (In passus 20 of the C text of *Piers Plow-*

man, Christ himself is portrayed as a knight, jousting in Piers's arms.)
In addition, during the century of the poem's composition, the ideals
of chivalry had probably assumed an importance unequaled in previous eras. Despite the decline in the viability of feudalism as a social
and economic system, the ideals of vassalic honor and fidelity continued to evoke a strong emotional response.[2] Richard Kaeuper, for example, notes: " We can easily be misled by older notions of the decline
of chivalry in the later Middle Ages. As is true with most ideal codes,
its practitioners and even more its theoreticians viewed practice in
their day as an intolerable slippage from the golden age. But perhaps
they decried the most vigorously what they saw as slippage as the
ideal actually took on more importance in life and thought all around
them."[3] He agrees in this respect with Arthur B. Ferguson, who also
argues for an increasing significance of the chivalric code during the
turbulent fourteenth century:

> The men and women of late medieval England were quite capable of,
> were indeed habitually given to, embalming general principles in tra-
> ditional forms and thereby isolating them quite effectively from the
> contingencies of daily existence. . . . And, by the same token, those
> tendencies which the historian finds most obviously working against
> the chivalric way of life could become actually instrumental in pre-
> serving the chivalric tradition, even perhaps in enhancing its signif-
> icance in the eyes of all but the most hard-headed observers.[4]

On the personal level, the feudal system united lord and vassal
through the act of homage. The oath of fealty, the second element in
the homage ritual, was sworn on holy relics and was considered irrevocable unless a serious breach of faith occurred on either side. The
Colyton oath, issued c. 943 in Edmund's third code, specifies that the
vassal "ought to be faithful to his lord, without any dispute or dissen-
sion, openly or in secret, favoring what he favors and discountenanc-
ing what he discountenances."[5] Bracton further specifies that once he
has done homage and sworn fealty, the vassal "cannot withdraw from
such lord or his homage without judgment, as long as he holds the
tenement . . . by which he is bound to homage."[6] In addition to taking the oath, the act of homage involved the *immixtio manuum*, the
placing of the vassal's hands within the hands of his lord—a posture

that became preferred for prayer over the course of the Middle Ages[7] and indicates the potential power of the feudal metaphor in a poem like *Cleanness*.

Both the importance of the feudal ideal and the solemnity of the contract imposed by the oath of fealty contribute to the structural and thematic framework of *Cleanness*. In the poem, as in medieval society (at least in theory), the vassal receives protection in return for obedient service. Postlapsarian humanity finds obedience difficult, however. As the exempla demonstrate, those individuals who maintain their vassal-lord relationship with God are able to escape the judgment leveled against all those around them who disregard the divinely ordained order. In addition, the poem itself, considered in toto as a final exemplum, provides a gift offering of the vassal/poet to God.

Turning to an examination of the feudal motif in *Cleanness*, we find that the poet goes to some pains to establish God as a feudal figure—that is, as a monarch and the head of a huge but well-managed household: "He is so clene in His courte, þe Kyng þat al weldez, / And honeste in His housholde, and hagherlych serued" (17–18); "In His comlych courte þat Kyng is of blysse" (546); "And to be couþe in His courte þou coueytes þenne, / To se þat Semly in sete and His swete face" (1054–55).[8] The poet uses the term "Soverayn" six times throughout the poem to emphasize further God's feudal role as suzerain of his people (780, 1152, 1225, 1289, 1313, 1643), as well as calling him the "proper Prynce þat paradys weldez" (195) and "þat Prynce of parage noble" (167).

Most convincing, though, is the portrayal of God in the opening parable of the wedding feast. As the head of a wealthy household—the feudal lord to whom others in the poem will be compared—he prepares a sumptuous feast in honor of his heir's marriage. When those initially invited refuse the invitation, he sends his messengers out to seek others. Despite the guests' lower station, the lord maintains courtesy and decorum:

> When þay com to þe courte keppte wern þay fayre,
> Sty3tled with þe stewarde, stad in þe halle,
> Ful manerly with marchal mad for to sitte,
> As he watz dere of degré dressed his seete. [89–92]

Even the simplest "watz serued to þe fulle, / Boþe with menske and with mete and mynstrasy noble, / And alle þe laykez þat a lorde aȝt in londe schewe" (120–22). The lord himself deigns to mingle among his unusual assortment of guests, an action that brings the one unworthy guest to his attention. Thus from the beginning the poet establishes God as a noble lord, courteous and generously hospitable, but incensed when confronted with "a gome vngoderly" (145).[9]

The severity of God's wrath calls into question the ultimate purpose of the poem. Is the poem designed to define *clannesse*? If so, we are still arguing over that definition. For example, Robert J. Menner holds that cleanness is chastity;[10] A. C. Spearing, that cleanness is the preservation of a divinely ordained order and classification of earthly existence;[11] D. S. Brewer, that cleanness is courtesy, with the far-reaching implications of that word in the fourteenth century;[12] Charlotte C. Morse, that cleanness is the avoidance of lechery and gluttony, sins that pollute the vessel of man's body and are analogous to idolatry and sacrilege.[13]

Not all critics agree, however, that the poet has set out to define cleanness. S. L. Clark and Julian N. Wasserman point out that the poem's title was chosen by its editor, not its author, and has been responsible for leading critics astray. Instead, Clark and Wasserman take their cue from the opening parable of the wedding feast and see the rest of the poem as a gloss for this parable of the Last Judgment.[14] T. D. Kelly and John T. Irwin also see the poem as dealing with Judgment. At the same time, they point out that the parable form itself is thematic, an "effective sign," a way of dividing the few who can grasp the parable's significance from the many who cannot.[15]

Clearly the poem does make a sharp distinction between those who find favor with God and those who do not. By implication, the poem's audience also will fall into one of these two categories. What, then, makes the difference between the two groups? It is the same ability, I would argue, that allows Noah, Abraham, Lot, Nebuchadnezzar, and Daniel to find favor with God—observance of the proper relationship between God and man, a relationship exemplified by that between feudal lord and vassal. Analyzing the exempla reveals that the use of reason, which allows man to grasp concepts of order and obligation, is an important element in maintaining proper feudal relations throughout the poem but one that becomes increasingly difficult to find.

While the positive characters in the poem display reason through skillful speech and proper behavior, especially in maintaining their vassal-lord relationship with God, those around them display an increasing disorder. In each exemplum, humanity moves further from the feudal ideal of order and comely service established in the opening parable. The deteriorating state of affairs on earth is shown both by the words and actions of those whom God judges and by the increasing disorder in the households of the righteous.

Scholastic tradition helps to explain why proper use of reason is an important concept. First of all, man is said to have been made in the image of God because, like his Creator—and unlike animals—he can reason.[16] Man, however, also possesses appetites of the flesh that must be kept in check by the reason, which directs the will. When a man allows his appetites to rule, he is no longer using his godlike qualities but has descended to the level of animals, which do as they desire without the medium of thought to direct their actions.[17] Indeed, Aquinas tells us, "Departure from reason is in itself evil. For the departure from the rule of reason is a turning away from God to whom man ought to be united by the use of right reason."[18]

Reason is also a quality closely linked with chivalry. For example, in Ramon Lull's *Libre del Ordre de Cauayleria* (*The Book on the Order of Chivalry*, c. 1280), which was widely circulated, reason forms an important part of the knight's armor: "The knight's horse is given a headpiece to signify that a knight ought to do feats of arms with reason. Just as the head of a horse goes before the knight, even so ought reason to go before all that a knight does. For all works without reason are vices in him."[19] Thus in *Cleanness* the concept of reason helps to form the link between religious precept and feudal ideal, establishing the lord-vassal relationship as the underlying metaphor of the poem.

First, the poem's emphasis on sins of the flesh—specifically, sins against natural sexual relations and proper use of food—should be considered in relation to reason. When appetites are no longer ruled by reason, man becomes bestial, a concept borne out in the poem through animal imagery. The misuse of reason dims within man the image of God, bringing divine wrath upon the offender. In addition, allowing appetite to overcome reason reverses the proper hierarchy of man's attributes; rebellion in the microcosm then naturally results in a chaotic macrocosm. Only divine intervention can restore order.

Second, the misuse of reason makes impossible the observance of vassalic obligations and hierarchy, for without reason man cannot enter into proper reciprocal relationships with fellow humans or the divine. Each exemplum of *Cleanness* illustrates a further weakening of the bonds that tie humanity to God, using the common medieval conception that society continues to decline from the first age.[20] The poet combines a theological concept (the use of reason as that which unites human and divine) and a sociohistorical reality of his time (the decline of feudalism, with a concomitant decline in its ideals of fealty and truth—that is, reason) to express his concern for the condition of his society.

In Noah's society as described by the *Cleanness*-Poet, we first see the consequences of the misuse of reason. Given one law to follow ("þer watz no law to hem layd bot loke to kynde," 263), the antediluvians transgress that law and instead give their appetites full sway. The poet tells us that they "controeuved agayn kynde contraré werkez, / And vsed hem vnþryftyly vchon on oþer, / And als with oþer, wylsfully, upon a wrange wyse" (266–68). When they allow their desires to run rampant, even uniting with the fallen angels, the result is a literal perversion of humanity, obvious in the external appearance of their giant offspring and also in their character: "And ay þe bigest in bale þe best watz halden" (276).

Significantly, the poet's description of Noah specifies what sets him apart from the others: "Þenne in worlde watz a wyʒe wonyande on lyue, / Ful redy and ful ryʒtwys, and rewled hym fayre" (293–94). The phrase "rewled hym fayre" indicates that Noah, unlike the others, is ruled by reason. God's words to Noah make this clear: "For þou in reysoun hatz rengned and ryʒtwys ben ever" (328).

The exemplum of Noah shows us many features of man's relationship with God that deteriorate as the poem progresses. First, Noah and God speak directly to each other, with no physical manifestation of the divine necessary, and no question or hesitation on Noah's part. He shows perfect obedience, as a feudal lord would expect from a worthy vassal, following complicated instructions to build the ark to God's specifications. In addition, his sealing of the ark "with clay alle aboute" (346) marks a close identification between God and man, and his preservation of each species to populate the world after the Flood imitates God's creation. Finally, we see that, unlike those around him,

> Frendez fellen in fere and faþmed togeder,
> To dryȝ her delful destyné and dyȝen alle samen;
> Luf lokez to luf and his leue takez,
> For to ende alle at onez and for euer twynne. [399–402]

None of the other victims in *Cleanness* evokes audience compassion.²⁴
Instead, as we shall see, each society we are shown progressively de-
parts from the image of God and a proper relationship with him.

In the next exemplum, Abraham is set before us as the righteous
man who finds favor with his Lord. Like Noah, a vassal who can recognize God's voice and offer a pleasing sacrifice, Abraham recognizes
the one God in his three guests and knows how to offer fitting hospitality. Abraham is the only righteous man in *Cleanness* who is not
defined by contrast with others; that is, he is not a virtuous man living
within an evil society. Rather, he and Sarah seem quite isolated on the
plain of Mamre. Perhaps because there is no contrast, we find no specific praise of his right use of reason. We do have proof of his likeness
to God in this respect, however, for as he accompanies God on the
road to Sodom, he dares to reason with him, though with appropriate
deference. His intercession is based on a rational argument that God
cannot rebut, and his humble speech and respectful address ("Sir")
keep intact the vassal-lord relationship:

> Sir, with Yor leue,
> Schal synful and saklez suffer al on payne?
> Weþer euer hit lyke my Lorde to lyfte such domez
> Þat þe wykked and þe worþy schal on wrake suffer,
> And weye vpon þe worre half þat wrathed þe neuer? [715–19]

As he continues to whittle the figure of just men from fifty to ten in
hopes of sparing the city, he continues to deprecate his own worth,
calling himself "bot erþe ful euel and vsle so blake" (747) and fearing
that he may "forloyne as a fol" (750). His humility only convinces us,
though, of his wisdom, and his "fayre speche" and "reken wordez"
(729 and 756) persuade God as well. Despite Abraham's belittling of
his wits, he and his Lord converse with ease, and it is through this
bond, rather than through a contrast with a surrounding society, that
we see Abraham as a man of reason.

In addition, Abraham proves his likeness to God by playing the part
of courteous host, recalling the opening parable but in appropriately

humbler terms. Abraham himself prepares a fitting meal for his three guests, placing simple food (bread, butter, milk, pottage) on a clean cloth beneath an oak tree. Showing himself a respectful vassal, "As sewer in a god assyse he serued Hem fayre" (639); that is, he serves his guests as if he were the chief servant of a noble hall.[25] David Herlihy notes that under the feudal system, the lord enjoyed the *droit de gîte*, or right to entertainment; such hospitality is central in the episodes of Abraham and Lot.[26]

Despite the similarities between Noah and Abraham as men of reason in both speech and action, we cannot help but notice a deterioration from the situation of the first exemplum. To communicate with Abraham, God manifests himself in human form. In addition, Abraham's household is less orderly than Noah's. Eavesdropping on the guests, Sarah laughs at the pronouncement that she will conceive, then later denies her laughter. Her scornful laughter shows a falling away from her husband's rule, although Abraham's three guests gloss over her disrespect in repayment of their host's courtesy. While Abraham knows how to reason with God and remains mindful of his subordinate station, Sarah's contact with the divine is limited to derision and then denial. Unlike Abraham, she does not exhibit the respect due one's liege.

With Lot, we return to definition by contrast with a surrounding society. He, like Noah, has kept the law of *kynde* despite the sexual perversions of those around him; the angels tell him that "þou art oddely þyn one out of þis fylþe" (923). In other words, he has retained the proper use of reason, allowing him, like Abraham, to recognize the divine nature of his guests. We see here, however, another falling away from the closeness between man and God. Whereas Noah and Abraham spoke directly to God, Lot speaks to his angels; whereas Noah communed directly with an unseen God, Abraham speaks to one God in the form of the Trinity, and Lot sees only two beings. But, as with Noah and Abraham, Lot's reason enables him to be a worthy vassal who knows how to speak fairly and offer pleasing food.

Specifically, like Noah and Abraham, Lot demonstrates reason through his manner of speech. Although the angels at first insist that they will sleep outdoors, they accept Lot's invitation of hospitality because of his "luflych wordez" (809). The Sodomites, however, disregard Lot's "mesurable wordez" (859) when he offers his daughters in exchange for his guests' safety. The Sodomites themselves speak "wyth a schrylle scharp schout" (840) and "harlotez speche" (874). The poet tells us,

> Whatt! þay sputen and speken of so spitous fylþe,
> What! þay ȝeȝed and ȝolped of ȝestande sorȝe,
> Þat ȝet þe wynd and þe weder and þe worlde stynkes
> Of þe brych þat vpbraydez þose broþelych wordez. [845–48]

Thus the Sodomites, in their perverse lust, literally foam at the mouth.

This figure of foaming at the mouth, a behavior usually associated with animals, makes a nice counterpoint in this exemplum to the motif of salt and yeast. Lot instructs his wife to use neither salt nor yeast as she prepares dinner, for these two ingredients signify a perversion of natural order. As appropriate punishment for her disobedience of his orders, she turns to salt when she looks back on Sodom, "and alle lyst on hir lik þat arn on launde bestes" (1000). Thus Lot's wife is associated with both unclean food and beasts. The motif of salt also appears in the lengthy description of the Dead Sea, "Þat euer of smelle and of smach smart is to fele" (1019). Landlocked but filled with salt water, the sea itself is a perversion of natural order and, appropriately enough, contains foaming asphalt, "spumande aspaltoun" (1038).[27]

We also notice the further deterioration in the order of Lot's household. Sarah mocks her guests but then, ashamed, denies it; Lot's wife brazenly disobeys orders. When she adds salt to the angels' food, the poet asks, "Why watz ho, wrech, so wod?" (828). By defying her husband's orders, for no purpose other than the pleasure of disobedience, she acts contrary to reason, so that she is "wod." When she disobeys later and turns into salt, the beasts that come to lick her signify again her lack of reason.[28]

Others in the poem share her disability. Although Lot's daughters obey his orders and are saved, their fiancés are not. When Lot wakes his future sons-in-law, they "token hit as tayt" (935) and ignore his warning. In the same way, the Sodomites who stand outside his gate do not perceive his wisdom when he offers to "kenne yow by kynde a crafte þat is better" (865). They are appropriately stricken "as blynde as Bayard" (886), another instance of animal imagery matching man's foolishness.[29] The sons-in-law and the rest of the city discover too late that Lot was the one rational man among them. He is therefore the only one to treat his guests respectfully—offering hospitality, protection, and obedience—in other words, recognizing himself as their vassal.

We should observe as well that when Lot and his daughters escape the destruction of their city, they are a broken household, a further proof of humanity's decline. Noah escapes with his family unit intact and with pairs of animals to replenish the earth; Abraham and Sarah receive God's promise to multiply; now Lot loses his wife, and his daughters lose their fiancés.

In the final exemplum, Belshazzar's feast, we are presented with more complex circumstances. Reason as a means of maintaining the proper order of society continues to function as a unifying theme, but there are two primary figures of reason—Nebuchadnezzar and Daniel—and one minor figure of reason, Belshazzar's queen. Daniel's assistance to two generations, father and son, emphasizes the increasingly swift decline of man's likeness to God. Appropriately, the temple vessels that provide the focus here were fashioned by Solomon, whose very name is associated with reason:

> Wyth alle þe coyntyse þat he cowþe clene to wyrke,
> Deuised he þe vesselment, þe vestures clene;
> Wyth sly3t of his ciences, his Souerayn to loue,
> Þe hous and þe anournements he hy3tled togedere. [1287–90]

Nebuchadnezzar, struck by the intricate beauty of Solomon's vessels, puts them away reverently and turns to God. But when he later sets himself up as God's equal, God punishes him by taking away what made him human—his reason—and Nebuchadnezzar descends for three years to an animal-like existence: "His hert heldet vnhole; he hoped non oþer / Bot a best þat he be, a bol oþer an oxe" (1681–82).[30]

This punishment is mild compared to Belshazzar's brutal death and the destruction of Babylon. Nebuchadnezzar's sin is pride, the error of thinking he could be equal to God. At least in *Cleanness*, this sin is not as serious as man's deliberately choosing to be *less* than human by perverting his reason. This idea also helps to explain the poet's observation early in the poem that Lucifer and Adam did not arouse God's full wrath. Their sins did not expressly involve a perversion of reason, a turning from human choice to animal instinct; rather, they attempted to turn from human limitations to divine omnipotence and omniscience. And, as Nebuchadnezzar was restored to health and kingship, so Adam's sin was amended by the "matchless maiden" and Lucifer's rebellion would not be wholly overthrown until the Last Judgment. Thus—at least for the *Cleanness*-Poet—pride, motivated by a desire to equal God, is a lesser evil and can eventually be remedied. For the antediluvians, the Sodomites, and Belshazzar, however, God's wrath is swift and irrevocable, for they have demolished the image of God within themselves by turning from reason.[31] In terms of the lord-vassal relationship, then, we might say that God prefers to have his power challenged (as frequently happened in the poet's society) than to see his vassals disregard feudal relations altogether in their concentration on satisfying their sensual appetites.

Belshazzar's attention to appetite and consequent disordered reason are apparent in many ways. As ruler, he has responsibilities to his own vassals. The disarray of his kingdom, though, is mirrored in his confused household and bestial desires. His household contains "a wyf," "a worþelych quene" (1351), but also "mony a lemman . . . þat ladis wer called" (1352). When he holds his feast, he expressly intends that his guests will "loke on his lemanes and ladis hem calle" (1370). Meanwhile, the queen herself is absent from the feast, for lines 1586–90 tell us that she knows nothing of the supernatural events in the hall until, from her chamber, she hears Belshazzar raging. The circumstances of Belshazzar's feast depict the final deterioration of household decorum in the poem and a mockery of the initial parable of the wedding feast, celebrating the lawful union of man and wife.

In addition, presenting the wife, rather than the husband, as a figure of reason underlines Belshazzar's irrationality and again demonstrates his disordered rule. As the king cries out and rends his clothes (1582), his queen hears his raging and enters the hall. She brings to mind the fittingly humble approach of Noah, Abraham, and Lot, who recognize their proper relationship to their feudal superior and speak and act accordingly: "Ho kneles on þe colde erþe and carpes to hymseluen / Wordes of worchyp wyth a wys speche" (1591–92). She reminds him of Daniel in terms that indicate her grasp of truth, for she describes Daniel as having "þe gost of God þat gyes alle soþes"

(1598). Even Belshazzar acknowledges her "gode counseyl" (1619), although when Daniel stands before him he begins, "hit is tolde me bi tulkes" (1623), disavowing his wife's help in this matter.

Belshazzar's lack of reason is also obvious from the description of the feast itself. Unlike Noah, Abraham, and Lot, Belshazzar cannot offer a decorous meal.[32] Instead, we see proof of the poet's observation that "Al watz þe mynde of þat man on misschapen þinges" (1355). In contrast to the simplicity of the poem's earlier meals, Belshazzar presents elaborate dishes decorated with paper ornaments of exotic beasts and birds, all carried in by men on horseback. The hall is noisy, and drink is plentiful enough to further damage his reason: "So faste þay weȝed to him wyne hit warmed his hert / And breyþed vppe into his brayn and blemyst his mynde" (1420–21). Then Belshazzar remembers Solomon's intricately made sacred vessels and calls for them so that his ladies can "lape," an example of animal imagery which complements the description of his action after the hand appears to write on the wall, that he "romyes as a rad ryth þat rorez for drede" (1543).[33] Solomon's sacred brass vessels are a telling counterpoint to the flimsy paper figures that ornament Belshazzar's platters. Solomon's vessels are properly used to feed the spirit and to keep man's attributes in divinely ordained order; Belshazzar intends to use them to feed the bodily appetite and give it preeminence over reason.[34]

That lack of wisdom prevails throughout the kingdom becomes evident when no one can interpret the runes on the wall. Belshazzar "bred ner wode" (1558); the point is repeated later that "wytles he wed wel ner" (1585). Without the governance of reason, Belshazzar has little self-control; the poet informs us that whenever his wooden gods do not grant his prayers, "He cleches to a gret klubbe and knokkes hem to peces" (1348). Now, when he finds that none of his learned men can interpret the writing on the wall, "he corsed his clerkes and calde hem chorles; / To henge þe harlotes he heȝed ful ofte" (1583–84). There is no doubt that he is a man ruled by passion; his is a worse madness than his father's, for Belshazzar has chosen to give up the proper use of reason, and with his father's example before him nonetheless dares to defy the Judaic God.

It is small wonder, then, that neither Belshazzar nor his "wise" men can read the mystical writing on the wall. Instead they must call on Daniel, who has "holy connyng" (1625) in his heart. Although a captive and therefore not bound to the king as a willing vassal, Daniel aids Belshazzar. Belshazzar has many models of reasonable behavior—both the queen and Daniel have served him well, and Nebuchadnezzar maintained the proper deference toward the God of the Israelites. In addition, Daniel proves his wisdom when he reads easily the "three signs in one," just as Noah had recognized the three persons of God and Lot had recognized the angels. Thus all the individuals touted in the poem for their favor with God (Noah, Abraham, Lot, Nebuchadnezzar, Daniel) recognize and reverence God—unlike Belshazzar, who "Se3 þese syngnes [Nebuchadnezzar's madness] with sy3t and set hem at lyttel" (1710). But whereas Noah and Abraham deal directly with God, Lot deals with two angels; Nebuchadnezzar sees God through Solomon's vessels; Daniel sees nothing but the writing on the wall, evidence that God was present at the feast. Thus, as evil has spread, God's presence in the world has lessened noticeably.

Having worked our way through the exempla, let us turn again to the opening parable. Many critics have observed the antithetical nature of the two feasts that frame *Cleanness*.[35] For example, those who are first invited to the wedding feast find excuses to stay away; those who are invited to Belshazzar's feast come willingly. Among the many properly attired guests at the opening feast, one man appears without a wedding garment and is cast out. At Belshazzar's feast, amidst the many revelers who defile the sacred vessels, one good man must be brought in, and he is given princely attire and elevated in power.

We must not overlook the significance of the feast itself, however. The wedding feast, of course, can be seen as a type of the marriage between Christ and his church (or between Christ and each of his followers), and it is usually interpreted as such.[36] It is also possible, though, to see in marriage a type of the proper union of body and soul, in which the body should take the part of the bride, being obedient to her wiser mate. And, even if nothing else, one sees in the wedding feast the establishment of a proper household, a microcosm for the ideal order of human society. In diametric opposition is Belshazzar's feast, in which the queen herself is absent and the concubines are raised to noble status, overturning the proper order of things. Wine and revelry, not reason, rule this feast, and so it is not surprising that the sacred vessels are turned to ignoble use. Belshazzar's feast has something akin to a carnival air, a veritable Feast of Fools in which natural order is deliberately inverted.[37]

Critics have pointed out the narrowing focus of the poet in the progression of the exempla: God judges and destroys, first, almost all of human society in the Flood; next, a particular area, Sodom and Gomorrah; and finally, one individual, Belshazzar, and his city.[38] In each judgment, the number of people favored by God also dwindles, from Noah's family with his three sons and their wives, to Lot and his daughters, to Daniel. This pattern lends the poem an apocalyptic urgency, with its concentration not only on the individual but also on the rampant spread of evil. At the same time, God's interaction with man diminishes, with his final manifestation merely a hand, and even that raised in judgment against the revelers, not extended toward the righteous. In addition, the household unit is shown in progressive decay: Sarah laughs; Lot's wife disobeys; Belshazzar overturns marital decorum; Daniel is a captive in a foreign land, with no household of his own.

Perhaps most chilling is the progressively worsening portrayal of human society throughout the poem. As noted above, the antediluvians were described as being so fair that they tempted the fallen angels of God, and although they allowed their sexual appetite to rule, they regained a poignant dignity in their death. The Sodomites, however, are portrayed as cruel, sneering fellows: "3ete vus out þose 3ong men þat 3ore-whyle here entred, / Pat we may lere hym of lof" (842–43).[39] Not only do they reject Lot's offer of his maiden daughters, but they also jeer at the man himself: "Wost þou not wel þat þou wonez here a wy3e strange, / An outcomlying, a carle?" (875–76). Their destruction seems well deserved and elicits no pity from the audience. Thus Lot's goodness is highlighted by the impressions we form of those around him.[40]

In the final episode, no distinction is made between God's people and the heathen who conquer them. In lines 1172–73, we learn that Zedechiah "of leauté . . . watz lat to his Lorde hende"—a reference to his slacking of feudal duties to God his suzerain—and, like Belshazzar, "He vsed abominaciones of idolatrye." Thus Nebuchadnezzar, who comes to reverence God, actually serves his cause more faithfully than did the Jewish leader. Belshazzar, inheriting his father's kingdom but not his wisdom, ignores God's warning even after Daniel has interpreted the writing on the wall. His only response is to heap material wealth upon Daniel—worthless honors since Belshazzar's reign does not last the night. When Darius conquers the Chaldeans, we are given no indication that the situation has changed for the better; one ruler has merely been exchanged for another. Indeed, the exemplum does not even make Daniel, the one righteous man, the focus of this episode, a paradigm which is adhered to in the previous cases. The audience hears nothing more of Daniel nor of the queen; our final image is of Belshazzar, carried drunk to his bed and beaten to death there, "Þat boþe his blod and his brayn blende on þe cloþes" (1788).[41] As he has ignored reason in his lifetime, so is his brain now literally mangled.[42] Appropriately, the final allusion to Belshazzar equates him with an animal: "Now is a dogge also dere þat in a dych lygges" (1792).

Overall, then, the poem gains momentum in its sense of apocalyptic urgency from the spread of evil throughout the population until God's people and idolaters are indistinguishable, and one can find wisdom in a heathen (the queen) in as rare an instance as among the Jews (Daniel). Minimizing the roles of these positive characters in the final exemplum further diminishes our sense of God's presence in the world. In addition, making Belshazzar the focus of the final exemplum enables the poet to give a new twist to the underlying theme of feudal relations. As Belshazzar does not recognize his proper relationship to the Judaic God, neither does he maintain proper feudal relations within his kingdom. He rules capriciously, at one point overturning marital decorum by celebrating his concubines at a public feast, then later showering a lowly captive with gifts and honors. Thus the final exemplum leaves us with the impression of an almost totally disordered society, unstable and unpredictable at all levels, no longer subject to feudal rules—perhaps the poet's vision of his own society.

Yet in this episode, as in the others, one person is singled out as the wise, pure individual whom God preserves. Despite the increasing difficulty of retaining God's favor, then, the poet offers proof that it *can* be done. And in each case, the key to God's favor appears to be the maintenance of suitable relations between vassal and Lord. This relationship relies on man's ability to reason, the ability which most closely links God and man, and is embodied in proper speech and action.[43] Noah follows God's instructions without hesitation, using a minimum of speech; Abraham reasons with God, even persuading him to moderate his judgment of Sodom; Lot uses his powers of persuasion to convince the angels to partake of his hospitality and attempts to dissuade the Sodomites from their evil intentions; Daniel interprets God's signs to warn the king of impending judgment.

In the first three instances, the actions of the reasonable man are consonant with his comely speech. Noah builds the ark and prepares a pleasing sacrifice; Abraham sets before his guests a wholesome meal and accompanies them for part of the journey to Sodom; Lot offers his guests food, lodging, and protection. But for Daniel, a captive in a foreign land, no action seems possible. His words *are* his actions; he counseled Nebuchadnezzar and now he counsels Belshazzar, but in the end his words go unheeded and Babylon is destroyed.

The poet himself, however, still trusts in the power of words to move others to good. By constructing a poem pleasing to his Lord, he acts as the diametric opposite of the unworthy guest at the wedding feast, who casts his eyes upon the ground and says nothing when questioned by the host. Furthermore, his choice of topic grants him special verbal powers, as we learn in the opening lines of the poem: "Clannesse whoso kyndly cowþe comende, / And rekken vp alle þe resounz þat ho by riȝt askez, / Fayre formez myȝt he fynde in forþering his speche" (1–3).

The "fayre formez" he employs, the exempla, are interwoven with simpler, homiletic material. This intricate structure has caused much debate about the overall organization of the poem. Basically, however, the message of links and exempla is the same; the links bear out the notion that *Cleanness* is primarily eschatological in nature, but they emphasize the individual's choice and grounds for hope in the matter of divine judgment.[44] The individual's responsibility for his works is the dominant message of lines 161–92, as the poet explicates the opening parable of the wedding feast, a parable of Judgment. He makes clear that the unworthy guest is attired in ignoble deeds and thoughts:

> Wich arn þenne þy wedez þou wrappez þe inne,
> Þat schal schewe hem so schene schrowde of þe best?
> Hit arn þy werkez, wyterly, þat þou wroȝt hauez,
> And lyued with þe lykyng þat lyȝe in þyn hert. [169–71]

He further elaborates by listing examples of deeds which will cause the sinner to forfeit the vision of God (177–88).

The links themselves emphasize that man cannot hide his thoughts or deeds from God; he is characterized as "þe gropande God, þe grounde of alle dedez, / Rypande of vche a ring þe reynyez and hert" (591–92). The final link alludes to the entire life of Christ by references to the Nativity and to Christ's breaking of bread, presumably at Emmaus (1069–1110). The New Covenant orientation of this link gives another dimension to "Þe gropyng so goud of God and Man boþe" (1102), for his touch heals. However, the link proceeds to warn against falling back into sin: "Bot war þe wel, if þou be waschen wyth water of schryfte. . . . Sulp no more þenne in synne þy saule þerafter" (1133, 1135).

The thrust of the poem, depictions of judgments linked by comments on judgment, puts the poet in God's service, following the model of Daniel.[45] Like Daniel, the poet cannot act except through speech; also like Daniel, who explains both "þe tyxte" and "þe mater" (1634, 1635) of the runes, the poet presents text (exempla) and matter (the commentary of the links). And if we accept the poem as dealing with Judgment, the poet follows Daniel as a spokesman for the apocalypse as well.[46] The poet's crafting of his material also links him to Solomon; as Solomon "fyled out of fygures of ferlylé schappes" (1459), "With alle þe syence þat hym sende þe souerayn Lorde" (1454), so does the poet carve out a poem dedicated to his Lord, using the wit he has been given.[47] At a more general level, however, the poet is linked with all the figures of righteousness depicted in the poem, for he proves himself a vassal of the divine, using his skill to produce a gift for his Lord and encouraging his audience to join him in homage.

Toward that end, in the final lines, the poet turns to another topic. He does not plead to walk in the light of reason, despite the emphasis on this attribute throughout and the culminating show of wisdom in Daniel's reading of the runes, a figure for our own reading of the poem he has wrought. And despite the metaphor of feudal relations established through the poem, he does not present himself as a vassal calling upon his sovereign for his rightful due. Instead, the poet begs for grace, an implicit acknowledgment that no matter what man's service or intellectual powers, in a world awash in evil, with Judgment surely imminent, he is lost without the grace of his Lord.

Notes

1. Elizabeth Armstrong believes the poet portrays Christ as a "perfect courtier," his life "a conflation of courtly love, courtesy, charity" ("*Purity*," *Explicator* 36 [1977]:31). The notion of God as feudal lord is introduced before Christ enters the poem, however. The opening parable suggests God the Father as feudal ideal, with the bridegroom (Christ) implicitly following the Father's example. A comparison with the final exemplum, in which Belshazzar deliberately turns away from *his* father's example, shows the breach between the realms of divine and human, ideal and real.

2. A concise analysis of the breakdown of the feudal system—its social hierarchy and its ideology—can be found in Paul Strohm's *Social Chaucer* (Cambridge, Mass.: Harvard University Press, 1989), 1–21.

3. *War, Justice, and Public Order: England and France in the Later Middle Ages* (New York: Oxford University Press, 1988), 196.

4. *The Indian Summer of English Chivalry: Studies in the Decline and Transformation of Chivalric Idealism* (New York: AMS Press, 1984), 27.

5. Richard P. Abels, *Lordship and Military Obligation in Anglo-Saxon England* (Berkeley & Los Angeles: University of California Press, 1988), 84.

6. *Bracton on the Laws and Customs of England*, ed. George E. Woodbine and trans. Samuel E. Thorne, 4 vols. (Cambridge, Mass.: Belknap Press, 1968), 2:233.

7. David Herlihy, ed., *The History of Feudalism* (London: Macmillan, 1971), 70–71.

8. All quotations are taken from *The Poems of the Pearl Manuscript*, ed. Malcolm Andrew and Ronald Waldron (Berkeley & Los Angeles: University of California Press, 1978). Citations in the text refer to line numbers in this edition.

9. In their introduction to the poem, Andrew and Waldron point out that "each reversion from narrative to direct moral comment (545ff., 1049ff., 1805ff.) brings the reader back to the picture of God as king in his court; the Wedding Feast parable, therefore, stands in a special explanatory relationship to the Beatitude that is the text of the whole poem, and particularly to its promise: 'they shall see God' " (26).

10. In *Purity*, ed. Robert J. Menner (New Haven, Conn.: Yale University Press, 1920), xlv.

11. "*Purity* and Danger," *EC* 30 (1980):301–6.

12. "Courtesy and the *Gawain*-Poet," in *Patterns of Love and Courtesy: Essays in Memory of C. S. Lewis*, ed. John Lawlor (London: Edward Arnold, 1966), 60–62.

13. "The Image of the Vessel in *Cleanness*," *UTQ* 40 (1971):202–16.

14. "*Purity*: The Cities of the Dove and the Raven," *ABR* 29 (1978):285–86.

15. "The Meaning of *Cleanness*: Parable as Effective Sign," *MS* 35 (1973):259–60. Connections between *Cleanness* and *Cursor Mundi* further indicate judgment as a dominant theme. Sarah M. Horrall argues for the *Cursor Mundi* as a probable source for *Cleanness*, concluding that the poet "understood the underlying pattern in *Cursor Mundi* of Paradise-Flood-Doomsday, and felt that it was also suitable for his own work" ("*Cleanness* and *Cursor Mundi*," *ELN* 22 [1985]:11). Following in the footsteps of Clark and Wasserman ("The Significance of Thresholds in the *Pearl-*

Poet's *Purity,*" *Interpretations* 12 [1980]:114–27) as well as Morse, Sarah Stanbury an-
alyzes the use of enclosure imagery throughout the poem, concluding that "motion
across a threshold, and particularly the motion that violates a sanctified space, is
itself the figure for judgment" ("Space and Visual Hermeneutics in the *Gawain-
Poet,*" *ChauR* 21 [1987]:487).

16. Aquinas specifies the relation between man's reason and his function as the
image of God:

> Meritorious knowledge and love of God is only possible through grace. There
> is, however, such a thing as natural knowledge and love of God. . . . and it is
> also natural to the mind that it has the power of using reason to understand
> God, and it was in terms of such a power that we said God's image remains
> always in the mind; *whether the image of God is so faint*—so shadowy, we might
> say—*that it is practically non-existent,* as in those who lack the use of reason; *or
> whether it is dim and disfigured,* as in sinners; *or whether it is bright and powerful,*
> as in the just, as Augustine says. [*Summa Theologica* 1a, 93, 8 ad 3]

17. Penelope Doob points out the appropriateness of Nebuchadnezzar's punishment in this regard: "Morally, Nebuchadnezzar represents any sinner who destroys
reason, the image of God, and thereby becomes bestial, mad, and an outcast. . . ."
(*Nebuchadnezzar's Children: Conventions of Madness in Middle English Literature* [New
Haven & London: Yale University Press, 1974], 69). Aquinas quotes Aristotle on this
subject: "Aristotle says that the reason why it is more shameful to be incontinent in
lust than in anger is that lust deprives man of the power to reason. In this vein he
also says that sins of intemperance are more reprehensible because we share these
same pleasures with brute animals (*Summa Theologica* 1a2ae 73, 6 ad 3)." Accordingly, Theresa Tinkle traces animal imagery throughout the poem ("The Heart's
Eye: Beatific Vision in *Purity,*" *SP* 85 [1988]:462, 464, 467).

18. *Summa Theologica* 1a2ae 73, 8 ad 3.

19. Trans. David Herlihy, in *The History of Feudalism,* 332.

20. See, for example, Chaucer's short poems "The Former Age" and "Lak of
Stedfastnesse."

21. We can assume that the poet was familiar with this tradition of the mystery
plays. One proof of familiarity is that the detail in ll. 1103–8, of Christ's breaking of
bread, was found only in drama—the *Ludus Coventriae,* the Towneley Cycle, and the
Shrewsbury *Peregrini* (Edward Wilson, *The Gawain-Poet* [Leiden: Brill, 1976], 75). For
a discussion of the usual portrayal of Noah and his wife in the mystery plays, see
Rosemary Woolf, *The English Mystery Plays* (Berkeley & Los Angeles: University of
California Press, 1972), 135–40.

22. Tinkle points out that through a grammatical ambiguity of the text, "those
who miss the *visio* become equated with beasts" ("The Heart's Eye," 462). Describing the panic of animals and humans, the poet conflates them in ll. 393–94 by writing "alle cryed" and "þay cryed."

23. Charlotte Morse describes this as "a reestablishment of order that contrasts
with the chaos in the kingdom of wild creatures when the Flood begins" (*The Pat-*

tern of Judgment in the "Queste" and "Cleanness" [Columbia: University of Missouri Press, 1978], 158).

24. Tinkle reads this passage less sympathetically; she emphasizes the poem's sight imagery, linked with the often overlooked portion of Matthew 5:8, the promise of a *visio dei*. In her reading, the antediluvians' final moments underline their separation from God: "As the defiled wedding guest looks to the earth, and Satan to himself, the lovers look to their partners" ("The Heart's Eye," 463).

25. See the note to ll. 639–42 in Andrew and Waldron, *Poems of the Pearl Manuscript*, 138.

26. Herlihy, *The History of Feudalism*, 73.

27. Later in the poem, Daniel will warn Belshazzar of his "froþande fylþe" (l. 1721), an image that links the two exempla.

28. For a fuller discussion of the detail of Lot's wife adding salt to the food, see O. F. Emerson, "A Note on the Middle English 'Cleanness,'" *MLR* 10 (1915): 373–75.

29. Tinkle notes the appropriateness of the Sodomites' punishment, for they refuse the *visio dei*, as does Lot's wife, who "looks back to the city, with vision once again demonstrating the heart's preoccupation" ("Heart's Eye," 464). Lynn S. Johnson (*The Voice of the Gawain-Poet* [Madison: University of Wisconsin Press, 1984], 122) and Earl G. Schreiber ("The Structures of *Clannesse*," in *The Alliterative Tradition in the Fourteenth Century*, ed. Bernard S. Levy and Paul E. Szarmach [Kent, Ohio: Kent State University Press, 1981], 139) also remark on the motif of sight.

30. Doob comments on two implications found in literary retellings of Nebuchadnezzar's story: "[F]irst, the presumptuous Nebuchadnezzar had to be made like a beast so that he could know what it was to be truly human; second, Nebuchadnezzar's external appearance and habitation are often taken as projections of the moral deformity and wilderness inside him"(*Nebuchadnezzar's Children*, 70).

31. Johnson, however, sees the exempla as moving from lust to avarice to pride, sins of increasing severity. She explains that Adam and Lucifer are included in the poem because their different fates highlight the theme of penance, of choice (*Voice of the Gawain-Poet*, 110–11). Morse sees Lucifer, Adam, and Nebuchadnezzar as types of the wedding guests who refuse the invitation: "God judges them all, but they do not make him as angry as do the hypocrites who unworthily accept his invitation" (*Pattern of Judgment*, 141–42).

32. Strictly speaking, of course, Noah does not offer a meal but rather a sacrifice. Thus even this detail illustrates the worsening human condition: the poem moves from Noah's sacrifice (involving no appetite and no uncleanness), to Abraham's wholesome repast, to Lot's sabotaged offering of clean food, to Belshazzar's outrageous feast.

33. According to the *Middle English Dictionary*, the verb *lapen* is usually associated with animals, especially dogs—"an apt association in view of Belshazzar's corpse later lying like a dog in a ditch" (Wilson, *Gawain-Poet*, 111).

34. Elizabeth Keiser concurs: "[T]he various departures from decorum manifest the inward failure to grasp the ideal of a life shaped in accord with reason. . . . the urges for display and for imaginative refinement of natural functions like sex, dress,

and food all lead to self-indulgent disorder in a mind governed by appetite" ("The Festive Decorum of *Cleanness*," *SMC* 14 [1980]:74).

35. See, for example, Clark and Wasserman, "Significance of Thresholds," 114–15; Johnson, *Voice of the Gawain-Poet*, 133; Kelly and Irwin, "Meaning of *Cleanness*," 247–49; and Spearing, "*Purity* and Danger," 296, 303.

36. As Kelly and Irwin point out, the marriage feast also recalls the union of God and man through the feast of the Mass. In addition, we should remember that Christ began his ministry at a wedding feast ("Meaning of *Cleanness*," 235–36).

37. Kelly and Irwin go so far as to associate the desecration of vessels at Belshazzar's feast with the Black Mass ("Meaning of *Cleanness*," 249).

38. See John Gardner, ed., *The Complete Works of the Gawain-Poet* (Chicago & London: University of Chicago Press, 1965), 68; and Morse, *Pattern of Judgment*, 159.

39. Morse observes, "The Sodomites' desire to seize the angels and assault them sexually parodies the true quest for the vision of God" (*Pattern of Judgment*, 169).

40. Even Lot's wife deserves her fate. Kelly and Irwin see her sin as more than disobedience; Lot's wife tries to overthrow the "fundamental principle of authority" ("Meaning of *Cleanness*," 241 n. 11) in a poem that characterizes God the Father as Authority (240). We can also see her disobedience as a trespass of her subordinate role in feudal marriage.

41. As Johnson notes, "This final Old Testament story differs from the first and second because there is no account of a safe landing, or of an escape" (*Voice of the Gawain-Poet*, 137).

42. Belshazzar's brutal death also mirrors his angry clubbing of idols, so that he "achieves ironic union with the false gods with which he has filled the true God's place," Jonathan A. Glenn asserts in his "Dislocation of *Kynde* in the Middle English *Cleanness*" (*ChauR* 18 [1983]:89).

43. Johnson observes that the poem focuses on the willfulness of human nature, an emphasis that links all the Cotton Nero poems in "personal recognition and choice, for through knowledge man may be released from his incomprehension and folly into the true freedom that is a gift of grace" (*Voice of the Gawain-Poet*, xvi).

44. Ruth Hamilton also sees the poem's links and exempla as counterpoint, so that the poem "alternates regularly between the hope of redemption and the threat of punishment" ("Repeating Narrative and Anachrony in *Cleanness*," *Style* 20 [1986]:187). Tinkle, however, defines another alternation: "The homiletic directness suggests the biblical *sermo humilis*, which makes spiritual truth easily accessible to the common man, while the narrative indirection, like the sublime beauties of Scripture, reserves its mysteries for the more contemplative and learned reader" ("The Heart's Eye," 470).

45. Hamilton suggests that "the poet sees himself, like the prophet Daniel, as divinely inspired" ("Repeating Narrative," 185). Schreiber goes so far as to locate the poem's unity in the concept of "poet as guide and teacher, the shaper of the vessel of truth, and the master of words who unlocks the secret meanings which ironically are not secret meanings at all" ("Structures of *Cleanness*," 148).

46. The inclusion of Jerusalem and Babylon in the final exemplum further supports Judgment as the focus of *Cleanness* (Johnson, *Voice of Gawain-Poet*, 137). Morse

agrees that the use of Babylon lends "apocalyptic urgency" to the poem (*Pattern of Judgment*, 137) and reminds us that each of the exempla is a type of the Last Judgment ("Image," 202).

47. Keiser describes *Cleanness* as "a highly ornate and aesthetically pleasing artifact" ("Festive Decorum," 63).

2 Imagining Feudalism in *Piers Plowman*

Attempts to Restore an Order

HE FOURTEENTH CENTURY in England was a period of massive social and economic change and ideological flux. Known for their descriptive conceptualizing of social structures, writers of the period were often at a loss when it came to reconciling the events of the century brought on by plagues, economic difficulties, and war with the centuries-old social models that never had corresponded to social realities.[1] Critical/theoretical discussions of the relation between reality in the external world and the linguistically generated reality of the text are not a concern of the medieval writers who generalize about the three orders: *oratores, bellatores,* and *laboratores*. Each of these groups had its place in medieval civilization, and in their proper configuration the groups were a *signum* of the Trinity.[2] One writer in the last half of the fourteenth century seems particularly occupied with social structure and with the obligations of feudal custom and practice as a means of reasserting stability in society. William Langland, in *Piers Plowman*—a poem written in at least three versions spanning almost thirty years in composition[3]—investigates the role of social order as the structure on which all systems of signification rest. For the poet, the loss of the feudal ideal signaled a coming eschatological event, most likely because he was unable to envision a world in which such an order was not present. Thematic studies of *Piers Plowman* have focused on the attainment of salvation, the use of temporal goods, and the practice of perfection, but this essay contends that, although these are important issues in the poem, they are subordinate to the theorizing about the social model of authority.[4] Of course, restoring a decaying social model by reasserting feudal custom and practice was not possible in the late fourteenth century; but Langland had to imagine that attempt verbally. That the feudal ideal fails in his poem does not indicate a lack of poetic craftsmanship but rather the realization that a society governed by greed or perhaps acedia,[5] as the dreamer envisions it in the Prologue, cannot be remolded into a world in which subordination, mandated by feudal society, is natural. In this essay, feudal custom and practice are limited to the feudal lord/tenant relationship. Clearly, there were problems at the latter level, but Langland is concerned with the obligation of peasant tenants—both free and bond—who have left their responsibilities on the manors to wander in search of higher wages or who have contributed to the growing number of the idle.

To understand Langland's imagining of the social ideal, we will concentrate on the first portion of the poem as it appears in the B text. Langland considers the matter of feudal obligations in the A text, but the A text breaks off without any clear alternative to the failed effort of feudal reorganization. The B text presents Langland's answer to social disharmony by moving to an investigation of the individual as the source of the problem. Restoring the *imago Dei* in the individual—also a sign of the Trinity—was more feasible than restoring the social model with feudal customs and obligations. This essay will focus on three "moments" in the text: the Prologue scene, the plowing of the half acre, and the action after the reading of the pardon as the conclusion to the imagining activity. But to understand Langland's manipulation of the ideology of feudal practice, we must look at the general conceptions of feudal society.

Two further points, however, need to be clarified. In the last decade, medieval studies has seen significant inroads made by modern critical theory—especially semiotics, deconstruction, feminism, and most recently, New Historicism or "critical historicism."[6] All of these have raised the question of the location of reality. In a critique of these theories and in particular of New Historicism, Gabrielle M. Spiegel notes the tendency to see reality as a linguistically constituted entity, not as something external to the text.[7] Critical-historical analyses of *Piers Plowman* treat the poem as a "parasitic reflector" of a reality external to the poem.[8] *Piers* has been more the possession of social historians than that of literary scholars.[9] The reality present in the text has been viewed as equivalent to the historical reality external to it. In this essay, the concept of reality lies beyond the text of the poem. Langland saw medieval society from a geographically limited perspective, but perhaps from a no less limited view than twentieth-century literary scholars who rely on an understanding of fourteenth-century history obtained from a modern historian's text. We cannot know the reality that Langland witnessed daily. What we can be sure of is that he is *not* a journalist. His poem follows Jacques Le Goff's notion that literature is "at once an expression, a reflection, and a sublimation or camouflage of the real society."[10] Here we are concerned with symbolic imaginings of that late medieval society.

Medieval studies must also take into account multiple uses of the term *ideology*. Marxist critics assign negative values such as false consciousness to this term. Here the term is understood as "less tenacious as a 'set of ideas' than as a system of representations, perceptions, and images that precisely encourages men and women to 'see' their specific place in a historically peculiar social formation as inevitable, natural, a necessary function of the 'real' itself."[11] Thus feudal custom constitutes an ideology that ties groups together in power situations and demands constant negotiations of that power.

Medieval Theories of Social Organization

Medieval theologians and philosophers were very conscious of social order in both a symbolic and a real sense. As Paul Zumthor notes, "We can no longer fail to take into account the high degree of semiocity of a culture—the Middle Ages—which thought of itself as an immense network of signs."[12] Central to this concept of network was a society whose organization was based upon a mutual functionality and usefulness.[13] The works of Gerard of Cambrai, Adalbero of Laon, Alfred the Great, Wulfstan, Aelfric, Gilbert of Limerick, and Humbert of Romans offer several conceptual models of social interdependence that bear elaboration as the basis on which Langland attempts, with the aid of feudal organization, to imagine medieval society in its correct signifying order.[14] In *Gesta episcoporum cameracensium* (1024),

Gerard of Cambrai contends that the earthly tripartite model is "homologous to the celestial order."[15] Thus earthly order is a sign of heavenly order. Adalbero of Laon (1025), focusing on functionality, elaborates on the role of each group:

> In the first rank of the nobles are the king and the Emperor; the rest of the nobles have the privilege of not having to submit to the constraint of any outside power, on condition that they abstain from crimes which royal justice represses. They are warriors, protectors of churches, defenders of the people great as well as small, and in doing this they assume their security. The other class is that of the serfs, a miserable race which owns nothing that it does not get by its own labour. Who can calculate the toil by which the serfs are absorbed? Their long journeys, their hard labour? Money, clothing and food—all are provided by the serfs. Not one free man could live without them. . . . These three groups exist together, they cannot be put apart. The services rendered by one are the conditions for those of the other. Each in turn is charged with the support of the whole. This triple assemblage is as one, and so the law may triumph and the world may enjoy peace.[16]

Other writers on social order conceive trifunctionality in geometric shapes. The most common of these is the triangle or pyramid, where the oratores are at the top, and the bellatores and laboratores occupy opposing sides at the base.[17] The king then occupies a position above all and ensures "equilibrium."[18] None of these conceptions of medieval society, however, was completely satisfactory. As Le Goff observes, there is an aristocratic orientation to the tripartite model. Even the designation of laboratores did not include all working peasants, but only those who had contributed innovations to the enterprise of work.[19] Nowhere were women included, and the growing merchant class, springing from the laboratores but distinct from them, was not included. And as Maria Corti writes, "[W]hat does not fit into the model does not exist at the level of the signs, the only level which in religious and cultural terms is endowed with meaning; it lives at an existential level as error, discord, an element that is negative and entropic (that is, pluralizing and centrifugal)."[20] And it is precisely this "existential level" that most concerns a writer of Langland's temperament. This term designates a category apart from what fixed models allow. Morton W. Bloomfield notes that as a "conservative radical" Langland is most concerned with "each class or order performing its proper duty," thus ensuring a just society.[21]

Feudal custom and practice energized the conceptual model of society. In England the king was the giver of the lands to his vassals. With the exception of the chartered towns, all land was held from the king.[22] In terms of signs, the fief was a sign of mutually acknowledged power and obligation between the king and his vassal. Churchmen even held fiefs from the king. Such a complete system of feudal organization left a clear mark on the landscape of England with its massive manors and castles—sites of social and economic power. The lord of the manor was to provide protection, land for rent, and some standard of compensation. The laborer—free and bond—in turn had obligations. He was to pay rent for land, to farm the lord's demesne, and to pay other duties for the right to participate in other services. M. M. Postan observes that the connection between lords and those who dwelt on their land was, in fact, fragile.[23] Although laws protected manorial activities, feudal organization in England was enervated by natural disasters such as the Black Death of 1348–49 and recurring plagues in the 1360s, the falling prices of agricultural commodities, and fewer laborers in combination with landlords who were competing for the remaining laborers by offering higher wages. In a system of implicit subordination as the key to power, peasants were becoming at times even more powerful than their lords.

Piers Plowman was written in the midst of this conceptual and actual change. The B text, assigned to the 1370s but not completed until after the Great Schism of 1378, contemplates growing economic and social problems.[24] Legislation, such as the Statutes of Labourers of 1351, was ineffectual in compelling workers to return to their feudal obligations.[25] Imaged in the B text, Langland's second attempt at addressing the problem of significative corruption brought on by social unrest imagines a feudal ideal but sees the ideal's own undermining by the forces of greed and false signification. Feudal custom and practice cannot be restored in late fourteenth-century England, but hope remains for the reform of the individual.

In the Prologue to the B text, Langland provides a vision of the manorial village in its decay but still within the realm of reform through the reassertion of feudal custom. In fact, the physical institutions which demarcate feudal organization are a part of the landscape. As the poem progresses, Langland moves from a description of society to a model of reformation, focusing on the group that most threatens feudal structure and the model of homologous signification that links earth and heaven.

Feudal Custom and Practice in the Prologue and Passus 1

The Prologue and the interpretive commentary by Holy Church in passus 1 introduce feudal society both in theory and in imagined actuality. Here we see the tension that is always present in the Langlandian model of social reform. The Dreamer falls asleep and imagines an ideologically charged landscape:

> [Ac] as I biheeld into þe Eest, an heiȝ to þe sonne,
> I seiȝ a tour on a toft trieliche ymaked,
> A deep dale byneþe, a dongeon þerInne
> Wiþ depe diches and derke and dredfulle of siȝte.
> A fair feeld ful of folk I þer bitwene
> Of alle manere of men, þe meene and þe riche,
> Werchynge and wandrynge as þe world askeþ. [Prol. 13–19]

Concerning this landscape, Holy Church notes

> "The tour on þe toft," . . . "truþe is þerInne
> And wolde þat ye wrouȝte as his worde teche
> For he is fader of feiþ, and formed yow alle
> Boþe with fel and with face, and yaf yow fyue wittes
> For to worshipe hym þerwiþ while ye ben here." [1.12–16]

Truþe is central not only to feudal custom and practice but also to discovering meaning in the poem. John A. Alford notes that "Truth is not simply an abstract loyalty, such as any society in any age could embrace, but a loyalty manifested concretely in the obligations of status, in the duties of knighthood, in the subordination of one individual to another."[26] The castle in which Truþe lives "was still viewed as a stronghold of feudal authority, not simply as a private residence. . . ."[27] In the late Middle Ages the fortunes of feudal estates were different in England from those of much of the continent; many powerful English families were able to maintain their castles without interruption. Many landlords actually profited from the declining number of

nobles.[28] "Matrimonial alliance and inheritance as well as . . . investment of the huge money profits which came from their proximity to
the king and from their political influence" made feudal organization
in England secure for a short time even during a period of decline.[29]

But in the Prologue the lord occupying the castle in the east is no
ordinary lord; he is God himself. As Ross G. Arthur notes, the concept
of truth here is absolute—"a name for God."[30] Here the poet is fusing
two levels of symbolic order in society. As noted earlier, the social
model was a *signum* of the Trinity; here the referent of the earthly sign
is occupying the position of the human lord who should be the sign of
divine authority. Langland has not made an error in signification; he
probably intends to show the divine presence in the human institution of social order and to suggest a feudal ideal. His presence also
highlights the shadowy, imperfect nature of the earthly institution.
That Holy Church reveals the meaning of the castle in this way is suggestive, particularly since medieval models of social organization are
ecclesiastically generated to support the visions of monarchy.

Truth, according to Alford, has six meanings in the poem.[31] Holy
Church's speech employs the word several times. First, as noted
above, it indicates the name of the lord of the castle. But later all humanity is encouraged to seek truth because "Whan all tresors arn
tried treuþe is the beste" (1.85). Internalizing the concept includes being "trewe of tonge" (1.88). Thus Holy Church has a hierarchical and
interconnected conception of truth in society. The presence of truth in
the world generates the concept of society.

The Prologue also introduces the concept of the manorial village.
The lord of the castle still has administrative control here. In fact, the
village provides additional profits. Plowmen represent the laboratores; both free and bondsmen are among the group. Merchants are
presented, but are not part of the ternary model. Various churchmen,
including anchorites and hermits but also pardoners and friars,
represent the oratores. They, too, are in a state of crisis, as are the laboratores—a point made abundantly clear throughout the poem.
Knights accompany the king who appears in the village, rounding out
the complete ternary model. But even here certain groups exist only
on an existential level—one that the model cannot accommodate. The
vision of the feudal world is tenuous, existing only as long as there is
agreement among the three groups: the king, the knights, and the
commons. The dreamer describes social theory in this way:

Thanne kam þer a kyng; kny3 thod hym ladde;
Might of þe communes made hym to regne.
And þanne cam kynde wit and clerkes he made
For to counseillen þe kyng and þe commune saue.
The kyng and kny3thod and clergie boþe
Casten þat þe commune sholde [hire communes] fynde.

[Prol. 112–17]

This statement revoices the theory in the selection from Adalbero of
Laon noted earlier. In a system of superior to inferior, one must provide goods for the other. But Langland was well aware that the commons were gaining control and threatening the system of obligations
that feudal society had long held as sacred. The fable of belling the
cat, with its clear political references, suggests that the older orders,
the upper portions of the pyramid, are no longer the dominant force
in society. Why Langland added the scene illustrating monarchical
and feudal theory to the B text is difficult to determine, but it likely
follows his established pattern of contemporizing his poem with each
successive rewriting. The commons were beginning to gain power in
Parliament; laborers were gaining power in their ability in some measure to control the conditions of work.[32] Such trends were, for a political and ideological conservative like Langland, dangerous. They
signaled the end of the feudal institution without putting in its place
a social model of organization that would result in peaceful relations.
Considered in terms of Clifford Geertz's notion of ideological formation, Langlandian theorizing is a product of strain: "It is a loss of orientation that most directly gives rise to ideological activity, an
inability, for lack of usable models, to comprehend the universe of
civic rights and responsibilities in which one finds oneself located."[33]
From this conceptualizing scene the poet moves on to imagine the
restoration of the feudal order in the search for Truth—a truth that
is mirrored in society. In a sense society revalorizes itself through
the action.

Feudal Custom and Practice on the Half Acre

The search for Saint Truth, encouraged by Reason, and the subsequent plowing of Piers's half acre, is the poet's most imaginative attempt to reassert the model of feudal authority. Saint Truth is

unknown to the professional pilgrim, who wears emblems of the growing religious mercantilism. Piers, who has worked for Saint Truth for forty years, provides the pilgrims with a set of allegorical directions that is too symbolic for the literal-minded company. That Piers deals at the conceptual level is significant. His attempt to reassert feudal custom and practice on his rented half acre is conceptually sound but not workable. Criticism of this scene is divided on the relation between the plowing of the half acre and the pilgrimage.[34] That the pilgrims are searching for Truth is indicative of the Langlandian ideology underlying the fiction. The pilgrimage to Truth is actually the establishing of feudal truth on the half acre, which itself is a portion of a manor. The scene, according to this reading, creates an imagined feudal reality.

When the pilgrims first meet Piers, he indicates that he knows Truth well. The description that he gives reflects the normative patterns of activity between a lord and his tenants:

> "I knowe hym as kyndely as clerc doþ hise bokes.
> Conscience and kynde wit kenned me to his place
> And dide me suren hym [siþþen] to seruen hym for euere,
> Boþe seow and sette while I swynke myȝte.
> I haue ben his folwere as þis [fourty] wynter,
> Boþe ysowen his seed and suwed hise beestes,
> Wiþinne and wiþouten waited his profit,
> Idyke[d] and Id[o]lue, Ido þat [he] hote.
> Som tyme I sowe and som tyme I þresshe,
> In taillours craft and tynkeris craft, what truþe kan deuyse,
> I weue and I wynde and do what truþe hote.
> For þouȝ I seye it myself I serue hym to paye;
> I haue myn hire [of hym] wel and ouþerwhiles moore.
> He is þe presteste paiere þat pouere men knoweþ;
> He wiþhalt noon hewe his hire þat he ne haþ it at euen."
>
> [5.538–52]

The relationship between Piers and Truth is an idealized conceptual relationship. Since Piers' only connection with Truth has been as a worker of Truth's fields, subordinate to him as feudal practice demands, the way for Piers to show the pilgrims how they may reach Truth is to engage them in work as he has done. The search for Truth, however, is multidimensional. At the same time that Piers is forming contractual agreements among the laborers and the knight, he is also conducting them on another level: a spiritual pilgrimage. John Burrow's notion that Piers is engaging in substitutionary pilgrimage needs this slight modification.[35] There are literal and symbolic pilgrimages under way simultaneously.

Piers' first effort is to engage the services of a knight to provide protection for the laborers on the half acre. When a knight volunteers to labor, Piers suggests rather that he perform the duties he has sworn before the king to perform:

"By Seint Poul!" quod Perkyn, "[for þow protest þee so lowe]
I shal swynke and swete and sowe for vs boþe,
And [ek] labour[e] for þi loue al my lif tyme,
In couenaunt þat þow kepe holy kirke and myselue
Fro wastours and wikked men þat [wolde me destryue],
And go hunte hardiliche to hares and to foxes,
To bores and to [bukkes] þat breken myne hegges,
And [fette þee hoom] faucons foweles to kille
For [þise] comeþ to my croft and croppeþ my whete." [6.24–32]

Knighthood had a clear place in medieval society and gave rise to a considerable number of texts that describe and determine its functions. Ramon Lull's *Libre del Ordre de Cauayleria* (*The Book on the Order of Chivalry*, c. 1280) mentions a similar obligation to protect the land:

The office of a knight is to maintain the land, for because of the fear that the common people have of the knights, they labor and cultivate the earth, out of terror lest they be destroyed. And out of fear of the knights they respect the kings, princes, and lords by whom the knights have their power. . . . The office of the knight also includes searching for thieves, robbers, and other wicked folk in order to have them punished. For just as the ax is made to hew and destroy evil trees, the office of the knight is established in order to punish trespassers and delinquents.[36]

To ensure the potential success of his plan, Piers makes an agreement with the knight that amounts to a verbal pledge of truth. Knowing the excesses of knighthood in reality, Piers warns the knight to "mysbede noȝt þi bondem[a]n, þe bettre [shalt] þow spede" (6.45). Such would

FIGURE 2. The Four-Ox Plough. B.L. MS Add. 42130, fol. 170. Courtesy of the British Library.

be a violation of truth and thus void the feudal institution that Piers is trying to reestablish on the half-acre. Mistreatment of tenants was widespread and seems to have increased as profits from the manors declined. J. L. Bolton notes that many were forced to work vacant land or to pay a fine if they refused.[37] Langland's knight, however, seems merely to provide a convenient moment for a thinly veiled observation on a contemporary problem. Unlike knights in fourteenth-century England, this knight does not appear to hold any fief from the king. He is probably a professional knight hired for the service of another knight. In reestablishing the order, the lord of the half acre is absent, but he has been identified earlier as God himself. At this stage, Piers has been effective in activating the formal structure of feudal authority that will restore signification in society. He has even been able to re-orchestrate all of the activities of the knightly class toward the production of a stable economy.

Piers next turns to the task of plowing, and he is immediately successful in encouraging others in his effort. The dreamer reports:

> Now is Perkyn and [þe] pilgrimes to þe plow faren.
> To erie þis half acre holpen hym manye;
> Dikeres and Delueres digged vp þe balkes;

Therwiþ was Perkyn apayed and preised hem [yerne].
Oþere werkmen þer were þat wroȝten ful [faste],
Ech man in his manere made hymself to doone,
And somme to plese Perkyn piked vp þe wedes.   [6.105–11]

Piers is a representative of the aristocratic laboratores, for he is an innovator. He engages those in labor who are not properly a part of the social model. David Aers notes that these peasants are from among the poorest, and are those who are wanderers after the Black Death.[38] From a single "moment" the poet realizes his attempt to imagine feudal order materially. Each of the two classes of society is performing the ideologically mandated activity. A state of interdependence exists among the groups. Clearly, the balance is a delicate one. Piers manages to further his enterprise not so much because of his "moral ascendancy"[39] but because he holds for the pilgrims the answer to the question of Truth's domain.

Piers' role in reasserting a feudal model of authority in late fourteenth-century England needs further observation. As a plowman, Piers represents a group that, in legislative terms, is one of the most resistant to manorial obligations. By offering Piers as the titular figure in the imagined feudal reorganization, Langland is offering an exemplar of his class. Some critics see Piers as a cleric at this point because of his understanding of biblical texts.[40] Although the priest who reads the pardon asks if Piers is a priest, there is no real evidence that the poet is offering anyone other than a spokesperson from among a group that was becoming by the 1370s the idle poor. The Commons' Petition against Vagrants in 1376 notes that "many of the said wandering labourers have become mendicant beggars in order to lead an idle life; and they usually go away from their own districts into cities, boroughs and other good towns to beg, although they are able-bodied and might well ease the commons by living on their labour and services, if they were willing to serve."[41] Piers indeed finds a group that is willing to serve, but he is unable to sustain that situation.

The feudal society of the half acre is short-lived. As Piers surveys the work at "heiȝ prime" (6.112) he notes that many of the workers are idle. Immediately their language reflects their corruption of the feudal ideal. Their words, "how trolly lolly" (6.116), do not signify truth. Faced with "strikes on the manor,"[42] Piers turns to the knight as the source of law to perform his appointed function on the manor. His warning, "Or þow shalt abigge by þe lawe, by þe ordre þat I bere!" (6.166), appears ineffectual. From Lull's description of knighthood's role in securing order, we can note the ominous potential that knighthood represents. But in an age when all parts of society are in need of reform, Piers' knight is no match for the problem. The feudal ideal of the half acre is not recoverable. As Jill Mann notes, "The society envisaged in this Passus is thus not ruled solely by moral law—nor even by the physical concerns exerted by one social group on another. It is ruled, ultimately, by the laws of physical nature."[43] The feudal ideal fails not because truth no longer exists, but because truth is no longer the pursuit of society as a whole. Individual desire undermines corporate needs—the principle on which feudal order depends.

As a final resort, Piers forces the idle laborers back to work through coercion—a method of dubious merit as it must continue to be present for the manorial system to operate. Hunger is indeed effective, but as Aers notes, "The appeal to Hunger is a desperate and ironically quite amoral wish for nature to reverse processes the poet has shown to be deeply rooted in his world."[44] Piers and Langland are keenly aware of social change and its possibility in blocking the search for truth. For truth to disappear as it is manifested in the feudal economy is a significative failure—an avenue to truth in the world is gone. A system of obligations and social practices must exist on its own terms and cannot be underwritten by the unnatural. The feudal ideal fails here because the lower levels of society wish it to fail.

The Limits of Langland's Feudal Model

Passus 7, involving Truth's granting a pardon—"*a poena & a culpa*" (7.3)—to Piers and his heirs, the reading of the pardon, and Piers' subsequent rejection of the plow for prayer and penance, is the final stage in the poet's attempt to imagine feudal custom and practice. Of the cruces in the B text, this is perhaps the most difficult to reconcile, in part owing to Piers' response at the reading of the pardon. Of course, not all critics believe that Piers has a pardon.[45] Such a reading, however, would undermine the credibility of Truth, who the text indicates purchased the pardon. In this passus, however, the pardon, as Rosemary Woolf notes, implies judgment rather than absolution.[46] The laborers on the half acre are under condemnation because they have failed in their activities. Had they fulfilled their obligations, they too would have a part in the pardon. As the dreamer indicates,

Alle libbynge laborers þat lyuen [by] hir hondes,
That treweliche taken and treweliche wynnen
And lyuen in loue and in lawe, for hir lowe hert[e]
Ha[dde] þe same absolucion þat was sent to Piers. [7.61–64]

Those who sing idle songs and refuse to work are not included in the social model of organization and are not within the domain of truth. The pardon is intimately connected with the concept of feudal order and practice.

At the reading of the pardon, the concept of Truth is again emphasized more in the unwritten text than in the written one. Leaving aside the question of carnal and spiritual readings of the pardon, we can see that Truth has given in his pardon an absolute statement: "*Et qui bona egerunt ibunt in vitam eternam; / Qui vero mala in ignem eternum*" (7.113–14). The implication is clear: those who have lived within the concept of Truth will be forgiven. And in the context of the poem, to live within truth is to perform the duties assigned according to feudal custom and practice. Piers' response to the priest, "*Si ambulauero in medio vmbre mortis / Non timebo mala quoniam tu mecum es*" (7.120–21), indicates that he places full trust in Truth and his pardon. That he destroys the pardon does not invalidate the pardon, but it may indicate that society in its present state is unable to participate in the stipulations of the pardon. While interpretation at this point must clearly remain speculative, we can be sure that Piers believes in Truth and its articulation in feudal society.

Piers' resolution to abandon his plow and to devote himself to prayer and penance cannot be explained merely as the change from an active to a contemplative life. And it does not indicate that Piers "recognizes he has been a fool."[47] The change of activity indicates that truth must first make an impact on the individual; then it can alter society. The feudal order is in crisis. He cannot alter that aspect of medieval society. Whether he postpones the reformation of society according to the feudal model to a later point in history or whether he abandons it altogether is unclear. What remains clear is that the concept of feudal custom and practice cannot be restored in the late 1370s and early 1380s.

Few writers of the late Middle Ages have been so engaged by the confrontation of the conceptual and the real as has the author of *Piers Plowman*. Evidencing an intense desire to pursue truth in his own day, Langland attempts to reassert the only model of authority that medieval civilization has to offer: the ternary model. Feudal custom and practice exist within the model as the energizing force. That the enterprise seems almost fated to end in failure does not limit the poet's ability to imagine its reorganization. At least one early reader of the poem—John Ball—saw the potential for social alteration as the object of the poem. Of course, Langland would not have approved Ball's eccentric reading of the text, in which Ball apparently believed that such a character as Piers might come to restore justice, but he would have approved the attempts to reestablish truth as the goal for society, from the individual to the three estates to the entire country and—finally—to all humanity.

Notes

Author's Note: I would like to acknowledge the support of the University of Tennessee at Martin Research Grant Fund and the National Endowment for the Humanities for this project.

1. Maria Corti, "Models and Antimodels in Medieval Culture," *NLH* 10 (1979):345–46.

2. Corti, "Models and Antimodels," 341.

3. Quotations from the B Text of *Piers Plowman* are from the George Kane and E. Talbot Donaldson edition (London: Athlone Press, 1975). For information on the dating of the poem, see Anne Middleton, *"Piers Plowman," A Manual of Writings in Middle English, 1050–1400*, vol. 7, ed. Albert E. Hartung (New Haven: Connecticut Academy of Arts and Sciences, 1986), 2218.

4. The following are used only as examples; the list is not exhaustive: Edward Vasta, in *The Spiritual Basis of Piers Plowman* (The Hague: Mouton, 1965), contends that the poem's theme is salvation. T. P. Dunning, in *Piers Plowman: An Interpretation of the A-Text*, 2d ed. (Oxford: Clarendon Press, 1980), maintains that temperance is the theme of the A text. Morton W. Bloomfield, in *"Piers Plowman" as a Fourteenth-Century Apocalypse* (New Brunswick, N.J.: Rutgers University Press, 1962), presents the theme as Christian perfection. Britton J. Harwood suggests that the original question about the salvation of the soul is suspended for consideration of social problems, but is "mediated" in Piers ("The Plot of *Piers Plowman* and the Contradiction of Feudalism," in *Speaking Two Languages: Traditional Disciplines and Contemporary Theory in Medieval Studies*, ed. Allen J. Frantzen [Albany: State University of New York Press, 1991], 91–114). The present chapter was written in summer 1990 and revised in fall 1991 after Harwood's article was published. Harwood's

argument is less concerned than is my own with the question of feudal custom and practice as a signifying system that relies more on semiotic models than on material reality. Clearly, Langland does not become sidetracked by social problems; they are integral to the question of personal salvation. I also disagree with Harwood's assumption that there is an implicit "contradiction" in feudalism as noted in the poem. For Langland to have seen such would have invalidated the feudal model as a *signum* of the Trinity.

5. John M. Bowers, *The Crisis of Will in Piers Plowman* (Washington, D.C.: Catholic University of America Press, 1986), 97–128.

6. Lee Patterson, "Introduction: Critical Historicism and Medieval Studies," in *Literary Practice and Social Change in Britain, 1380–1530*, ed. Lee Patterson (Berkeley & Los Angeles: University of California Press, 1990), 1–2. Patterson suggests that medievalists use this term because of its broader frame of reference.

7. "History, Historicism, and the Social Logic of the Text in the Middle Ages," *Speculum* 65 (1990):59–64.

8. Jean E. Howard, "The New Historicism in Literary Study," *ELR* 16 (1985):25.

9. Anne Middleton, "Introduction: The Critical Heritage," in *A Companion to Piers Plowman*, ed. John A. Alford (Berkeley & Los Angeles: University of California Press, 1988), 2–4.

10. *Time, Work, and Culture in the Middle Ages*, trans. Arthur Goldhammer (Chicago: University of Chicago Press, 1980), 88.

11. James H. Kavanagh, "Ideology," in *Critical Terms for Literary Study*, ed. Frank Lentricchia and Thomas McLaughlin (Chicago: University of Chicago Press, 1990), 310.

12. *Speaking of the Middle Ages*, trans. Sarah White (Lincoln: University of Nebraska Press, 1986), 30.

13. Rufus William Rauch, "Langland and Medieval Functionalism," *RPol* 5 (1943):441–61.

14. This list was compiled from the studies of medieval social order in Georges Duby, *The Three Orders: Feudal Society Imagined*, trans. Arthur Goldhammer (Chicago: University of Chicago Press, 1980), 13–109; and Corti, "Models and Antimodels," 342–50.

15. Duby, *Three Orders*, 34.

16. "*Gesta episcoporum cameracensium*," in Rodney Hilton, *Bond Men Made Free: Medieval Peasant Movements and the English Rising of 1381* (London: Temple Smith, 1973), 54.

17. Corti, "Models and Antimodels," 340–41.

18. Le Goff, *Times, Work, and Culture*, 57.

19. Corti, "Models and Antimodels," 341, 346; Hilton, *Bond Men*, 53–54.

20. Corti, "Models and Antimodels," 341.

21. "*Piers Plowman*," 46.

22. Joseph R. Strayer, "Feudalism," in *Dictionary of the Middle Ages*, 13 vols., ed. Joseph R. Strayer (New York: Charles Scribner's Sons, 1982–85), 5:54.

23. *The Medieval Economy and Society: An Economic History of Britain in the Middle Ages* (London: Weidenfeld & Nicolson, 1972), 73–75.

24. Middleton, "*Piers Plowman*," 2218.

25. David Aers, *Community, Gender, and Individual Identity: English Writing, 1360–1430* (London: Routledge, 1988), 26–35; Helen Jewell, "*Piers Plowman*—A Poem of Crisis: An Analysis of Political Instability in Langland's England," in *Politics and Crisis in Fourteenth-Century England*, ed. John Taylor and Wendy Childs (Gloucester, Eng.: Alan Sutton, 1990), 64–71.

26. "The Design of the Poem," in *A Companion to Piers Plowman*, ed. John A. Alford (Berkeley & Los Angeles: University of California Press, 1988), 33.

27. Alford, "Design of the Poem," 32.

28. Georges Duby, *Rural Economy and Country Life in the Medieval West*, trans. Cynthia Postan (Columbia: University of South Carolina Press, 1968), 316.

29. Duby, *Rural Economy*, 316.

30. *Medieval Sign Theory and "Sir Gawain and the Green Knight"* (Toronto: University of Toronto Press, 1987), 89.

31. *Piers Plowman: A Glossary of Legal Terms* (Cambridge: D. S. Brewer, 1988), 159–60.

32. May McKisack, *The Fourteenth Century, 1307–1399*, vol. 5 of *The Oxford History of England*, ed. George Clark (Oxford: Clarendon Press, 1959), 384–97.

33. *The Interpretation of Cultures* (New York: Basic Books, 1973), 219.

34. Early criticism of the poem saw the pilgrimage and the plowing of the half acre as separate activities and noted that the pilgrimage was apparently abandoned. John Burrow was the first to note that the plowing of the half acre was substituted for the pilgrimage; see his "The Action of Langland's Second Vision," *EC* 15 (1965):247–68.

35. "Action of Langland's Second Vision," 247–68.

36. In *The History of Feudalism*, ed. David Herlihy (New York: Walker & Co., 1970), 315, 318–19.

37. *Medieval English Economy, 1150–1500* (Totowa, N.J.: Rowan & Littlefield, 1980), 212–14.

38. *Community*, 42.

39. Elizabeth D. Kirk, *The Dream Thought of Piers Plowman* (New Haven: Yale University Press, 1972), 74.

40. The connection between plowmen and preachers in the Middle Ages was a commonplace based on Gregory's *Moralia*. See Stephen A. Barney, "The Plowshare of the Tongue: The Progress of a Symbol from the Bible to *Piers Plowman*," *MS* 35 (1973):261–93.

41. In R. B. Dobson, *The Peasants' Revolt of 1381*, 2d ed. (London: Macmillan Press, 1983), 74.

42. Aers, *Community*, 41.

43. "Eating and Drinking in 'Piers Plowman,' " *Essays and Studies* 32 (1979):29.

44. Aers, *Community*, 17.

45. Denise N. Baker, in "From Plowing to Penitence: *Piers Plowman* and Fourteenth-Century Theology," *Speculum* 55 (1980):715–25, rejects the validity of the pardon. Rosemary Woolf sees the pardon as valid after it is torn ("The Tearing of

the Pardon," in *Piers Plowman: Critical Approaches*, ed. S. S. Hussey [London: Methuen, 1969], 70).

46. Woolf, "Tearing of the Pardon," 70.

47. Baker, "From Plowing to Penitence," 722.

Containing Change

Modifying Feudal Ideals of Order

———————————————————————— ❧

THE FACT THAT the feudal ideal of order was not inviolable presented numerous problems to those who would conservatively appropriate forms of feudal custom and practice in order to shape or
stabilize society. Reasserting the paradigm of feudal order to no avail
no doubt would have been the worst of these problems to arise. But
even when such results occurred, as was often the case in the later
Middle Ages, vestiges or elements of the former ideal might be articulated or brought into play to assert order. Such is the argument of the
first essay in the second part of this collection.

In "Potency and Power: Chaucer's Aristocrats and Their Linguistic
Superiority," Jean E. Jost approaches the subject of social and political
stability and coherence from the perspective of linguistic power. It is
her contention that where order is not established through procedure,
as in the world of the Canterbury pilgrims, it may at least be secured
by giving voice to the principles that once were fundamental to feudal
custom and practice. To that end, her study demonstrates how Chaucer, in perceiving the changing social relationships in his world, has
his male aristocrats—the Knight and his son, the Squire—maintain a
superior attitude in their discourse for the purpose of defending
against intrusion into their ranks by members of the new, emerging
lower social orders, individuals who would infringe on their age-old,
presumed position of authority. The Knight, who reveals a profound
understanding of the problems inherent in discourse, achieves this
end by assuming a secondary power of creation in his tale, through
both his use of history to convey philosophy and his dignified style,
and thereby maintains confidence about his place in the world. The

Squire, while failing to achieve the standard set by his father, especially as his representation of the ideal is transformed into an illusory and magical reality, nevertheless remains confident in at least the form—if not the content—of what he is saying. The Knight and the Squire are optimistic about the potency of their language despite the fact that their linguistic stance underscores further the vulnerability of the feudal ideal of order.

When it became necessary to reestablish social and political stability by appropriating features of the feudal ideal of order, it was not always clear which aspects of that ideal would be the most appropriate and effective for each situation. It goes without saying that such uncertainty often led to modification of the perceived ideal. Indeed such modification would sometimes necessarily involve the outright rejection of particular features of the ideal in favor of others to make possible the successful and expeditious negotiation of actual circumstances. This type of modification or "redefinition" is treated by Liam O. Purdon and Julian N. Wasserman in the second essay in this part entitled "Chivalry and Feudal Obligation in Barbour's *Bruce*."

In this Scottish national epic concerning the wars fought for independence from the English, Purdon and Wasserman contend that John Barbour has two objectives in mind as he recounts Robert Bruce's rise to power. First, he demonstrates the ineffectuality and potential danger of the age-old chivalric ideal through the character and the exploits of Edward Bruce, which proved to be fatal to the Scottish cause in Ireland. Second, and more importantly, he argues for the use of a modified version of feudal obligation in the form of an "egalitarian" specific vassal homage embracing the importance of the individual as the most efficacious means of unifying a realm at war under the rule of militant kingship. That the Scots win their fight as the result of a determined belief in their cause cannot be argued. Barbour, however, repeatedly emphasizes that this cause gains support only through the appropriation and modification of certain practical features of conventional feudal custom and practice. In other words, Barbour indicates that the shaping of the new Scottish order comes about as the Scots reinvent the ideal of feudal order, sometimes rather hastily but never imprudently, as they fight and defeat the English armies invading their homeland.

3 Potency and Power

Chaucer's Aristocrats
and Their Linguistic Superiority

————————————————————————————— ✤

N HIS epilogue to Ramon Lull's *The Book of the Ordre of Chyualry*, William Caxton writes: "O ye knyghtes of Englond, where is the custome and usage of noble chyvalry that was used in tho dayes? What do ye now, but go to the baynes and playe at dyse? And some, not wel advysed, use not honest and good rule, ageyn all ordre of knyghthode."[1] Perhaps every age bemoans what it perceives as the moral degeneration of the innovative and modern. And perhaps each idealistically conceives the previous zeitgeist and mores, deprecating its own untested ethical world view. William Caxton was not alone in lamenting the decline in values and knightly expectations of his time; on an even grander scale, historians after him have magnified his concern.[2]

It is no accident that feudalism is said to have "declined." For one thing, after the twelfth century, the knight's function as warrior-knight had changed. According to Carl Stephenson,

> To the decline of the feudal aristocracy various military changes of the later Middle Ages gave added impetus. . . . It was demonstrated that . . . masses of pikemen could solidly withstand cavalry charges; that longbowmen and crossbowmen, since their arrows would easily penetrate ordinary mail, could be used to good effect for defense or for offense. These lessons in warfare, though not always appreciated

49

at the time, eventually inspired a new tactical system in which the feudal warrior had no place.[3]

The ethical dimension informing the bond of fealty that had, by extension, once provided a framework and context for chivalric behavior, had now disappeared along with the oath of fealty.

Furthermore, a landless knight from the merchant class, or one newly entering the ranks as a mercenary, would have no independent means of support, a serious drawback in an era when paid wages were notoriously unreliable. How would the *parvenu* support himself and provide needed military supplies during conflict when he could not rely on family wealth? What would he do in peacetime, without means of self-support? Looting and plundering were the inevitable consequence, further degrading what was intended as a highminded, selfless profession.[4]

Even in the heyday of chivalric feudalism, tension between the real and the ideal, the actual and the desired, the accepted and the aspired to, characterized an aristocratic society embroiled in defending its preeminent social and political position and power, justifying its means.[5] Sometimes, in its bid to glorify chivalric values, literature—most often romance—reinforced such an idealistic vision.[6]

But the presumed inborn superiority of the aristocracy was questioned neither in social theory nor in romance. Social class distinctions and a hierarchal power structure were simply assumed. The aristocratic milieu had little in common with that of peasant society. Its privileged status was a given; only the degree or extent of its privilege varied. As David Herlihy claims, chivalry

> had the function of providing to one of the great classes of traditional European society a justification for its privileges and position. For centuries . . . [after its inception], the European nobles pretended that God had given them the sword for the repression of evil and the defense of the good. But apart from its close association with a privileged class, chivalry further defined for a larger group of individuals how a gentleman should appear and how he should act in love and war. No doubt the ideal was honored more in the breach than in the observance.[7]

The nobility preserved that prerogative, that privileged role and its attendant compensations, with a veneer of "courtesie" and an exalted code of behavior instituted to protect clergy, women, and peasants in paternalistic fashion. If the aristocracy had tenaciously maintained its view of superiority during chivalry's prime, even more strongly did it insist upon its privilege during its decline. When the aristocracy's position was threatened, it resolutely asserted its dominance. In Georges Duby's words, "Although in the early thirteenth century the French nobility formed a united and homogeneous group, linked by a feeling of inborn and hereditary superiority and by a common respect for the ideals of chivalry, as a class it also felt itself to be threatened. In face of the threat it closed its ranks and strengthened the bonds which held it together."[8] Challenged by an upstart bourgeoisie in political, social, and economic arenas, the nobles reacted with defensive resistance to the intrusion of *vilains* and wealthy merchants into their ranks. The attempt to protect their status despite changing economic realities ultimately proved futile; but it was the source of tension and struggle felt across social lines. As the marginalized wealthy bourgeoisie made inroads into the privileged ranks, threatened nobles struggled vainly to maintain control. As Jennifer Goodman puts it, "Manuscripts, book lists, and tournament records of the late fourteenth and fifteenth centuries show a rising preoccupation with details of chivalric practice, in life as in the new verse and prose romances."[9] No doubt this tenacious grasp of a past glory would inevitably extend to the literary domain.

Geoffrey Chaucer, fourteenth-century social historian as well as author, keenly perceived the changing social relationships of his world. As Paul Strohm points out, Chaucer's "equivocal evocations of vassalage ultimately suggest growing trouble for the social institution on which they depend."[10] In creating his pilgrimage including different travelers, he draws on this tension between individuals, professions, and particularly social classes at every turn, and in many ways. According to Strohm, for each of Chaucer's tales, "the social assumptions borne by the narrative form, the apparent social perspective of its teller, and the ways in which the assignment heightens the audience's sense of social implications [are] . . . complicated by a further, characteristic maneuver, in which Chaucer introduces his own tacit criticisms, both of the social assumptions of his narrative and the social perspective of his teller."[11] But of greatest interest is his method of linguistic interplay, as he orchestrates narrators who reinforce, contradict, *quite,* undercut, and best each other through discourse.[12] Chaucer's *Canterbury Tales* thus dramatizes how the social problems of the fourteenth century affected his aristocrats. To that end, Chaucer expresses the tension of a class threatened in its privilege and power through aristocratic narrators who confirm their highborn status by nuanced discourse. If we can grant them a measure of psychological realism—treat characters as people who think and, possibly, even connive—we will discover certain common linguistic traits uniting the members of the nobility. Harold Bloom's spirited defense of such an approach endorses such a methodology. Pointing to what Shelley called "forms more real than living man," Bloom finds

> What is virtually without precedent in Shakespeare is that [Chaucer's] characters *change themselves by pondering upon what they themselves say.* In Homer and the Bible and Dante, we do not find sea changes in particular persons brought about by those persons' own language, that is by the differences that individual diction and tone make as speech produces further speech. But the Pardoner and the Wife of Bath are well along the mimetic way that leads to Hamlet and Falstaff. What they say to others and to themselves partly reflects what they already are, but partly engenders also what they will be. And perhaps even more subtly and forcefully, Chaucer suggests ineluctable transformations going on in the Pardoner and the Wife of Bath through the effect of the language of the tales they choose to tell.[13]

What Bloom suggests is germane to the following discussion of language usage, but assumes further a justification for conceiving characters as persons for the purpose of critical inquiry. David Aers makes a similar argument for viewing Criseyde as a person in less emotional, but strongly definitive terms.[14] Grounded in such support, this discussion likewise presumes the legitimacy of seeing characters as real, speaking human beings, reflecting, among other things, their social class.

The *Canterbury Tales,* encompassing multiple social classes, offers a perfect forum in which to investigate various levels of linguistic skepticism, trust, ambivalence, confidence, and doubt, both in the nature of language itself, and by any given narrator. Each one, reflecting his or her social level, struggles to capture truth in the appropriate genre and with the requisite degree of linguistic decorum. As Robert Jordan has recently observed, "Chaucer's poetry exhibits many forms of ambivalence about truth and considerable self-consciousness and anxiety about its own validity as an instrument of truth. While seemingly confident, often even flamboyant, in its command of the verbal medium, Chaucer's poetry also expresses . . . a fragmented and problematic outlook, an uncertainty about fundamental truths, including the truth of poetry—indeed of language—and about the role and status of the poet."[15]

In fact, Chaucer is concerned with the validity and reliability of the word, with language in general and poetry in particular. His doubts about a poetic able to convey truth continue into the *Canterbury Tales,* a work Derek Traversi has called "essentially open-ended and distrustful of the human capacity for final statements."[16] Chaucer's skepticism, however, may delve deeper than "final statements." The tellers' certainty about the truth they attempt to represent may be undermined by their own often self-deprecatory statements and the way they make words function in their tales, especially if they lack confidence. They, too, are conscious of the limited truth-value in their own articulated or literary product. But even more strongly than they doubt the power of language to tell truth, they distrust discourse for what it can *do:* deceive, humiliate, antagonize, control. How words actually function in the *Canterbury Tales* to reveal or mask reality, how individual pilgrims perceive language operating—indeed, *make* language operate in prologues and tales—and how words control reality, are as "diverse" as the travelers and their tales.

Social standing is one indicator of how language is perceived and utilized. Not all characters evaluate language function negatively, and some hold complicated positions about its varied capabilities. Indeed, the various tellers create a heteroglossia consisting of every conceivable linguistic form; their tales presume and reinforce their hesitation, doubt, or certainty about the potency of discourse, and reveal exactly what it can do. Some tellers find language efficacious and persuasive—that is, a means to effect good; others see it as impotent, unreliable, deceptive, dangerous, or destructive. Some oppose language to deeds, preferring one to the other; others utilize both, finding them mutually reinforcing. In each case, the tale mirrors the linguistic position of the teller.

Chaucer's two primary representatives of the feudal aristocracy, the established Knight and the youthful Squire, reveal contrasting assumptions about acting within their stations in life; in other words, they differ about their right to assume truth, to state it convincingly, and to demand public attention. The first wisely tempers his inherited position with judicious restraint, while the second injudiciously uses it without measure. Each simultaneously reveals his philosophical position about the ideal and the real in his language and the type of tale he chooses—or is capable of offering. Strohm notes that Chaucer assigns different genres to particular social strata, the dignified, to that of the knight: "The Canterbury pilgrims describe the *Knight's Tale* as a *storie* (ll. 3110–11), presumably meaning to compliment its dignity, its venerability, its value as instruction . . . traditionally situated characters like the Knight, the Squire, the Monk, and the Prioress tend toward narrative punctuated by assertion of the atemporal and transcendent."[17] The Squire, on the other hand, tells a fantastic romance, what Goodman calls a "composite courtly romance,"[18] less tied to any particular historical reality and hence less venerable. For both the Knight and Squire, a certain confidence accompanies the distinction of aristocratic social class, naturally exhibiting a concomitant linguistic security. But how each expresses this confidence, and what each perceives as real or ideal, indeed varies.

Chaucer's Knight, veteran of the wars, is sophisticated and experienced enough in worldly matters to realize security is neither easily won nor automatically presumed. Although his tale ultimately resolves with some satisfaction, it is gained only through pain experienced by the characters, and work for the teller. Perhaps closer in time to the waning ideal of chivalry, the Knight wants to idealize the noble way of life, to valorize it by his tale in its dignified, ritualized style, its grand epic scope, its deference to Theseus's power, and its attempt to orchestrate action and display order and power. As Strohm suggests, "The Knight's narrative finally rejects a conception of history as a record of human accomplishments and embraces a conception of providential history subject to intervention from above."[19] Such a notion presumes the superiority of hierarchal rank over individual merit. Conversely, the Squire does not use providential history as his escape; nor has he yet learned the chastening lessons of human suffering and labor. One generation later and caught in the throes of worsening social chaos, he attempts to escape from his world to a magical reality, out of touch with concrete daily life or its responsibilities. His confidence in language and his assumption about his skill as a teller, however, are unfounded. He lacks the breadth and depth, the wisdom of moderation, of his father, which his father has gained from living. What is more, his privileged class affords him no escape from a linguistic rout. His perception of reality is unduly optimistic. Thus, while the Knight's view of life is primarily realistic, and the Squire's is ideal, if somewhat preposterous, both involve a linguistic confidence originating in their social heritage. Neither of them questions the potency of language, and while they display language's capacity for tricking and damaging, neither would ever think to dismiss or reject such a linguistic power.[20] These aristocratic representatives, then, exemplify a complacent self-perception, and exhibit an inflated sense of self-importance through the language of their tales, one based on their privileged social status.

Much debate has arisen over the chivalric reputation and merits of Chaucer's "worthy knyght" since he is part of that landscape of shifting ethical ground Caxton laments shortly thereafter. In 1907, John Matthews Manly noted, "When Chaucer painted this portrait, the figure which served him as model and the ideals which it embodied were already doomed. Gunpowder and cannon had come to take away the occupation and the prestige of the knight, and almost exactly at the same time Genoa and Venice had given the first great demonstration that 'business is business' and that the ideals of chivalry must give way to the ideals of commerce."[21] And in 1957, F. N. Robinson commented that "Although chivalry in the fourteenth century was in its decline and had a very sordid side, Chaucer has wholly refrained from satirizing the institution."[22] But Terry Jones would disagree, showing that in depicting his Knight, Chaucer reveals an authorial awareness of feudal deterioration. Whether or not this Knight is a mercenary, or a scurrilous character Chaucer meant to malign, as Jones believes, his personal status is certainly in decline, for

> . . . he is not endowed with any physical beauty or grace, there is no mention of any family background, no coat-of-arms, no shield, no belt (crucial to the truly "gentil" or noble knight), no manorial estates. He shows no interest in the courtly pastimes of hunting, hawking, or

courtly love. His dress is shabby, his retinue small, and his life-long career on the battlefield has been exclusively abroad and has apparently missed out on all the great English victories of the period—such as Crécy, Poitiers and Najera—on which the reputation of English chivalry in the fourteenth century rested.[23]

This description need not negate the aristocratic status of the Knight, but shows to what degree he has fallen within it. David Aers, agreeing with Jones, contends that "the *Knight's Tale* is not an unequivocal celebration of Theseus as the principle of law and order we are to worship. It is a critical, often highly ironic, exploration of secular rule, its forms of power and its uses of language."[24] If chivalry were here presented as so corrupt, and aristocratic privilege so threatened, does the character of the Knight indicate any such awareness, or act to assert or preserve it? Just how conscious of the chivalric decline did Chaucer intend him to be? His actions and his speech suggest he is highly aware of the changing social climate. Whether Chaucer's Knight was indeed modeled on Henry of Grossmont, First Duke of Lancaster (1310–61), or his grandson Henry of Derby (later Henry IV, 1382–1439), as A. S. Cook suggests,[25] is irrelevant. Rather, the Knight and his compatriots, regardless of their current economic condition and despite their decline, believe in their superior status, and linguistically reveal that sense of privilege in the face of declining deference to the ideal that once informed their social standing.

Although the Knight discriminatingly relies on his characters' and his own words to convey meaning, beginning with " 'Now let us ryde, and herkneth what I seye' . . . with right a myrie cheere" (I.855, 857), the rest of his tale indicates a deeper perception of the problems inherent in discourse. Life, truth, and communication are not easy. Unlike the Squire, who chooses to create an original tale, the Knight repeats one "as olde stories tellen us" (I.859), firmly grounded in history, military exploits, and Greek mythology. These are his realities. Further, he pays a debt to authority and the past by drawing on them, hence displaying a measure of humility in his choice. On the other hand, he is not so tied to tradition that he is unable to use it, in fact, to anachronize it if he chooses, as in transforming the legendary King Theseus into a venery-loving medieval duke.

Not only what, but how the Knight tells his tale, the style he chooses, reveals his aristocratic heritage. As Knapp suggests, "In keeping with its address as authorized discourse, the tale represents, not the fast-paced, suspenseful up-for-grabs quotidian world, but the world of ideas . . . the leisurely manner of the tale enacts this symmetry over and over."[26] His leisurely approach and dignified solemnity bespeak a confidence and assurance in the tale and in his own importance, even in the face of personal decline, which demands the pilgrims' attention. In speaking of the opening five lines, C. David Benson says, "Although its style and vocabulary are relatively simple, the passage moves with a leisurely stateliness that is appropriate to the tale's exalted themes. . . . Theseus is introduced by name . . . both familiar and impressive to the reader [and] assigned a series of titles ('lord,' 'governor,' and 'conquerour') . . . [which] suggest power and control and are suitably grand without being grandiose."[27] What is more, power and control are second nature to the Knight, as is implicit in his attitude and self-expression. Charles Muscatine believes that in the *Knight's Tale* "form and style are so functional that they point directly to the meaning. The pace of the story is deliberately slow and majestic . . . a great deal of [the] descriptive material has a richness of detail far in excess of the demands of the story. . . . Like the descriptions and narrator's comments, the direct discourse in the tale contributes to its slowness. . . . When we look at the form in which these materials are organized, we find symmetry to be its most prominent feature."[28] Accordingly, dignity of word-choice and pacing, carefully followed ritual, and precise protocol mark the Knight's approach to his tale. Impressions are important. In his bid to be impressive, he carefully structures his tale, and, in endorsing the value of his way of life, fully elaborates on chivalric customs and practices. Muscatine notes that "the chivalric aspects of the scene are described with minute particularity . . . swoons and cries, fallings on knees, and sudden palenesses . . . a symphony of howls, wails and lamentations."[29] While the content may be excessive, the style is controlled, deliberate, convinced, secure, and as solid as the Knight wishes his class status to be perceived. The slow, deliberate pacing, the orderly symmetry—Palamon, Arcite, and Emily paired with Venus, Mars, and Diana, funerals with weddings, times with places, movements with speeches—comprise an attempt to validate and valorize order, hierarchy, the crumbling social class system. In other words, the Knight recounts minute particulars of aristocratic life to endorse its value, to reinforce its significance, to ensure its continuance. Muscatine is right in calling it

> a sort of poetic pageant. Its design expresses the nature of the noble life . . . love and chivalry, but even more important is the general tenor of the noble life, the pomp and ceremony, the dignity and power, and particularly the repose and assurance with which the exponent of nobility invokes order. . . . The society depicted is one in which form is full of significance, in which life is conducted at a dignified, processional pace, and in which life's pattern is itself a reflection, or better, a reproduction, of the order of the universe.[30]

Such a harmonious state of affairs, however, is more wish than reality; although the Knight and his tale both display the secure stance and confident demeanor that mark his own perceived social status, his personal reality has been diminished by world events. In the face of obvious loss, he insists on and ensures by his formalized construct a past ideal reality, a society in which everyone knows his or her place and stays within it.

Thus the Knight assumes a certain secondary power of creation, both in style and content—in that he can orchestrate and manipulate his tale as he wishes—when he states, "And thus with victorie and with melodye / Lete I this noble duc to Atthenes ryde" (I.872–73). He seems to be granting permisssion to his characters. Simultaneously, he displays a control of subject matter not unlike that with which the young Squire will later struggle unsuccessfully, claiming:

> And certes, if it nere to long to heere
> I wolde have toold yow fully the manere
> How wonnen was the regne of Femenye . . .
> And of the grete bataille for the nones
> Bitwixen Atthenes and Amazones . . .
> But al that thyng I moot as now forbere.
> I have, God woot, a large feeld to ere. [I.875–77, 879–80, 885–86]

Surely he has a clear sense of his purpose, and goes after it. Accordingly, he identifies the reality he will examine: noble, military, romantic, heroic, mythic, tragic. His narrative is direct, controlled, uninterrupted, and punctuated with structural markers for the audience's benefit. With sophisticated rhetorical maneuvering, he mentions what he will not discuss to provide a context for his immediate story of the captive widows' plight. Here he attains the proper balance of emotion and restraint. Here, also, the widows' words are efficacious: Theseus declares war on Creon, demanding proper burial for their slain husbands. As noted above, some critics have found this brutal retaliation—killing Creon and his knights and putting innocent folk to flight—damaging to the Knight. Interestingly, the widows want the corpses to bury and pray over, involving both action and ritual words, which they believe will have a certain salvific effect. The status of Theseus ensures the power of the Knight's words to enact deeds in a parallel fashion, for he, too, is part of the powerful aristocratic society. Yet his wisdom has moderated any elitist arrogance or unwarranted hyperbole. He concludes the episode by stating, "But shortly for to telle is myn entente" (I.1000).

A decade ago, Robert W. Hanning argued that precariousness of control constituted

> a main theme of the Knight's Tale, linking the Knight's ad hoc artistic activities with the political, and finally philosophical, program of Theseus by which the Athenian duke attempts to solve the potentially disruptive problems of Palamon and Arcite. And behind Theseus lies yet a deeper level of unresolved tension: the ambivalence of the Knight about life's meaning, as revealed in his treatment of his characters. At this last, most profound level, Chaucer confronts the paradoxes inherent in chivalry, and thereby transforms Boccaccio's literary tour de force into a troubling anatomy of an archaic but, in his day, still influential ideal of the noble life.[31]

Indeed, upheaval and control is a major issue within the tale and the Knight's society, assuredly binding Theseus and the narrator. The latter's unresolved tension and ambivalence about life are a natural consequence of the current social environment in which he is posited as living. No doubt a nostalgic desire to reclaim an orderly, predictable past in the face of current social disruption partly motivates the Knight's well-orchestrated narrative. Chivalric paradoxes could hardly have escaped Chaucer, who imposed them on his fictional figure. But it is unclear why Hanning finds Chaucer's Knight to have "difficulties in discharging his unaccustomed artistic responsibilities [that] surface most spectacularly in his description of Arcite's funeral rites"[32] when the Knight engages in a very conscious and purposeful *occupatio*. Considering the circumstances and the task at hand, the Knight manipulates a complicated, multivalenced tale with multiple perspectives and discourses like a master chess player, perhaps more successfully than any other pilgrim. Relative, if not perfect, order obtains.

Nonverbal discourse is also efficacious in the *Knight's Tale*, as in the scene where the two prisoners lie nearly dead, unable to speak. While speech itself is ineffective here,

> . . . by hir cote-armures and by hir gere
> The heraudes knewe hem best in special
> As they that weren of the blood roial
> Of Thebes, and of sustren two yborn. [I.1016–19]

Semiotics has made its way to the Theban battlefield! Concluding Theseus's conquest, the Knight opines, "what nedeth wordes mo?" (I.1029). They have conveyed their message, so why belabor the point? The narrator-Knight has, of course, used rhetorical tropes to paint this impressive nonverbal scene, evincing his own linguistic power, once again with self-confident *sprezzatura*. Next, May's injunction to "Arys, and do thyn observaunce" (I.1045) brings Emily to stroll in the garden beneath the now-recovered prisoners, "And as an aungel hevenysshly she soong" (I.1055). But it is the sight of her, not her words or even her unproductive voice, that moves first Palamon and then Arcite to voluminous, unproductive protestations—comically demonstrating that all aristocratic discourse is not sacrosanct.

Recognizing the power of nonverbal discourse, the Knight chooses to depict elaborate wall paintings, lavish tournaments, dramatic pageantry, all emblematic of his power. Not limited to linguistic communication, he sees the value of creating tableaux to convey and reinforce his aristocratic station. He is confident in adding new colors to his palette, especially to endorse chivalric life. Yet he does not eschew verbal power. While his tale is comparatively long within the *Canterbury Tales* framework, it is remarkably contained and circumscribed compared to Statius's and Boccaccio's versions. And since he begins the game and thereby sets the standard, no other pilgrim could consider his tale of verbal and semantic communication long or uncontrolled.

Palamon's cry "A!" (I.1078) effectively elicits verbal communication, eleven lines of Arcite's sympathy and Palamon's explanation. But both speeches complicate the situation, for they draw Arcite's attention to Emily. Arcite's protestation of love evokes Palamon's injured retort that Arcite has thus betrayed him, broken their vow of brotherhood "Ysworn ful depe . . . Neither of us in love to hyndre oother" (I.1132, 1135). A rupture in the discourse occurs, however, for their mutual pledge, spoken with sincere conviction, has failed to bind. Palamon challenges "false Arcite" to deny it: "thou darst it nat withseyn" (I.1140). Thus, language becomes dangerous—it is no more predictable or reliable than their changing reality. Palamon ruminates inconclusively about this aspect of language as he considers the cruel gods who govern the world "with bynding of your word eterne" (I.1304) without regard to true guilt or innocence.

If the young Palamon's and Arcite's words are deceptively ineffective, those of the established Duc Perotheus carry weight: at his request, Arcite is released from prison when he vows not to return to the kingdom. But this confidence in the strength of language is undermined when Arcite bemoans his wrong decision to leave the tower and the sight of Emily. The Knight-Narrator playfully ends Part I with a question: Who is worse off, the prisoner watching his lady from afar or the free man unable to see her at all? The answer is as nebulous as whether or not language tells truth.

Part II flies in on Mercury's wings, but the Knight treats this apparition in Arcite's dream as realistically as he does other divine beings, grounding it firmly in the concrete. His injunction to return to Athens is more effective than Arcite's weeping and lamenting. The Knight bemoans a second failure of language in humbly disclaiming his ability to recount Palamon's seven-year anguished imprisonment:

> Who koude ryme in Englyssh proprely
> His martirdom? For sothe it am nat I;
> Therfore I passe as lightly as I may.   [I.1459–61]

But after his escape, Palamon sums up the deceitful Arcite's behavior with true words: "[Thou] hast byjaped heere duc Theseus, / And falsly chaunged hast thy name thus" (I.1585–86). When they are caught fighting by Theseus, Palamon exclaims, "what nedeth wordes mo? / We have the deeth disserved bothe two" (I.1715–16). His confession of their identities condemns both himself and Arcite, the escaped prisoner and the exile who promised never to return. Facts are facts, and mere words will not change them. Here Palamon claims language is futile, impotent to alter the situation. But the duke, and perhaps the Knight, see it differently: Theseus *will* be moved by the ladies' begging tears to forgive the recreants if they swear loyalty and peace to him and his country. The duke and, perhaps by extension, the Knight whose surrogate he is trust discourse, even in the face of Palamon's and Arcite's recent treachery. And endorsing the efficacy of words, Theseus forgives their past trespasses while establishing a tourney to determine Emily's husband. Not his words, but valiant action, will ultimately fulfill their destiny.

With his own voice, the Knight begins Part III fearing lest men think him negligent in not telling all—in this case, all Theseus provided for the extravagant lists determining Emily's fate. This conscientious awareness of his own language power marks the Knight as a responsible tale-teller of reality, here describing the elaborate physical preparations and temples erected for the tourney. He does it well. Both the rhetorical flourish and the extended length of his descriptions display a certain sprezzatura. And the verbal pictures he creates derive from nonverbal communication—paintings on the temple walls recounting mythic history. This fantastic reality is nevertheless treated with respect and dignity to lend it a measure of credibility, and thus ground it in the real. But the most significant evidence of the Knight's trust in discourse occurs in the gods' promises, which, however seemingly incompatible, are indeed fulfilled as promised. Verbal commitments that appear to represent impossible, unrealistic, even idealistic fulfillment of all desire, ultimately prove real.

Notably, the Knight is not overly impressed by these pagan deities, treating them with an ironic distance, even disdain, from a stance of confident security. As F. Anne Payne points out,

> [T]hey are actual gods with Roman names, have a dramatic objectivity equivalent to the other characters, and are a part of a traditional mythological system to which the Knight pays no attention. Saturn, instead of uttering the words of a Golden Age god, berates the assembly with an account of the evil he presides over. Jupiter, instead of acting as the awesome controller of all things, is the harried, unsuccessful ruler trying to keep peace in the family.[33]

Not accustomed to being excessively deferential, the Knight treats the gods as equals at best, perceiving their weaknesses and satirically observing their shortcomings. Nevertheless, they have their role in the story.

First Palamon prays to Venus, successfully communicating his pain, confusion, and desire—not for victory, but for Emily. His disclaimer "Allas! I ne have no langage to telle / Th' effectes ne the tormentz of myn helle" (I.2227–29) is that and no more, for his language does successfully evoke Venus's pity. Lacking audible words, the Venus statue signals by a shaking of the idol and "made a signe, wherby that he took / That his prayere accepted was that day" (I.2265–66). Then, Emily begs three things of the goddess Diana: to protect her from vengeance and ire, keep her "a mayden al my lyf / Ne nevere wol I be no love ne wyf" (I.2305–6), and send her rivals love and peace. But the realistic girl makes accommodation lest her wish be impossible: if not, "sende me hym that moost desireth me" (I.2325). Her words as well seem efficacious, judging by the responsive fires on Diana's altar, which die out, rekindle, and, whistling, finally die out again. Even more indicative of Emily's verbal potency are the clattering of Diana's arrows and her sudden apparition, reporting the gods' decree for her marriage:

> . . . by eterne word written and confermed
> Thou shalt ben wedded unto oon of tho
> That han for thee so muchel care and wo,
> For unto which of them I may nat telle.   [I.2350–53]

Finally, Arcite begs Mars for Emily, and hence the victory that would merit her. His words and the promise of his beard and hair evoke a clattering of temple doors, a brightening of the fires, a sweet smell from the ground, a ringing of Mars's hauberk, and a murmuring of "Victorie!" In each case the Knight creates discourse that all presume is true and reliable. His confident assumption is thus reassuring to his audience(s) as well. Never are the gods' predictions doubted in this divine world that, to the Knight, is itself unreal or false. The Knight remains emotionally uninvolved—with Palamon and Arcite's lovesickness, with their conflict over this maid they have yet to meet, with Emily's wish to remain virginal. He stands apart—not aloof, but distinct from the action of the drama. More like Theseus than any other character, he looks benignly on the comings and goings of a past long gone and possibly also on the recent past he may have experienced, and whose passing he may well mourn.

Part IV begins with Theseus's tournament stipulations to prevent "destruccion of blood" (I.2564); words thus control life-and-death activity on the playing field. To a certain degree they are successful: when Arcite bests Palamon, Theseus stops the games, awarding Emily to the victor. But this realistic, human world of mortal combat is subservient to the divine one, in which gods and goddesses ultimately exercise control. Saturn reassures the weeping Venus that although Arcite won the battle, the game is not over. He is right. Arcite's precipitate fall and subsequent death mean he wins the victory, which was his prayer, but leave Palamon free to collect the prize. In fact, on his deathbed the generous Arcite offers his blessing, verbally endorsing the union of Palamon and Emily. Words continue to exert a great force on events and regularly prove true and reliable sources of information. Yet they have their limits. At Arcite's death, the Knight exclaims:

> His spirit chaunged hous and wente ther,
> As I cam nevere, I kan nat tellen wher.
> Therfor I stynt; I nam no divinistre;
> Of soules fynde I nat in this registre,
> Ne me ne list thilke opinions to telle
> Of hem, though that they writen wher they dwelle. [I.2809–14]

The Knight's scrupulous honesty is the main reason language is so truthful on his lips. What he does not know, he directly acknowledges, admitting neither overstatement, greater knowledge than he has, nor false protestations. Words can detail Arcite's funeral pyre ceremony, so the Knight does provide some description while disclaiming knowledge. "But shortly to the point thanne wol I wende / And maken of my longe tale an ende" (I.2965–66), he retorts with much self-conscious awareness of his narrative.

As Aers points out, the tale ends with a long parliamentary oration expressing a will for dominance, no doubt as a counter to the dominance he feels eluding him and his noble knights. Aers contends, "Through the speech itself, Chaucer shows how theological language can serve those in power. It enables them to present thoroughly limited class and nationalistic self-interests as universal ones dictated by a transcendental being to whom they have special, indeed monopolistic, access."[34] Such privilege regarding the Godhead is assumed by those who hold privilege elsewhere, in the societal domains they control. Moral self-assurance justified through theological language thus parallels social self-assurance, a conviction that the noble class is right and justified in all things.

The *Knight's Tale* concludes with the behest of Theseus, whose powerful words based on philosophic reasoning effect a long-awaited resolution. At his suggestion, Palamon and Emily finally wed, verbally pledging their troth after several years' mourning for Arcite. Theseus's authority carries the day. Throughout the tale, language has always proved dependable and reliable. Reality has conformed to verbal descriptions of it. People (and gods) have kept their word. Theseus enjoins Emily and Palamon to follow his words of advice to marry, and to use language wisely, not complainingly, for "whoso gruccheth ought, he dooth folye" (I.3045). Perhaps the Knight feels the same way. The final words of the tale also sound much like the Knight's ideal of perfect language use, almost as sacred as their marriage pledge: "Nevere was ther no word hem bitwene / Of jalousie or any oother teene" (I.3105–6). Verbal accord has thus marked the entire tale; perhaps an aristocratic Knight would have expected and experienced such harmony.

Does such assurance redound upon an entire class used to success and fulfillment? Perhaps if a courtly teller relies on surety and confident achievement in an ideal world, he might thus assume the same surety about language and its ability to tell truth accurately and truly. In the figure of the Knight, Chaucer has carefully created an exemplary self-conscious artist, aware of his task and craft, with which to initiate his tales.

If aristocratic society has reinforced the Knight, offering him confidence about his place in the world, it has similarly endorsed his son, the young, dashing Squire. While the Knight's perspective on life is reasonable, rational, and generally realistic, however, the Squire presents no such discipline. Further, his military conduct is also questionable. Stanley J. Karl speculates,

> If the Knight was one of the last of the *defensores fidei,* his son was certainly cast in the mold of one of the "new men" of the court of Richard II. His "crusade" was the miserable affair led by the bishop of Norwich for purely political reasons. . . . The new recruits to the

expedition, consisting largely of London apprentices and others of the same sort, could hardly be considered "gentil," and in fact are described by Professor McKisack as "an undisciplined rabble, interested only in loot." The Squire's participation in armed raids . . . is a good example of much of the highly unchivalrous fighting of the Hundred Years' War.[35]

The idealism previously held in such high regard has become tarnished, politicized, and made common by the changing circumstances. Those among the aristocratic ranks were no longer necessarily noble, marking a further chivalric decline.[36] Yet despite the emergence of the new generation, Derek Pearsall is right in noting that "The *Squire's Tale* affirms its kinship with the *Knight's Tale* and the *Franklin's Tale*, as indeed one would expect, since the former is told by his father and the latter by the man who would like to be his father. . . . The values implied and presented for our admiration are the same, namely those of romance."[37] But the execution of the tales indicates a disparity in narrative skill.

When the host invites him to tell a tale of love, knowing as much as any on that topic, the Squire gently demurs, and assents to

> . . . seye as I kan
> With hertly wyl, for I wol nat rebelle
> Agayn youre lust; a tale wol I telle.
> Have me excused if I speke amys;
> My wyl is good, and lo, my tale is this. [V.4–8]

Surely the Squire displays courteous gentility, true or feigned, and a headlong enthusiasm. But, incapable of telling a coherent, meaningful tale, he chooses to communicate indirectly, metaphorically, symbolically. David Lawton points to the "frequent incongruities and instability of tone" critics have imputed to the Squire and the tale's rhetoric, but the noble youth appears oblivious.[38] He enters a romance fairyland, what John P. McCall has named "Wonderland"—idealistic and unreal—when his tale begins.[39] Although fictional narratives per se are never literally true, they do posit language that may or may not reveal truth despite their qualification of the "fictional genre." In true romance style, realistic for the genre if not life, a knight carrying a mirror and sword, and wearing a gold ring, rides in upon a brass steed "With so heigh reverence and obeisaunce, / As wel in

FIGURE 3. Knight and lady in a garden. B.L. MS Harley 4431, fol. 376.
Courtesy of the British Library.

speche as in contenaunce" (V.93–94). Clearly the Squire values verbal
competence, although his own type of story is rambling rather than
shaped. His tale is of people of his own social class[40] and, in that regard, more likely to be realistic; but King Cambyuskan is of Tartary, or
Southern Russia, rather remote from the Squire's experience, and the
King's qualities are unrealistically ideal. The extreme traits and description of this idealized King begin the fantasy, for no king

> . . . was of so greet renoun
> That ther was nowher in no regioun

So excellent a lord in alle thyng:
He lakked nought that longeth to a kyng. [V.13–16]

Furthermore, he kept all religious laws, always maintained a royal estate, and was hardy, wise, rich, piteous, just, trustworthy, benign,
honorable, courageous, young, fresh, strong, fair, and fortunate. So,
what does he lack? Not children, for he has two sons and a daughter,
to describe whose beauty, the Squire claims,.

It lyth nat in my tonge, n'yn my konnyng;
I dar nat undertake so heigh a thyng.
Myn Englissh eek is insufficient.
It moste been a rethor excellent
That koude his colours longynge for that art,
If he sholde hire discryven every part.
I am noon swich, I moost speke as I kan. [V.35–41]

Such hyperbole, what Vincent J. Dimarco calls "an elaborate example
of the 'inexpressibility' topos"⁴¹ describing Cambyuskan's qualities
and the Squire's inability to relate Canacee's virtues, suggests unrealistic idealism and perhaps disingenuous humility. The Squire admits
his language is insufficient, and even that "Ther nys no man that may
reporten al" (V.72), but the rest of the rambling tale belies his sincerity.
Had he in fact doubted his abilities, he would not have plunged forward with such headlong daring, such unrestrained recklessness. Not
actually believing himself inadequate, he blunders on with little sense
of organization or self-possession. His innate confidence in himself,
engendered from birth in those of his station, prevents him from conceiving equal linguistic competence in others. No doubt he is oblivious to the fact of his narrative's failure.

According to Pearsall, "it would betray a certain lack of humour to
attempt to penetrate [the plot's] obscurity . . . the only person who is
confused is the poor Squire."⁴² Nor does he know how to use language. For one thing, he indulges in a long exposition of the seasons,
Cambyuskan's riches, and characters' virtues, among other topics, to
no purpose. His second use of the modesty topos occurs in conjunction with the praise he offers the successful rhetor, the knight who

. . . with a manly voys seide his message,
After the forme used in his langage,

Withouten vice of silable or of lettre;
And for his tale sholde seme the bettre,
Accordant to his wordes was his cheere,
As techeth art of speche hem that it leere.
Al be that I kan nat sowne his stile,
Ne kan nat clymben over so heigh a style,
Yet seye I this, as to commune entente:
Thus muche amounteth al that evere he mente,
If it so be that I have it in mynde.   [V.97–109]

Here the Squire describes his own aesthetic and communication theories, that a speaker should utter his message in strong voice and
proper form, with emphasis on syllables and letters. Content and organization seem irrelevant. Immediately, he disclaims his own ability
to achieve the rhetorical heights he has just created for his character!
But as a matter of fact, the Squire succeeds at that rhetoric that he denies, while failing in the larger narrative issue of coherence. Our modern sense of unity, so well displayed by the Knight, is here wanting.

The Squire's world is purely fantastic, if creatively ingenious. Magically, his horse flies, his ring translates animal language, his mirror
reveals infidelity, and his sword severs or heals as the wielder prefers.
The young man feels compelled to emphasize the veracity of these virtues, claiming of the sword's powers, "This is a verray sooth, withouten glose" (V.166), and of the horse's immobility, "But sikerly,
withouten any fable. . . . It stant as it were to the ground yglewed"
(V.180, 182). But not everyone accepts these mysterious phenomena.
One skeptic claims:

. . . He lyeth, for it is rather lyk
An apparance ymaad by som magyk,
As jogelours playe at thises feestes grete.   [V.217–19]

Others discuss the magical nature of the gifts, such as the sword,
inconclusively:

They speken of sondry hardyng of metal,
And speke of medicynes therwithal,
And how and whanne it sholde yharded be,
Which is unknowe, algates unto me.   [V.243–46]

Although people verbally hypothesize about the sword, neither they nor the narrator knows the secret. As Pearsall notes, "the tone of 'algates unto me' implies the valuelessness of what is not known to the speaker, rather than the modesty of ignorance."[43] The Squire's self-confidence and social class endorsement might well allow him such a condescending view. What is more, his diatribes arrogantly suggest that anything he might say is worth attention, though they are simply smokescreens masking the inconclusive direction his tale is taking. Thus language itself is effective in hiding the ineffective use to which he puts it.

The Squire's next disavowal of knowledge is equally disingenuous:

> Who koude telle yow the forme of daunces
> So unkouthe, and swiche fresshe contenaunces,
> Swich subtil lookyng and dissymulyngs . . .
> No man but Launcelot, and he is deed.
> I sey namoore. [V.283–87, 289]

While the possibility of communication remains foregrounded, the Squire continues to send mixed messages: Yes, certainly language is effective, for look at the marvelous tale in which I am engaged; but, simultaneously, no, for no one else is competent to match the complexity or intensity of reality. If he actually believes the scene to be indescribable, he holds a mental reservation for himself. His aristocratic position offers a secure sense of his linguistic worth, but that trust is not transferable to others. Others cannot share in his confidence, nor does he place his confidence in those not so socially privileged.

An example of this latter attitude can be heard from the brass horse rider within the tale, who refuses to spin out his explanation of the magic courser; he succinctly claims, "Ther is namoore to seyne" (V.314). Although this knight seems not to value long discursive passages, he yet spends twenty lines describing his horse's virtues. Certainly, the Squire believes the king can interpret the data: "Enformed whan the kyng was of that knyght, / And hath conceyved in his wit aright / The manere and the form of al this thyng" (V.335–37); *then* joy reigned, until "The hors vanysshed, I noot in what manere" (V.342). The Squire seems unable to control his own narrative. Its fantastic unreality gives it a life of its own, unwieldy and elusive, if not downright deceptive.

When Canacee hears the sorrowful plight of the falcon with her magic ring, she believes her words, since experience has never led Canacee to doubt language veracity. Mentioning her status and social class authority, she would rely on their power to alleviate the falcon's pain. Like the Squire, who holds similar assumptions, Canacee has aristocratic confidence, here extending to a trust in her ability to cure the bird:

> . . . as I am a kynges doghter trewe,
> If that I verraily the cause knewe
> Of your disease, if it lay in my myght,
> I wolde amenden it er that it were nyght . . .
> To heel with youre hurtes hastily. [V.465–68, 471]

This lament presumes that if the falcon tells Canacee the words of her pain, Canacee's words might cure it. Such an idealistic notion is in keeping with the idealistic setting in far-off Tartary, the idealistic gifts with unqualified benefits, and the idealistic characters in their perfect lives. There is no touchstone of reality with the royal family. The falcon's story, however, reveals how false, deceitful words can cause pain. Despite his oaths of fidelity, a tercelet has betrayed the falcon. She concludes that "sooth is seyd, goon sithen many a day, / 'A trewe wight and a theef thenken nat oon' " (V.536–37). In other words, only a guilty creature is likely to be suspicious or distrustful of words. The duplicitous tercelet reveals his doubleness and feigning in his entreaties and language to his mate, who "thoughte he was so trewe" (V.588).

The Squire has continued this tale at great length, with great confidence, and to no purpose. The falcon's story seems not to fit into a larger pattern, and its function is unclear. Unlike the purposefully planned and carefully orchestrated symmetrical pattern of the *Knight's Tale*, the Squire's rambles without design. When it trails off inconclusively, he attempts to establish a new order, apparently no more structured than his previously drawn-out material.

Fortunately the Franklin steps in to save the young man, and all the company, from more of the same.[44] The Squire, with all his self-assurance intact, fails to realize the failure of his tale; his inflated linguistic sense of worth, however aristocratic, is unfounded. The rest of that fair company perceive his ineptitude clearly and none rebukes even the social-climbing parvenu for the much-needed interruption. The Franklin's hyperbolic praise of his eloquence is a calculated effort not to deflate the Squire's aristocratic ego, although it includes an appropriate qualification: "Considerynge thy yowthe . . . For of thy speche I have greet deyntee" (V.675, 681). He wishes his own son would "commune with any gentil wight / Where he myghte lerne gentillesse aright" (V.693–94). This desire assumes such verbal communication would have its effect in establishing his son in the right socially mobile class, an advantage that the young Squire has used to his own benefit. Yet, by any standard, the Squire has failed. The feudal ideal of service in the real world, of chivalry in every arena, of dedication to worthy causes, of preserving that noble life ineluctably slipping away, have in his tale been transformed to illusory ideals and magical reality, false if not ignoble. The grand epic reality of his father has slipped into a series of fantastic diversions lacking coherence and order. Yet despite his apparent failure, his confidence never wanes. Although his aristocratic standing has not made him a better rhetor, it has provided a firmly confident psychological stance from which to offer a tale with an unfortunately unwarranted ease and certainty.

Thus both tales are concerned with the veracity of language, the first showing its success despite seeming contradiction, the second describing its importance in conveying meaning, especially in the revealing mirror and translating ring. Although a confidence in their world view and in the language used to describe it marks each tale, in the first, such confidence is shown to be warranted, but in the second, as foolish at best because not fully grounded in reality. Perhaps the recent critical interest in youth and eld, experience and inexperience, will further enlighten the contrasting approaches taken to present the tales of these aristocrats.

Some twenty years ago, Herlihy reminded us that Marc Bloch's historical method, examining the "total social environment" of a previous society, had developed a rhetoric of its own: "The rhetorical question, suggesting a conclusion, frequently replaces the confident affirmation of the older academic historian. . . . The history of feudal society, illuminated by this and other methods, should attract not only those interested in the Western past but all who are concerned with the dynamics of human change."[45] Muscatine and others have since concurred with the necessity of reading history from multiple perspectives, using data from various relevant disciplines. Language is one of them. Whether we wish to read history from literature or vice versa, a scrupulous examination of language is essential. Ever fascinated by the nuances of language and voice, Chaucer could not but have been compelled by the challenge of how to create one—or several—linguistic constructs for these once-great, still-refined, always-confident scions of a fading social order. With the magnificent subtlety we have come to expect from him, the rich complexity of approach we have come to rely upon, and the linguistic versatility we can hear from his voice as well as his quill, Geoffrey Chaucer has surely preserved the bastions of a disappearing reality—the world *as in his tyme*—and the language that makes it come alive.

Notes

Author's Note: An earlier version of this article was delivered at the Twenty-Fourth International Congress on Medieval Studies in Kalamazoo, Michigan, in May 1989.

1. William Caxton, Epilogue to *The Book of the Ordre of Chyualry*, the translation of Ramon Lull's *Le Libre del Ordre de Cauayleria*, ed. Alfred T. P. Byles, EETS, o.s., 168 (London: Oxford University Press, 1926).

2. Leon Gautier, *Chivalry*, ed. Jacques Levron, trans. D. C. Dunning (New York: Barnes & Noble, 1965). Gautier and others contend that chivalry flourished in the eleventh and twelfth centuries and steadily declined thereafter. According to F. L. Ganshof, "from the end of the thirteenth century [feudal institutions] ceased in Western Europe to be the most fundamental element in the structure of society, lying behind and influencing every aspect of its life and thought" (*Feudalism*, rev. 3d ed. [New York: Harper and Row, 1964], 168). Although Elizabeth A. R. Brown's comprehensive survey of the notion of feudalism and her admonition about using the labels "feudal" and "feudalism"—as ambiguous and simplistic explanations of reality—must be borne in mind, the utility and convenience of these terms, which she readily grants, justify their use in this essay ("The Tyranny of a Construct: Feudalism and Historians of Medieval Europe," *AHR* 79 [1974]:1063–88).

3. Carl Stephenson, *Mediaeval Feudalism* (Ithaca, N.Y.: Cornell University Press, 1967), 102.

4. John Gower believed that "Since the poor but proud man does not have the wherewithal to conduct himself with pride, he lives everywhere by plundering" (*The Major Latin Works of John Gower: The Voice of the One Crying and the Tripartite Chronicle*, ed. and trans. Eric W. Stockton, "Vox Clamantis," VII, IV 260). Ramon Lull concurs, claiming a squire without equipment and wealth with which to defray his expenses "will perhaps have to become a robber or a thief, traitor or beggar, or have some other vices which are contrary to chivalry" (*The Book of the Ordre of Chyualry*, trans. W. Caxton, ed. A. T. P. Byles, 63).

5. Instituting the Sumptuary Laws is one case in point, an attempt to satisfy the perceived need to emphasize the hierarchies of social status. In Portugal in 1340, all "peons,"

> those who [did] not have enough wealth to possess horses and who were residing in towns, were forbidden to wear furs and jewelry because it did not become their station. . . . As social categories became more fluid (entrance into the nobility, for example, increased as noble families died out through war and pestilence; fiefs entered the hands of bourgeois by purchase), there was an atavistic attempt to maintain the rigid distinctions nostalgically associated with an earlier period and to do so especially by means of laws on dress . . . it was not conspicuous consumption itself that was reprehensible—that was expected of and appropriate to the nobility—but conspicuous consumption by bourgeois and parvenu non-nobles that seemed to threaten the social order. [*Dictionary of the Middle Ages*, 13 vols. ed. Joseph R. Strayer, (New York: Charles Scribner's Sons, 1982–89), 11:506, 507.]

6. Sumner Ferris speculates that "late medieval literature presents a picture of the knight and of chivalry that is based on actualities of the time, but so heightened and idealized that the result is misleading, even falsified" ("Chronicle, Chivalric Biography, and Family Tradition in Chivalric Literature," in *Chivalric Literature: Essays on Relations Between Literature and Life in the Later Middle Ages*, ed. Larry D. Benson and John Leyerle [Kalamazoo: Western Michigan University Pub., 1980], 25). Joseph R. Ruff, however, finds that "Late medieval romances often present puzzling combinations of realistic material from contemporary society and idealistic material from literary tradition" ("Malory's Gareth and Fifteenth-Century Chivalry," in *Chivalric Literature*, 101).

7. *The History of Feudalism*, ed. David Herlihy (London: Macmillan, 1970), 285.

8. *The Chivalrous Society*, trans. Cynthia Postan (Berkeley & Los Angeles: University of California Press, 1977), 182.

9. "Chaucer's *Squire's Tale* and the Rise of Chivalry," *SAC* 5 (1983):128.

10. *Social Chaucer* (Cambridge, Mass.: Harvard University Press, 1989), 93.

11. *Social Chaucer*, 130.

12. I follow Peggy Knapp's definition of *discourse* as discussed in her *Chaucer and the Social Contest* (New York and London: Routledge, 1990), 2. This definition was first offered by Catherine Belsey: "a domain of language use; a particular way of talking (and writing and thinking) . . . [which] involves certain shared assumptions which appear in the formulation that characterizes it" (*Critical Practice* [London: Methuen, 1980], 5).

13. Introduction, *Modern Critical Interpretations: Geoffrey Chaucer's "The Knight's Tale,"* ed. Harold Bloom (New York, New Haven & Philadelphia: Chelsea House, 1988), 2–3.

14. "Criseyde: Woman in Medieval Society," *ChauR* 13 (1979):177–200.

15. *Chaucer's Poetics and the Modern Reader* (Berkeley & Los Angeles: University of California Press, 1987), 1–2.

16. *The Canterbury Tales: A Reading* (Newark: University of Delaware Press, 1983), 146.

17. *Social Chaucer*, 130, 167.

18. Goodman maintains, "The composite romances are marked by precisely those elements that have annoyed the modern reader in *The Squire's Tale*: meticulous attention to the niceties of courtly life joined with an inexhaustible appetite for marvels . . . [with] a propensity for treating segments of earlier romances as building blocks for new and more flamboyant structures" ("Chaucer's *Squire's Tale* and the Rise of Chivalry," 129). In a time of social disintegration, this nostalgic use of earlier tales reveals the yearning for a lost ideal.

19. *Social Chaucer*, 131.

20. Social class, however, is not the only determinant of actual or linguistic security. The Miller, Reeve, Pardoner, Wife of Bath, Merchant, Friar, and others, for example, trusting their rhetorical skills, create tales in which language, deceptively or rightly used, brings the desired resolution. Their views of reality have no social class foundation; but their worlds are often fraught with solvable problems, albeit by magic, violence, trickery, or other means. Their confidence must derive from a source other than class—perhaps from an ability to interact socially, or their evident linguistic competence. But the nature of their linguistic certainty differs from that of the aristocracy.

21. "A Knight Ther Was," *Transactions and Proceedings of the American Philological Association* 38 (1907):90.

22. *The Complete Works of Geoffrey Chaucer*, 2d ed., ed. F. N. Robinson (Boston: Houghton Mifflin, 1957), 652n.

23. *Chaucer's Knight: The Portrait of a Medieval Mercenary* (Baton Rouge: Louisiana State University Press, 1980), 2.

24. *Chaucer* (Brighton: Harvester Press, 1986), 24.

25. *The Historical Background of Chaucer's Knight* (New Haven: Transactions of the Connecticut Academy of Arts and Sciences, 20, 1916; rpt. New York: Haskill House, 1966).

26. *Chaucer and the Social Contest*, 19.

27. *Chaucer's Drama of Style: Poetic Variety and Contrast in the Canterbury Tales* (Chapel Hill: University of North Carolina Press, 1986), 67.

28. "Order and Disorder," in *Modern Critical Interpretations: Geoffrey Chaucer's "The Knight's Tale,"* ed. Harold Bloom, 13–15.

29. "Order and Disorder," 15.

30. "Order and Disorder," 18–19.

31. " 'The Struggle Between Noble Designs and Chaos': The Literary Tradition of Chaucer's *Knight's Tale*," *Literary Review* 23 (1980):80.

32. " 'Struggle Between Noble Designs and Chaos,' " 79.

33. "*Sic et Non*: Discarded Worlds in the Knight's Tale," in *Modern Critical Interpretations: Geoffrey Chaucer's "The Knight's Tale,"* 105.

34. *Chaucer*, 30.

35. "Chaucer's *Squire's Tale* and the Decline of Chivalry," *ChauR* 7 (1973):208. May McKisack's comment is found in *The Fourteenth Century, 1307–1399* (Oxford: Clarendon Press, 1959), 432.

36. F. J. C. Hearnshaw finds one reason for the decline of chivalry to be "the indiscriminate knighting of persons not 'gentil' by birth, such as 'wealthy burgesses'

(who were prepared to pay heavily for the honor)" ("Chivalry and Its Place in History," in *Chivalry: A Series of Studies to Illustrate Its Historical Significance*, ed. Edgar Prestage [New York: Knopf, 1928], 27).

37. *The Canterbury Tales* (Boston & London: Allen & Unwin, 1985), 139.

38. *Chaucer's Narrators* (Cambridge: Boydell & Brewer, 1985), 114.

39. "The Squire in Wonderland," *ChauR* 1 (1966):103–9.

40. Goodman points to what she calls the Squire's "snobbish aside" in arrogantly discussing the lower class, particularly the crowd:

> Of sondry doutes thus they jangle and trete,
> As lewed peple demeth communly
> Of thynges that been maad moore subtilly
> Than they kan in hir lewednesse comprehende. [220–23]

Notice also the use of "lewed" and "lewednesse" of a people who "jangle and trete," all of which are pejorative terms.

41. "Notes to the *Squire's Tale*," in the *Riverside Chaucer*, ed. Larry D. Benson (Boston: Houghton Mifflin, 1987), 891.

42. "The Squire as Story-Teller," in *Sonderdruck aus Geoffrey Chaucer* (Darmstadt: n.p., 1983), 297.

43. *Canterbury Tales*, 140.

44. Lawton rejects the notion of the Franklin's purposeful interruption, claiming that we have "seen the phenomenon of the 'finished fragment', and the Epilogue to the Tale . . . is raised to the status of a merciful interruption. . . . But it does not read like an interruption . . . the lines . . . do not bear the weight of an interruption; they would be suitable at the real narrative conclusion of the Squire's Tale or . . . any other tale assigned to the Squire" (*Chaucer's Narrators*, 115, 116). Although Lawton may be right, we have no conclusion to the tale, and cannot reasonably posit one. Until new textual discoveries offer alternatives, all we can do is to accept the text as received.

45. *History of Feudalism*, xxvii.

LIAM O. PURDON AND
JULIAN N. WASSERMAN

4 Chivalry and
Feudal Obligation
in Barbour's *Bruce*

ECENTLY, scholars have begun to demonstrate how, in *The Bruce*, John Barbour manipulates poetic convention and historical fact for the artistic and poetical purpose of creating a rousing pro-Scots account of the early fourteenth-century wars for independence. Interestingly enough, this growing critical appreciation for the form and content of the oldest extant Scottish "national epic"[1] has repeatedly drawn attention to the poem's curiously deliberate rejection of "chivalry," especially in its treatment of Edward Bruce.[2]

To understand Barbour's treatment of chivalry and chivalric custom, one must first place the poem in the context of the growing concept of the individual that was taking place during the fourteenth century, especially in England where such ideas were to have profound effects on the nature of feudalism and feudal obligation.[3] Indeed, the Scottish war for independence and even the need for a Scottish "national epic" may be taken as manifestations of the development of the sense of the individual and of individual "rights." In fact, the Scots' revocation of claims of vassalage to the English monarch may be viewed as an at-large application of the developing right of *exfestucatio* or *diffidatio*, the repudiation of the feudal contract by a vassal if the lord did not fulfill his duties and overstepped contractual bonds,[4] itself a reflection of a growing sense that the Pauline doctrine of the complete subjugation of the part to the whole was no longer a viable means of organizing a society in which workers made increasing demands for control of their property and conditions of employment.[5] Yet if the growing sense of the individual as manifested by feudal exfestucatio or diffidatio was a force that Barbour wished to encourage for the sake of Scottish independence, it was also one that needed to be carefully circumscribed, as the same impulse to individual identity that separates the Scots from the rest of Britain might also work against Scottish unity, breaking the people into individual clans incapable of sustaining the unified front necessary for national independence. To extend the Pauline metaphor, the force that leads the arm to declare its independence from the body might also lead the hand to separate from the arm.

Barbour's method of fostering and at the same time maintaining control over that impulse is to call his readers' attention to the limitations of chivalry in order to enable his audience to perceive the value of feudal obligation, a less attractive but by no means less practical part of feudal custom and practice.[6] In short, Barbour's strategy is to separate feudal obligation, the subsuming of the individual to the greater whole, from the secondary effect of personal glory through individual gallantry, demonstrating the social as well as political value of using a system of feudal obligation to unify a people under militant kingship.

To understand this secondary effect, it is perhaps helpful to turn to the literary model par excellence of medieval chivalry, the tales of King Arthur. The fourteenth-century *Alliterative Morte D'Arthur* provides an instructive example of the type of chivalry that Barbour explicitly rejects. For example, Arthur's repudiation of vassalage owed by himself to the Roman emperor Lucius provides a striking parallel to the Scottish revolt against English King Edward.[7] And the spirit of individualism, the nationalism that serves as the first cause of the revolt against Lucius, is directly reflected in the way in which the war for British independence is fought. Within the *Alliterative Morte,* battles are primarily the sites of individual acts of courage and nobility by knights such as Gawain or Kay, or, in the end, Gawain against Mordred or Arthur against Mordred. Indeed, the actual battle with the Romans is begun by the rash acts of one individual, Gawain. And even the final revolt against proper vassalage, the revolt against Arthur, grows out of an individual's ambition. Mordred's usurpation is, in a sense, simply the ultimate expression of individuality, of the self that places itself above all else. The great masses of soldiers are little more than backdrops for the exploits of individual knights who in the end even have the potential to eclipse Arthur. This is exactly the type of individual performance of which Barbour is suspicious.

One place in which Barbour's concern for the individual in warfare is seen arises in his rejection of chivalry in favor of strategy, or what is now called guerrilla warfare. This is a move that certainly constitutes a departure from advocating an ordered, predictable way of fighting, though not necessarily a departure from the military strategical thinking found in a work like Vegetius's *De re militari*, a work that would have been available and of great interest to Barbour and the heroes of his "romanys,"[8] especially as they faced armies that were greater and more powerful than their own. In a sense, guerrilla war is faceless, a series of skirmishes between companies of men without the independent personal duels that mark chivalric warfare, and so is, in essence, the antithesis of the formally staged battles in the *Alliterative Morte*. Such tactics do find a parallel, however, in another series of fourteenth-century tales, the stories of Robin Hood, whose antichivalric guerrilla tactics are likewise employed in the renunciation of obligation to an unjust lord.[9]

While at least one scholar has argued that *The Bruce* should end after Barbour's blow-by-blow description of the Battle of Bannockburn,[10] such a revision would vitiate the effect of the whole work, not only because it would eliminate memorable episodes[11] but also because it would preclude any mention of the disastrous Scottish campaign in Ireland. This campaign was a major military venture during the Scottish wars for independence, and for that reason alone could not be ignored by Barbour. But more important than that, it was not the kind of subject to be passed over, unflattering as it might be to the Scottish cause, because it provided Barbour with an appropriate historical means of demonstrating the inherent weakness of the chivalric ideal and the strength of feudal obligation. Through his account of Edward Bruce's administration of the campaign, Barbour uses this costly Scottish defeat to inform his audience of the virtue of feudal obligation.

According to Barbour, Edward Bruce is a capable, chivalrous knight—one "stoutar . . . yan a libard" (14.2). Barbour first develops this view of Robert Bruce's brother in the episode concerning the re-

FIGURE 4. Bruce versus de Bohun at Bannockburn. Corpus Christi College, MS 171, fol. 265r. Courtesy of the Masters and Fellows of Corpus Christi College, Cambridge.

taking of Galloway. By this time in the wars for independence, most of Scotland north of the Scottish Sea, except for Galloway, is loyal to Bruce. Edward wants to subdue Galloway and, when given the chance, does so, winning at Dalbeattie. "Throw his [Edward's] chewalrous chiwalry," says Barbour, "Galloway was stonayit gretumly / And he dowtyt for his bounte" (9.541–43). This victory inspires further acts of chivalry, one of which, recounted by Sir Alan of Cathcart, involves Edward's daring attack with fifty mounted knights on an English force consisting of at least thirty times that number:

> Schyr Eduuard yat gret ʒarnyn had
> All tymys to do chewalry
> With all his rout in full gret hy
> Folowyt ye trais quhar gane war yai . . . [9.588–91]

Edward may be given to chivalry, but the narrative focus is actually on "his rout." The battle is really one between "companies"—"he and his cumpany" (594), the "Inglis cumpany" (601), and "schyr Eduuardis cumpany" (614), as the audience is thrice told within a short span of time. While Edward is the flower of chivalry (and a lucky soldier, as this account of the battle in the mist indicates), he is more attentive to the fulfillment of his chivalric ambition, his individual glory, than to the details of feudal warfare, such as the strategy shown here of transforming potential enemies into close allies by securing their loyalty through feudal obligation.

This tendency toward impracticality on Edward's part is brought into sharp focus later, when, beginning the Irish campaign, Edward forges alliances based solely upon the word or verbal bond of his potential enemies—in short, using words exchanged between individuals as individuals so that peace is negotiated much as chivalric war is fought. Chivalry, individual distinction in warfare, results in individual bonds of fealty, peace between institutional leaders rather than between the companies of men who have waged war. And it is here that the growing notion of the individual that made it conceivable to break the feudal bond between the Scottish vassals and their English Lord through exfestucatio or diffidatio makes the newly forged bonds vulnerable to rupture. Walter Ullmann notes:

> The very idea of *diffidatio* contains as an integral element the concept of *fides*, for *diffidatio* is nothing less than the withdrawal of loyalty

from the lord by the vassal. This loyalty was not institutionalized, but was intensely personal: it was the bond which kept lord and vassal together and had reference exclusively to the lord as an individual person. In contrast to the descending theme of government, one is here presented with a definite individual-personal relationship, that kind of relationship which, by virtue of the institutionalization of faith, could not and did not exist in the descending form of government, in which not the individual but the office constituted the essential ingredient.[12]

As his army makes its way southward, for example, Edward bargains with the Irish, enlisting their support to help him drive the English from Irish shores. What he works out, at first, is simply an agreement or a *hycht* (14.16), which, later, he reaffirms as all of Ulster "his pes haly cummyn wer" (14.98). But this does not stop the attacks on the Scottish forces. Again, after the success at Dundalk and the routing of Sir Richard of Clare's fifty-thousand-man army in the battle near the forest of Kilross, Edward accepts just the word alone of his potential enemies. In this instance, the term *fewte* or fealty (14.331) is used as an Irish king named O'Dempsey invites Edward to accompany him to see his Irish realm. But like the previously sworn allegiance that does not secure a peace for the Scottish, this new verbal bond also proves to be without substance as the Irish actually attempt to drown Edward and his entourage. Edward's approach to unifying Ireland behind the Scottish cause is somewhat reminiscent of his brother's nearly fatal indenture agreement with John Comyn,[13] and reminiscent of another similar agreement made during the wars, involving King Edward of England and Sir Aymer de Valence. King Edward promises Valence a reward in the form of vast tracts of land in return for the destruction of Robert Bruce and his army. While service and reward—that is, elements of feudal reciprocity—are stressed in this instance, the bond is again only verbal, resulting in a fortunate disregard for King Edward's order to kill all prisoners.[14]

Indeed, it is only after Robert Bruce and his army come to Ireland at Edward Bruce's request that Edward begins to secure allegiance through feudal obligation. On the return to Carrickfergus, for example, we hear for the first time during the entire campaign that the Irish kings are rallying behind Edward, swearing to be his men:

Ye kingis off Irchery
Come to schyr Eduuard halily
And yar manredyn gan him ma
Bot giff yat it war ane or twa. [16.305–8]

Although this use of vassal homage (*manredyn*) finally secures the peace in Ireland, however, Barbour is quick to point out that this political arrangement is subsequently undermined by Edward's inability to control himself and to plan his deeds with greater care. The implication in the narrative account of the waywardness of Edward's chivalry is that, had he established his control of Ireland "with mesure" and not been given principally to feats of gallantry and boldness, then the Scottish rule in Ireland would have remained intact.

This mistake of not consistently securing the service and support of the Irish through feudal obligation during the entire Irish campaign costs many—like Gib Harper—their lives, and the Scots, their control of Ireland. As tragic as Edward's ignominious defeat and subsequent death are, however, they serve to emphasize, by comparison, how valuable feudal obligations can be when establishing the social and political unity of a realm. They put in relief Robert Bruce's careful, nearly systematic way of building alliances through feudal obligation.[15] More important, they invite us to consider the virtue of feudal obligation itself and the practical and ethical implications of social and political order based in a system of feudal obligation.

According to Barbour, the kind of feudal obligation that once secured Scotland's freedom and independence—and must now, in the uncertain early years of the Stuart dynasty, be rejuvenated in order to secure anew that very same freedom and independence[16]—consists of the traditional components of homage, fealty, and fief, with homage being the most important.[17] What is more, as in traditional treatments of this vassal homage, Barbour adds, this relationship is most effective when it is specific or individual, binding each to the other in obligations of reciprocity, in essence paralleling Ullmann's observations concerning personal rather than institutional loyalty in the feudal contract. This is demonstrated by Barbour early in the poem shortly after King Edward dissolves his feudal relations with Robert Bruce, who will not be his vassal, and James of Douglas, whose vassalage he will not accept.[18] As Douglas meets Robert Bruce at Moffat and tells him of his plight, he recognizes Robert Bruce as his true lord and king and does homage:

> & quhen Dowglas saw hys cummyng
> He raid and hailyst hym in hy
> And lowtyt him ffull curtasly,
> And tauld him haly all his state
> & quhat he was, & als how-gat
> Ye Clyffurd held his heritage,
> And yat he come to mak homage
> Till him as till his rychtwis king. [2.152–59]

This specific homage is then followed by a homage done by the entire barony, who are also loyal to Bruce's cause.[19] Although Barbour does not identify the homage in this second instance as "specific" or "individual," such is the implication. The fact that the barons' friendship is attained along with the homage, as Barbour indicates, suggests a degree of familiarity that could result only from an individual interview with Robert Bruce:

> Bot off yar nobleis, gret affer,
> Yar seruice na yar realte
> Ʒe sall her na thing now for me,
> Owtane yat he off ye barnage
> Yat yidder com tok homage,
> And syne went our all ye land
> Frendis and frendschip purchesand
> To maynteym yat he had begunnyn. [2.183–89]

Barbour reintroduces this idea of a specific vassal homage later in the poem when Douglas begins the process of reclaiming his heritage from Clifford. The specific nature of the vassalage in this case is emphasized through its association with an individual. What is different about this association—what, in other words, enhances its importance here—is that the individual who does the homage to Douglas is Thom Dicson, one of many common men introduced and named in the poem.[20] Douglas knows at this point in the campaign that, because Clifford is a formidable opponent, he must be shrewd and work by sleight if he is to reclaim his heritage. When he arrives in Douglasdale to begin the campaign, Dicson, an old servant, summons every good man and more to do homage to Douglas. What is more, like Ubbe in *Havelok the Dane*,[21] he is the first to do homage to his lord:

> Sa wrocht he throw sutelte
> Yat all ye lele men off yat land
> Yat with his fadyr war duelland
> Yis gud man gert cum ane & ane
> And mak him manrent euerilkane,
> And he him selff fyrst homage maid. [5.292–97]

The implication here is that *each* man becomes Douglas's man. What is different is that vassal homage is no longer restricted to the noble or warrior class but now extends down to the commons. In short, the fealty is sworn to the Douglas as a person rather than to the institution or position that Douglas represents or holds. Ullmann makes an interesting point concerning the dual roles that a king holds:

> One must divide kingship into two parts: first, there was the king by the grace of God—the theocratic king *par excellence*—who, because he alone had received the power to rule from God, stood above his subjects . . . who could not call him to account; secondly, next to this theocratic function every medieval king was also a feudal lord. In many vital respects this feudal function was diametrically opposed to the theocratic function; thus, every medieval king was an amphibious creature, because as a theocratic king his will alone counted, while as a feudal king he had entered into contractual relations of an individual nature with his tenants-in-chief and thereby had become one of them.[22]

The difference between Edward Bruce and his brother Robert is that Edward, in chivalric fashion, has forged his allegiances to others as a theocratic lord, while Robert has adopted the mode of a feudal one and has, as we shall see, become one of the people he would lead.

This downward extension of vassal homage is introduced at least one other time in the poem—not long, interestingly enough, after Clifford's defeat. In this second instance of "egalitarian" vassal homage, however, it is not Douglas but rather Bruce to whom the commons do homage. While Bruce is on the run from Sir Amery, he enters a house inhabited by a "howswyff." After introducing himself as a traveling man, he talks to the woman and listens to her praise

"Robert ye Bruys." When it seems appropriate to reveal his disguise, Bruce does so. The woman is confused at first; she does not expect her king to be in the area unescorted. As soon as she learns of her countryman's plight, however, she responds, first, by saying the situation is not correct, and then offers Bruce her two sons. Barbour neither uses the term homage nor an equivalent here, but homage is implied in the woman's subsequent reference to her sons as now Bruce's "sworn men":

> ". . . Yai sall becum ȝour men in hy."
> As scho diuisyt yai haiff done,
> His sworn men become yai sone. [7.266–68]

More examples of conventional vassal homage involving the noble or warrior class are used by Bruce and Douglas during the rest of the struggle; combined with these "egalitarian" forms, they help unite the Scots in their cause for freedom and independence. These instances are not as fully developed as the early examples of vassal homage in the poem, but they are no less significant. An illustrative example, for instance, occurs after Bruce routs the English and pro-English forces in the Battle of Loudon Hill. Seeing that the outnumbered Scottish forces have won the day by cunning and strategy, many who live nearby offer their support to the prospering Scottish cause by doing homage to Bruce. The term "homage" is used here. What is more, the homage is again a specific homage as each new vassal goes before Bruce to become his man:

> Swa war yai blyth withowtyn dout,
> For fele yat wynnyt yaim about
> Fra yai ye king saw help him swa
> Till him yar homage gan yai ma. [8.387–90]

The Scottish forces' defeat at Loudon Hill of an army five times their size in number is no small feat. More significant for the cause and to the outcome of the poem, however, is Barbour's imaginative association here between this Scottish victory as a turning point in Scottish military fortunes and a large-scale unification of the Scots behind the cause by means of vassal homage.

A variant form of conventional vassal homage is also introduced by Barbour later in the struggle as the Scots gain the upper hand, as it were, against the English. Specific or individual like the previous examples considered so far, this kind of vassal homage—a homage of atonement—addresses the need to gain support of those whose loyalty had formerly been given to the English crown. During a skirmish in the forest of Selkirk, Sir Thomas Randolph, King Edward's nephew and one of Bruce's long-time foes, is captured by Douglas. Rather than let discontent fester, Bruce decides not to imprison and ransom Randolph but rather to forgive him. He offers this forgiveness in addition to an earlship involving control of the lands of Murreff in return for Randolph's loyalty and cooperation. Randolph, as the text indicates, neither kneels before his new lord nor swears an oath of fealty to Bruce. Homage and fealty are suggested here, however, as Barbour states that Bruce trusts in Randolph's new "worthi wasselage" (10.270). Moreover, that Bruce gives Randolph "syndry landis" and makes him "ryche . . . off land & fe" (10.274) also introduces enfeoffment, the third part of the conventional tripartite vassal homage ritual. The assured loyalty resulting from Randolph's vassal homage is evidenced not long afterward as Randolph, relying upon the ingenuity and help of Will Francis, captures Edinburgh Castle, a crushing blow to English prestige.[23]

The emphasis Barbour places on various forms of specific vassal homage in *The Bruce* reveals Barbour's understanding of the immediate, actual implications of this feudal practice. The secured and inviolable relationship between a lord and his man may not be as attractive as Edward Bruce's show of chivalric prowess, Barbour suggests, but it is much more practical and substantial. It unites, as has been shown, people from different levels of society, and from different sides of a conflict.

What is more, it provides a quasi-legal means of defining and protecting property, and an effective means of uniting and reassuring people emotionally as well as psychologically—again, in a way that loyalty to descending institutional authority does not. The former, illustrated several times in the poem, involves usually either protection of property or assurance of heritability. The first example of this is presented most noticeably in the memorable episode concerning the Scottish appropriation of Rathlin Island early in the history of the struggle. As the Scots alight on Rathlin shores, vassal homage in the form of homage and fealty is used to secure the peace between the island's population and the Scottish forces, which have been joined by Earl Lennox and his men. The agreement and bond gives Bruce ready access to a large fighting force comprised of the island's men and their pages and to all the provisions his men might need. In return for this support, the people are assured that their possessions and property will be protected from depredation or confiscation:

> And yai as lord suld him ken,
> Bot at yar possessioune suld be
> For all his men yar awyn fre.
> Ye cunnand on yis wys was maid,
> And on ye morn but langer baid
> Knelyt and maid ye king homage,
> And yarwith swour him fewte
> To serve him ay in lawte,
> And held him rycht weill cunnand,
> For quhill he duelt in-to ye land. [3.750–60]

The protection of the heritability of property is often suggested in the various instances of vassal homage done either to Bruce or Douglas, but it is dramatically enunciated on the eve of the Battle of Bannockburn. In this episode, Bruce reminds the troops they are fighting for the freedom and honor of the Scottish people. He chooses his words carefully because he knows the army with which his thirty-thousand-man force is about to clash is a "wonder to see." Understanding the value of disinformation, he tells his men that the English look bad, and reminds his followers that they are fighting for the right to be free, a right for which they must be prepared to make the supreme sacrifice as they bear themselves manfully. As he comes to the end of his speech, he offers a promise. He asserts that, if any man shall die on the morrow, that man's heirs will be assured their rightful inheritance. In other words, whatever happens, his men's possessions and property cannot be alienated in perpetuity:

> And ik hycht her in leaute
> Giff ony deys in yis bataille
> His ayr but ward releff or taile
> On ye fyrst day [his land] sall weld
> All be he neuer sa ʒoung off eild. [12.318–22]

If growth of the individual is defined as the increased ability to control one's property, then Barbour, through *The Bruce*, argues that the best guarantee of heritability—hence, the individual—is, paradoxically, the seeming subordination of the individual through feudal loyalty, which protects heritability.

Vassal homage as an effective means of uniting people emotionally and psychologically is usually emphasized by Barbour either in terms of acts of loyalty, such as the support Bruce receives from his vassals as they wait out the winter at Loch Lomond, or, more important, in terms of the fraternal and familial bond that is the basis of feudal reciprocity. This kind of bond is remarked in several ways in the poem. It is apparent, for example, in Bruce's and Douglas's relationships to their men, illustrative examples of which follow the Battle of Loudon Hill and the Black Douglas's fight with Sir Robert Neville, respectively. Not far from Inverarie, on the way to Mounth, for instance, Bruce takes ill and becomes so sick that he can neither ride nor walk. This dramatic change in their leader's health distresses Bruce's men. Barbour describes the emotion of their response as if it were the emotion expressed by one brother to another under similar circumstances:

> Yen wyt 3e yat his men war wa,
> For nane wes in yat company
> Yat wald haiff bene halff sa sary
> For till haiff sene his broder ded
> Lyand befor him in yat steid
> As yai war for his seknes,
> For all yar confort in him wes. [9.42–48]

Likewise, as soon as Douglas's men have defeated Sir Robert Neville near Berwick March, Douglas allows his followers to seize what they can from the battlefield. The men collect their booty, which Douglas, in turn, divides among them. When he refuses to take any for himself, Douglas's action is described by Barbour as the action of one who is almost paternal—whose concern is for the welfare of his men as if they were members of his family:

> Ye prayis amang his menze
> Eftre yar meritis delt he
> And held na thing till his behuff.

Sic dedis aucht to ger men luff
Yar lord, and sua yai did perfay.
He tretyt yaim sa wisly ay
And with sa mekill luff alsua
And sic a-wansement wald ma
Off yar deid yat ye mast cowart
He maid stowtar yen a libart,
With cherysing yusgat maid he
His men wycht and of gret bounte. [15.539–50]

Another way in which the psychological and emotional unity created by vassal homage is expressed in terms of the familial/fraternal
bond is in Barbour's treatment of women. There are, to be sure, many
pro-Scots and pro-English women in the poem. As might be expected,
too, the former outnumber the latter. It is not, however, the women's
numerous war-related activities or even direct involvement in vassalic
obligation[24] that Barbour principally links with the fraternal/familial
nature of the feudal relationship. Rather, it is the stereotypic view of
woman that Barbour uses to throw in relief the reciprocity informing
the feudal cohort. The frailty of women and the need for them to be
sent away for their protection during the winter at Loch Lomond,
for example, emphasizes the dogged loyalty that exists between a
lord and his men. Bruce's halting of his entire army in Limerick to
accommodate a humble washerwoman in childbirth, likewise, may
suggest a Scottish belief in the sanctity of human life and the family,
but, by the same token, proves to be an expeditious means of reaffirm-
ing and expanding feudal order. While the narrator identifies Bruce's
act as being one of "full gret curtasy," he also adds that the Irish
who have witnessed this courtesy do homage ("manredyn") immediately thereafter.

The most obvious way the fraternal/familial basis of vassal homage
is emphasized is in the coronation of David and his subsequent marriage to Edward III's sister Joan toward the end of the poem. What is
interesting about this example is not that it includes specific homage
from nobles as well as commons or that it is associated directly with
family through the marriage of David and Joan. What underscores the
fraternal/familial in this marriage/homage event is Bruce's inclusion of
the "tailʒe," or entail, to provide for succession in the event that an
heir to the throne does not result from the new union:

Ye king maid yaim fair welcumyng
And efter but langer delaying
He has gert set a parleament
And yidder with mony men is went,
For he thocht he wald in his lyff
Croun hys ʒoung sone & his wyff,
And at yat parleament swa did he.
With gret fayr and solemnyte
Ye king Dawy wes crownyt yar,
And all ye lordis yat yar war
And als off ye comynyte
Maid him manredyn and fewte.
And forouth yat yai crownyt war
Ye king Robert gert ordane yar,
Giff it fell yat his sone Dawy
Deyit but ayr male off his body
Gottyn, Robert Stewart suld be
Kyng and bruk all ye realte
Yat hys douchter bar Mariory,
And at yis tailʒe suld lelyly
Be haldyn all ye lordis swar
And it with selys affermyt yar. [20.119–40]

Barbour's emphasis upon feudal custom and practice rather than the chivalric ideal is an obvious response to the political realities affecting late fourteenth-century Scottish succession. Through vassalic obligation—that is, through the relationships resulting from vassal homage—Barbour demonstrates that social and political unity can be achieved. The attraction or illusion often associated with the chivalric is nowhere to be found in the practical feudal relationships resulting from homage, fealty, and fief. But those superficialities, Barbour reminds his audience in his treatment of Edward Bruce, are more a liability than an asset. Unburnished as it may be, the relationship that mutually benefits a lord and his men is, finally, the basis of a free and independent feudal monarchy. Furthermore, that relationship, Barbour indicates, can and must be additionally secured by extending specific vassal homage to all levels of society—that is, to the commons as well as the nobility.

Notes

1. *Barbour's Bruce*, 3 vols., ed. Matthew P. McDiarmid and James A. C. Stevenson, The Scottish Text Society (Edinburgh), 4th ser., 12 (1980), 13 (1981), 15 (1985). Hereafter references to this edition of the poem will appear in the text.

2. On Barbour's treatment of chivalry in general and Edward Bruce in particular, see Lois H. Ebin, "John Barbour's *Bruce*: Poetry, History, and Propaganda," *Studies in Scottish Literature* 9 (1971–72):223–24; Bernice W. Kliman, "The Idea of Chivalry in John Barbour's *Bruce*," *MS* 35 (1972):493–95; Bernice W. Kliman, "John Barbour and Rhetorical Tradition," *Annual Medievale* 18 (1977):110; Bernice W. Kliman, "The Significance of Barbour's Naming of Commoners," *Studies in Scottish Literature* 11 (1974):111; and Anne M. McKim, "James Douglas and Barbour's Ideal of Knighthood," *Forum for Modern Language Studies* 17 (1981):176–79.

3. Walter Ullmann, *The Individual and Society in the Middle Ages* (Baltimore, Md.: Johns Hopkins University Press, 1966), 64.

4. For a discussion of renunciation, see Jacques Le Goff, *Time, Work, and Culture in the Middle Ages*, trans. Arthur Goldhammer (Chicago: University of Chicago Press, 1980), 246–48. See also Marc Bloch, "Les formes de la rupture de l'hommage dans l'ancien droit féodal," in *Mélanges historiques*, 2 vols. (Paris: S. E. V. P. E. N., 1963), 1:189–209; and *Glossarium Mediae et Infirmae Latinitatis*, 12 vols., ed. D. Du Cange (Niort, 1884), 3:453–54.

5. See 1 Cor. 12:4ff. For a discussion of the rise of the individual in the context of "class struggle," epitomized by the revolt of 1381, see David Aers, *Community, Gender, and Individual Identity: English Writing, 1360–1430* (London: Routledge, 1988). In particular, Aers sets the growing sense of the "individual" not against the traditional Pauline metaphor invoked by medieval authors but against the "received cultural categories" of contemporary critics and traditional views of a fixed hierarchy based on an assumption that the authors who espoused such views did so for all classes (see especially pp. 6–10). Of course, the development of the concept of the individual is an ongoing phenomenon not limited to the fourteenth century. For a more "traditional" discussion of the roots of the medieval concept of the individual, see Colin Morris, *The Discovery of the Individual, 1050–1200* (Toronto: University of Toronto Press, 1972).

6. The contrast between chivalry and feudal obligation conforms to Barbour's use of pairs of opposites as structuring devices within *The Bruce*. On the epistemological informing structural principle in the poem, see Judith Grossman, "The Correction of a Descriptive Schema: Some 'Buts' in Barbour and Chaucer, " *SAC* 1 (1979):43–44; Kliman, "The Idea of Chivalry," 481; Kliman, "John Barbour and Rhetorical Tradition," 112; McKim, "Barbour's Ideal of Knighthood," 173; Walter Scheps, "Barbour's *Bruce* and Harry's *Wallace*: The Question of Influence," *Tennessee Studies in Literature* 17 (1972):24 n. 8; Jacqueline Trace, "The Supernatural Element in Barbour's *Bruce*," *Massachusetts Studies in English* 1 (1968):56, 63–65; and Ian C. Walker, "Barbour, Blind Harry, and Sir William Craigie," *Studies in Scottish Literature* 1 (1964):204–6.

7. For an excellent example of chivalric warfare between individual knights, see in particular *The Alliterative Morte Arthure, A Critical Edition*, ed. Valerie Krishna

(New York: Burt Franklin, 1976), ll. 2044–94. Moreover, it is important to note that the conflict with the Emperor Lucius is over a matter of "homage" (l. 99).

8. For the poetical version of the *De re militari*, see, for example, *Knyghthode and Bataile*, ed. R. Dyboski and Z. M. Arand (EETS, o.s., 201 [1936], 19–35). For the Scottish prose version, see Diane Bornstein, "The Scottish Prose Version of Vegetius' *De re militari*," *Studies in Scottish Literature* 8 (1971):177–83. For further discussion of Vegetius in the Middle Ages, see Philippe Contamine, *War in the Middle Ages*, trans. Michael Jones (New York: Basil Blackwell, 1984), 170, 210–12, 214, 251–52, 297.

9. In regard to the historical Robin Hood and the origins of the legend in the fourteenth century, see John Bellamy, *Robin Hood, An Historical Enquiry* (Bloomington: Indiana University Press, 1985). Bellamy notes that allusions to "bastard feudalism and the legal and social institutions it contained," such as the "giving of liveries and fees, distraint knighthood, the office of sheriff and the administration of the forest" in the *Gest of Robyn Hode*, locate the origins of the legend in the fourteenth rather than the thirteenth or fifteenth centuries (58). Interestingly enough, an example of the conversion of former enemies through personal feudal obligation (some might say "cooption," others "appropriation") may well be found in Bellamy's historical Robin Hood, who, according to account books, was taken into Edward II's court as, among other positions, a member of the "valetz de chambre" during the early 1320s.

10. W. A. Craigie, "Barbour and Blind Harry as Literature," *The Scottish Review* 22 (1893):179–80.

11. See, for example, the Black Douglas's victory at Lintalee, Robert Bruce's care for the pregnant washerwoman, the Battle of Byland, the raid on Weardale, or the Treaty of Northampton.

12. *Individual and Society*, 65.

13. Robert Bruce's indenture agreement reads as follows:

> And [Robert] said, "Sen ȝe will it be swa
> I will blythly apon me ta
> Ye state, for I wate yat I have rycht,
> And rycht mays oft ye feble wycht."
> Ye barownys yus accordyt ar,
> And yat ilk nycht writyn war
> Yair endenturis, and aythis maid
> To hald yat yai forspokyn haid. [1.507–14]

14. Valence not only disregards Edward's order to kill his prisoners but also employs homage as a way of securing their loyalty after the English victory at Methven. This strategy is exemplified in the case of Thomas Randolph:

> And to ye king off Ingland sone
> Yai wrate haly as yai haid done,
> And he wes blyth off yat tithing
> And for dispyte bad draw and hing
> All ye presonneris yocht yai war ma.

Bot Schyr Amery did nocht sua,
To sum bath land and lyff gaiff he
To leve ye Bruysis fewte
And serve ye king off Ingland
And off him for to hald ye land
And werray ye Brws as yar fa.
Thomas Randell wes ane off ya
Yat for his lyff become yar man. [2.455–67]

15. Walker, "Barbour, Blind Harry," 205.
16. Ebin, "John Barbour's *Bruce*," 206.
17. See, for example, *A Source Book of Mediaeval History*, ed. Frederic Austin Ogg (New York: American Book Company, 1908), 216–28; see also Marc Bloch, *Feudal Society*, 2 vols., trans. L. A. Manyon (Chicago: University of Chicago Press, 1961), 1:146–62; Le Goff, *Time, Work, and Culture*, 237–65; Carl Stephenson, *Medieval Feudalism* (Ithaca, N.Y.: Cornell University Press, 1942), 5–14, 17–24.
18. According to Barbour, the Scots naively invite Edward I to adjudicate the Scottish succession after the death of Alexander III in 1286. The Scottish barons, Barbour indicates, forget that Edward had previously placed the Welsh in bondage and conducted his "foreign" policy by force and cunning. This point is demonstrated by Barbour in his account of how Edward installs and then deposes a puppet king, John de Baliol, in Scotland as a pretext for seizing that realm. Forgotten or omitted from this retelling of history is any treatment of John de Baliol's rebellion against the English crown or of Robert Bruce's sworn fealty as earl of Carrick to Edward in 1296. Added to this revision of history, too, is the offer to Robert Bruce of a lordship over the fief of Scotland in exchange for vassalic obligation to Edward. While Barbour emphasizes that this offer is unacceptable to Robert Bruce, the manipulation of history of which it is a part is more important to the poem, not only because it establishes the context within which the Scottish wars for independence are justified but also because it introduces an abuse of vassal homage. Edward's attempt to secure Robert Bruce's fealty is not for the mutual benefit of Scotland and England but rather for Edward's individual benefit and political aggrandizement. Edward's designs upon Scotland in general, and upon Robert Bruce in particular, are put in contrast in the latter part of the prologue by Barbour's account of Edward's disregard for James of Douglas's claim to the hereditary right of his father's lands and knight service. Whereas Edward would make Robert Bruce— a king—his vassal, in Douglas's case he ignores the issue of immunity and does not permit the legitimate heir to property within the realm to do homage and become his man. This unwillingness to accept James of Douglas as a vassal is not a perversion of the vassalic relation, as it is in Robert Bruce's case, but rather an outright rejection of vassal homage.
19. McKim, "Barbour's Ideal of Knighthood," 169–70.
20. Kliman, "Significance of Barbour's Naming of Commoners," 109.
21. *Havelok*, ed. C. V. Smithers (Oxford: Clarendon Press, 1987), 60–64, ll. 2173–2274.

22. Ullmann, *Individual and Society,* 66–67.

23. Two other notable homages of atonement are included in the poem. One, involving the Lord of Lorne's men, occurs after the fight at the Bander Pass (10.123–35). The second concerns Lawrence of Abernethy (13.564).

24. The example in which a woman is directly involved in vassalic obligation arises in the poem's episode in which the Scottish forces return to the mainland, landing on the shores of Turnberry. The people the Scots encounter for the most part are afraid to show support for the Scottish cause. A lady who is distantly related to Bruce ignores the English threat and offers Bruce men who are in her service:

> Bot a lady off yat cuntre
> Yat wes till him in ner degre
> Off cosynage wes wonder blyth
> Off his arywyng, [and] alswyth
> Sped hyr till him in full gret hy
> With fourty men in cumpany
> And betaucht yaim all to ye king. [5.133–39]

Disenfranchising Women

Limiting Feudal Ideals of Order

THE ABILITY TO secure social and political order through the assertion of class difference or the modification of vassalic obligation, the emphasis of the preceding part of this collection, attests to the inherent vitality of the feudal ideal of order in people's thinking and action. But although the ideal could be expressed in multiple ways or even molded to accommodate unanticipated or unpredictable circumstances, its worth and effectiveness were seriously limited by its relegating women's actual social, political, and even legal experience to a position of subordinate importance. Cynthia Ho's essay, "As Good As Her Word: Women's Language in *The Knight of the Tour d'Landry*," calls attention to this fact in its examination of the work's treatment of gendered language.

Ho's argument is that Landry uses the restrictions inherent in feudal codes as a justification to teach his daughters obedience to a system that subjugates them. Knowledge of these restrictions—that is, understanding the ethical danger of gendered language use or, in this case, of the discourse that empowers women to work outside Christian and feudal hierarchies—enables Landry's daughters to become paragons of feudal loyalty but not fully developed individuals in their own right. Thus, while medieval men tested their chivalric prowess and courage in definable places and were judged by their deeds or actions, Ho demonstrates that, for Landry, medieval women had no choice but to test their mettle in less clearly defined spaces and were judged primarily by their judicious use of gendered language that would not threaten the feudal order circumscribing what little power or freedom they were allowed to enjoy.

In "Men's Theory and Women's Reality: Rape Prosecutions in the English Royal Courts of Justice, 1194–1222," Patricia Orr approaches the flaw of restrictiveness in the feudal ideal of order from a legal standpoint by demonstrating how women complainants in rape prosecutions confronted the failed ideals of the feudal legal system, found what few practical remedies they could, and managed, despite their suffering, to get on with their lives. According to Orr, the legal system, rapidly developing in the area of land law, was at its worst in criminal law. Toward 1222, there is evidence that the prospects of complainants of rape were taking a decided turn for the worse. Most women declined to sue their cases to a conclusion in the courts. Indeed, only 20 percent of their cases were brought before the justices. And these yield a surprising result: while some ended in acquittal of the defendant, those that did not had outcomes unlike those in modern law. In some of these cases a settlement or concord was reached between the parties. After paying the court for the privilege of settling, the defendant usually rendered something of value to his victim. In some instances this was a monetary payment. In others, more shocking to modern thinking, the assailant married his victim, an outcome that probably had its practical advantages to a woman who may have feared that her marriageability, and thus her livelihood, had been damaged by the attack.

Thus for most women who brought charges of rape, the prospects were poor. Corporal or capital punishment was rarely imposed on the defendant, and most women did not even find it worth their while to prosecute their cases. Indeed, there are strong indications that victims of rape did not fit well into the legal system, regardless of the jurists' stern pronouncements against this particular crime. While the legal system was undergoing a transition from feudal principles to those of a more centralized government, the apparent purpose of the court remained simply to provide a place in which women might use their own initiative to gain settlement or some other benefit.

5 As Good As Her Word

Women's Language in
The Knight of the Tour d'Landry

E *LIVRE DU Chevalier de La Tour-Landry pour l'enseignement de ses filles*, Geoffrey Landry's collection of entertaining popular tales aimed at teaching Christian womanhood to his three daughters, is both a literary and social document. To judge by the twenty-one extant copies of Landry's manuscript, it was a great favorite in fourteenth-century France. This popularity endured and spread throughout Europe so that by the sixteenth century a German translation went into thirteen printings.[1] Two Middle English versions are known, one by an anonymous translator in a handwriting that dates it during Henry VI's reign, and one by William Caxton, which he printed and entitled *The Booke whiche the knyght of the toure made to the enseygnement & teching of his doughters.*[2] While the single unnamed manuscript translation is usually considered the most literary rendering of the original French text, it is abridged, and thus the six surviving copies of Caxton's version provide the only complete, although at times utilitarian, English version of Landry's text.

The Knight's Prologue not only provides practical information on the production of the text, but it also introduces his important thematic concerns. The Knight begins his introduction by telling how, in 1371, the sight of his daughters in the family garden compels him to produce a book to guide the motherless girls in proper feminine deportment. While sitting in the April bower whose "gay and lusty" singing birds "enlust" him and remind him "how love hadde holde" him in his time of "servyce," he succumbs to reminiscences—of his dead wife, of his own bachelorhood, of the other men he has known. He thinks specifically of conversations with other knights who brag of the women they have loved. These men deceive women by "grete othese," perjury, and forswearing, thereby making the women suffer "vylanous diffames without cause and withoute reason" (12). With these thoughts occupying his mind, he looks up and sees his daughters walking toward him. The young girls' innocent presence in this garden, which for their father has obvious courtly associations, causes him to juxtapose in his mind the kinds of love he has known: the right order of marriage and the deleterious effect of selfish romance. Here, at the beginning of the text, the tension that is played out throughout the book between the social stability offered by feudal ideals and the anarchy resulting from "fin amours" is figured as motivation for creation of the text itself, for Landry has a "grete desyre that they shold torne to honoure above alle other thynge" (11). Landry's sensitive reflection on and protestation against men's abuse of their power over women is not a preamble to a text which will help empower his daughters, however. Rather, Landry clearly intends to use restrictions inherent in the feudal codes as a justification to teach his daughters obedience to the system that subjugates them. The Knight's introduction amply illustrates that masculine language is an emphatic force capable of seducing and shaming women. In response to this threat, Geoffrey Landry, father and noted chevalier, attempts the most delicate of balances between love for his daughters and desire to defend the male's privileged place in the social order. He does this by proposing that the victim, and not the perpetrator, be properly educated. Because "they ben yong and litil and dysgarnyssshed of al wytte and reson," he realizes the need to teach the girls by examples and doctrines, reputable words of authority which will supplant in their youthful minds the possible "sayenges" that snare women. Thus, Landry makes his contribution to fourteenth- and fifteenth-century female conduct literature by devoting attention to admonishing and disciplining through the use of language. In his ambition to place his daughters outside the economy of unlawful desire, he banishes them altogether from the world of the free exchange of words. *The Book of the Knight* is thus a conduct book for a woman's tongue, because the honor of both herself and her family hangs on her beneficial or harmful language.

Significantly, Geoffrey runs from the romantic garden setting and immediately begins assigning priests and clerks to research stories for inclusion in his book that will teach his daughters "to govern themselves." He tells us that his investigators assemble didactic stories and moral truisms concerning religious and social conduct, which he then compiles into a finished text with over 140 exempla embedded in the loose discursive frame. The book is roughly divided into four intermingled parts: a long collection of short directives followed by exempla that provide positive and negative models of female behavior, prolonged comparisons of Eve and Mary, a debate between the Knight and the Lady of the Tower, and a final exemplum about Cato. Clusters of exempla on the same topic, often in pairs, though not necessarily one positive and one negative, support the book's objective of exploring conflicting discourses. Sometimes the pairings contrast a biblical tale with a historical tale; at other times, a well-known exemplum balances an experience from Landry's own life. Just as the grouped tales throughout the work contextualize each other, the Knight's lengthy conclusion, containing both a debate and an extended exemplum, reinterprets the *sentence* of the tale collection as a whole.

Landry's central concern is gendered language use, and as the work progresses, he attempts to expose the errors of discourses that dangerously empower women to work outside Christian and feudal hierarchies. In the end, he extensively shows that in gender politics, language is the battleground for power. His love for his daughters and his desire to protect them from harm are unmistakable; yet he presents a construct in which women can succeed only in the negative sense: they must strive not to be blamed. Most, but not all, of Landry's tales involve the marriage relationship. Even when the topic is woman's conduct in society, the moralization, employing a product-oriented ideology, leads to consideration of the impact of her behavior on her husband.[3]

Verbal Fidelity and Feudal Order

Landry's marital ideology incorporates the concepts of loyal service and oath-giving fundamental to Christianity and hierarchal medieval feudalism. Social and religious theorists of medieval Europe presented man's necessary obedience to God as the pattern for acknowledging the authority of earthly lords and performing acts of loyalty for them. Romans 13:1–2 is but one of many biblical citations that support the religious basis of social hierarchies: "Let every soul be subject to higher powers: for there is no power but from God: and those that are, are ordained by God. Therefore he that resists the power, resists the ordinance of God. And they that resist purchase to themselves damnation." In this chain of fidelity, the husband serves as a vassal to his lord, and the wife, ordained by God to serve in private, not public roles, must mirror vassalic behavior in obedience to her "liege" lord, her husband. In the social reality of woman's subordination is seen a reflection of theological truth, for all women are inferior through Eve's secondary creation and through her willful participation in the fall. This verity binds her to obey man even as he must obey his human superiors and God. Saint Thomas Aquinas's teleological reading of the biblical account of man's creation sees a divine origin of social reality, that woman was created to be man's helpmate. Female subservience predates the fall and is a "civil" hierarchy instituted by God, for, as Aquinas wrote, "order would have been wanting in the human family if some were not governed by others wiser than themselves. So by such a kind of subjection woman is naturally subject to man, because in man the discretion of reason predominates."[4] The only proper sphere of influence for the inferior female is in private life as supporter of the leader of the family.

The highest goal of the feudal relationship is absolute, loving loyalty. As feudal society was preserved from complete anarchy only by the mutual contracts between lords and vassals, it was essential that all levels observe their contracts faithfully. The ballad "The Bachelor at Arms" proclaims: "You must cherish your lord's rights / And above all guard his lordship."[5] The feudal spirit of society naturally conceived of relations of service in terms of fealty, and it is especially noticeable that feudal Christian marriage patterns the modes of the wife's loyalty for her husband on those of the vassal for the lord. Since the woman was the proven inferior who must serve the superior, she must, as both a good Christian and a good member of society, follow the directive for loyalty. Advice on the loyalty of wives of course abounds. Saint Louis IX of France writes to his daughter Isabella, Queen of Navarre, famous and typical advice of his day: "Dear daugh-

FIGURE 5. A fifteenth-century wedding. Pierpont Morgan MS 394, fol. 9v, detail. Courtesy of the Pierpont Morgan Library.

ter . . . Obey your husband humbly in all that is pleasing to God."[6] Also a loving father, Landry attempts to inculcate in his daughters' minds the importance of obedient feminine support for feudal ideals in areas such as dress, piety, posture, and most importantly, language. The famous letter of Bishop Fulbert of Chartres to Duke William of Aquitaine in 1020 outlines the ideal image of feudal relations which Landry mirrors in his feminine standards: "He who swears fealty to his lord must always remember these six things: harmless, safe, honorable, useful, easy, possible."[7] Theoretically determined position, not merit, is the basis of honor. In chapter 112 Landry offers "Examples of many good ladyes of tyme presente" who have honored and attended their husbands well. The motif that holds all these stories together is that none of the husbands deserves obedience or devotion. The heroine of the 134th exemplum "oughte to be preysed . . . For her lord was over lytell of persone crokbacked goglyed and uncurtoys . . . but the good lady loued and worshipped hym . . . and dradded and served hym so mekely that many man had wonder therof" (149). As a practical matter, Landry instructs his daughters that a wife should be submissive to her husband regardless of the unreasonableness of his request, for husbands are by right intolerant of disobedient wives. The eighteenth exemplum tells "How a woman sprange upon the table" (35). This tale echoes the Prologue in its emphasis on the inequality of standards applied to male and female action; men are allowed broad amnesties for inappropriate behavior, while women are carefully monitored and reproached. Three merchants engaged in idle chatter begin to boast to each other about the obedience of their wives. Each decides to bet a jewel on his wife's submission. The first wife fails the test by asking "Why?" when told to jump into a basin, "And her husbond waxe moche angry and felle and gafe her a buffet." The second wife "was beten as the other was." The third wife, however, wins the wager for her husband and provides merriment for the men when she nervously anticipates her husband's commands to such an extent that she jumps on the dinner table, when all he had wanted was some salt. Landry appends a lengthy moralization to this tale that "thus ought every good woman to fere and obeye her lord & husbonde and to doo his commaundement is hit right or wrong" (37). Not surprisingly, Landry also offers standard examples of women, such as Delilah (100), who ruined their men through betrayal.

In feudal culture, fealty was uttered as a word, an oath of allegiance. The actual oath as a person's bond, then, is a symbol eminently suited to express other commitments as well. The pledge of betrothal is a domestic version of essentially the same relationship: a wife's oath of fidelity to her lord-husband binds her to her husband just as the husband's words bind him to his lord. Infidelity, that is, a lack of loyalty in any way, breaks the sacred marriage vow. As J. Douglas Canfield has illustrated, fidelity to words is a master trope in English literature.[8] Geoffrey Landry's choice of tales for his daughters emphasizes the society's concern for the word as a sign of loyalty and as a locus of potential transgression and betrayal. With any misuse of words, either in failing to enhance her husband's situation or in actively subverting his purposes, a wife betrays her oath of loyalty to her husband. In this model of fidelity, potential threats to domestic success do not come from outside forces but dwell at home, residing in the mouth of the female spouse. This explains why Landry can document the unethical and immoral rhetoric men use with women in his Prologue, but not actively work to censure it. For although men's lies may transgress social mores and cause women great personal sadness, they do not threaten social stability, since men's trickery of women does not subvert important bonds of loyalty.

Women should aspire after submission in marriage, not equality in public. Landry shows that society is structured so that women can never better men in a war of words. In two different tales, women with legitimate complaints attempt to confront male culprits, only to be ridiculed while the men go free. In the thirteenth exemplum (chapter 14), a woman who accuses a man of cheating at dice ends up unfairly implicated in sexual immorality (30), while in the twenty-second, three women seduced by one man become objects of ridicule (42). Judicious use of words assures a woman a marriage, but if she speaks unwisely while being courted, she will certainly forfeit that chance of matrimony, as tales 10 and 12 report in chapter 22. The King of Denmark's two oldest daughters lose the King of England to their youngest sister because she speaks the least (25), as does the King of Aragón's oldest daughter, who loses the King of Spain because she articulates too haughtily "through her teeth." He chooses instead her younger sister who is "humble and softe of speche" (29). Inserted between these two historical exempla is Landry's own tale of courtship. The knight goes with his father to interview his potential wife, but she mistakenly attempts a light-hearted courtly repartee on the topic of prisoners of love. He complains that "she was ful of wordes & when we shold depart she was aperte for she praid me two or thre tymes that I should not leve." He and his father agree to forgo the match, and he counsels his daughters, "al gentyl wymmen . . . ought to be softe humble rythe stedfast of estate and of manere of lytel speche to answere curtoisly" (28).

Through careful selection and pairing of tales, Geoffrey sets up a series of contrasting situations that amply illustrates that both maidens' and married women's virtue rests in their discerning governance of words. Landry's own aunt exemplifies the truth that women who use their language carefully and judiciously can reform their husbands. This aunt felt no jealousy over her lecherous husband although he came to her bed after visiting other women. By gently reproving him in private, and showing excessive care for him despite his sordid treatment of her, she was eventually able to convert him with her excellent words (34). The submissive wife is answerable to her husband, who can punish her for disobedience or inappropriate language. In exemplum 17, a husband entreats his wife to guard her words, and when she will not, he knocks her to the ground, kicks her face, and breaks her nose so that she is forever ugly: "It had ben moche better for her that she had holden her stylle and hadde suffred yet it is reson and ryght that the husbonde have the hyhe word and it is but honoure to a good woman to suffre and hold her pees and leuve the haultayn langage to her husband and lord" (35). Chapter 63 points out that even if the wife is innocent, as in the case of Herod's wife (92), or morally correct as was Vastys the Queen of Assyria (94), no wife has the right to presumptuously speak for herself. Women must know when to speak and when to remain silent.

Traditional complaints against women contend that women err so frequently with their copious speech that talking is the characteristic feminine weakness. In asserting that women talk more than men because they have more superfluous humidity which enables their tongues to move more quickly and easily in their mouths, the Dominican friar Robert Holcot gives a dubious biological justification for a prejudice against women long held by clerical misogynists. He adds that "The Gloss says that it is a matter of astonishment that women, who have fewer teeth than men (and teeth are needed for talk) should yet have, not less to say than men, but a great deal more."[9] One of the most popular and often represented medieval demons in both art and literature is Tutivillus, whose special task is to record women gossips in the church, illustrating the extremes of which the female tongue is capable. Because garrulity is a disease associated with women, he appears in great numbers of tale collections such as *Handlyng Synne* and *Jacob's Well*. The devil performs his typical slapstick antics in Landry's twenth-seventh (48) and twenty-eighth exempla, comically hurting himself while trying to write down all the women's vain and trite words (49). The powerful designation here of women's concerns as "trite," opposed to the implied significance of the male world, reflects the self-confirming "social dialect" of feudal, masculine language.[10]

In religious and secular literature, fear of a woman's promiscuous loquacity is often coupled with the dangerous vision of her unbridled personal freedom. Thus, restraints on women's activity must begin with their words. Proverbs 7 insists the wordsome woman is "loud and wayward, her feet do not stay at home; now in the street, now in the market, and at every corner she lies in wait." Holcot insists, "This is the whole end and apparatus of womanhood, that it should be garrulous and wandering, impatient of quiet, not wishing to stay at home."[11] Landry's first set of exempla concerning female self-control begins, conventionally enough, in chapters 1–5 with prayer, the act of linguistic submission to God's will. A maiden's obediently suitable use of communication with God will set the pattern for the relationship with her husband since prayerful dedication restrains unbound female language and guides it to appropriate avenues of expression. In Landry's tales, subjugation of feminine language practically prevents uncontrolled action. As always, the standards for judging good words are clearly focused on benefits to the husband. Several tales make the direct connection between copious or inappropriate words and dissolute actions. In the third exemplum, chapter 6, a certain knight had two daughters. While the first was devout, the second "was suffred to have all her wylle." When this wanton daughter marries, she refuses to be instructed by her husband's "faire spekyng" just as she refuses to spend the appropriate amount of time at her prayers. One night her husband wakes to find her not in the bed, and he discovers her with her servants who "japed to geder eche with other." In his anger, he maims her, puts out her eye, and becomes the first of many to abandon her. The moral Landry provides is that she lost her eye, her husband (who loved another because of her ugliness), and eventually her household for her wickedness, all because of her mother's indulgence: "she had gyven her the reyne overlonge in suffryng her to do all her wylle." Landry faults her in comparison to her sister, whose prayers lead her to live happily ever after: "It is good to say houres and here all the masses" (19). Tale 24 is a similar example of a good but young lady who is ruined because her husband is overpermissive when she makes requests. She will not do her husband's will, goes to feasts alone, and of course comes to ill repute for enjoying those freedoms appropriate only to men (44).

Eve and Mary

The cluster of moral statements and exempla concerning Eve and Mary forms an important segment of Landry's argument. The bifurcation of the image of women into daughters of Eve or of Mary is an established medieval conception. Peter Damian, the eleventh-century reformer poet, plays on this idea in his well-known use of the Latin anagram involving Ave and Eva:

> That angel who greets you with 'Ave'
> Reverses sinful Eva's name.
> Lead us back, O holy Virgin,
> Whence the falling sinner came.[12]

The central difference in the two women is often figured as one of Eve's disobedience, particularly in her lack of humble consent to the preeminence of God's and man's authoritative language. Iconographically, Satan seducing Eve frequently appears in close juxtaposition with Gabriel speaking to Mary. Gothic annunciation manuscripts always involve the angel delivering words to a silent and complacent Mary, the obedient agent of redemption who bore Christ, the second Eve who cancels out the first. In contrast to Eve, who condemned mankind with her foolish tongue, Mary is noted for her brevity. Repeating a medieval commonplace, the *Ancrene Wisse* states that "seinte

Marie the ah to alle wummen to beo forbisne wes of se lutel speche that nower in hali writ ne finde we that has spec bute fowr sithen."[13] Eve essentially sins in feudal terms with her treasonous disloyalty to Adam. During the climax of the liturgical drama *La Jeu d'Adam et Eve*, Adam cries out in his fury and dismay: "Oh, evil woman, full of treason, / Forever contrary to reason / Bringing no man good in any season."[14] Eve doubly betrays Adam, for not only is she guilty of stepping out of her correct role and inappropriately advising her liege lord, but she is also responsible for the damning content of that advice. Her lack of concern for the correct ordering of power in the feudal system and for the esteem accorded to Adam originating from that power causes her to encourage Adam in his own treachery. Through her faults, he turns aside from his rightful lord and accepts a new one, Satan.

Landry's juxtaposition of Eve and Mary in his discourse to his daughters focuses on this matter of "folly" versus discretion. The exemplum of Eve and her conversations especially pertains to Landry's argument because in the world outside Eden feudal government may fall all too easily to the temptations of disorder. Eve commits eight follies—four sins of the mouth and four sins of action generated from too loose an appreciation for language protocols, emphatically proving that lack of vigilance over women's speech leads to complete loss of control over their actions. Each enumerated folly heads a chapter with a moralization and supporting exempla.[15]

"The First Folly of Eve," Caxton's Chapter 39, introduces Eve's fall by explaining that our first mother was given exceptional freedoms and power over the earth which she wantonly disregarded in pursuit of personal satisfaction. Landry says she held a "parliament" with Satan, a word having the same denotation and connotation in Middle English as in Old French.[16] Landry here implies that Eve, in her presumption of parity with Satan and her inappropriate seizure of the right to negotiate on Adam's behalf, displays the disobedience which brings about her eternal "servage" (62). Satan cleverly takes upon himself the visage of a female peer, reinforcing Eve's bent toward feminine pride: "he hadde a face ryght lyke the face of a woman And spack ryght mekely." Landry divides this folly into a series of blunders. First, Eve puts herself in a position to be tempted, and second, she does not immediately turn away from Satan's words. In previous tales, Landry has clearly established that women should not be out alone, subject to temptation or tempting others. From Eve's example, he hopes his daughters will learn never to put themselves in the unchaperoned position of listening to a man's seductions: "The Serpent found Eve ferre froo her lord and allone Wherfore atte his best leyser he shewed her his deceyvable purpose and false langage" (63). An interesting support for the conviction that Eve should not have been away from Adam's company appears later in chapter 71, which tells the biblical tale of the murder of the woman of the tribe of Ephraim. In Landry's version, an angry wife willfully leaves her husband's home to return to her father, fatally puts herself in harm's way (she is raped and murdered), precipitates her husband's going to war in revenge, and causes many innocent men to die for no reason except that an obstinate woman did not stay by her husband's side (101). When Satan arrives, Eve, instead of returning to Adam, stays to listen. If not for this crucial misstep, all would have been well, for her quick return to Adam's side would have defeated the foe: "But hadde she come to her lord she hadde dyscomfyted and overcome hym to grete shame" (63).

Eve's second folly is that after indulging in a conversation out of Adam's presence, she answers without consulting her husband first: "she withoute takyng ony counceylle of her husbond answerd and helde with hym talkyng." Unmindful of the rights of male prerogative, she replies on her own, "For the answere was not conuenyent to her but it longed and apperteyned to her lord Adam." Eve clearly sins in not demurring to answer, "and therefore she myghte have answaerd that she shold speke to her lord and not to her" (63). At this point in the text, Landry supports his gloss with a modern tale on the same theme. When a prince proposes "foule love" to the "good lady of Acquyllee," she replies that she will have to ask her husband first, an answer which, not surprisingly, cools the ardor of the prospective lover. Landry concludes, "And soo ought euery goode woman doo and not answere after her owne wylle" (64).

In her third folly Eve misrepresents God's command in her conversation with Satan. Ignorant of the potency of words, she forgets the "defence of god whiche he made to her and to her lord" (64), and by daring to respond, she encourages the temptation: "Her symple and folysshe answeer gaf to the serpent lucifer gretter boldeness to speke to her more largely and to tempte her more playnly." By feigning acquiescence to her power and bowing to her words, Satan mimics the subversive discourse of courtly love and sets out to woo Eve. Eve's speaking of her own volition is the pivotal event of the fall, for once the devil sees her seize her own language he correctly understands that she is developing an appetite, a prideful and sensual hunger, for further power over herself. These desires, clearly inappropriate in a right-ordered world, are the target of Satan's further temptation, "ye shold be as fayre as bryght shynyng and as myghty as he hym self is." Eve's craving for autonomy approximates her desire for dominance over all creation. Justin Martyr's image that in the temptation "Eve conceived the word of the serpent" is appropriate here. Out of control, the seduced Eve falls to Satan's "faire spekynge" (66). Eve's next four follies involve indulging three other senses—looking, touching, tasting—all brought on by the stimulation of unbridled conversation.

As Proverbs warns,[17] emancipated words incite unfettered actions. After having gratified herself inappropriately, both emotionally and physically, the first woman disloyally subverts all of creation in bringing on the fall of her lord Adam through her bad guidance. Landry tries to explain the fine distinction between a wife's appropriate and inappropriate advice. He counsels wives, following an Italian conduct book, on advice-giving to "take care thou dost on no account say to him 'My advice is better than thine,' even though truly it were better, for by doing so thou couldst easily drive him into great anger against thee and great hatred." Landry insists that a good wife can give good advice, within careful boundaries: "Here thenne is a good ensample for yf ony woman counceylle ony thyng to her husbond he ought first to thynke yf she said well or nought and to what ende her counceylle shall mowe come or that he to her counseylle gyve ony consent" (68). The Knight provides a tale from his own experience of a baron who dies through his wife's bad advice. The moral once again puts the relationship in terms of feudal practice: "Therfore every good woman ought to thynke wel what counceylle she wyll gyve to her lorde and that she counceyl hym not to doo ony thyng wherby he or she may have ony shame or damage in acomplysshynge her foolysshe wylle" (68).

Eve's ninth folly was in excusing herself. When God asks her why she made her lord to fall in sin, she blames others. God's anger is clearly directed at her for her lack of loyalty to Adam, "Wherfore it semed that god therfore was mor angry thenne . . . by cause she deceyved her lord by hir folysshe counceylle and that she wolde have excused her synne" (69). Women are supposed to make satisfaction for their husband's sins, certainly not bring them into reproof. In exemplum 121 of chapter 100 Landry tells of a wicked man who is saved three times by the prayers of his wife. The moral concludes that a wife "ought to make grette abstenences and good dedes" for her husband's spiritual benefit (133). Eve's desire to save herself at the expense of Adam clearly reverses the flow of beneficial obligatory service.

After the follies of Eve, several loosely structured tales intervene before Landry, in Chapter 107, presents the story of the "gloryous and blessyd vyrgyne Marye," which clearly contrasts with the earlier tale of Eve, the destroyer of paradisaical prelapsarian language. Since Eve destroyed not only her own and Adam's unimpeded communication with God but also the world in which perfect communion existed, Mary must make double compensation for defective speech in the fallen world. Like Eve, Mary interacts with a spiritual entity bearing a special message. Holy Scripture praises Mary's retiring attitude, "by cause she dradde & was aferd as the Aungel salewed her," and Mary's quiet questioning contrasts with Eve's gullible acceptance: "She wold fyrst knowe how it myght be But thus dyd not Eue she dyd byleve to lyghtely as this day done many sumple wymmen whiche lyghtely byleeuve the fooles wherefore afterward they be broughte to doo folye they enquere not ne behold not the end to thwich they shall come as dyd the gloryous and blessyd vyrgyn Marye whiche enquyred of the aungel the ned of the faytte or ded" (144).[18]

Mary's first great attribute is, then, that she accepts God's word as uncontested truth. Her second, also in contrast to Eve, is her obedience—an example to all women. No amount of cunning praise will encourage her to attempt to rise above her preordained, vassalic station: "She took no pryde therfore within her self but sayd that she was his chammberer or servaunt / And that hyt shold be done after his playsyre." The application of this attribute is clear: "And therfore is here good Ensample how every good woman oughte to humble her self toward god toward her lord and toward the world" (145).

Landry's Conclusion: The Debate on Courtly Love and Cato's Exemplum

The first half of Landry's lengthy conclusion contains a debate between Geoffrey and his dead wife over conflicting discourses. Feudal language demands an acceptance of hierarchies, and systems which encourage disruption of these orderly loyalties are necessarily dangerous. Courtly love, as a subversive system which involves skewed fidelity and abhorrent word use, appears in Landry's text as a system detrimental to social continuity and peace. When the stereotypical submissive male lover uses this language, he shows excessive deference for the woman, thus reversing the important balance of fealty necessary for marital success. Since both the lover's inferior position to the lady and his supplications to her are patterned on the model of feudal fealty, Landry views the language of courtly love as an upended, inappropriate parody of "service." As Wendy Morgan points out, courtly love appears dangerous because it negates the intellectual imperatives to loyalty.[19] The hierarchal bonds of vassalage conflict with the fashion of courtly love and expose the female's threat to it under the influence of a traitorous code that granted her dominance. Landry is obviously familiar with courtly love and often discusses the practical and legal aspects of the cult; and yet his frequent condemnations of courtly behaviors, especially female adultery, create an ironic frame for his later defense of courtly love. Despite the traditional courtliness of Landry's home region, Anjou, he fully accepts the feudal and ecclesiastical attitudes that demand strict moral guidelines for women.[20] For example, he repeatedly points out to his daughters that if a woman once loses her reputation for chastity, she is scorned by all worthy people.

Deciding the authorial intent of the final debate on courtly love, which continues the examination of the topics explored in earlier sections, is one of the most difficult critical challenges of the text. Landry defends the benefits of courtliness while his wife answers him point by point, countering his exempla with her own. Because of the moral outlook in the early chapters of the book, most critics agree with Sidney Painter that the text is a disclaimer against courtly love and that "the ideas put in the lady's mouth" are the Knight's.[21] If the debate is really a literary device, why does Landry portray himself as a supporter of a system he despises, and why does he allow the wife to proclaim the politically "correct" position? The explanation that the Chevalier's arguments reflect opinions that he had held in his younger days is not completely satisfying. In chapter 122 the Knight/ Husband remembers for his daughters an argument with his now dead wife on the appropriateness of courtly love, "that a lady or da-moyselle myght love peramours in certayne caas" (163). Since the original argument had been in the presence of the daughters, this is a mutually remembered event which the father now urges his daughters to recollect as he does; he asks them to align their own memories with his, filtering all meaning through the masculine voice.

In the shared human linguistic community, all of our language is of course a patchwork of words we have heard before and reproduced for our own purposes. But as Bernard Cerquiglini observes, the most clandestine manipulation is assigning our own discourse to other speakers: "a constant discursive drift, a strategy of feigning, which makes linguistic exchange less a kind of social commerce and more a warfare."[22] The father thus begins by stating the benefits of courtly love as they might be viewed from the feminine viewpoint. This intriguing argument echoes his Prologue without referring specifically to it, for the advantages of illicit enjoyment, which seem female-centered, are in fact beneficial only to the male. Landry's supposed argument for courtly love in fact supports the premise of the complete conduct manual that women can prosper only by adhering to the loyalties inherent in feudal obligation. In the course of the debate, Landry carefully lists and destroys the premises of courtly love. First, he asks why ladies cannot love paramours since it is honorable for the woman and it benefits the man by encouraging him in feats of arms, the more to please his lady. This clearly refers to the ideas also espoused, probably ironically, by the twelfth-century churchman Andreas Capellanus, who offered specific rules of behavior that dictated the manners and methods of wooing and winning a lady. Andreas emphasizes the ennobling elements of courtly love: "Love causes a rough and uncouth man to be distinguished for his handsomeness: it can endow a man even of the humblest birth with nobility of character."[23]

The wife answers that first "these wordes are but sport and esbatement of lordes and felawes in a langage moche comyn" (164). She accurately responds, then, that these are just words with no moral force, mimicking the language of the Knight himself in the Prologue when he speaks of men's debasement and contortions of the language to achieve their own ends. At this juncture we should not be surprised at the lack of a genuine female voice, for it can be argued that the very concept exists in only a very few examples in medieval literature. Although women speak in many texts, their language is that imagined by the male author, and thus is free of "the discordant demands of an alienated individuality."[24] Landry then follows this agenda of evoking a vivid reality, not from the woman's point of view, but based on a male presumption that female compliance will be appropriate and nonthreatening. The invented wife at this point takes an unusual step in exhorting the daughters to ignore their father's advice, "Therefore I charge yow my fayre doughters that in this mater yee byleuve not your fader." Her argument here seems puzzling: because he is a man, the Knight's masculine language cannot be trusted. While it may seem that she is subverting filial loyalties, she actually acknowledges the rhetorical trap that he attempts to lay for the female members of the family. He posits his argument not as the father and lord of the family, but as a man open to the idea of courtly love, and she responds to him on that basis. She then instructs her daughters that there are two reasons why a paramour's love is bad for women: first, love distracts women from their primary devotion, the Church, and second, men are inherently bad. We will remember that the father himself has taught this repeatedly. The mother has taken over the father's role, and she continues by employing his method of teaching by presenting her own exempla, one on the origin of Venus and another on the ruin of two women. In protesting that while men offer worship, they eventually dispense mockery and blame, she relentlessly repeats the same tenets the father has urged all along.

Here we see an implicit comparison between the problems of Satan's persuasions and those of courtly love, for just as listening to Satan's siren song of power caused Eve's fall, so the fourteenth-century woman's listening to the beguiling promises of courtly love will lead to her irrevocable ruin as well. Both temptations invite a call to rebellion against forces of male-dominated social peace. Men who use courtly language to gain a woman's love destroy that woman just as Satan, who promised Eve extraordinary self-determination, propelled her into further bondage. By putting himself in the position of proponent of courtly ideals, the Knight, in a strange recreation of the tale of Eden, tempts his wife and daughters to accept the premises of courtly love and its implicit subversion of powers just as Satan seduced Eve. The mother advises her daughters well in chapter 124 not to repeat Eve's error of being a gullible listener. Instead, they should turn a deaf ear: "a womman ought not here the wordes or talkynge of hym that requyreth her of love . . . to the ende ye be not deceyved . . . and yf one begynne to resonne and talke with yow of suche matter lete hym alone." A woman's best protection is that which Eve did not do, to call in a witness, "Or els call to yow somme other body to here hym say what he wil and thus ye shalle voyde and breke his talkynge" (167).

To support her admonition that women must do everything they can to avoid the appearance of capricious language, the wife rebuts the Knight with a tale from his own youth, which he had already told in chapter 12 for the purpose of alerting his daughters to the dangers of imprudent speech. The wife correctly reminds him that he had developed a significant fright at a young lady's courtly language which she innocently tried to use in the wooing game. Since Landry's former conclusion contrasts with his courtly protestations, she accurately recalls for him that in his telling of the tale he had insisted, "but by cause that she whiche was not wyse ynough to ansuere yow curtoysly and wel ye demaunded her not" (168). Landry here enhances the didactic effectiveness of the pseudowife by showing her to be both credible and wise. Interestingly, the only verifiable quotation traded in the debate, or offered in the entire text, is the Dame's, since the transcript of the father's original courtship tale validates her accurate repetition.[25] In the interests of truth, she generates the retelling and further boosts her legitimacy as authority figure.[26] Here also the wife's argument mirrors the advice of Reason to Lover in *The Romance of the Rose*, that all "fin amours" are linguistic conceits that must be forsaken.[27] Although Landry risks subverting himself by allowing such expertise on the part of the wife, her later support of his ideologies justifies the artifice.[28]

The Knight, defeated in his contention that young girls can take lovers, turns to consider wives' courtly suitors. It comes as a surprise so late in the text that the wife has had her own chance at extramarital love. In chapter 131, "How a knight loved the lady of the toure," the knight first challenges her truthfulness and claims that perhaps she has had her paramours. She replies that when men speak to her of love, her cunning manipulation of discourse can "breke theyr wordes"; she is a woman so savvy with words that she is prepared for all contingencies. In her own personal exemplum she tells of defeating a potential courtly lover who, silenced by her words, "prayd that I shold kepe my pees therof." The only flaw in the mother's tale is her nonsupplication to her liege lord for help. Interestingly, she takes possession of the word-trading game men control and works out her own solution. We might wonder whether this is Landry's slip, that in imagining himself in the same situation, he assumes a "manly" linguistic solution to the affront. Nevertheless, this oversight is not remarked on, and Dame Landry quickly tells another tale of her friend who also defeats courtly temptations more in accord with the precepts of the book. The tale of "The Lady of the Fucille" presents a perfect picture of how a woman should react to temptation. This lady is one of the type that refuses to "disporte them with none other than with theyr lord," and thus she calls in her uncle to protect her by eavesdropping on the visit of a potential lover. Her rejected suitor calls it a "treasonous" act (173), but his attempt to unbalance her defenses by invoking encoded feudal terms goes unrewarded.

The debate over courtly love ends, and the father's views triumph. The Knight's concern with controlling female words takes its fullest reign in this section, for in retelling his wife's conversation, he takes authority over the record of her *sentence*, literally taking the words right out of her mouth. Of course by this point we have already suspected that the Dame is an imitation wife, a product of the male writer expropriating female speech. She does not show a woman's impotence in the presence of male language that we might expect, nor does she show appropriate reticence, because she is Landry himself. The dream wife shouts down all the allures of a discourse that threatens the secure relationships embodied in feudalism. Even when tempted by a beguiling demonic voice, mimicking the allures of romance, she holds firm in her loyalty to her husband, espousing the precepts he has carefully presented throughout the text. Landry's didactic imperatives necessitate the creation of Dame Landry the counterfeit wife as well as Landry the counterfeit mother. In addition, the acquiescing feminine voices within the work create a web of confirmation with the Prologues of both Landry and his editor, Caxton: by recording the laudatory reception of their ideologies by female audiences, each points out that "real" women sanction the accuracy of the texts' fictionalized female pronouncements.[29] In his prefatory moves, Landry tells us he got the idea of writing a conduct book from the Queen of Hungary

"whiche fayre and swetely chastysed her doughters and them endoc-
tryned as is conteyned in her book" (1). Caxton as translator and editor appends his own introduction to the author's in which he upholds
Landry's didactic purpose. Caxton addresses his text to "yong gentyl
wymen" and endorses the opinion of a matron who so highly approved of the book for her own daughters that she requested a translation by Caxton.[30] Thus, before we come to the text we are reassured
of women's as well as men's confirmation of the precepts of the work.

The second half of the conclusion presents the extended exemplum
of Cato. In this traditional tale, Cato gives his son Cathonet three
pieces of wisdom. First, do not take an office with your lord, because
you can be ruined by rumors. Second, do not respite any man who
deserves to die. Third, essay your wife to know whether she can keep
secrets. Each of these traditional morals teaches a man to control and
order his world for his greatest personal security, a master plan in
which the wife's loyalty is the third and most important component.
After Cato dies, the son breaks the first two rules and only then remembers the third. His subsequent elaborate scheme to test his wife's
ability to keep secrecy not only discloses the disloyalty of his wife but
also proves all three of his father's sayings to be true. In the conclusion, the emperor agrees that it is unremarkable that women cannot
keep a secret, "for hit is not of newe how that a woman can not kepe
secretly that whiche men sayen to her in counceylle" (191). The author
sends two important messages in the conclusion of this last tale. It is
now the close of his advice book to his daughters, and the father, Geoffrey Landry, reminds his daughters of the importance of a father's advice. Cathonet proclaims, "Now have ye herd how it is happed to me
by cause I dyd not byleuve the counceylle of my fader which was so
trewe and wyse a man" (191). After confirming his authority, the
Knight informs them of the most important moral lesson of not only
this tale but of the entire tale collection: women must be paragons of
feudal loyalty, sacred keepers of the word. Landry reminds his daughters to "kepe the counceyll of your lord and not telle it to no body"
(191). The word is an arrow out of the mouth that cannot be recalled.
In his final word, he follows his established structural pattern and
confirms the traditional tale with a personal sentiment gleaned from
his own experience: "For many one i knowe whiche have loste moche
of theyre goode and suffred many grete evyls for to have spoke to

lyghtely of other and for to have reported suche wordes as they herd saye of the whiche they had nought to doo all for none so wyse is that may know what to him is to come" (191). As always, watch your word.

Notes

Author's Note: Research for this project was assisted by a National Endowment for the Humanities Summer Seminar at the Newberry Library and a Davidson College Faculty Research Grant.

1. The *Livre* enjoyed great popularity in France, England, and Germany. The French version also appears in two early sixteenth-century printings, an interesting example of the tenacity of the feudal ideal (John Grigsby, "A New Source of the *Livre Du Chevalier De la Tour Landry*," *Romania* 84 [1963]:171–207).

2. *The Book of the Knight of La Tour-Landry, Compiled for the Instruction of his Daughters; Translated from the Original French into English in the Reign of Henry VI*, ed. Thomas Wright (New York: Greenwood Press, 1969); M. Y. Offord, ed., *The Book of the Knight of the Tower Translated by William Caxton* (EETS, s.s. 2 [New York: Oxford University Press, 1971]). Because these two editions do not agree on chapter numberings or headings, I refer exclusively to those in the Caxton translation. All parenthetical citations refer to page numbers in the Caxton translation. As the exempla are not marked or numbered in either edition, those designations are my own.

3. There are many excellent studies of medieval women and their status in the medieval marriage. For a sampling, see Georges Duby, *Medieval Marriage*, trans. Elborg Forster (Baltimore, Md.: Johns Hopkins University Press, 1978); Barbara Hanawalt, *The Ties That Bound* (New York: Oxford Universtiy Press, 1986); Joel T. Rosenthal, ed., *Medieval Women and the Sources of Medieval History* (Athens: University of Georgia Press, 1990); Susan Mosher Stuard, ed., *Women in Medieval Society* (Philadelphia: University of Pennsylvania Press, 1976); Erika Uitz, ed., *The Legend of Good Women*, trans. Sheila Marnie (Mount Kisco, N.Y.: Moyer Bell, 1988).

4. *Basic Writings of Saint Thomas Aquinas* (New York: Random House, 1945), 1:881.

5. Eustache Deschamps, "Du Bachelier d'Armes," trans. Diane Bornstein, in *Chaucer: Sources and Backgrounds*, ed. Robert P. Miller (New York: Oxford University Press, 1977), 159.

6. *Acta S. S. Bollandists*, 5th Aug., p. 588, trans. in Bede Jarrett, *Social Theories of the Middle Ages* (Westminster, Md.: Newman Bookshop, 1942), 75.

7. *Recueil des historiens des Gaules et de la France*, 10:463, quoted in *Readings in Medieval History*, ed. Patrick J. Geary (Lewiston, N.Y.: Broadview Press, 1989), 404.

8. *Word as Bond in English Literature from the Middle Ages to the Restoration* (Philadelphia: University of Pennsylvania Press, 1989), xii.

9. *In Proverbia Salamonis*, lect. 5, fol. lxi, trans. in Jarrett, *Social Theories*, 84.

10. On the dialects of power, see Carroll Smith-Rosenberg, *Disorderly Conduct: Visions of Gender in Victorian America* (New York: Oxford University Press, 1986), 43–44.

11. Jarrett, *Social Theories*, 85.

12. Quoted in Henry Kraus, *The Living Theatre of Medieval Art* (Bloomington: Indiana University Press, 1967), 47. See also *The Lay Folks' Catechism*, eds. Thomas F. Simmons and Henry Edward Nolloth (EETS, o.s. 118 [London: Kegan Paul, Trench, Trubner, 1901]), 12, ll. 184–87.

13. J. R. R. Tolkien, ed., *Ancrene Wisse* (London: EETS, 1962), 44.

14. Translated in Henry Kraus, *The Living Theatre of Medieval Art*, 50.

15. For a source study of Eve's follies, see Grigsby, "New Source," 178–201.

16. *Oxford English Dictionary*, 2 vols. (Oxford: Oxford University Press, 1981), 2:2080.

17. See, for example, chaps. 14, 15, and 22.

18. Even when Mary does speak in her "Magnificat," she reiterates God's words in the form of biblical quotation rather than creating any particular, individualized language.

19. " 'Who was Then the Gentleman?': Social, Historical, and Linguistic Codes in the *Mystère d'Adam*," *SP* 79 (1982): 101–21.

20. Sidney Painter, *French Chivalric Ideas and Practices in Medieval France* (Baltimore, Md.: Johns Hopkins University Press, 1940), 138–40.

21. Painter, 140.

22. "The Syntax of Discursive Authority: The Example of Feminine Discourse," *Yale French Studies* 70 (1986):183–98.

23. *The Art of Courtly Love*, ed. John Jay Parry (New York: Columbia University Press, 1941), 31.

24. Parry, *Art of Courtly Love*, 189.

25. George W. Savran, *Telling and Retelling: Quotation in Biblical Narrative* (Bloomington: Indiana University Press, 1988), 7–11. Savran discusses the "verifiable" qualities of the different categories of "quoted direct speech."

26. Meir Sternberg discusses "narrator" versus "character generated" retellings ("Proteus in Quotation Land," *Poetics Today* 4 [1982]:107–56).

27. Guillaume de Lorris and Jean de Meun, *The Romance of the Rose*, trans. Charles Dahlberg (Hanover, N.H.: University Press of New England, 1983), 96.

28. The wife appears as an extremely discerning didact. Landry's text was often printed in the fifteenth century together with ladies' instructional works featuring Dame Prudence, such as "The Tale of Melibee" and Christine de Pizan's *Le Livre des trois vertus* (Lee Patterson, "What man artow?" *SAC* 11 [1989]:150).

29. For a discussion of male editorial self-confirmation, see Nancy K. Miller, "Rereading as a Woman: The Body in Practice," in *The Female Body in Western Culture: Contemporary Perspectives*, ed. Susan Rubin Suleiman (Cambridge, Mass.: Harvard University Press, 1985), 358.

30. See N. F. Blake's argument that the sponsor of the text is Elizabeth Woodville ("The 'Noble Lady' in Caxton's 'The Book of the Knyght of the Towre,' " *Notes and Queries* 210 [65]:92–93).

6 Men's Theory and Women's Reality

Rape Prosecutions in the English
Royal Courts of Justice, 1194–1222

————————————————————————————————— ✌

OMEN WHO COMPLAINED of rape in an English judicial system still heavily marked by feudalism[1] found
their position to be paradoxical; the position of women
in feudalism, the bond of mutual loyalty between fighting men, was at best anomalous.[2] In legal theory women were to be
protected from rape, and the legal treatises set out fierce punishments
for the crime.[3] However, as complainants in a crime in which accusers
were invariably women and defendants always men, they would
seem to have been at a distinct disadvantage in a legal system administered exclusively by men. The court must have been a discouraging
place for them; in the period covered here the court rarely convicted
and never severely punished a defendant in a case of rape, and most
women did not even bother to prosecute their cases.[4] On the court's
behalf it must be said that those few women who prosecuted their
rape cases usually saw them resolved favorably to themselves, and
that its treatment of complainants of wounding, a nonfatal crime of
violence in which the victims were almost always men, was not much
better (see table 6.4). On the other hand, the evidence suggests that,
in the latter part of this period, rape plaintiffs' chances for a favorable
outcome were worsening in a way that was not true of plaintiffs of
wounding (see table 6.10). On the whole, the court seems to have operated less to dispense justice than to provide a forum for women to

get a settlement,[5] and it is to the women's credit that, when the courts did little for them, they were able to do something for themselves and win the means to put the past behind them and to begin rebuilding their lives.

The two great jurists of twelfth- and thirteenth-century England were agreed: rape was a serious crime and deserved a severe punishment. The author of the treatise attributed to Glanvill, writing in 1179, thought the punishment for rape should be the same as for any felony, presumably including capital punishment.[6] The treatise called by the name of Bracton specified a fierce corporal punishment, blinding and castration, in the case of rape of virgins. The ideas of the treatise's anonymous author on how far the protection of the law should extend have a modern sound; the rape of any woman, be she virgin, married woman, widow, or even prostitute, was a crime and was to be punished.[7] There was a large gap, however, between the declarations of legal theory and the practice of the legal system. In part this discrepancy was due to deficiencies in the judicial system itself; though developing rapidly in the area of land law, it came only slowly to rationalize the criminal law and was impotent to handle the criminal cases presented to it.[8] It was particularly so in cases of rape.

This was not because rape was a trifling offense. The violence of many assaults is attested by even these laconic court records. Christiana daughter of William son of Norman was dragged from the road on which she was walking and raped. Jurors or court officials attested that Malot Crowe was raped and seen bleeding, that Sibba daughter of William had been beaten and raped, and that the assailant of Aubrey, daughter of another William, not only raped but also bound and shamefully treated her.[9] Several women were imprisoned as well as raped; one was held for eight days. Alice de Grendon said that Ralph de Beauchamp took her into his house and raped her, and then used three armed men to take her to another of his houses and hold her there for three days. The court took her allegation seriously; it ordered that Ralph's lands be taken into the hand of the king and that he be distrained to come into court and answer her. Stephen Hoket took Lucia sister of William Ballard into his booth and raped her and kept her there all night, and when she cried out, his family members came and put a lock on the door to keep her from raising the hue and cry.[10] Perhaps the purpose of imprisoning these women was to impede their ability to begin their prosecution and thus to invalidate their suits. The possibility of gang rape, suggested by the accomplices or multiple defendants who appear in several cases,[11] cannot be verified in these records; they do not make clear what part the additional defendants played in the offense.[12]

It was the responsibility of the rape victim to initiate and pursue her own prosecution in the court. Rape prosecutions were invariably begun by appeal, which was not, as in modern legal practice, the retrial of a case in a higher court, but a procedure in which an injured party initiated a case by coming into court and making a complaint of the wrong done to him or to her.[13] Unlike homicide or robbery, rape was not a subject of presentment; that is, it would not be brought to the attention of the court by the report of a presentment jury. There was only one tentative approach to a presentment for rape, a case in 1195 in which the jurors said they had heard a rumor that the daughter of John de Childrinton had been raped; no action was taken on the report.[14]

In accordance with the belief that an appeal should be brought by the injured party, women complainants themselves appealed their alleged assailants,[15] and the legal records thus give a strong impression that women were acting on their own in bringing their appeals. If families or other interested parties were involving themselves in the actions of the complainants, the court only occasionally took notice. In a few cases, fathers of the complainants are noticed because they appeared in an official capacity; they served as pledges that the complainants would prosecute. In one case a man from the community helped the opposing parties to come to a secret settlement, and in one unusual case the parents of a complainant pursued her appeal when she did not appear herself.[16] It seems likely that a wise woman would seek all the support and assistance available to her, and that families would take a strong interest in the progress of the cases, but from the evidence of the rolls the women conducted their own cases, and it may well be that they took a prominent part in them.

Correctly conducting her appeal, that is, her prosecution, was essential to the success of a woman's complaint of rape, and the steps of the appeal, called the suit, had to be very carefully made if the appeal was not to be quashed when it came before the justices. The process may have been a particularly trying one for women who had been raped. First the appellor, the person bringing the charges, had to prove that a crime had been committed by finding witnesses to the condition in which she had been left after the attack. An example of the action expected of her is given by Glanvill: "A woman who suffers in this way must go, soon after the deed is done, to the nearest vill and there show to trustworthy men the injury done to her, and any effusion of blood there may be and any tearing of her clothes."[17] She was then to show the same evidence to the reeve of the hundred and to repeat her claim at the next county court.[18] The exposure of injuries of so private a nature may have posed a hardship for women; Eileen Power has presented evidence that even in an age that put little value on privacy women felt considerable hesitancy about exposing their bodies to men.[19] But the demonstration was for the purpose of proving that the crime had indeed taken place, and was of the same sort that was expected of a man who made an appeal of wounding; the law made no exceptions for the sake of any putative feminine modesty.

Once the charges were made in county court, it was the responsibility of the appellor to continue appearing in the court until the defendant was brought into court and tried, or until he was outlawed, or some other disposition was made of the case. A woman who failed to do so was liable to be amerced or, if she was too poor to find pledges, imprisoned.[20] Even so, an astonishing number of women failed to prosecute their cases. Their reasons no doubt varied; the reports of most cases are too brief to give any reason for the appellor's default. A typical example reads, "Goda daughter of Hugh appealed William Reiskele of rape; she has not prosecuted. Let her be taken and amerced."[21] It is likely that some appeals were false and were abandoned for that reason, but such a large proportion of unprosecuted appeals cannot be explained on the grounds of falsity alone. It is not possible to tell if pregnancy played a part in the failure to prosecute. Later writers expressed a notion that pregnancy signified consent, grounded in the belief that a woman, like a man, could play her part in conception only if she gave her consent;[22] the rolls and the treatises are silent on this point. In some cases, no doubt, suit had been incorrectly made. Failure to sue correctly could be fatal to the appeal, as mentioned earlier. Lady Stenton suggests that in the highly formal appeals process it was easy for any appellor to make "some technical fault"; women, who were much less likely than men to have attended

Table 6.1 Cases of Rape

Outcome	Number of Cases	Percentage
Not prosecuted	129	64
Withdrew	2	1
One party died	10	5
No conclusion	26	13
Appellor lost	13	6
Outlawed	13	6
Concorded	9	5
Prosecuted until punishment imposed	0	0
Total	202	100

the courts on a regular basis, were less familiar with legal procedure and so perhaps more likely to make mistakes.[23] And women, however knowledgeable, who had felt distaste for revealing their injuries to lo- cal officials and thus had skipped that essential step may have felt it was not worth their while to appear in court. Perhaps others stayed away because they felt that a court in which severe punishment was so seldom imposed would not be sympathetic to their complaints.

For whatever reason, among the majority of women who brought appeals, there was a strong disinclination to prosecute them to a con- clusion in the courts. As we see in table 6.1, of the 202 women who brought appeals of rape in the rolls, fully 129, like Goda daughter of Hugh, failed to prosecute them. Two other women came into court and withdrew before their suits were completed. Elena de Escaude said she had been coerced into making her appeal by the local con- stable, who was perhaps a personal enemy of the accused, and Emma daughter of Thomas de Aymunderby gave no reason for withdrawing, even though the jurors had attested that her suit had been reasonably made.[24] In all, just under two-thirds of the women, 131, or 65 percent, abandoned the appeals they had begun. In addition, there were ten other appeals that could not continue because one or the other of the parties had died; thus 141 cases, some 70 percent, were not prose- cuted because of the default of the complainant or the death of one of the parties.

Of the remaining sixty-one cases, there are twenty-six that come to no conclusion in these rolls. In two of these the scribe left the record of the case unfinished. In seven other cases the scribe completed the record of the case but left no indication of any judgment for or against the defendant, as when the men of Grimesbi were amerced because they did not attach a man appealed of rape, or when a certain Roger's pledges were amerced because Roger did not appear to answer charges of rape against him.[25] Seventeen other cases were postponed to await another step in the process. The appeal brought by Yllaria daughter of Hemeric de Dunton was to await the assembling of a jury,[26] and in the case of Sarah daughter of John Bosse, a certain Richard Curteis asked for more time to get the defendant into court; Richard had seized eighty-four loads of wheat from the defendant's chattels and still had hopes of forcing his appearance.[27]

This leaves only thirty-five cases, just a little over one-sixth of the total, that actually came to a conclusion in court. Women who persevered this far with their appeals found their chances for a decision in their favor were surprisingly good. To be sure, some women suffered setbacks; women lost thirteen cases outright when the judgment of the court went against them, even in two cases in which the defendant had fled. In the remaining cases women could be said to have made some gain; in thirteen cases their opponents had fled and were outlawed,[28] and in nine cases they made concords under the purview of the court. Thus women could be said to have received decisions favorable to themselves in twenty-two cases, while losing only thirteen. There was no case, however, in which a woman prosecuted her case against a defendant who was present in court until a punishment was assessed. A breakdown of the outcomes of all the rape appeals can be seen in table 6.1.

Table 6.2 gives a clearer picture of the outcome a woman could expect when she brought her appeal. Note the high percentage of unprosecuted cases: 70 percent of the cases were dropped, either because of lack of prosecution or because one or the other of the parties had died. Women could expect to sue their cases to some sort of favorable conclusion in only twenty-two, or 11 percent, of the cases, and in no case did a woman sue her case to the point that her opponent was convicted and a punishment was assessed. We also note, however, that defendants were acquitted in only thirteen of the cases that were concluded in the court; this makes only 6 percent of the cases that ended in favor of the defendant. In the thirty-five cases that

Table 6.2 Cases of Rape Not Sued

Cases Not Sued	Number of Cases	Percentage
Not prosecuted	129	64
Withdrew	2	1
One Party Died	10	5
Total	141	70
Cases Not Concluded	26	13
Defendant Acquitted or Not Penalized	13	6
Some Gain Made by Plaintiff		
Defendant Outlawed	13	6
Concorded	9	5
Total	22	11

Table 6.3 Cases of Rape Sued to a Conclusion

Cases Sued to a Conclusion	Number of Cases	Percentage
Defendant Acquitted	13	37
Some Gain Made by Plaintiff	22	63
Total	35	100

were brought to a conclusion, as table 6.3 shows, appellors had a reasonable chance for success.

Women who achieved this measure of success had vigorously pursued their suits, missing few if any of the steps involved; their cases sometimes elicited sympathy from the justices. Yvette daughter of Rannulf appealed William of Winceby of rape and of imprisoning her for two days. William denied the charge, but testimony was all in Yvette's favor. The jurors and Andrew, the keeper of the pleas of the crown to whom she had come as soon as she was freed, attested that she was bloody and had been shamefully treated, that is, had suffered other mistreatment as well as the rape, and the whole wapentake[29] testified that she had come to the next meeting of its court and made her appeal. William relented; he and Yvette put themselves in the king's mercy for a license to concord. William had to pay an amercement, but the court showed its sympathy for Yvette by pardoning hers.[30]

Prompt and vigorous suit also helped one woman who had been held captive for a longer time after the assault. Leviva daughter of Siwat was raped and held prisoner for eight days. After she escaped from the house where she had been held, she went to the serjeant and made her complaint, and she later sued at both the wapentake and the county courts; she concorded with the defendant for one-half mark, the equivalent of just under seven shillings. In the case of Lucia sister of William Ballard, Stephen Hoket, whose family helped him keep Lucia in his booth all night, claimed that Lucia was lying and that she had been his mistress for a year before she had made her appeal. But the serjeant attested that she had been seen bleeding, and the justices showed their opinion of Stephen's behavior by amercing him five marks for the concord he made with Lucia; the terms of this concord will be discussed later.[31]

Failure to prosecute, on the other hand, may have predisposed the justices to disbelief, at least in the early years of the period, or at any rate provided grounds for dropping proceedings, as in one case in which no further steps were taken even though the jurors said that the defendant had fled immediately after the crime. The justices had apparently first ordered that the defendant be outlawed, but then decided that because the appellor had not prosecuted they could do nothing.[32]

Failure to make adequate suit, that is, to go through the process of raising the hue and cry, showing evidence of the assault to the proper officials, and declaring the offense in the local courts, seriously weakened an appeal; so did changing the language of the appeal. Juliana de Clive committed both errors. She first said that Robert son of Nicholas had raped her; later she said only that he had lain with her by force. Moreover, she had not made suit. The appeal failed when the jurors, who had reported the lack of suit, gave it as their belief that Robert was not guilty.[33] At other times no reason for disbelief is apparent. David de Westbiria fled to a church for sanctuary for a rape, but when the appellor, a minor, came to sue her appeal, testimony was given that he had not raped her. The appeal went no further.[34]

Other appeals failed because of a strong presumption that they were the result of a grudge on the part of the appellor and not of an actual offense. Some had been brought by women whom the court decided were discarded mistresses. Agnes Tredgold appealed William de Smithfield of having raped, beaten, and robbed her. William denied this, saying that she had been his mistress, and gave one-half mark for an inquest and to have his judgment, that is, for the court to decide his case without delay. The jurors said that she was his succuba, or paramour, before and after the alleged offense and that she was making the appeal because he had become affianced to someone else.[35] Marjorie daughter of Albric lost her appeal when the jurors said that Reginald son of Amfrid had "had her for a long time and for two years in her father's house" and that no hue and cry had been raised. In another case the jurors said that Aldusa de Eton had appealed Simon son of Alan because, after she had been his mistress for a year, he had married another.[36]

These women and others like them may have suffered very real wrongs, wrongs that a breach of promise suit might have rectified, but according to the ideas of the time it was extremely unlikely that they had been raped. The existence of the long-term relationship itself seems to have been thought of as conclusive evidence that no rape had occurred; the jurors' mention of Marjorie's omission of the hue and cry seems to be a confirming circumstance, with no hint of the idea that a rape could occur within such a relationship.[37]

It was equally the jurors' opinion that Maud daughter of Henry de Spermour appealed Henry son of Eullar of Sheffield out of malice. Maud's father had been at the scene of a homicide and had fled. The fugitive was later found in a wood in the company of Maud, her sister, and some fifteen sheep of uncertain provenance by Henry son of Eullar of Sheffield, who had raised the hue and cry, forcing Maud's father to flee again. Maud herself was arrested and held until pledges were found to guarantee her good behavior. The jurors thought that these events, and not a genuine offense of rape, were the basis of Maud's appeal.[38]

A grudge may also have been the basis of the appeal made by Aleis widow of Elias Clerk. She alleged that Baldwin Druell came to her house at night with accomplices, lay with her, wounded and bloodied her, and then abducted her daughter by force. Aleis declared she had made proper suit, showing wounds to both the sheriff and the lord chancellor. Baldwin denied all this and said he had solemnly married the daughter with Aleis's consent. Unfortunately this is one of the cases that, though the opponents were given a further day in court,

FIGURE 6. Two ladies captured. Trinity College, MS 0.9.34. Courtesy of
Trinity College, Cambridge.

were not concluded in these rolls, so we cannot tell if events were as
Aleis described them or if, on the other hand, it was a case of a custody battle that became violent.[39]

Comparing appeals of rape with wounding reveals that women
were not alone in facing difficulty in getting redress for a crime of vio-

lence against themselves. Of all the criminal actions available in the royal courts, wounding is the best for comparison to rape because it was the only other nonfatal crime of violence against the person. Since complainants of wounding were almost invariably men, results of wounding cases will reveal any bias against women, if such a bias existed. Wounding and rape were linked by both *Glanvill* and *Bracton*, each of which says that a woman may appeal for rape just as she may appeal for any injury to herself,[40] and the offenses share several characteristics. Like rape, wounding was a crime of violence but was not fatal. If a wounding caused the death of the victim, the case immediately became one of homicide and lesser charges were not considered, as is illustrated by the case of Robert son of Roger, who still lay with the wounds given him by a man who had later fled. The case was to be postponed to a later coming of the justices, presumably to see whether Robert would live or die.[41]

Like rape, wounding was not a felony and was not normally brought by presentment; it was the responsibility of the injured person to make an appeal and follow it up in court. In both wounding and rape, the appellor was required to show evidence of the offense to responsible men of the community if the appeal was to succeed. In each, as it happens, a large proportion of cases was not prosecuted—although the rate of failure to prosecute in appeals of wounding was nothing like that in appeals of rape—and in both the prescribed penalty or penalties were much harsher than any that the rolls record as actually having been imposed.[42]

Still, there was no exact correspondence between the prosecution of appeals of rape and wounding. There were a great many more appeals of wounding than of rape; there are 366 cases of wounding in these rolls, including appeals of mayhem, as compared with only 194 appeals of rape. It is quite likely that appeals of rape in the thirteenth century were underreported;[43] appeals of wounding may have been overreported by complainants eager to settle old grudges or to continue in court disputes or even fights that had ended unsatisfactorily elsewhere.[44] On the other hand, there may simply have been more fights that ended in woundings than incidents of rape.

Plaintiffs in cases of wounding may have been more optimistic about their chances of success; they were much more likely than complainants of rape to prosecute their appeals. As is set out in table 6.4,

Table 6.4 Comparison of Outcome of Cases of Wounding and Cases of Rape

Outcome	Wounding (Percentage)	Rape (Percentage)
Cases Not Sued		
Not prosecuted	27.0	64
Withdrew	8.5	1
One Party Died	3.6	5
Total	39.1	70
Cases Not Completed: Procedural Reasons	32.5	13
Defendant Acquitted	10.1	6
Some Gain by Plaintiff		
Outlawed	4.6	6
Concorded	11.2	5
Total	15.8	11
Guilty: Punishment Assessed	2.5	0
Total	100	100

of the 366 wounding appeals, ninety-nine, or 27 percent, were not prosecuted by the plaintiff, as compared to the roughly 64 percent that were not prosecuted in appeals of rape. More plaintiffs in appeals of wounding withdrew after having begun their suits: thirty-one, or 8.5 percent, as opposed to only 1 percent in appeals of rape. The death of one of the parties halted proceedings in 3.6 percent of wounding cases, close to the 5 percent in cases of rape. Wounding appeals were much more subject to delay within these rolls than were appeals of rape; there were 119 cases, or 32.5 percent, that were postponed for some reason: to await judgment, to bring defendants into court, to consult a jury, or to be heard by an ecclesiastical court because the defendant was a clerk, as compared with only 13 percent in cases of rape.

At first glance, appellors of wounding would seem to stand a greater chance of losing their cases than complainants of rape. In cases that were sued to a conclusion, appellors of wounding saw the defendant acquitted in a greater proportion of their appeals: thirty-seven, or 10.1 percent, of the defendants in wounding cases were acquitted, as opposed to 6 percent in appeals of rape. Only sixteen wounding cases ended with the outlawing of a defendant who had fled; along with one case in which the defendant fled to a church and abjured the realm, this makes 4.6 percent of the cases. In rape appeals, some 6 percent of the defendants were outlawed.

On the whole, however, appellors of wounding, who brought a higher percentage of their appeals than did appellors of rape, also had a larger proportion of cases end in their favor. They were more effective than appellors of rape in settling cases by concord; forty-one of them, or 11.2 percent, did so, as did only 5 percent of appellors of rape. Eight appellors of wounding were able to do something no appellor of rape did, that is, prosecute their cases to a conclusion in which the defendant was declared guilty and punishment was imposed. When one case in which the defendant came and made fine for his crime is added to these, we see that ten, or 2.5 percent, can be said to have won their appeals.

One probable reason for the smaller number of delays in rape appeals is the justices' practice of dealing expeditiously with appeals of rape. There was seldom a delay for a jury, for example; if a defendant requested one, the justices seem to have turned to the jurors at hand, perhaps to the presentment jury. In appeals of wounding there were more occasions for delay. Battle and, before 1215, the ordeal were used to decide cases of wounding; and there was always a delay between the ordering of battle or the ordeal and its being carried out. The larger numbers of persons involved in incidents of wounding caused further delay; a single fight might produce several appeals. Often one case, perhaps the first to be brought or the one concerning the most serious wound, would be decided first and the others would be postponed; if the case to be decided was to go to the ordeal or to a jury, for example, the others would have to await its outcome.[45] Even without such obvious reasons for postponement the justices may have been inclined to temporize; they might postpone a case without giving any reason whatever.[46] Appeals of wounding usually resulted from fights or assaults that either created hard feelings between the parties or grew out of long-standing disputes or enmities. The potential for disruption of the community was such that the justices may have pre-

Table 6.5 Cases of Wounding and Cases of Rape Sued to a Conclusion

Outcome	Wounding		Rape	
	Number of Cases	Percentage	Number of Cases	Percentage
Defendant acquitted in plaintiff's favor:	37	35.6	13	37
Defendant outlawed	17	16.3	13	37
Concorded	41	39.4	9	26
Guilty: Punishment assessed	10	8.7	0	0
Total: Plaintiff's favor	68	64.4	21	63

ferred to give time for tempers to cool and hope that the parties could reach reconciliation in a concord.

Such a judicial policy would also account for the large proportion of concords reached in cases of wounding: 11.2 percent, as compared to only 5 percent of rape cases. There is a higher percentage of outlawry in rape cases than in appeals of wounding; perhaps the men accused of rape were more likely to be transients, as was the wandering merchant who assaulted Agnes, niece of John, and fled to Ireland, and as were, on a different level, two emissaries of the Emperor Otto who were parties to a case arising from their assault of a woman named Wimarc in London.[47]

Nevertheless, appellors of wounding were also more likely to make some gain from their appeals than were appellors of rape. This was partially because appellors of wounding more often pursued their cases, but even if only those appeals that were sued to a conclusion are considered, the appellor of wounding had a slightly better chance for a favorable outcome than did the appellor of rape, as is seen in table 6.5.

The margin of plaintiffs who won favorable outcomes in cases of wounding as opposed to that in cases of rape is slight, even though a higher percentage of appellors of wounding made concords and some sued their cases to a conviction. Some 64.4 percent of cases of wounding ended favorably for the plaintiff, as compared with 63 percent of the cases of rape, and when we go behind the statistics to the events as described in the cases, we see that appellors of wounding had to face hazards that appellors of rape never saw.

The judicial duel posed problems for both appellors of wounding and appellors of rape, though in different ways. There has been some speculation that women's inability to fight the duel had an adverse effect on their bringing of criminal appeals: "A woman, unlike a man, never had to risk her life in prosecuting a charge of felony."[48] The chief effect of this inability was the restriction of the appeals that a woman could bring, but it also may have contributed to skepticism of even those appeals that were within women's province. An appeal that put a defendant at risk without a corresponding risk to the appellor may not have met with the legal system's fullest confidence.

Appellors of wounding were confronted with the opposite problem, the necessity of fighting again the persons who had wounded them in the first place. The opportunity to use the legal system to continue the fight may have been attractive to some appellors, but few wanted to put themselves to the danger of a duel. Duels were adjudged in only eight appeals of wounding and actually fought in only two.[49] The justices' caution is in part the reason for the scarcity of duels; in six of these cases the justices decided that there should be a duel only after it was attested that the appellor had indeed been seriously wounded.[50] In another case there was to be a duel even though the appellor had shown only "a little wound."[51] Once his duel had been awarded to him, however, the appellor chose to withdraw and put himself in mercy; perhaps the justices had expected him to repent of what was, in the context of the time, a trivial appeal. In most cases nothing more is recorded in these rolls after the judgment that battle lay between the opposing parties except perhaps that a day had been given them on which they were to come armed.

Of the two duels that were fought, the appellor was victorious in one, the appellee in the other. One appeal was the result of a civil action in land that led to violence when the defendant, who had essoined for bedsickness, was found to be up and about and working in his fields. Richard son of John said that Geoffrey of Shireford had come to his sickbed where he lay after he had been given an essoin of bedsickness in a civil plea and had beaten and wounded him, and then had wounded his wife Emma when she raised the hue and cry. Geoffrey, Richard's opponent in the civil plea, denied all this. He said that he had come to Richard's fields, found Richard plowing instead of lying on his sickbed, and tried to capture him, but the men of the prior of Coventry took Richard away. Geoffrey tried to explain away Emma's wound by saying that when she raised the hue and cry someone pushed her down on a rock. But because Richard had made suit properly a duel was waged; when it was fought, Geoffrey was the victor and was acquitted. Richard was arrested, probably until he made fine for the accusation his loss of the duel had "proven" false.[52]

The other case was a more straightforward case of wounding. George of Nitheweie, who accused Thomas son of Estmar of mayhem, had to fight Thomas after it was decided that George's wound in the arm had not in fact maimed him. Thomas had denied George's accusation and put himself on a jury of the neighborhood, but all factors in the case appeared to be in the accuser's favor: the wound had been shown, suit had been reasonably made, and the jurors said they knew Thomas was guilty. The duel was waged and fought, and George was victorious. The record says that Thomas, the vanquished defendant, was blinded and mutilated.[53] The ferocity of the punishment, unique in these rolls, probably reflects the certainty on the part of all concerned of the guilt of the accused, but the accuser had had to risk himself in the duel and win the battle before judgment was rendered in his favor.

A few men who brought appeals of wounding and mayhem had to face a hazard no appellor of rape ever faced in these rolls: the open hostility of the judges. These men claimed to have been maimed or to be beyond the age for fighting and thus unable to fight a duel; the court may have looked with disfavor upon their attempt to force their opponents to a duel, in spite of their well-founded suits and the injury that had obviously been done to them. Astinus de Wispington appealed Simon de Edlington of tearing out one of his eyes and thus maiming him, and Astinus had made sufficient suit. The justices, hearing all this, adjudged that there be an ordeal but, rather than send Simon to the ordeal, they directed that this same Simon, the defendant, be allowed to choose which of them was to carry the hot iron. Simon naturally chose that Astinus should carry it. Not surprisingly, the two men later came before the justices and put themselves in mercy, a reasonably good sign that they had reached an agreement.[54]

The justices gave the same choice of who was to carry the hot iron to defendants in two other cases in the same eyre; one was an appeal of mayhem, and the other was an appeal of wounding in which the defendant was over the age to fight the duel, that is, over the age of sixty. In each case the plaintiff withdrew; one paid three marks for the privilege.[55] The chief of the justices of this eyre was the much-admired Simon de Patishall, so it is unlikely that the judgments were mistakes arising from judicial inexperience.[56] The common thread seems to be animosity toward appellors who put defendants to the ordeal, even though their injuries were severe ones. Perhaps the justices suspected that old enmities lay behind the appeals and preferred to force an agreement rather than allow further injury, even that attendant on the judicial ordeal.

In yet another case of mayhem in the same eyre, an appellor was treated summarily in spite of his very grievous injuries. Thomas son of Lefwin appealed Alan the reaper of attacking him on the road, carrying him off to Alan's house, breaking his arm, robbing him of his cap and his knife, and holding him while Alan's wife Emma cut off one of his testicles and Ralph Pilate cut off the other. Once Alan had returned him to the road, Thomas raised the hue and cry and made his suit. The king's serjeant went to Alan's house and found the knife and the testicles as Thomas had said, but he found no sign of the cap, and moreover the county court attested that Thomas had never mentioned a broken bone in his arm before. The appeal was quashed, not before Alan had offered the court two marks to have his judgment. The two marks aside, the reason for Thomas's loss was probably the variance in the appeal. A variance alone could be fatal to an appeal, and in addition Thomas's claim to have been maimed, had it been believed, would have enabled him to avoid the duel and have Alan sent to the ordeal, an alternative to which the justices, in the three cases previously cited, seem to have been demonstrating distaste. Privately the justices no doubt believed, as did Lady Stenton, that the attack was in retaliation for an attack on a woman of Alan's family. In sum, they preferred to leave matters as they stood, and Thomas was amerced for his false claim.[57] No appellor of rape seems to have been treated quite so shabbily.

The question remains why so many appeals were brought only to be dropped. If women expected little benefit from continuing their suits, why did they bring them in the first place? The bringing of an appeal was no light matter; it involved the finding of pledges that the appeal would be prosecuted or, in the case of impecunious plaintiffs, the swearing of a personal oath to sue. If the plaintiff did not prosecute, she and her pledges, if any, were amerced, and if she had no pledges and no money, the justices would direct that she be arrested and jailed for her default. That women did bring appeals of rape into the courts, even if they later defaulted on them, argues that they hoped for some benefit worth the risk of amercement or imprisonment.

The cases that were sued to a conclusion favorable to the plaintiff give a hint of the nature of such a benefit. As we have seen, except in those cases in which the defendant was outlawed, the conclusion in every case was a concord rather than a conviction (see table 6.5). We are seldom told the terms of these agreements, but those of which we are told are suggestive. Leviva daughter of Siwat, who said that Simon son of Agnes had raped her and held her in her house for eight days and then kept possession of her chattels, agreed to settle with Simon for one-half mark which he was to pay her on the next Sunday.[58] Sibba daughter of William, who had been raped and beaten until she was bloody, accepted the larger sum of twenty shillings from her assailant William son of Hugh of Bolton. The court tried to facilitate this agreement by forgiving William's amercement, and the sheriff undertook to see to it that the money was delivered to her.[59]

In the other cases whose terms are revealed in these rolls, the settlement was uncongenial to modern thinking: the attacker married his victim. Stephen Hoket, whom Lucia sister of William Ballard had accused of raping her and, with the connivance of his relatives, confining her in his booth all night, paid five marks for a concord by which he was to become her husband.[60] Malot Crowe, who as the jurors attested had been raped and seen bleeding, ended her appeal by marrying her attacker, as did Marjory daughter of Henry the smith.[61] This solution to the appeal, unsatisfactory as it is by modern standards, may have made good economic sense to the women concerned; it helped them to guarantee their marriageability.

It was a time when, although women who could afford it might remain single or marry for love if they so desired,[62] marriage was the most likely source of a woman's livelihood; and a guarantee of marriage may have appealed to women who were afraid that their prospects of marrying had been harmed by the rape. Such fears were not groundless.[63] Not that medieval English society was entirely rigid in requiring that women be continent before they married; Agnes de

Weston, for example, lived with one man until he died, apparently out of wedlock, and then married his brother, and Mabel de Acton, who had a son by a priest, later married and had another son.[64] These cases, however, seem to be exceptional. They are the only ones mentioned in the rolls.

The case of Isabelle daughter of Robert of Shukeburgh may be instructive concerning contemporary views. Isabelle was carried off during "King Stephen's war" (guerra regis Stephani) by an itinerant knight named Warin who had previously sought her in marriage without success; Warin kept her for several years and had a son by her while supporting himself by robbery. During the reign of Henry II, Warin was captured and put in the pillory; he died there. Isabelle then returned home to her father, who received her, as the rolls say, because she had gone with Warin against her will. Soon she was courted by a man named William, whom she married, bringing with her a maritagium of four virgates of land. By him she had another son.[65] Two points can be gleaned from this account: one is that Isabelle's unwillingness was considered worthy of mention as a condition of her return to her father's house, from which she was married, and the other is that marriage to her was made financially attractive not only by the maritagium but by her standing as her father's only heir.

Isabelle's capture and the sexual relations that followed it had, by all accounts, been against her will. The histories of Agnes and Mabel show that lack of virginity was not an insuperable obstacle to marriage, and Isabelle's case is an example of the effectiveness of both a perception of the woman's unwillingness and her economic standing in smoothing her entry into marriage. Indeed, Agnes and Mabel themselves both had land that might have played a part in their attractiveness as marriage partners. If vengeance was beyond their reach, women could work toward a very practical goal, the restoration of any damage to their marriageability caused by the rape.

The concords arrived at in court are the most obvious example of the achievement of such a practical goal. The terms of six such concords are given in the rolls;[66] in four out of those six the assailant married his victim, thus guaranteeing her the relative economic stability of marriage in the most direct way possible. In the other two the women agreed to a payment of money, in one case a half mark and in another twenty shillings. It may be that they preferred to maintain their independence; one may have already been in possession of a house and chattels.[67]

Had women preferred marriage, they would have found even a small monetary settlement useful as a sort of maritagium provided by the attacker. The purchasing power of money in the early thirteenth century is difficult to define with precision, but from these rolls it appears that half a mark would buy a cow or roughly a dozen sheep, and that twenty shillings would go much further. Twenty shillings is the value given to ten and a half loads of oats, one load of winter wheat, and an ox in one case, and to the lease for four years of two virgates of land and five houses worth five marks along with assorted chattels in another.[68] Such an amount may have done much to aid the marriage of a poor woman or even a woman in moderate circumstances.

The practicality of these settlements throws a different light on the failure of any rape appeal to go to the punishment phase when both assailant and accuser were present; rather, when the jury had declared the guilt of the defendant, the parties involved reached an agreement. The offense of rape was not only a crime of violence; it also could be viewed as a sort of property loss in which the "property" was an intangible one, the marriageability of the woman concerned. Women may well have preferred, if the occasion arose, to allow their assailants to do something toward making amends for that loss. Evidently the courts concurred in such a view; they certainly were willing to allow the making of concords.

The records suggest the possibility of some prejudice against a married woman who brought an appeal of rape. Of the four cases in which women who were married, perhaps after the commission of the crime, brought appeals of rape, none ended in a way that was favorable to the appellor. Two were not prosecuted, and in one of these the jurors declared that the defendant was not suspected of the crime.[69] Of the other two cases, one resulted in an acquittal and the other was one of the two cases in which a defendant had fled for the crime but nevertheless was not outlawed. Each of these two appeals was complicated by other deficiencies in the appellor's case. In one case the appellor changed the words of her appeal from "raped by force" to "lay with by force," thus creating a variance; she also had not made proper suit, and her husband, whose existence she had not mentioned to the court, had not appeared in court to sue with her. The jurors declared the defendant not guilty.[70] In the other case the scribe seems to be listing reasons why nothing can be done: the appellor had a husband, and the defendant, who was a wandering merchant and did not live in Bristol, where the offense occurred, had fled into Ireland, and was not suspected by the jurors.[71] We are not told whether or not the husband was present in court.

That three out of four appeals brought by married women ended in acquittal is striking; regrettably, there is no case that clearly expresses the court's attitude toward a married appellor of rape, and the number of cases we do have is too small and their circumstances are too ambiguous to allow any firm conclusions. At any rate, those women who brought their cases to a successful conclusion seem to have had no objection to accepting a settlement that either guaranteed a marriage for them or possibly aided them in securing one for themselves, and the court seems to have viewed such an outcome as appropriate, possibly even frowning on an appeal brought by a woman who was already married.

The much larger proportion of women who brought appeals only to let them lapse poses a more difficult question; did these women get some benefit that was worth the effort and the possibility of imprisonment, or was their appeal a mere futile gesture? If there was no benefit to be gained, why were the appeals brought at all? The rolls provide a partial answer; five of the women who did not prosecute are known to have made secret concords with the defendant before their cases came up in court. No doubt the assailants were motivated to offer the agreement by the bringing of the suit. Making a concord without the permission of the justices could be expensive; the plaintiff was amerced or arrested and the defendant was amerced as well. One defendant was forgiven his amercement because he was poor and another was merely placed under pledges, but the plaintiff in another case was assessed twenty shillings and in yet another the defendant was to pay a mark, the equivalent of just over thirteen shillings. In the remaining case a third party who had made peace between accusor and accused was to be amerced.[72] It may be that many other such agreements were made, with greater care taken to keep them from the knowledge of the court.

In only one case do we know the terms of the agreement. The jurors attested that Marjory daughter of John of Turgitorp had married Walter son of Simon whom she had accused of rape; it was she who was assessed a penalty of twenty shillings. Her choice, like that of others, had been to assure herself of a marriage, even though it was to the man who had assaulted her.[73]

It need not be assumed that practical considerations alone went toward the making of such a marriage. The feelings of the women involved do not come down to us, but perhaps the assailant had, after the offense, gone to some lengths to ingratiate himself to her. This was the case in a startling modern parallel to Marjorie's settlement. In December 1986, Natalia Estefania Benites and Ramon Vargas, the man who only a month before had raped her, threatened her, and left her in a field, were married by the judge who was to have presided over Vargas's trial, with the prosecutor and defense attorney as their witnesses. The couple had been dating for about three months before the assault, and after Vargas was arrested and imprisoned he had begun calling Benites on the telephone. He was persuasive; first he talked her out of being angry with him, and finally she accepted his proposal of marriage. The charges against Vargas were dismissed. The judge, in the same spirit as the justices who pardoned the amercement of Yvette daughter of Rannulf when she concorded her suit against William of Smithfield, declined to ask for the $25 fee usually charged for the performing of a marriage ceremony. Though shocked at this unusual outcome to a rape case, all who were present at the ceremony were said to have enjoyed themselves; perhaps a similar spirit of reconciliation and optimism attended thirteenth-century concords of marriage.[74]

The large majority of appellors of rape who did not prosecute leave no record of why they abandoned their appeals. Even so, they may have done more than air their grievances; they may have begun the process of bettering their lot. Like Isabelle daughter of Robert of Shukeburgh, they may have seen the value of public knowledge of their own unwillingness. Even if they could not or for some reason did not wish to continue their appeal, bringing it may have helped them to counteract the uncertainty of rumor, spread abroad their own account of events, and ease their return to normal life. Some, like Marjory, may have secured concords without a further appearance in

FIGURE 7. Page from Bracton's Law-Book. B.L., MS Add. 11353, fol. 9. Courtesy of the British Library.

court; others may simply have gone back to their usual way of life. The abandoning of an appeal was not necessarily the sign of a defeat; the bringing of the appeal alone may have sufficed for the purposes of some women.

Rape complainants' effectiveness in court, however, declined over the period encompassed in this study. The period breaks naturally at the year 1215, when civil war halted the operation of the courts for three years, during which Magna Carta was forced on the king, the ordeal was abolished, and John's close personal supervision of justice was replaced by the bureaucracy that functioned as part of his son's regency government. Rape cases split fairly evenly, with ninety-seven having been brought before 1215 and 105 after. The rate of failure to prosecute remained surprisingly constant, given the prolonged suspension of judicial activity before 1215; sixty-one, or 63 percent, of rape appeals were not prosecuted before 1215, compared with sixty-eight, that is, 65 percent, after that year.

Women who sued their cases to a conclusion, however, found that their prospects for success changed dramatically for the worse. Before 1215, eight defendants were outlawed and seven agreed to settlement in open court; thus in fifteen cases, or 15 percent, plaintiffs could be said to have brought their cases to a successful conclusion. In only four out of the ninety-seven was the defendant acquitted, meaning that women lost, so to speak, only about 4 percent of their cases. Or, to present the figures in another way, out of the nineteen cases that were brought to a conclusion, women were successful in fifteen, nearly 80 percent of them.

After 1215, however, only five out of one hundred defendants were outlawed, and only two came to an agreement in open court; women made some gain in only 7 percent of the appeals they brought. By contrast there were acquittals in eight, or 8 percent, of the appeals that were sued to a conclusion; acquittals were edging out successful suits for women who persisted in their appeals after 1215. It is unlikely that women suddenly began to accuse a much larger proportion of innocent men; reasons for the change must be sought in some other direction.

Like other plaintiffs, women who brought appeals of rape were affected by the conditions that surrounded the loss of the ordeal as a means of trial in 1215. The ordeal itself meant little in appeals of rape;

it was not used in any rape appeal in these rolls, nor did *Glanvill* give any indication that it should be. But the increasing use of the jury and the growing inclination for the legal system to take a hand in pursuing appeals that formerly had been left to appellors alone left its imprint on the prosecution of appeals of rape, an imprint that can be discerned by comparing cases in which the jury participated before 1215 with those after that date.

In the years between 1194 and 1202, juries had a small role in appeals of rape. In one case jurors attested that Yvette daughter of Rannulf had been seen bloody and shamefully treated, and in another they said that Agnes Tredgold had been the succuba or paramour of William de Smithfield; otherwise they only attested to the innocence of a mother whose son had come to her house after he had committed a rape, or confirmed that a third party had arranged the concord between opposing parties, or were summoned for an inquest whose result does not appear in the rolls, or presented testimony which damage to the roll has left illegible. If a plaintiff did not sue her case, it almost invariably lapsed because of the failure to prosecute; it was not considered necessary that a jury be consulted.[75]

The year 1208, seven years before the abolition of the ordeal, marks a turning point in the adjudication of cases that had not been prosecuted by the appellor, and the cases from that year deserve to be studied in detail. Of the fourteen cases recorded from that year, eleven were not prosecuted. Two of the cases lapsed as they would have in earlier years; the defendant was adjudged to be without day, that is, he was not to be given a day on which to appear in court again to face that particular charge.[76] Though being allowed to go without day was probably not the equivalent of an acquittal, in which the defendant was adjudged to be *quietus* or "quit" of the charges, the practical effect was the same.

In nine out of these eleven cases, however, it is clear that the appeal did not lapse as it usually would have in previous years. Five entries are remarkable in that the defendants themselves elected to carry on the case. Four of these entries record that the plaintiff did not appear but that the defendant in each case offered the king a half mark to have his judgment anyway; in each case the ruling was that the defendant go without day.[77] In the remaining case, even though the plaintiff, Aubrey, daughter of William, was not present, testimony was heard that she had been bound and shamefully treated. The defendant, William son of Roger de Belebi, gave the sizable sum of twenty shillings to have a judgment; like the others, he was allowed to go without day.[78] Even more mysterious is the action of defendants in two other unprosecuted cases who did not even seek a judgment; they simply appeared and gave money to the justices, a half mark in one case and a mark in the other. No reason is given for their behavior; the entries merely record that the plaintiff did not appear and the defendant came and rendered payment.[79]

There is no indication why in 1208 it became important to follow even an unprosecuted case to its conclusion. The preliminary impression is that defendants themselves were taking the initiative in seeking a judgment that would clear them of the charge; perhaps defendants, previously content to go their way when a suit was not prosecuted, suddenly became very conscientious about having their names cleared. It is more likely that the initiative came from the court at some point in the proceedings before the case came before the justices and began to be recorded in the rolls. In a time when King John was in strained circumstances, a desire for revenue may be suspected, but there may also have been an increasing strictness in the court's attitude toward men accused of rape. Though the judgments were uniformly in favor of the defendants, each of whom was granted something very like an acquittal, the amounts they paid to have the court pass judgment in their cases, a half mark to twenty shillings, were strikingly similar to those tendered as settlements in final concords.

After 1215, once appeals of rape once again appear on the rolls, the court was clearly taking the initiative in continuing a considerable portion of rape appeals that plaintiffs had allowed to lapse. The use of the jury was cautiously expanding, and it was to the jury that justices were likely to turn when a woman did not follow up her appeal of rape. In thirty-four of the sixty-eight cases that were not prosecuted by the appellor between the years 1215 and 1222, the court asked the jury, probably the presentment jury since there is no indication that a special jury was empaneled, whether or not its members suspected the defendant. This was also done in three cases in which the appellor had died, making thirty-seven cases in all. As a general rule the jury did not suspect the defendant. In thirty of the cases they acquitted him by declaring that they did not suspect him or that they did not believe him to be guilty.[80] In only six did they suspect him or believe him to be guilty;[81] in the remaining case they merely acknowledged that suit had been reasonably made.[82] Generally a conviction was followed by an order for the defendant's arrest; it is recorded that one defendant quickly made fine for a half mark.[83] Jurors also contributed to two of the remaining cases by reporting that a concord had been made between the two parties.[84]

Another two cases in which further steps were taken did not involve the jurors at all. In one the justices were told that the offense had been committed in another wapentake and decided to ask whether the plaintiff had sued there; in the other, the defendant simply came to court, as some had in 1208, and paid a half mark without awaiting a verdict.[85]

Usually the justices followed up a plea that the plaintiff had allowed to lapse only when the defendant was present; if he were absent, the justices, if they took any action, might content themselves with amercing his pledges, the men who had sworn to produce him in court.[86] Even so, two of the five convictions just described were rendered against absent defendants; perhaps their offenses were particularly notorious or flagrant ones.

The courts also used the jury, sometimes at the request of an appellor who pleaded an exception of *odio et atia* (a complaint that the appeal was malicious and not based on a true offense), to assist in the judgment of a case when the appellor prosecuted her suit. Sixteen cases were prosecuted to a conclusion in the years after 1215; of those, seven ended in favor of the plaintiff, whether by concord or outlawry of the defendant, and nine ended in acquittals (see table 6.7). These results are a significant change from those of the early years of the period, during which cases that were sued to a conclusion had gone lopsidedly in favor of the plaintiff, with fifteen ending in the plaintiff's favor and only four acquittals, as table 6.7 shows.

The reason for this change is not immediately apparent; as in the cases that were not prosecuted, however, the jury played a part. In the sixteen cases sued to a conclusion, the jurors were consulted on eleven occasions; in eight out of the eleven they declared the defendant not guilty,[87] even in at least one case in which the defendant had fled for the crime.[88] This meant that jurors were responsible for eight

Table 6.6 Cases Not Prosecuted in Which Jurors Gave Verdict

Outcomes:	Acquittals	Convictions
Cases Not Prosecuted	27	6
Appellor Died	3	0
Totals	30	6

Percentage of Total:	Total	Percentage
Acquittals	30	83
Convictions	6	17
Totals	36	100

Table 6.7 Cases Prosecuted to a Conclusion

Outcomes	Number of Cases	Percentage
Early Years:		
Acquittals	4	21
Favor of Plaintiff		
Concords 7		
Outlawry 8	15	79
Totals	19	100
Late Years:		
Acquittals	9	56
Favor of Plaintiff		
Concords 2		
Outlawry 5	7	54
Totals	16	100

of the nine acquittals that defendants won. The ninth case was lost without ever reaching the jury. For one thing, it was an attempted rape instead of an accomplished deed; even though it was only the prompt action of the men of the vill in answer to the appellor's screams that stopped the act from being completed, the offense was not considered to be a rape. Moreover, a third party had tried to make amends between the two, and the appellor had later taken a husband. All things considered, the appellor was not deemed to have a case worthy of the court's further attention.[89]

On the other hand, the jurors' opinion supported the plaintiff in four of the six cases that ended in the plaintiff's favor. Three of these were against defendants who had fled and who were to be outlawed.

Table 6.8 Appeals Decided by Recourse to Jury

Outcomes:		Number of Cases	Percentage
Acquittals:			
Not prosecuted or appellor died	30		
Sued to a conclusion	7	37	79
Plaintiff's Favor:			
Not prosecuted	6		
Sued to a conclusion	4	10	21
Totals		47	100

In one of these the jurors' support was lukewarm; the appellor was to sue until the defendant was outlawed because "they better believed him to be guilty than not."[90] The remaining case is remarkable in that it was the only one in which the verdict went against a defendant who was present in court. The defendant denied the charges, but the jurors declared that he was guilty and that suit had been reasonably made; he concorded to marry the plaintiff.[91]

There are other examples in the rolls of persons who fled for a crime but were not believed to be guilty, and the jurors did not declare against women in every case. But, in the later period when they were being frequently consulted, jurors disbelieved more appeals of rape than they believed. The extent of the jurors' influence can be seen by comparing the results of all the rape appeals in which the jury declared an opinion in the years after 1215, as is done in table 6.8.

This evidence is suggestive, but does not of itself prove much about jurors' attitudes toward women who brought charges of rape; in fact, there are reasons why a drop in judgments against defendants need not surprise us. It has been shown that jurors were prone to engage in jury nullification, the practice of giving acquittals against the facts when, for example, they thought that the defendant was unlikely to commit further offenses, or they thought the punishment prescribed by law was more severe than the offense warranted.[92] It is instructive to compare jurors' verdicts in cases of wounding, whose plaintiffs were usually men, to find out whether the jury had any particular effect on plaintiffs in rape cases.

The records show that, in cases of wounding, the jury was likely to declare in favor of the plaintiff whether or not the plaintiff elected to prosecute. In the period after 1215, the jury was consulted in thirty-

Table 6.9 Jurors' Declarations in Cases of Wounding after 1215

	Favor of Plaintiff		Favor of Defendant	
	Number of Cases	(Percentage)	Number of Cases	(Percentage)
Brought to a conclusion	14	(70)	6	(30)
Not prosecuted	11	(65)	6	(35)
Totals	25		12	

seven cases of wounding; they declared in favor of the plaintiff in twenty-five, or 68 percent, of the cases, and in favor of the defendant in only twelve, or 32 percent. As might be expected from what we have seen in rape cases, jurors were most favorable to plaintiffs who sued their cases to a conclusion. There were twenty such cases; the jurors declared in favor of the plaintiff in fourteen, or 70 percent, of the cases, and in favor of the defendant in only six, or 30 percent. Results were only slightly less favorable for plaintiffs who did not appear and prosecute their cases. There were seventeen cases in which the plaintiff did not prosecute but the court chose to consult the jury; in these the jurors ruled in favor of the plaintiff in eleven, or 65 percent, of the cases, and in favor of the defendant in six, or 35 percent, of the cases.

The contrast with jurors' declarations in cases of rape could hardly be more pronounced. Overall, as is set out in table 6.10, jurors declared in favor of plaintiffs in only 21 percent of rape cases, but declared in favor of plaintiffs in 68 percent of wounding cases. The jurors were disposed to favor rape plaintiffs in fewer than a quarter of their cases, while favoring plaintiffs of wounding in fully two-thirds of theirs.

Women's prospects for a favorable outcome were further dampened by a drop in the number of concords arrived at openly in court. As is shown in table 6.7, there were seven such concords arrived at before 1215, but there were only two in the period after that year, even though there were more appeals of rape brought after 1215 than before, 105 as opposed to 97. The jurors' tendency to give acquittals may have cleared some men who otherwise might have found it expedient to concord with the appellors; the courts may also have been growing less receptive to concords as a settlement of criminal appeals.

Table 6.10 Jurors' Declarations in Cases of Rape and Cases of Wounding after 1215

	Rape		Wounding	
	Number of Cases	*Percentage*	*Number of Cases*	*Percentage*
Favor of Plaintiff	10	(21)	25	(68)
Favor of Defendant	37	(79)	12	(32)
Totals	47		37	

Women may have compensated for the decline in judgments favorable to them by making more private concords after 1215 than they had been making before that date. Only one secret concord was brought to the attention of the justices before 1215; in the period after that year, however, four such concords were said to have been made.[93] Caution is necessary in evaluating this information; the numbers are too small to yield conclusions and do not necessarily represent the true figures in an activity that the parties concerned probably did not wish to have brought to the court's attention. Moreover, the numbers may reflect an increase in reporting of such concords as the jury came to be used more frequently in cases that were not prosecuted. But it is also possible that the figures represent a real rise in private concords made outside the court. Whatever the reason, it is clear that after 1215 women were making more concords outside the court than in it, that they must have considered their own negotiations to be of more value to them than any they could conduct in the court.

Castration and blinding as punishment for rape have been conspicuous by their absence in this study, as they are in the rolls, but may have had more effect on the behavior of juries, appellors, and defendants than the lack of such punishments in the rolls would indicate. That no such punishment was ever assessed in this time does not mean that it was a foregone conclusion that none ever would be, or that it was not at least spoken of in rolls that are lost to us, and the possibility that it might be inflicted may have lurked in the minds of all concerned. Jurors might have hesitated to convict acquaintances who on the whole had led orderly lives, even if they had committed the rape, unless the offense was a particularly flagrant one. If so, the effect on defendants would have been twofold. Most may have felt it worth their while to come into court, deny all charges, and rely on the clemency of their neighbors; but some, especially if their offense had been flagrant, may have felt they would do better to avoid appearing in court by persuading the appellor to come to a private agreement and drop her formal suit in the *curia regis*.

The court must have seemed an inhospitable place to women appellors of rape; most dropped their prosecutions, and, after 1215, those who pursued their cases were more likely than not to lose them. But a predisposition, found even among historians, to treat women as helpless victims is not entirely justified; women and those who supported them were working quietly to aid themselves. To a woman who was willing to forgo the punishment of an assailant, the prospect of a concord, private or arrived at in court, was probably an attractive one. Punishment, even if well-deserved, was of little practical use, but a half mark could serve as a maritagium for a woman of humble status, and a marriage would solve at once the problem of future marriageability. The sums men paid, whether to the appellor or to the court, were hardly ruinous, but they represented a reasonable capital investment and might have served as a reminder not to commit the offense again, especially if the man had been in some anxiety that the most extreme punishment, however rarely administered, might be assessed in his case.

There is some evidence of activity outside the court on rape complainants' behalf. City officials once meted out rough justice to two offenders. Segwin and Marcman, citizens of Cologne and messengers for the Emperor Otto, complained to the court that officials of London had thrown them into jail with thieves and refused to release them until they had paid three marks; testimony in the case showed that the two men were appealed of the rape of a woman named Wimarc who had raised the hue and cry against them and made proper suit. The officials were no doubt taking advantage of an opportunity to practice a little informal extortion; in the course of doing so, they made these emissaries quite literally pay for their crime.[94] Some families who wanted the attacker to suffer corporal punishment may have taken matters into their own hands, as two cases, one of castration and one of blinding, suggest.[95]

The paradox for women was that, in a court which did not deliver the protection of the harsh sentence its own legal thinkers promised to victims of rape, and whose modernization seems to have harmed their prospects, it was their own activity that had the most effect on their situation. An interest in abstract justice, in the form of assiduously investigating cases and punishing the guilty to the full extent of the law, is not to be found in these rolls. The chief benefit women derived from bringing appeals of rape was the direct outcome of their own actions; they proclaimed and made public their own unwillingness, they worked behind the scenes to make private settlements, and they contracted marriages or won amounts of money that would help them to secure a marriage or even to live more comfortably on their own. Feudal protection may have been slight and modernization not very promising, but the courts did act to provide women appellors of rape an arena for their own efforts, and they were able to use the courts in their own way to mend the damage done to them, secure their own future, put the past behind them, and begin rebuilding their lives.

Notes

1. Doris M. Stenton argues that English women, after having had relative autonomy and influence during the Anglo-Saxon period, became virtually powerless after the Norman Conquest brought feudalism to England (*The English Woman in History* [London: George Allen & Unwin, 1957], 1–30). Lady Stenton's position is reiterated by Christine Fell, Cecily Clark, and Elizabeth Williams's *Women in Anglo-Saxon England and the Impact of 1066* (Bloomington: Indiana University Press, 1984). There is no reason, however, to think that real women were as bound as theory would suggest; Darryl Dean James finds considerable activity by women after 1066 in the Abingdon Chronicle ("A Translation and Study of the 'Chronicon Monasterii de Abingdon,' " Ph.D. diss., Rice University, 1985, 64–68).

2. Feudal landholding, dependent on the relationship between lord and man, was being replaced by true ownership of property; Robert C. Palmer argues that this development had taken place by the year 1200, though feudal relationships were still important as social constructs and conduits for patronage ("The Origins of Property in England," *Law and History Review* 3 [1985]:22–24, 47).

3. *The Treatise on the Laws and Customs of England Commonly Called Glanvill*, ed. and trans. G. D. G. Hall (London: Thomas Nelson & Sons, 1965), 176; *Bracton on the Laws and Customs of England*, 4 vols., ed. and trans. Samuel E. Thorne (Cambridge, Mass.: Belknap Press, 1968, 1977), 2:414–15.

4. The eyres, the itinerant royal courts on circuit, were the venue where most rape cases were heard; it was easier and less expensive to bring them there than in the central courts of justice at Westminster. (See Sir Frederick Pollock and Frederick William Maitland, *The History of the English Law Before the Time of Edward I*, 2 vols., 2d ed. [Cambridge: Cambridge University Press, 1898; reissued 1968], 1:200–2; 544–45.) For the outcomes of rape cases see table 6.1.

5. Roger D. Groot concludes that society as a whole thought reparation, rather than punishment, was appropriate for the crime of rape ("The Crime of Rape *temp.* Richard I and John," *Journal of Legal History* 9 [1988]:324–34, see 325, 332).

6. *Glanvill*, 175.

7. *Bracton*, 2:414–19.

8. Pollock and Maitland, *History of the English Law*, 2:521, 557. S. F. C. Milsom, *Historical Foundations of the Common Law*, 2d ed. (Toronto: Butterworts, 1981), 403.

9. *Pleas Before the King or His Justices*, vols. 1 and 2 (1198–1202), vols. 3 and 4 (1198–1212), ed. Doris M. Stenton, Selden Society, vols. 67, 68, 83, 84 (London, 1948–67), 2:337, 395, 4:3424, 3491.

10. *The Earliest Lincolnshire Assize Rolls, A.D. 1202–09*, ed. Doris M. Stenton, Publications of the Lincolnshire Record Society, vol. 22 (Lincoln Record Society, 1926), 916; *Rotuli Curiae Regis*, 2 vols., ed. Francis Palgrave (Record Commission, 1835), 2:82; *Pleas Before the King or His Justices*, 4:3424; and see *The Earliest Lincolnshire Assize Rolls*, 590.

11. There are some twenty such cases; see, for example, *Curia Regis Rolls Preserved in the Public Record Office*, 10 vols. (London: His Majesty's Stationery Office, 1922–49), 1:148; *Rolls of the Justices in Eyre . . . For Yorkshire in 3 Henry III (1218–19)*, ed. Doris M. Stenton, Selden Society, vol. 56 (London: Bernard Quaritch, 1937), 653, 784, 836, 957; *The Earliest Lincolnshire Assize Rolls*, 236, 950, inter alia.

12. Record evidence for Renaissance Venice shows that gang rape was a more or less common occurrence there, although the records do not yield enough information to reveal the group dynamics involved in the attacks (Guido Ruggiero, *The Boundaries of Eros: Sex Crimes and Sexuality in Renaissance Venice* [New York & Oxford: Oxford University Press, 1985], 98).

13. Bringing the appeal was the responsibility of the accuser in any criminal case; he or she initiated the procedure by making a formal complaint before the court and offering proof, usually trial by battle (Pollock and Maitland, *History of the English Law*, 2:605–6).

14. *Three Rolls of the King's Court in the Reign of King Richard I, A.D. 1194–95*, ed. Frederick William Maitland, Publications of the Pipe Roll Society, vol. 14 (London, 1891), 96. The presentment jury was a special jury convened for the purpose of putting before the court all that the community knew or suspected about felonies committed since the last visitation of the justices in eyre; presentment is the ancestor of the modern process of indictment (Pollock and Maitland, *History of the English Law*, 2:642–43). Rape did not become an indictable offense until the Statute of Westminster II in 1285, according to Barbara A. Hanawalt ("Women Before the Law: Females as Felons and Prey in Fourteenth-Century England," in *Women and the Law: A Social Historical Perspective*, vol. 1, *Women and the Criminal Law*, ed. D. Kelly Weisberg [Cambridge, Mass.: Schenkman Publishing Co., 1982], 181). Naomi D. Hurnard found two presentments of rape in the pipe roll of 1180 ("The Jury of Presentment and the Assize of Clarendon," *English Historical Review* 56 [1941]:374–401). Groot, noting these examples, believes the jurors' report of the rumor concerning the daughter of John de Childrington is "clearly such a presentment" ("The Crime of Rape *temp.* Richard I and John," 325). He suggests that, since the jurors were not fined, presentments for rape may have been considered proper. Their extreme

rarity argues against this; the court may simply have been lenient to the jurors in question.

15. There is one case in which the parents, both mother and father, either brought or continued an appeal of the rape of their daughter; they appeared in court but the daughter failed to sue. The defendant was present and denied the charge. The justices allowed the question to go to the jurors, who said that the daughter had been raped and the suit had been correctly made but the appellee was not guilty of the crime (*Pleas of the Crown for the County of Gloucestershire*, ed. Frederick William Maitland [London: Macmillan, 1884], 482). There is no other example in these rolls in which the appeal was brought by any person other than the woman concerned.

16. Fathers appear as pledges that their daughters will prosecute in *Rolls of the Justices in Eyre . . . for Yorkshire*, 649, 1044; and in *Pleas of the Crown for the County of Gloucestershire*, 6. A man who is not identifiable as belonging to either family helped the parties reach a private settlement in *The Earliest Lincolnshire Assize Rolls*, 826; for the parents who continued their daughter's appeal, see n. 14, above.

17. *Glanvill*, 176.

18. The county court was a royal court, but was local in character and was presided over by the sheriff. It generally met every four to six weeks and was taken over by the royal justices when an eyre was held in the county. See Pollock and Maitland, *History of the English Law*, 2:535–39; and Robert C. Palmer, *County Courts of Medieval England* (Princeton, N.J.: Princeton University Press, 1982), 198.

19. The medical treatise written for women by Trotula, "Dame Trot of nursery lore," was translated into English, the language literate women were most likely to be able to read, so that, according to the translator's preface, "every woman lettered read it to other unlettered (women) and help them and counsel them in their maladies withouten showing their disease to man . . ." And a woman doctor in Paris, prosecuted in 1322, defended her right to practice by pointing to her many successful cures and by arguing that women doctors were needed because many women were ashamed to reveal infirmities to a man and had often died rather than do so. (See Eileen Power, *Medieval Women*, ed. M. M. Postan [Cambridge: Cambridge University Press, 1975], 86–88, and *The Medieval Woman's Guide to Health: The First English Gynecological Handbook*, trans. Beryl Rowland [Kent, Ohio: Kent State University Press, 1981], 4–11.)

20. Amercement was the most common punishment in the royal court; it was imposed for technical infractions. In theory the king could confiscate all the possessions of the offender; in practice the courts imposed standardized amounts for most infractions (Pollock and Maitland, *History of the English Law*, 2:514–15); in the case of default of prosecution, it was probably imposed for taking the court's time and placing the accused in jeopardy for a suit the plaintiff did not care to continue.

21. *The Earliest Lincolnshire Assize Rolls*, 653.

22. Ruth Kittel, "Rape in Thirteenth-Century England: A Study of the Common-Law Courts," in *Women and the Law: A Social Historical Perspective*, ed. D. Kelly Weisberg, vol. 2, *Property, Family, and the Legal Profession* (Cambridge, Mass.: Schenkman Publishing Co., 1982), 104–5.

23. *The Earliest Lincolnshire Assize Rolls*, lxviii. Some of the women, of course, may have had help from knowledgeable men in their families.

24. *Curia Regis Rolls*, 7:98. The justices may have been skeptical; they freed Elena only after she agreed to make fine for a half mark, but the constable was not amerced (*Rolls of the Justices in Eyre . . . for Yorkshire in 3 Henry III (1218–19)*, 1029).

25. *The Earliest Lincolnshire Assize Rolls*, 529, 599.

26. *The Earliest Lincolnshire Assize Rolls*, 938.

27. *Rolls of the Justices in Eyre . . . for Lincolnshire 1218 and Worcestershire 1221*, ed. Doris M. Stenton, Selden Society, (London: Bernard Quaritch, 1937), 53:500.

28. Outlawry was no small matter for the defendant on whom it was imposed; his lands were confiscated, he was subject to capture by any citizen who cared to make the attempt, and, at least in theory, he could be killed if he resisted arrest. (See Pollock and Maitland, *History of the English Law*, 2:449.) Groot regards outlawry as having been imposed for the offense of contempt against the king rather than for the offense of rape ("Crime of Rape," 327), but its imposition was by no means automatic; it seems to have been intended as punishment for the rape as well as the flight.

29. A wapentake was a division of the county in areas where Scandinavian settlement had been heavy; it held its own court at regular intervals (Pollock and Maitland, *History of the English Law*, 1:556).

30. *The Earliest Lincolnshire Assize Rolls*, 590.

31. *The Earliest Lincolnshire Assize Rolls*, 916; *Pleas Before the King or His Justices*, 2:395.

32. *Pleas of the Crown for the County of Gloucestershire*, 341. Another woman's appeal apparently failed on the grounds of lack of suit alone (*Curia Regis Rolls*, 1:33).

33. *Pleas of the Crown for the County of Gloucestershire*, 76.

34. *Pleas of the Crown for the County of Gloucestershire*, 127.

35. *The Earliest Lincolnshire Assize Rolls*, 909.

36. *Rolls of the Justices in Eyre . . . for Gloucestershire, Warwickshire, and Staffordshire, 1221, 1221*, ed. Doris M. Stenton, Selden Society, vol. 59 (London: Bernard Quaritch, 1940), 966; *Rolls of the Justices in Eyre . . . for Yorkshire in 3 Henry III*, 669.

37. It is possible that these women may have considered themselves to be married if, for example, they had exchanged words of future consent, which committed the parties to a marriage in the future, without understanding that such words did not constitute a valid marriage in themselves. Even if they had exchanged words of present consent, which the Church understood as creating a valid marriage whenever and wherever spoken, they may have neglected to have witnesses present, thus making the marriage very nearly impossible to prove if the spouse denied it. (See R. H. Helmholz, *Marriage Litigation in Medieval England* [London & New York: Cambridge University Press, 1974].) Such speculations are beyond proof with the materials we have, but I am grateful to Robert C. Palmer for giving me this new perspective on the possible circumstances of these appeals.

38. *Rolls of the Justices in Eyre . . . for Gloucestershire, Warwickshire, and Staffordshire*, 751.

39. *Curia Regis Rolls*, 7:335.

40. *Glanvill*, 176; *Bracton*, 419. Wounding will be treated here as encompassing mayhem, because the two appeals differ in degree rather than substance, with maiming being a wounding that permanently incapacitates the victim; moreover, the two are not always easy to distinguish from each other as recorded in the rolls.

41. *Rolls of the Justices in Eyre . . . for Gloucestershire, Warwickshire, and Staffordshire*, 939.

42. For the penalties for wounding and mayhem, see Pollock and Maitland, *History of the English Law*, 2:488–89. In theory both capital and corporal punishments could be imposed for wounding and mayhem; in practice Maitland found no examples of the death penalty and mentions only one case in which an offender was punished by mutilation, though the mutilation was savage. See the discussion later in the chapter of the appeal of George of Nitheweie.

43. Hanawalt, *Women Before the Law*, 183–84.

44. See the appeal of Richard son of John, discussed later in the chapter.

45. For example, in *Curia Regis Rolls*, 1:39, five appeals; in *Pleas Before the King or His Justices*, 2:289–91, three appeals—two await the concord being reached in the third.

46. *Pleas Before the King or His Justices*, 4:3444–48.

47. *Pleas of the Crown for the County of Gloucestershire*, 484; *Curia Regis Rolls*, 4:54.

48. Kittel, "Rape in Thirteenth-Century England," 101.

49. *The Earliest Lincolnshire Assize Rolls*, 638; *The Earliest Northamptonshire Assize Rolls, A.D. 1202 and 1203*, ed. Doris M. Stenton (Publications of the Northamptonshire Record Society, 1930), 99; *Rolls of the Justices in Eyre . . . for Gloucestershire, Warwickshire, and Staffordshire*, 919, 1322; *Pleas of the Crown for the County of Gloucestershire*, 87, 434; *Rolls of the Justices in Eyre . . . for Yorkshire in 3 Henry III*, 579, 911.

50. Presumably the appellor in question had recovered sufficiently to do battle, since in theory he could not legally field a champion in his behalf; Pollock and Maitland, *History of the English Law*, 1:633.

51. *The Earliest Lincolnshire Assize Rolls*, 638.

52. *Rolls of the Justices in Eyre . . . for Gloucestershire, Warwickshire, and Staffordshire*, 919.

53. *Pleas of the Crown for the County of Gloucestershire*, 87. The nature of the mutilation is obscure and Maitland himself does not attempt to clarify it, but cites a miracle story from the same eyre about a defeated champion who was blinded and mutilated but miraculously healed by Saint Wulfstan, to whose service the man then dedicated himself. Maitland suggests that "it may be that these horrible sentences were not always very punctually obeyed" (*History of the English Law*, 142).

54. *The Earliest Lincolnshire Assize Rolls*, 595; Groot considers the judgments in this and the following two cases to have been to the advantage of the plaintiff, because they allowed him the opportunity to prove his case ("Crime of rape," 334). The plaintiff, however, faced with the necessity of carrying the red-hot iron when, by custom the defendant should have done so, probably would have disagreed. These cases look like forced settlements.

55. *The Earliest Lincolnshire Assize Rolls*, 843, 851.

56. *The Earliest Lincolnshire Assize Rolls*, xx.

57. *The Earliest Lincolnshire Assize Rolls,* 773, 773a, 773b; lix.

58. *The Earliest Lincolnshire Assize Rolls,* 916.

59. *Pleas Before the King or His Justices,* 4:3491.

60. *Pleas Before the King or His Justices,* 2:395.

61. *Pleas Before the King or His Justices,* 2:337; *Rolls of the Justices in Eyre . . . for Yorkshire in 3 Henry III,* 959.

62. Ralph V. Turner notices that Roger son of Reinfrid offered King Richard ten marks for custody of an heir so he could grant the profitable custody to his daughter Bonanata, apparently providing for a daughter who had not married (*The English Judiciary in the Age of Glanvill and Bracton* [Cambridge: Cambridge University Press, 1985], 61). And Magna Carta envisages the possibility that widows may have preferred not to remarry, as their payments to the king for the privilege of not marrying would seem to attest (J. C. Holt, *Magna Carta* [Cambridge: Cambridge University Press, 1965], 319).

63. Thus, the Avogadori in Renaissance Venice frequently sentenced rapists to give dowries to their victims, in one case the very large sum of fifty gold ducats, in order to ensure their marriageability. Generally these dowries were given to underage victims, those who were twelve years of age or younger; the court feared that women of marriageable age who brought charges of rape were lying in an attempt to gain dowries for themselves (Ruggierro, *Boundaries of Eros,* 96–101).

64. *Curia Regis Rolls,* 9:237–38; *Rolls of the Justices in Eyre . . . for Gloucestershire, Warwickshire, and Staffordshire,* 1125. Hanawalt writing about the fourteenth century, thought that virginity before marriage was more the concern of moralists than of prospective husbands and quotes a case in which a woman slept with three men and married the last two; the final one became her legal husband *Ties That Bound,* 195–96).

65. *Rolls of the Justices in Eyre . . . for Gloucestershire, Warwickshire, and Staffordshire,* 390. These facts emerged in the course of a suit between the grandson of the robber knight, who had somehow come into possession of the whole four virgates although his father, the son of Isabelle and Warin, had been granted only one-half virgate for his use, and the son of Isabelle's legal husband. They were concorded, with the grandson of the robber knight retaining only the half virgate his father had been allotted and giving up the rest for five marks; both were considered to be too poor to pay for the license to concord.

66. *Pleas Before the King or His Justices,* 2:337, 395 and 4:3491; *Rolls of the Justices in Eyre. . . . for Yorkshire in 3 Henry III,* 959, 1086, *The Earliest Lincolnshire Assize Rolls,* 916.

67. *Curia Regis Rolls,* 10:73–74; *The Earliest Lincolnshire Assize Rolls,* 702, 802; *Pleas Before the King or His Justices,* 1:19.

68. *Earliest Lincolnshire Assize Rolls,* 826; *Rolls of the Justices in Eyre . . . for Gloucestershire, Warwickshire, and Staffordshire,* 902; *Rolls of the Justices in Eyre . . . For Yorkshire,* 649, 946, 1044.

69. *Rolls of the Justices in Eyre . . . for Yorkshire in 3 Henry III,* 848, 935.

70. *Pleas of the Crown for the County of Gloucestershire,* 76.

71. *Pleas of the Crown for the County of Gloucestershire,* 484, table 3.

72. *The Earliest Lincolnshire Assize Rolls,* 826; *Rolls of the Justices in Eyre . . . for*

Gloucestershire, Warwickshire, and Staffordshire, 902; *Rolls of the Justices in Eyre . . . for Yorkshire in 3 Henry III,* 649, 946, 1044.

73. *Rolls of the Justices in Eyre . . . for Yorkshire in 3 Henry III,* 946.

74. "Bride's 'I do' Frees Groom," *Houston Chronicle,* December 10, 1986, evening final ed., sec. 1, p. 25.

75. *The Earliest Lincolnshire Assize Rolls,* 590, 826, 909, 938; *The Earliest Northamptonshire Assize Rolls,* 42, 38.

76. *Pleas Before the King or His Justices,* 4:3459, 3463.

77. *Pleas Before the King or His Justices,* 4:3475, 3476, 3477, 3490.

78. *Pleas Before the King or His Justices,* 4:3424.

79. *Pleas Before the King or His Justices,* 4:3406, 3437.

80. See, for example, *Pleas of the Crown for the County of Gloucestershire,* 155; *Rolls of the Justices in Eyre . . . for Lincolnshire 1218 and Worcestershire 1221,* 1074; *Rolls of the Justices in Eyre . . . for Lincolnshire, Warwickshire, and Staffordshire,* 759; *Rolls of the Justices in Eyre . . . for Yorkshire in 3 Henry III,* 545, 689, 803.

81. *Rolls of the Justices in Eyre . . . for Yorkshire in 3 Henry III,* 594, 688, 763, 955, 957; *Pleas of the Crown for the County of Gloucestershire,* 341.

82. *Rolls of the Justices in Eyre . . . for Yorkshire in 3 Henry III,* 955.

83. *Rolls of the Justices in Eyre . . . for Yorkshire in 3 Henry III,* 957.

84. *Rolls of the Justices in Eyre . . . for Yorkshire in 3 Henry III,* 649, 946.

85. *Rolls of the Justices in Eyre . . . for Gloucestershire, Warwickshire, and Staffordshire,* 826; *Rolls of the Justices in Eyre . . . for Yorkshire in 3 Henry III,* 614.

86. See, for example, *Rolls of the Justices in Eyre . . . for Yorkshire in 3 Henry III,* 984, 985, 988, 991, and 996, in which the court showed no interest in the defendants, who had not been attached; see also *Rolls of the Justices in Eyre . . . for Yorkshire in 3 Henry III,* 768 and 1019, in which the defendant's attacher, or pledge, was amerced.

87. *Rolls of the Justices in Eyre . . . for Yorkshire in 3 Henry III,* 669, 934, 974; *Rolls of the Justices in Eyre . . . for Lincolnshire and Worcestershire,* 1124; *Rolls of the Justices in Eyre . . . for Gloucestershire, Warwickshire, and Staffordshire,* 751, 966; *Pleas of the Crown for Gloucestershire,* 76, 301.

88. *Pleas of the Crown for Gloucestershire,* 301.

89. *Rolls of the Justices in Eyre . . . for Lincolnshire and Worcescestershire,* 1182.

90. *Rolls of the Justices in Eyre . . . for Gloucestershire, Warwickshire, and Staffordshire,* 858.

91. *Pleas of the Justices in Eyre . . . for Yorkshire in 3 Henry III,* 959.

92. Thomas Andrew Green uses homicide cases, about which there is more information, to show this (*Verdict According to Conscience: Perspectives on the English Criminal Trial Jury, 1200–1800* [Chicago & London: University of Chicago Press, 1985], 22–27, 52). It would be instructive to compare juries' verdicts in rape cases with his findings.

93. *Rolls of the Justices in Eyre . . . for Gloucestershire, Warwickshire, and Staffordshire,* 902; *Rolls of the Justices in Eyre . . . for Yorkshire in 3 Henry III,* 649, 946, 1044.

94. *Curia Regis Rolls,* 6:54.

95. See text at n. 57.

Experiencing Feudal Realities

Enduring Feudal Ideals of Order

————————————————————————————————— ✦

ANOTHER LIMITATION of the feudal ideal of order embodied in the
reciprocity between lord and vassal often resulted from the complexity
of feudal allegiances established in a world that was itself becoming
more complex. Individuals as well as groups or classes of individuals
were affected, sometimes fortuitously and sometimes intentionally, by
overlapping fidelities, misunderstandings, or even acts of treachery.
In "*Par amur et par feid*: Keeping Faith and the Varieties of Feudalism
in *La Chanson de Roland*," William T. Cotton demonstrates the effect
of the intricacies of vassalic obligation on the individual—on Roland
himself.

Cotton argues that the conflict within Roland's character results
from the vastly different faces Roland must turn toward enemies and
friends. Roland does this because vassalic reciprocity in his world extends to all social relations—between the individual and the group,
friends and enemies, even men and women. What is more, because
this reciprocity is complex and often mutable, much effort has to be
devoted to resolving its social and ideological stresses and ambiguities. The search for resolution in the chanson involves numerous examples, including Roland himself. Indeed, the conflict between
Roland's personal ideals of chivalric heroism and social ideals of service to seigneur, people, Christendom, and God is central to the
poem. Interestingly, the very qualities that make Roland both great
and, to a large degree, useful to his emperor and his people—namely,
courage, initiative, and a sense of self-worth—are inevitably carried
to excess and become their opposites, especially when overlapping allegiances are in conflict. Thus, for contemporary readers, the chal-

lenge presented by the *Song of Roland* is to move beyond simplistic judgments of appropriate or inappropriate behavior of characters in order to understand the rich and varying interplay of conflicting ideals within the individual experience.

Ill-defined or complex feudal allegiances also often resulted in unfulfilled vassalic obligation and its consequences. In "When Feudal Ideals Failed: Conflicts Between Lords and Vassals in the Low Countries, 1127–1296," Karen S. Nicholas argues that, while princes and kings consolidated their power in the Low Countries, a growing tension between rulers and nobility arose, one that was not uncommon in other medieval principalities and realms. In chronicles treating this particular part of Europe at this time, Nicholas demonstrates, one rarely hears of extraordinary or even ordinary acts of loyalty but rather of acts of treachery. Many of these conflicts are attributed to lords' and vassals' failure to fulfill obligations imposed by their relationships. Sometimes multiple homages produce conflicts of interest; sometimes lords are unwilling to accept limitation of duty or knight-service. Whatever the reason, escape from comital authority or imposition of punitive settlements estranged lords from vassals, vassals from lords.

Numerous examples of this kind of estrangement in the Low Countries can be found in chronicles and records from the time of the murder of Charles the Good to that of the murder of Floris V. In the case of border vassalage, for example, numerous instances of hostilities between lords and vassals can be identified. Further, grievances between princes and nobles often led to wars and even murder. The highest nobles often resented and disputed princely consolidation of power and exercise of authority. Nobles also frequently resented and disputed kings' and princes' assertions of comital rights and reliance upon lesser nobles and *ministeriales* in their attempts to consolidate power. Thus the ideals of order resulting from feudal custom and practice often had no place in the twelfth and thirteenth centuries in the Low Countries, where vassals resented the misdeeds of their lords and lords exacted unreasonable punitive settlements from their vassals.

7 Par amur et par feid

Keeping Faith and the Varieties of Feudalism
in *La Chanson de Roland*

————————————————————————————— ❧

PAR AMUR ET PAR FEID (through love and loyalty) is a formulaic phrase occurring frequently in *La Chanson de Roland*
(in that form at lines 86, 3460, 3801, 3893; in the slightly different form *par feid et par amur* at 2897, 3770, 3810)[1] as part of a
feudal vow that emphasizes the importance of keeping faith with another person, a community, a way of life, or a cultural ideal. The de-
termination to keep the faith is not a simple one, however, because
several objects of faith-keeping compete for an individual's allegiance.
Most evidently, faith-keeping in a feudal system built upon an exchange of faith (as the etymology of *feudal* suggests)[2] is a reciprocal
relationship between vassal and seigneur. Many competing focuses of
faith-keeping both mimic this central relationship and may challenge—and certainly complicate—it. These "focuses of faith" are set
out in the list that follows. The focus is given first, followed by the
specific conflict evidenced in *La Chanson de Roland:*

1. Self (as *prudhom, chevaler, baron; vassal*)
   Conflict—demands and expectations of honor/shame culture
   (*proz, hunte, blasme*)
2. Peers (*compaignons, duz pers*)
   Conflict—Guenes vs. Roland, Oliver vs. Roland

3. Family or clan (the agnatic family; *parenz*)
   Conflict—a later development, not much in *Roland* but dominates other *chansons*

4. Immediate feudal lord (*seigneur;* donates *honur, fief* in return for *auxilium, consilium,* and *féodalité,* or faith-keeping)
   Conflict—not extensive in *Roland,* whose actual historical setting is prefeudal, but in other later chansons

5. Ultimate feudal overlord (*liege, suzerain; reis, emperere*)
   Conflict—"King's Two Bodies" (Carles as individual or symbol)

6. People or nation (*li Franceis; dulce France, belle France*)
   Conflict—national patriotism vs. imperialism

7. Carolingian empire (more or less coterminous with Christendom)
   Conflict—secular-sacred split (little felt in poem)

8. Christendom (*li chrestiens, chrestientet*)
   Conflict—social version of Christianity versus individual, spiritual version of it

9. God (*damne deus, veir paterne*)

Notice that *par amur et par feid* is a formula for faith-keeping in two different senses. It is a legal term, serving as an essential part of the oath of fealty. And it is an oral-formulaic unit, the length of a hemistich, serving as one of the building blocks of the jongleur's style. The seven uses of the formula in the poem exemplify both functions. At line 86 Marsile of Saragossa instructs his emissaries to promise Carles that the Saracen "serai ses hom par amur et par feid." During the judicial combat to settle Guenes's fate, the formidable Pinabel appeals to Tierri for a compromise, promising "Tes hom serai par amur et par feid" (3893). When Carles has saved Naimes's life during the battle with Baligant's forces, the two old men embrace and personally renew their devotion, "Puis sunt justez par amur et par feid" (3460). The weak judges of the court at Aix recommend that the traitor Guenes be let off easy this time, on promise of good behavior: "Puis si li servet par amur et par feid" (3801). There is an oral-formulaic doubling, in its alternate form, when they actually deliver their verdict to the emperor in the following *laisse:* "Puis si vos servet par feid et par amur" (3810; the two versions of the formula are rhythmically similar but allow for different assonance). In his own defense Guenes is not above taking the near-sacred formula for fealty in vain, claiming that in avenging

FIGURE 8. The vassal doing homage. Heidelberg, MS Cod. Pal. germ. 164, fol. 6v (Lehnrecht, 24, 2). Courtesy of Universitätsbibliothek Heidelberg.

himself on his obstreperous stepson he had not broken faith with his lord: "servei le [Carles] par feid et par amur" (3770). In his lament for his dead nephew, the king expresses himself not only in familial terms but also in feudal ones as Roland's seigneur: "Carles le pleint par feid et par amur" (2897).[3]

Clearly, it is important not to sentimentalize the terms of this oath of fealty, and particularly not its aspect that we are tempted to translate simply as "love," from the word *amur*. In a close semantic analysis of *par feid et par amur* and its variants, George F. Jones shows the terms *in context*—of the whole poem, of other chansons de geste, and of other versions of the Roland story.[4] For him, the phrase amounts to almost "a legal formula" indicating "political rather than emotional ties."[5] Instead of personal affection, the *amur* element indicates a social or political relationship (and usually one of subordination) which is an agreement between the parties to keep peace with one another, make peace, or form an alliance. "By such formulas a vassal acknowledged that he owed both his land and his wealth to his liege," Jones explains; however, "the *amur* that is offered is not love or friendship, but rather servitude."[6]

In fact, the verb *amer* should not be understood always to imply personal affection or emotional attachment. It could just as well indicate an appreciation of a person's *value*, as in Carles's lament for the loss of Roland not only as a beloved relative but also as a military ally. "Even personal affection," Jones insists, "in the *Song of Roland* is seldom disinterested."[7] This becomes more evident if we consider the kiss, *par amistiet*, like the one exchanged by Guenes and the Saracens to seal the bargain for betrayal (1530). Such a kiss, Jones explains, "involves a contract" and has little to do with affection. Similarly, the word *amistiet*, when it is used to designate the relation between seigneur and vassal, describes a bond that is radically different from the tie of friendship. A sign of this is that a person refers to close friends or subordinates as *amis*, but never to superiors, simply because, in the feudal relationship, no equality is involved.[8] Modern readers are most likely to sentimentalize the "touching friendship" of Roland and Oliver, but according to Jones, even this relationship is much involved with concerns for honor and shame, as the prominence of terms like *vergoigne* (1705; disgrace) and *hunte* (1707; dishonor) reveals.[9] The ties between the *compaignons* are close social and even political ones, and their bond might be seen almost as much an alliance as a friendship. "Love and friendship in the *SR* are readily subordinated to considerations of honor," Jones concludes,[10] and, we might add, to considerations of political power, all leading to conflicts of value.

The oral formula for declaring fealty, *par amur et par feid*, must be understood, then, in light of semantic analysis, especially of the element arising from the verb *amer*, so that there will be no tendency to sentimentalize the feudal relationship. It is a close, personal bond between individual consenting parties, but it is also a legal contract, quid pro quo. This is exemplified by the seven instances in which the phrase or its variant appears in the poem. Faith-keeping became such an essential element of medieval culture that its dictates dominated people's lives in the various "focuses of faith."

Feudalism is commonly thought of as a political and social arrangement having to do with the power relationships of land ownership, maintenance of security, and class standing. However, as feudalism appears in *The Song of Roland* it is a much more encompassing network of relationships amounting to a total culture.[11] If we think of feudalism as primarily the reciprocal sharing of service and protection between an individual male of the land-owning class and his immediate over-lord, the poem shows how that apparently two-way reciprocation actually extends to all of a person's social relations—between individual and group, friends and enemies, countrymen and foreigners, men and women. Thus the individual's outward social contact, far from being binary (vassal-seigneur), can probably better be conceived as extending in seven directions (see the following schema). The individual is involved in contacts with (1) his peers (*compaignuuns*—in Roland's case, Oliver, Turpin, and the rest of the *duz pers*); (2) his family or clan, including household retainers (*parenz*); (3) his immediate feudal overlord (*seigneur*, to whom he is *vassal*); (4) his ultimate feudal monarch, the king or emperor ("*Carles li reis, nostre emperere magnes*"); (5) the nation (*dulce France*) or people (*li Franceis*) that the ruler represents; (6) European Christendom as a whole (*li chrestiens*); and (7) the Christian God (*damne deus, veir paterne*).

Schema

SEVEN VARIETIES OF FEUDALISM

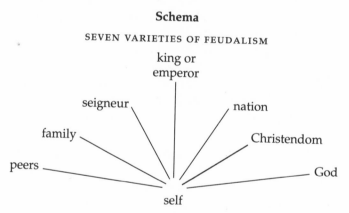

The degree to which this schema offered by the poem is paradigmatic for a representative man is qualified somewhat by complicating factors in Roland's case. For instance, Roland's ultimate feudal overlord, Carles, is also a member of his family, his maternal uncle. On the other hand, Roland's nemesis, his stepfather Guenes, is also a close family member, although not a blood relative. There is apparently no intermediate layer of feudal obligation between Roland and Carles (vaguely reflective of actual conditions in early Carolingian feudalism), yet Roland himself is the seigneur of some members of his rear guard. Nevertheless, the seven-part schema of relationships basically pertains. It is hierarchal yet also complex and mutable. Much of the substance of the epic is devoted to exposing and resolving its social and ideological stresses and ambiguities.

Several areas of actual and potential conflict arise between the seven types of allegiance, and these conflicts impel the action of *Roland*. To begin with, the interests of the individual and his supporters—peers or clan—often clash with those of the seigneurial overlord. This is less true of Roland than it is of his antagonist Guenes, who disastrously implicates his champion Pinabel and thirty of his *parenz* in his self-defense in the fourth section of the poem. The conflicting claims to service coming from immediate and ultimate feudal overlords bulk less large in the poem than they probably did in eleventh- and twelfth-century European politics. But such claims do complicate life for Marsile of Saragossa: if he were to seriously entertain the proposal of holding Spain in fief from Carles, instead of using the proposal as a ruse, he would be in trouble with his pagan overlord, the Emir of Babylon. Central to the poem, however, is the conflict within the hero between the personal ideals of chivalric heroism (leading Roland, for instance, to the *desmesure* of refusing to blow Olifant at Oliver's insistence in order to summon Carles) and the social ideals of service to seigneur, people, Christendom, and God. A radical conflict between secular and spiritual ideals of behavior and service is one more likely to be felt by a modern reader than by the audience of a poem composed for a crusading age; nonetheless, such a conflict is latent in the *Chanson*, and its successful resolution intensifies the beauty of Roland's death or Carles's fifth dream in the last laisse. The fact that the social Christendom and religious fervor of the society tend to define themselves in terms of opposition—*paiens unt tort e chrestiens unt dreit; damne deus* is opposed by the unholy, parodistic trinity of Apollon, Tervagant, and Mahoun—is itself enough to determine that there will be a significant degree of antagonism among the competing poles of allegiance. For the poem's world is one of struggle, and not all of the choices are as clear-cut as the characters frequently declare them to be.

The central and determining cause of these conflicts is the one between personal and social ideals because the feudal culture has its matrix in an even broader culture, the honor/shame culture that seems to have existed in most times, places, and social strata (see the four classic studies of honor/shame culture listed in note 4). The qualities highly valued by an honor/shame culture that make Roland both great and, to a large degree, useful to his emperor and people—courage, initiative, sense of self-worth—are inevitably carried to excess and become their opposites—foolhardiness, insubordination, and pride. These peripeties occur at critical junctures in the narrative when the areas of influence typified by the seven poles of allegiance overlap. The challenge that *Roland* presents to modern readers is to get beyond simplistic judgments of what is appropriate behavior on the part of characters, what is right or wrong by our standards or those of the time of "Turoldus," to see the rich and various interplay of conflicting ideals.

A useful approach will be to locate several significant nodes of conflict to see how these highlight the relationships between individual, peers, family, seigneur, monarch, nation, Christendom, and the deity, and in particular to look at instances where resolutions are either achieved or suggested. The examples discussed have been chosen on the basis of a survey of the text that has picked out more than three hundred fifty instances of feudalism with these valences attached:

F = feudalism

$F \downarrow$ = feudal relationship (for example, *nurriture*) from *seigneur* to *vassal*

$F \uparrow$ = feudal relationship (*servise*) from *vassal* to *seigneur*

$F \rightarrow$ = lateral feudal relationship (*prozdom, recreantise*) between equals

$F_{h/s}$ = feudalism and the manifestations of honor/shame culture

F_c = feudalism and what later came to be called chivalry

F_f = feudalism and the claims of family

F_x = Feudalism and Christianity (or F_x = other religion)

During the last one hundred fifty years of *Roland* criticism, attention has come to be focused on a few key incidents in the poem and the conflicts in value arising out of them. These are cruces of interpretation rather than textual cruces. In the following pages I shall focus on a half dozen such nodes of conflicting values and then consider five (not entirely congruent) moments of resolution that show how varieties of feudal relationship can be seen as the matrix of *Roland's* drama. Five of the first grouping are taken for simple convenience in their narrative order, whereas the sixth, which I shall consider at greater length, encompasses the entire action of the poem. Some, though not all, of the moments of resolution can be seen as addressed to specific nodes of conflict.

(1) Critics—particularly those of a rationalistic turn of mind, such as Dorothy Sayers in the introduction to her still-popular Penguin Classics translation of 1957—have been troubled by the apparently fated quality of the choice of the embassy to the Saracens (LL. 8–27), with the selection falling upon Guenes, to practically no one's satisfaction, and marked by Carles's inexplicable helplessness. This choice is shortly afterwards balanced (LL. 58–63) by the similarly fated episode of the selection of the rear guard, to the satisfaction only of Guenes and to the consternation of Carles. (2) The once-renewed dispute between Oliver, Roland, and Turpin (LL. 80–88, 128–35) over the propriety of sounding Olifant is the most important node in the poem for the conflict between the requirements of feudal duty and the expectations of honor/shame chivalry. (3) The technical legal dispute among Guenes and Pinabel versus Carles, Naimes, and Tierri (LL. 272, 277) highlights from a different direction the conflict between personal rights to revenge for slighted honor and social requirements for the subordination of the individual's code to the needs of feudal seigneur, monarch, nation, and people. (4) The poem displays (but does not emphasize) two distinct methods of conversion to Christianity, the coercive treatment of the people in Marsile's capital of Saragossa (L. 266), and the gentle persuasion successfully practiced on Queen Bramimonde (LL. 266, 290); the modern temperament is likely to be more concerned than the poem's original audience about this contrast between a militant Christianity and one whose proselytism is secure enough to trust in gentler means. The fact that it is a noble *woman*, Bramimonde, who is the beneficiary of gentle persuasion shows a nascent sense of chivalry even in this archetypal chanson de geste. (5) Although it is not insisted upon, in the last laisse of the poem there seems to be a conflict within Carles himself between his final calling to Christian duty, in the fifth dream, versus his secular,

feudal duty to stay home and protect France. Or perhaps the reservations he feels about going to the aid of King Vivien in Imphe simply reflect the fact that Carles is a tired, weakened, disappointed old man who has lost his best supporters and one of his closest relatives and has seen the treason and ill will of his people. (6) Overarching all of these is the conflict within Roland's character, which has been the source of so much interpretive debate over the poem. Roland can be insolent, insubordinate, wild, proud, fierce, violent, and downright destructive to opponents and yet also faithful, gentle, courteous, forgiving, tender, and solicitous to friends.[12] It is not so much a mere double standard that operates in his behavior as a veritable schizophrenia in his being. For indeed, it is truly a different Roland from the one known to Turpin who is seen by Guenes and the Saracens; Oliver may have some inkling of the complexity.

Of these six nodes of conflict, the first and third—the fated quality of the choices of the embassy and the rear guard, and the dispute over Guenes's right to revenge—might be identified as the problem of the monarch (as ultimate feudal overlord, *suzerain* = *souverain*), calling into question who and what he is. The second and sixth nodes—the contention over the sounding of Olifant, and the conflict between the two sides of Roland's character—could be called the problem of the hero. In that case, the fourth and fifth nodes—the two methods of conversion to Christianity, and the debate within Carles over his Christian duty—might be a problem of the Frankish Christian culture as a whole.

In some respects, what I call five moments of resolution address themselves to some of these nodes of conflict. (1) For example, the four miracles or instances of God's intervention on Carles's behalf— the signs and portents accompanying Roland's death (L. 110), the prolongation of daylight so that Carles can complete his defeat of Marsile's forces (L. 180), the sending of Gabriel to bolster Carles's spirits in his duel with Baligant (L. 261), and later the strengthening of Tierri so that he can defeat Pinabel in the judicial combat (L. 286)— address themselves to items five, four, and one: the conflict within Carles, the conversion methods of Christianity, and the apparent weakness of the emperor in the face of breakdowns in the feudal system. The four miracles or interventions all indicate God's approval of the course Carles takes. Thus Christian feudalism *ratifies* imperial feudalism. (2) Tierri's coming out of nowhere[13] to act as Carles's champion against the party of Guenes when the Franks as a group seem ready to cave in to extortion and emotional blackmail, and his success despite his unprepossessing physique, indicate the worthiness of Carles's and Roland's cause and therefore answer the contention raised by Guenes over personal honor and the right to revenge (in the third node (while reinforcing the sense of how the conflict within Carles (in the fifth node) is to be resolved. (3) There are indications, almost amounting to what we expect of character motivation in novelistic narrative, that Bramimonde on her own is well on the way to rejecting paganism, for she twice blames, curses, and rejects the false trinity (LL. 187–88, 195–96). The fact that she is herself thus moved by grace at least partially justifies the operation of two modes of conversion (node four), for some pagans *deserve* greater consideration. Many commentators have noted the limited generosity extended to pagan enemies from time to time by the narrative voice; it almost becomes a formula that some pagan fighter is such a fine physical figure and is so brave that he would be a worthy *baron*, if only he were Christian. An extension of this is seen in (4) the episode (L. 264) of Marsile's death from shame and despair when he hears of his feudal overlord Baligant's defeat and death at Carles' hands. This poignant passing of an enemy somewhat validates the pagans' feudalism (they too can keep the faith) while exposing its weakness (it is the wrong faith). As such, it represents an indirect comment on the failures or near failures of Frankish feudalism (the first, third, and fifth nodes). (5) Applicable to all the cruces listed node (but particularly to the second and the sixth node) is Roland's apotheosis at the time of his death (LL. 168–76), uniting all varieties of feudalism, sometimes within the space of just a few lines. This is one reason why the death scene is central to the poem.

The scene of the Frankish council near the beginning of the poem (LL. 8–27) has long been a focus of attention and indeed a critical crux, and the same can be said of the choice of the rear guard which balances and completes it (LL. 58–63). Readers have been puzzled by the apparently *fated* quality of the choice of the embassy to the Saracens (Guenes) and of the leader of the rear guard (Roland). Fate weighs heavily in the classical and northern pagan epics (Homer's *moira*, Virgil's *fatum*, Beowulf's *wyrd*) but is less to be expected in a poem whose medieval universe sees this quality in terms of a some-how less ominous Fortuna. Note that two of the strongest instances of foreshadowing in *Roland* appear within these nineteen laisses. At the end of the catalogue of Carles's chief counselors, the narrative voice declares, "Guenes i vint, ki la traisun faist. / Des ore cumoncet le cunseile mal prist" (12.178–79). When Guenes (intentionally?) drops the emperor's right gauntlet, extended as a sign of transfer of feudal authority, the onlookers are horrified (25.334–35). Perhaps more perplexing is Carles' apparent helplessness in the grip of these events. He is easily swayed by contrary arguments, he reacts emotionally, and he ends up asserting his authority in the wrong way and at the wrong time, thus falling into Marsile's trap, widening the rift between stepfather and stepson, and practically assuring a disaster. A puzzle similar to the one of why Carles cannot control his council and the outcome of its deliberations is the whole question of the bad blood between his nephew and the nephew's stepfather. Why do these two hate one another? It is not very helpful to hypothesize knowledge from the oral tradition of the poem, now lost to us.

At least some of the questions can be answered, however, if we look at the complex varieties of feudal relationships at work in the scene. The "problem of the monarch" is compounded by a breakdown of the feudal duty to the monarch on the part of Guenes and Roland primarily, but also of other counselors, because of personal animosity and the resort to vendetta to which it leads.

When Roland first nominates Guenes for the embassy (L. 20), he *specifies* that the man is his stepfather (20.277–80). It is not clear why the younger man should do so, but evidently the family relationship is significant. Guenes' immediate reaction is one of fear and outrage (20.286–91). Guenes assumes he *will* be sent, even though Carles has refused several previous nominations (289—the fated quality), and he swears revenge (290–91), which is his basis at the time of the trial for a claim that his betrayal of the rear guard was simply the working out of his personal right to vengeance. Here we see the complication of family quarrels and chivalric honor taking precedence in at least one character's mind over his feudal duty to his lord and ultimately to monarch and nation.

When Roland once again volunteers to go on the embassy himself, however, Guenes perversely refuses, for the demands of the honor/

shame-bound chivalric portion of the feudal code will not allow him to refuse now to accept the emperor's command. Guenes has been backed into a corner, as it were:

Guenes respunt: "Pur mei n'iras mie!
Tu n'ies mes hom ne jo ne   F ↑
suit tis sire.   F ↓
Carles commandet que face
sun servise,   F ↑
En Sarraguce en irai a Mar-
silie.
Einz i frai un poi de legerie,

Que jo n'esclair ceste meie
grant ire."
Quant l'ot Rollant, si
cumençat a rire. AOI.
Quant ço veit Guenes que ore
s'en rit Rollant,
Dunc ad tel doel pur poi d'ire
ne fent,
A ben petit que il ne pert le
sens;
E dit al cunte: "Jo ne vus aim
nient,

Sur mei avez turnet fals juge-
ment.

Dreiz emperere, veiz me ci en
present,
Ademplir voeille vostre com-
mandement."   F ↑

Ganelon replies, "You will not go in my place!
You're not my vassal and I'm not your lord.
Charles orders me to render him a service,
So I'll go to Saragossa, to Marsile.
But I'll do something a bit ill-advised,
Before I purge this great anger of mine."
When Roland heard him he began to laugh. AOI.
When Ganelon sees that Roland is laughing at him now,
He has such a fit of anger that he is ready to burst,
He very nearly goes out of his mind;
And he says to the Count: "I don't care what happens to you now.
You have arranged to have this rotten nomination fall on me.
Rightful Emperor, I stand here before you,
I wish to carry out your orders." [LL. 21–22]

Note that Guenes partly refuses Roland's offer because " 'Tu n'ies mes hom ne jo ne suit tis sire' " (298). Despite his fear and his strong objections, Guenes accepts Carles's command (22.309). The central tenet of feudalism, the vassal's obligation to serve his seigneur, is being carried out; but its validity is entirely undermined by the complicated circumstances and by the corrupt spirit in which the duty is accepted.

In laisse 24, when Guenes renews his defiance of the *duz pers*, he practically admits that his *conseil* to the monarch, a recognized feudal duty, has been bad (24.322–30). Earlier Roland had warned Carles to refuse Marsile's overtures and complete the military conquest of Spain, because the Saracens were not to be trusted, as their treacherous beheading of the emissaries Basile and Basan had indicated (14.207–14), and yet here Guenes fears, " 'mais n'i avrai guarant: / Nu l'out Basilies ne si freres Basant' " (24.329–30). When his own life is on the line, Guenes virtually reverses his earlier stand, but no one present at the council seems to notice. The conflict between varieties of feudalism, then, can only work itself out in further conflict heightened into fatal violence.

Similarly, at the time of the delegation of the rear guard (LL. 58–63), Carles seems paralyzed by a mysterious inability to judge and act. When Guenes nominates his stepson for the dangerous position, Roland, Carles, and their supporters seem to compete with one another in their haste to fall into the traitor's trap. The fated quality is heavy in laisse 58.743–50. Carles reacts venemously to the nomination: " 'Vos estes vifs diables,' " he growls to Guenes. Carles's helplessness is emphasized in 61 when "Ne poet muer que des oilz ne plurt" (773). Why, then, is it impossible for the emperor simply to refuse the nomination? Is it because the event is *fated*? In accepting, Roland boasts that he will fulfill his feudal obligations impeccably (59). But then he bitterly curses his stepfather, taunting him that Roland will never drop to the ground the gauntlet of feudal authority if it is donated by Carles to him.

Quant ot Rollant qu'il ert en la rereguarde,	Hearing that he will be in the rear guard,
Ireement parlat a sun parastre:	Roland spoke angrily to his stepfather:
"Ahi! culvert, malvais hom de put aire,	"Oh! you dirty son of a bitch,
Quias le guant me caist en la place,	Did you expect me to drop the gauntlet to the ground

F ↑

Cume fist a tei le bastun de- vant Carles?" AOI.	The way you let the staff fall before Charles?" AOI. (L. 60)

If Roland is so willing to accept the nomination, as he appeared to be in 59, why is he now so angry about it? Roland, too, is in the grip of conflicting forces. His common sense tells him the Saracens are not to be trusted. Yet his personal honor requires that he accept this challenge, and his feudal duty would *seem* to require that he take on the command of the rear guard if Carles tells him to.

It may be that in these two episodes of ill-fated decision, the *Chanson* has risen beyond any realistic absorption of the circumstances of feudalism, in all their complexity, into a realm of the mythic. Perhaps the two-hundred-year-old Emperor Charlemagne is a *mythic* figure of such stature that he cannot be expected to function politically in the world. Who he is matters more than what he does.

The double crux of the contention among Roland, Oliver, and Turpin over whether or not to sound Olifant (LL. 80–88, 128–35) is crucial to the "problem of the hero," for here is brought out in its starkest terms the way in which the honor/shame ethos inevitably falls into competition with the social and communal ethos of feudalism.

Ironically, the first contention is introduced by Roland's great credo on the nature of *vasselage*. When the observant Oliver warns him that a terrible battle is in the offing, Roland responds:

. . . "E Deus la nus . . . otreit!	"May God grant it to us!
Ben devuns ci estre pur nos- tre rei:	We must make a stand here for our king:
Pur son seignor deit hom sus- frir destreiz F ↑	One must suffer hardships for one's lord
E endurer e granz chalz e granz freiz,	And endure great heat and great cold,
Sin deit hom perdre e del quir e del peil.	One must also lose hide and hair.
Or guart chascuns que granz colps i empleit	Now let each see to it that he employs great blows,
Que malvaise cançun de nus chantet ne seit! F$_{h/s}$	So that no taunting song be sung about us!

Paien unt tort e chrestiens unt dreit.	F_x F_x	Pagans are in the wrong and Christians are in the right.
Malvaise essample n'en serait de mei." AOI.	$F_{h/s}$	I shall never be cited as a bad example." AOI. [LL.79:1008–16]

Here is seen the admirable martial ethic of service and suffering—suffering great hardships *pur son seignor* (1010), enduring great heat and cold, losing (somewhat humorously) *del quir e del peil* (1012)—balanced by vigorous action—dealing great blows, thus fulfilling the medieval stoic ideal of *agere et pati*. The innocent simplicity with which this is uttered is based on the simple, direct early medieval universe that Auerbach explained so admirably: " 'Paien unt tort e chrestiens unt dreit.' " But complicating this is the self-referential quality of the poem: Roland desires " 'Que malvaise cançun de nus chantet ne seit! /. . . . Malvaise essample n'en serat ja de mei' " (1014, 1016). Here is the epic concern for fame and against shame. This short passage thus contains one of the strongest statements in the poem of the ideal of feudal service to one's lord (F ↑), along with an insistent comparative valuation of Christianity and its competitor religion (F_x—F_x), and a lively sense of the demands of an honor/shame culture (F_c or $F_{h/s}$). At this point the three ideals are mutually supportive, but two of them are soon in conflict with one another when Oliver requests that Roland blow Olifant to summon aid.

Oliver's reasoning is simple: at the sound of Olifant, their feudal seigneur will rush to fulfill *his* duty to his vassals by rescuing them (1051–52). But Roland refuses on the grounds that honor/shame forbids it and he would " 'perduire mun los' " (1054). He doesn't want his kinsmen or his countrymen to incur blame on his account (1063–64) or suffer reproach (1076). He expects the men in his party to behave *vassalment* (1080), in a knightly fashion, or "courageously" (Brault's translation of the word at this point). Considering how ridiculously high the odds against them are, Oliver avers; he can see no " 'blasme' " (1082) arising out of calling for aid—it is merely prudent, standard military tactics. But, of course, prudence is not one of Roland's virtues. As the narrative voice magnificently sums up, "Rollant est proz e Oliver est sage" (1093). It is at points like this that the stark paratactic style of the poem rises to something like mystery. True, we have seen these Rolandian and Oliverian qualities in action, but unfortunately they sometimes work at odds with one another, as now. And yet the narrative goes on to claim, "Ambeduie unt meveillus vasselage" (1094). The direct comparative valuation of Roland and Oliver seems to hold most true if we consider that *together* the two of them make up an ideal *vassal*.

It is a truism of *Roland* commentary that some of the most crucial developments in the plot are signaled by similar *laisses*, and this certainly holds for the second Olifant passage (LL. 133–35, when Roland sounds the horn).[14] It is two earlier laisses, 129 and 131, however, that are crucial in the contention between personal honor and feudal duty. The tables are turned when Oliver speaks out against blowing the horn, using Roland's standards against him, saying that to call for aid at this point would be " 'Vergoigne' " (1705; 'dishonorable'), would amount to " 'reprover a trestuz vos parenz' " (1706), bringing" 'hunte' " (1707; 'shame'); " 'Ne serait vasselage' " (1715; " 'That would not be a heroic deed!' "). When Roland persists, despite a slightly veiled threat from Oliver that Roland will not be allowed to marry Oliver's sister Alde, then Oliver sternly rebukes Roland:

. . . "Cumpainz, vos le feistes, . . .		"Comrade, you brought it on yourself,
Kar vasselage par sens nen est folie;		For heroism tempered with common sense is a far cry
	F_c	from madness;
Mielz valt mesure que ne e- stultie.		Reasonableness is to be preferred to recklessness.
Franceis sunt morz par vostre legerie.		Frenchmen have died because of your senselessness.
Jamais Karlon de nus n'avrat servise.	$F\uparrow$	We shall never again be of service to Charles.
Sem creisez, venuz i fust mi sire,	$F\downarrow$	If you had believed me, my lord would have come,
Ceste bataille oüsum faite u prise,		We would have fought or won (?) this battle,
U prise u mort i fust li reis Marsilie.		King Marsile would be captured or slain.
Vostre proëce, Rollant, mar la veimes!	F_c	We have come to rue your prowess, Roland!

Karles li magnes de nos
n'avrat aie.   F ↑
N'ert mais tel home desqu'a
Deu juise.

Vos i murrez e France en ert
hunie.   F~h/s~
Oi nus defalt la leial cumpai-
gnie,
Einz le vespre mult ert gref la
departie." AOI.   F→

Charlemagne will not have
any help from us.
There shall never be such a
man again until Judgment
Day.
You will die here and France
will be dishonored.
Today our loyal companionage
comes to an end,
Before nightfall, our parting
will be very sad." AOI.
[131.1723–36]

There is a noticeable difference between heroism (*vasselage*) and madness (*folie*). Roland is virtually accused of *desmesure* (although the
word itself is not used, only its positive form referred to negatively in
1725). The feudal obligation of using the rear guard to support Carles's cause has been abrogated (1727–30), whereas Roland's great chivalric qualities, such as *proëce* (1731), have been foolishly squandered.
To call for aid in these circumstances really would bring dishonor (*hunie*, 1734) on his people. In the following laisse Archbishop Turpin
tries to serve as peacemaker and accurately predicts the course of the
rest of the poem: Carles will come to their rescue when he hears the
horn, in time to grant them Christian burial and avenge their deaths.
But this is hardly sufficient to heal the rift between the two *cumpai-
gnons*, for it is a rift that runs clear down the center of the poem and,
indeed, its world.

The apparent helplessness of the all-powerful monarch to assert his
feudal sway and maintain the feudal structure against those who
would inadvertently or unintentionally subvert it, is even more
strongly evident in the fourth section of the poem at the trial of
Guenes (LL. 270–89).[15] Again, Carles himself seems unable to counter
effectively Guenes's specious arguments in his defense. (Of course,
Carles is not aware of all Guenes's machinations; for instance, Carles
does not know that Guenes falsified the original offer to Marsile by
claiming that Roland was to get half of Spain in fief.) Carles can only
embody the appropriate reply by his example as a divinely appointed
monarch (as he was seen to be subsequent to being crowned Emperor
by Leo III in 800), but he cannot *articulate* it—that duty falls to a loyal

vassal. Thus the "problem of the monarch." There is a notable break-down (if only temporary) of monarchical control in the face of the more basic honor/shame tenets of personal revenge.

At the beginning of the trial, once Carles has charged him, Guenes offers a four-part defense. There has been some sort of prior grudge between stepfather and stepson: " 'Rollant me forfist en or e en aveir' " (3758; compare 3778), although the nature of this supposed wrong is left unspecified. (Would Guenes simply be referring to his earlier being named to the embassy?) Nonetheless, Guenes is deter-mined he has committed no treason: " 'Mais traïsun nule n'en i otrei' " (3760). This, he claims, is because he formally challenged Ro-land and the *pers*: " 'Jo desfiai Rollant le poigneor / E Oliver e tuz lur cumpaignun' " (3775–76). Thus he was legitimately carrying out a personal revenge, according to the honor code, and no political trea-son was involved on a specifically feudal level: " 'Venget m'en sui, mai n'i ad traïsun' " (3778). Note, however, that the narrative voice has previously prejudged Guenes, "Guenelun, ki traïsun ad faite" (3748), and that voice evaluates him in the formula used often for Sa-racens, "Cors ad gaillard, ed vis gente color, / S'il fust leials, ben re-semblast barun" (3763–64). Nonetheless, his kinsman Pinabel supports his cause and demands for him the right to trial by combat (3789–90).

At this point a crux occurs in the competing varieties of feudalism in *Roland*, when Carles's council at Aix backs down before the implied threats of Guenes and Pinabel and their supporters (275.3798–805). This temporizing by the panel of judges selected from vassals repre-senting the center of Carles's empire is one of the great failures in the poem, as far as the requirements and expectations of feudalism are concerned. The judges' immediate expediency might seem to be served by avoiding a civil war between Carles and one of his most powerful vassals that would necessarily involve them. But short-term peace would be gained only at the expense of undermining the hier-archal order of Frankish feudalism, which, although it is a contractual agreement between social equals, depends on a system of political subordination. Does the judges' failure arise out of their fear? Or the expectation of a bribe? Or some unexplained demoralization? They whine, " 'Mult sereit fols ki . . . se cumbatreit' " (3804), which would seem to indicate the former, although perhaps all reasons are germane. Carles fully realizes what is wrong with this counsel but seems paralyzed to refuse it: "Ço dit li reis: 'Vos estes mi felun!' " (3814; he "sees that all have failed him," 3815). He must wait passively ("Quant Carles veit que tuz li sunt faillid, / Mult l'enbrunchit e la chere e le vis, / Al doel qu'il ad si se cleimet caitifs," 3815–17) for a champion to appear—a sort of feudal grace—as occurs in the next laisse.

Tierri of Anjou's accusation of Guenes directly balances feudal duty against personal honor and values the former: " 'Que Rollant a Guenelun forsfesist, / Vostre servise l'en doust bien guerir! / Guenes est fels d'iço qu'il le trait, / Vers vos s'en est parjurez e malmis' " (3827–30). The key terms here are *fels* ("felonious"), *parjurez* ("perjured"), and *malmis* ("false"). In laisse 278, Pinabel formally accepts the challenge, "Met il el poign de cerf le destre guant" (3845), according to feudal protocol. Carles wisely demands thirty hostages as a bond for Guenes's bail (3846–49). The judicial duel in laisses 280–86 highlights at least three of the varieties of feudalism working either in concert or conflict with one another. Christian feudalism is paid its respects when both the combatants confess, hear mass, and make offerings (3846–49), and the king himself prays, " 'le dreit en esclargiez?' " (3891). The duel opens with some initial verbal skirmishing in which the combatants in a series of patterned speeches offer, refuse, counter-offer, and counter-refuse clemency to one another in specifically feudal terms:

Dist Pinnabel: "Tierri, car te recreiz!	F ↑	Pinabel said: "Thierry, concede defeat!
Tes hom serai par amur et par feid,	F ↑	I shall be your vassal in friendship and in good faith,
A tun plaisir te durrai mun aveir,		I shall give you what I have to your heart's content,
Mais Guenelun fai acorder al rei!"		But reconcile Ganelon with the King!"
Respont Tierri: "Ja n'en tendrai cunseill,	F ↑	Thierry replies: "I shall not give this matter any thought,
Tut seie fel se jo mie l'otrei!		I'll be damned if I consent to it in the least!
Deus facet hoi entre nus dous le dreit!" AOI.	F_x	Let God this day show which of us is in the right!" AOI.

Ço dist Tierri: "Pinnabel,
mult ies ber,
Granz ies e forz, e tis cors
ben mollez,
De vasselage te conoissent ti
per. F_c
Ceste bataille car la laisses
ester,
A Carlemagne te ferai
acorder. $F \uparrow$
De Guenelun justise ert faite
tel, $F \downarrow$
Jamais n'ert jur que il n'en
seit parlet."
Dist Pinnabel: "Ne placet
Damnedeu! F_x
Sustenir voeill trestut mun
parentet, F_f
N'en recrerrai pur nul hume
mortel,
Mielz voeill murir que il me
seit reprovet." $F_{h/s}$

Thierry said: "Pinabel, you
are very brave,
You are big and strong and
your body is well built,
Your peers recognize you for
your courage.
Leave off fighting this duel,

I shall reconcile you with
Charlemagne.
But such justice shall be done
to Ganelon
That no day shall pass with-
out it being mentioned."
Pinabel said: "May it not
please the Lord God!
I wish to sustain all my kins-
men,
I shall not concede defeat for
any man alive,
I'd rather die than incur blame
for this." [283–84:3899–909]

Once the fighting becomes pitched, God intervenes directly on Tierri's behalf (3923), and he guarantees the proper outcome to the combat: "A icest colp est li esturs vencut" (3930). Throughout the scene,
the fickle Franks serve as a kind of chorus, approving of Tierri's intervention, " 'Or avez vos ben dit' " (3837), and in effect reversing
their earlier judgment by applauding Tierri's triumph and condemn-
ing Guenes and his supporters (286.3931–33).

The quick close of the poem at this point is remarkable. In two
laisses (288–89) the execution of Guenes and his party is dispensed
with (3932–33); the narrative voice diverts our attention with two sen-
tentiae which offer a direct and simple moralization (but take no account of the indirect path by which the decision has been arrived at):
"Ki hume traïst sei ocit e altroi" (3959) and "Hom ki traïst altre nen est
dreiz qu'il s'en vant" (3974). Then the conversion of Bramimonde and
Carles' anticlimactic fifth dream take place in the last two laisses, 290–
91. The sheer *speed* of the narration here might signify a successful

resolution of tensions between personal honor and the social demands of feudalism. Or it might betray a haste to wrap up the story while seeking to diminish any sense of a conflict of incompatible values that are supposed to support but end up undermining one another.

Similarly, especially for the modern reader, there is a distinct conflict between the ideals of martial and Christian feudalism in *Roland*. The Christianity of Archbishop Turpin of Reims is muscular indeed. The crises of this conflict occur in the instances of conversion in the poem. We can speak of two modes of conversion, the normal and the unusual.

The normal mode of conversion, that accorded to most Saracens, is forcible, either in fact or by threat: your belief or your life. When Carles's forces invade Marsile's capital of Saragossa,

Li emperere ad Sarraguce prise.		The Emperor has taken Saragossa.
A mil Franceis funt ben cercer la vile,		Orders are given for a thousand Frenchmen to search the city,
Les sinagogues e les mahumeries.	F_x	The synagogues, and the mosques.
A mailz de fer e a cuignees qu'il tindrent		Holding iron hammers and axes,
Fruissent les ymagenes e trestutes les ydeles,		They smash the statues and all the idols,
N'i remeindrat ne sorz ne falserie.		No sorcery or false cult will remain there.
Li reis creit Deu, faire voelt sun servise,	F_x	The King believes in God, he wishes to serve Him,
E si evecque les eves beneissent,		His bishops bless the waters,
Meinent paien entresqu'al baptisterie.		They lead the pagans to the baptistery.
S'or i ad cel qui Carle cuntredie,		Now if there is anyone who opposes Charles,
Il le fait prendre o ardeir ou ocire.		He orders him to be taken prisoner, burned, or put to death.

Baptizet sunt sez plus de .C.
milie
Veir chrestien. . . .

Well over a hundred thousand
are baptized
True Christians. . . .
[266.3660–72]

Evidently "Saracens" means both Jews and Muslims. The Christian soldiers indulge in an orgy of iconoclasm. And then the converts are "led" to baptism. This is what the irenic spirit of Duke Naimes's advice in the first council (16.239–42) has come to. Carles's original offer of clemency to Marsile, as guilefully delivered by Guenes, had emphasized conversion prior to feudal submission. The alternative to willing, peaceful conversion was harsh (33.433–37). The guileful note is the lie Guenes adds about Roland's being given half of Spain in fief (36.470–74). (In his report of the embassy, of course, Guenes does not mention this addition—54.692–97.) If the alternative "convert or die" (or lose your lands) offered to the Saracens seems harsh, keep in mind that they are not always allowed any such choice. After the second battle of Rencesvals, no attempt is made to capture or convert the fleeing forces of King Marsile (180:2461–74). Those who are not slaughtered in revenge for the deaths of Roland and the *duz pers* drown in the Ebro River trying to escape, to the great satisfaction of the pursuers.

The unusual mode of conversion to Christianity, by means of gentle persuasion, is reserved for one Saracen character alone in the entire poem, Marsile's widowed queen. At the end of the laisse narrating the forcible conversion of all the survivors of the seige of Saragossa, Carles expressly orders her rescued from that harsh treatment: ". . . ne mais sul la reine: / En France dulce iert menee caitive, / Ço voelt li reis par amur convertisset" (266.3672–74). The basis for Carles's reservation of Bramimonde seems to represent a nascent sense of chivalry on his part. Typical of the earliest stages of chivalry, there are two double standards operating in the emperor's choice: it favors a woman over any man, and a noble person over any commoner. The penultimate stanza of the whole poem is devoted to her actual conversion, back at Aix after Guenes's trial and just before Carles's fifth dream (290.3975–87). The concluding line of the laisse might seem to imply that all other modes of conversion do not lead to sincere changes in faith: "Chrestiene est par *veire* conoisence" (3987; emphasis added).

The very fact of the Saracens' willingness or ability to change faith in significant numbers (albeit normally under duress) is not only a judgment on the falsity of their own faith but could also indicate the possibility that Christianity too does not necessarily enjoy the whole-hearted support of all its believers. Some of them, no doubt, are timeservers, only out for what they can get (for example, support in battle) and ready to turn on any gods who do not deliver. Perhaps Christianity, too, is susceptible to these imperfections? But this is certainly not the central attitude of the poem, which does not openly recognize any conflict between martial and Christian feudalism. Roland is Carles's knight *and* God's, and Guenes is a traitor to his people *and* his God, as much as if he had turned Saracen.

The melancholy quality of the poem's last laisse has struck many commentators, and I have remarked already on the speed of the narrative at this point. (Even the last laisse itself can be broken down into brief sections: lines 3988–89 review the justice meted out to Guenes; 3990 refers to the conversion of Bramimonde in the previous laisse; the central bloc, 3991–4001, is devoted to Carles's dream with its renewed call to duty; and the last line, 4002, carries the poem's enigmatic *explicit*). On the surface, the emperor's reluctance to accept the renewed call appears to be purely personal: "Li emperere n'i volsist aler mie: / 'Deus!' dist li reis, 'si penuse est ma vie!' / Pluret des oilz, sa barbe blanche tiret" (291.3999–4001). He is old ("barbe blanche"), he is tired (" 'si penuse est ma vie' "), he is sad ("Pluret des oilz"). The line introducing his reaction seems almost litotic in its starkly simple expression: "Li emperere n'i volsist aler mie" (3999). Is this merely a straightforward expression, or are we right to detect a tone of reluctance on Carles's part to fulfill God's command willingly and quickly? The narrative ends without any statement that Carles has complied or will do so. Nevertheless, dreams in the poem up to this point have always served as omens or prophecies, which are borne out by subsequent events, leading to a presumption that this last one must carry an equal force.

If there is a tone of reluctance in Carles's reaction as described in line 3999, perhaps that feeling is not simply a personal one reflecting his human limitations; perhaps it also indicates a conflict in duties, between secular-feudal and religious-feudal obligations. For note that the King Vivien who requires succor is not called one of Carles's vassals; the appeal is that he is a leader of a *Christian people* who require Carles's aid: "Li chrestien te recleimet et crient" (3998). Political expediency would suggest that Carles should remain at his capital, Aix, or at least within the bounds of his kingdom, regrouping his forces, healing the wounds caused by the execution of one of his major lords and that man's family, and finding some way to replace his lost right arm, Roland. But the demands of Christendom and the demands of empire may not coincide. It is not putting too much pressure on this single laisse to see in it such a conflict of the two social varieties of feudalism. European monarchs of the eleventh through the thirteenth centuries no doubt faced versions of such a conflict, when a call came from Rome for a crusade.

Of the conflicts between competing varieties of feudalism discussed so far, the most crucial one, however, must be that *within* the hero himself. Roland is the paradigm of the Auerbachian "paratactic man," having within his scope two distinct ranges of behavior that exist side by side but are not resolved. Toward opponents he can be insolent, insubordinate, wild, proud, fierce, violent, destructive. Yet toward friends he is unfailingly faithful, gentle, courteous, forgiving, tender, solicitous. And the change between the one Roland and the other can occur almost within a single breath.

This paratactic Roland is summed up briefly in one laisse, number 91:

. . . cil de France le cleiment a *guarant*.	F ↓	. . . the men of France called him their protector.
Vers Sarrazins reguardet *fierement*		He looks fiercely toward the Saracens
E vers Franceis *humeles* e *dulcement*,		And amicably and gently toward the French.
Si lur ad dit un mot curteisement. . . .	F→	And he spoke to them in comradely fashion. . . . [91.1161–64; emphasis added]

The same Roland who looks *fierement* toward the Saracens looks *humeles* and *dulcement* toward his own people, who confidently expect him to be their *guarant*.

The picture of Roland presented by his nemesis-stepfather at the time of the blowing of Olifant shows him as wild, foolish, and insubordinate (134.1773–81). Guenes condemns Roland for 'pride' (*orgoill*, 1773), reminds Carles of an instance of military insubordination and bloody-mindedness at Noples (1775–79), and mocks him as a mere trifler who would sound an enormous elephant-tusk trumpet at the death of a hare (1780–81). This condemnation comes from one who will shortly be an avowed enemy, and between whom and Roland there are already some unspecified grounds for bad blood, so that such an opinion must be largely discounted. But not entirely, as Roland's own actions and demeanor during the story indicate.

Roland's behavior toward his stepfather during the appointing of the embassy and rear guard may be motivated by a desire to endanger and embarrass him; it is certainly gauged to mock and humiliate him. When Guenes gets angry over his nomination and starts making threats, Roland "cumençat a rire" (302). His reply to his stepfather, " 'Orgoill oi et folage, / Co set hom ben, n'ai cure de manace' " (292–93), is certainly not the deference from a younger man to his elder expected in this society. When Guenes turns the tables by nominating Roland to the perilous leadership of the rear guard, the tone of Roland's reply is possibly in doubt (59: 751–59). "Sire parastre, mult vos dei avec cher" ("Sir stepfather, I am much indebted to you," 753) sounds like sarcasm. There is no question, however, about the tone of Roland's further reply in laisse 60:

Ireement parlat a sun parastre:		Roland spoke angrily to his stepfather:
"Ahi! culvert, malvais hom de put aire,		"Oh! you dirty son of a bitch,
Quias le guant me caist la place,	F ↓	Did you expect me to drop the gauntlet to the ground
Cume fist a tei la bastun devant Carles?"		The way you let the staff fall before Charles?"[60.762–65]

What courteous knight would call anyone (least of all his elder) a coward, or in Brault's quaint rendering, a dirty son of a bitch?

The other Roland, who is warm *cumpaignun*, brave leader, and wise seigneur, comes out in adversity, when his forces are being defeated by overwhelming enemy numbers. In laisse 140 he laments his dead soldiers and takes responsibility for them as his *vassals* (1856) whom he should have been able to preserve. The best of this Roland comes out in three laments, two for Oliver and the last for Turpin. In the first lament for the dead Oliver, Roland generously voices the basis of *compaignage* when he declares, " 'Ensemble avum estet e anz e dis, / Nem fesis mal ne jo nel te forsfis' " (2028–29; F→). There is no clearer expression in the poem of the claims of the feudalism of peer relationships, unless it be in the similar statement one hundred lines later. Roland's ultimate praise for his friend comes in the second lament, at laisse 163 (2207–14). The lament for Turpin in laisse 167 shows Roland's recognition of the claims both of chivalric feudalism (" 'gentilz hom, chevaler de bon aire,' " 2251) and Christian feudalism (2252–58).

The most engaging example of Roland's fairness comes when he receives his sternest test, as the blinded and stricken Oliver tries to brain him. Definitely, the Franks of the *chansons* are men of a word and a blow, the blow sometimes not waiting for the word. But Roland, in laisse 149, is a model of loving restraint:

A icel colp l'ad Rollant reguardet,		After this blow, Roland looked at him,
Si li demandet dulcement et suëf:	F→	He asked him softly and gently:
"Sire cumpain, faites le vos de gred?		"Comrade, sir, are you doing this on purpose?
Ja est ço Rollant, ki tant vos soelt amer!		Look, it's Roland who loves you so!
Par nule guise ne m'aviez desfiet!"		You haven't challenged me in any way!"
Dist Oliver: "Or vos oi jo parler.		Oliver said: "I hear you speaking now.
Jo ne vos vei, veied vus Damnedeu!		I do not see you, may the Lord God see you!
Ferut vos ai, car le me pardunez!"	F$_c$	I struck you, please forgive me for this!"
Rollant respunt: "Jo n'ai nient de mel,		Roland replies, "I have suffered no injury,
Jol vol parduins ici e devant Deu."		I forgive you this here and before God."
A icel mot l'un a l'altre ad clinet,	F→	After he said this, they bowed to each other;

| Par tel amur as les vus de-sevred! | See them now parting with such affection! (1998–2009) |

Instead of retaliating instinctively, as might be expected in the midst of a pitched battle, Roland addresses his compaignon *dulcement et suëf*; when Oliver asks pardon for an act carried out in blindness, Roland immediately forgives him with full graciousness, and the lifetime companions, about to part forever, "l'un a l'altre ad clinet" (2008). If anyone in the poem understands the limitations of Roland's nature and is sensitive to the tensions within him, it is his friend Oliver, who is here the recipient of the best in the hero's nature.

Roland's apotheosis at the time of his death (LL. 168–76), uniting all the varieties of feudalism, sometimes within the space of a few lines, has called forth some of the finest efforts of modern exegesis, especially in analyses of the three similar laisses on the disposal of Durendal (171–73) and the three describing the actual death (174–76). The absolute climax of the scene is, of course, the third similar laisse on the death, number 176, which, although it does not contain all seven varieties of feudal relationship in explicit form, has at least five of them in some of their most significant expressions in the entire poem: the feudalism of self, with its manifestation of chivalry (F_c); the feudalism of peers and family, with the intense concern for honor and shame in the social context ($F\rightarrow$ or F_f or $F_{h/s}$); the central feudalism of service to a lord and the people he symbolizes ($F\uparrow$) and of course its reciprocal in the lord's protection and reward ($F\downarrow$); and finally the fullest manifestation of Christian feudalism in Roland's actual apotheosis (F_x). This climactic laisse is reproduced below with the valences indicating varieties of feudalism marked on it:

Li quens Rollant se jut desuz un pin,		Count Roland lay beneath a pine tree,
Envers Espaigne en ad turnet sun vis.		He has turned his face toward Spain.
De plusurs choses a remem-brer li prist:		He began to remember many things:
De tantes teres cum li bers cunquist,	F_c	The many lands he conquered as a brave knight,
De dulce France, des humes de sun lign,	$F\rightarrow$ F_f	Fair France, the men from whom he is descended,

De Carlemagne, sun seignor, kil nurrit.	F↓	Charlemagne, his lord, who raised him.
Ne poet muër n'en plurt e ne suspirt,		He cannot help weeping and sighing.
Mai lui meisme no volt mettre en ubli,	F$_x$	But he does not wish to forget prayers for his own soul,
Cleiment sa culpe, si priet Deu mercit:		He says his confession in a loud voice and prays for God's mercy:
"Veir Patene, ki uncs ne men-tis,	F$_x$	"True Father, who never lied,
Seint Lazaron de mort resur-rexis		Who resurrected Saint Laz-arus from the dead
E Daniel des leons guaresis,		And saved Daniel from the lions,
Guaris de mei l'anme de tuz perilz		Protect my soul from all perils
Pur les pecchez que en ma vie fis!"		Due to the sins I committed during my life!"
Sun destre guant a Deu en puroffrit,	F↑	He proffered his right gaunt-let to God,
Seint Gabriel de sa main l'ad pris.	F$_x$	Saint Gabriel took it from his hand.
Desur sun braz teneit le chef enclin,		He laid his head down over his arm,
Juntes ses mains est alet a sa fin.		He met his end, his hands joined together.
Deus tramist sun angle Cherubin	F↓	God sent his angel Cherubin
E seint Michel del Peril,		And Saint Michael of the Peril,
Ensembl'od els sent Gabriel i vint.		Saint Gabriel came with them.
L'anme del cunte portent en pareis.	F$_x$	They bear the Count's soul to Paradise. [176:2375–96]

Note the intensity with which varieties of feudalism are juxtaposed in lines 2378–80. Roland remembers "De tante teres cum li bers cunquist" (F$_c$; 2378); "De dulce France" (F→; 2379a); "des humes de sun lign" (F$_f$; 2379b); "De Carlemagne, sun seignur, kil nurrit" (F ↑, F ↓; 2380). In the latter half of the laisse the focus shifts exclusively to spiritual feudalism (2382–92). In Roland's prayer of 2382–88 he commits his soul to God (F$_x$). Perhaps the most startling conflation—at least to modern expectations—in the whole poem of secular feudalism and religious feudalism is Roland's proffering his *destre guant* to God and Gabriel's accepting of it, in sign of Roland's final resignation of his feudal duties in life and God's signification of ultimate reward (2390; F ↓ and F$_x$). After this, as Roland has physically composed himself for death in the pose of a funerary statue (2391–92), his assumption into heaven borne by Cherubin, Saint Michael of the Peril, and Gabriel is even more climactic. Along with the mighty warrior Archangel Michael, who was instrumental in casting the rebel angels out of Heaven, the Angel Gabriel had many strong associations with the pilgrimage routes in southern France. Gabriel was the angel with Daniel in the lion's den (2386), he was the messenger of the Annunciation, and he will blow his horn to announce the Judgment. In this chanson, when *damne deus* intervenes, he commonly employs Gabriel as his agent (encouraging Carles in the Baligant duel, 261.3619–11; the fifth dream, 291.3992; the miraculous extension of daylight mentions only "an angel," 179.2452; however, in saving Tierri there is no intermediary: *Deus le guarit*, 285.3923).

The conflation of varieties of feudalism in the preceding laisses, 168–75, is not quite so intense and might best be laid out in a kind of tableau display that should be adequate to indicate nearly twenty instances of various kinds of feudal relationships called up by Roland's death scene.

Varieties of Feudalism in Laisses 168–175

No.	Laisse	Lines	Type	Circumstances
1	168	2261–62	F$_x$	Roland prays to God to accept peers; prays to Gabriel
2		2263	F$_{h/s}$	Roland protects Durendal and Olifant with body, *que reproce n'en ait*
3	169	2278	F$_c$	Saracen body robber *e de grant vasselage*

No.	Laisse	Lines	Type	Circumstances
4	170	2287–91	F_c	Roland brains Saracen with one blow from Olifant
5	171	2298–2305	$F_{h/s}$	Roland can no longer protect Durendal and must destroy it
6		2306–9	F ↑	with Durendal Roland has conquered many lands for Carles
7	172	2318–21	F ↓	donation of Durendal to Roland by Carles—one of the most important instances in poem of *feudal investiture*
8		2322–34	F ↑	full catalogue of Roland's conquests for Carles using Durendal
9		2335–37	$F_{h/s}$	that France should not be dishonored by Roland's losing Durendal
10	173	2345–50	F_x	Roland reviews the four relics in hilt of Durendal; therefore it has sacred as well as martial value
11		2351	$F_{h/s}$	"Ne vos ait hume ki facet cuardie!"
12		2352	F ↑	Roland's conquests for Carles with Durendal (cf. nos. 6 and 8)
13	174	2357–63	$F_{h/s}$	Roland lies down at advanced position *facing* Spain
14		2363	F_c	Roland's ultimate pride—he dies as a conqueror
15		2364–65	F_x	Roland as vassal of God: "Pur ses pecchez Deu en puroffrid lo guant"
16	175	2368–74	F_x	Roland's act of contrition
17		2373–74	F_x	Roland offers glove; angels descend toward him (therefore God accepts)

What this inspection of laisse 176, as well as the quicker survey of laisses 168–75, which portray Roland's death and apotheosis, proves is that all the varieties of feudalism are compatible with one another and can be unified into a viable whole. They conform to one another and, as a matter of fact, are essential to one another. Far from being in contention with one another, they are mutually supportive, in the experience of an epic hero who can embody all of them. This moment of resolution at Roland's death, then, offers a solution to the tensions we noted in the six nodes of conflict of varieties of feudalism in the poem, but especially of the second and sixth ones, which constituted the "problem of the hero."

The structured interrelationships among varieties of feudal behavior in *La Chanson de Roland* provide the poem's action, its underlying conflicts, its governing motif of faith-keeping as expressed in the formula of the oath of fealty, its characteristic imagery; they help to determine its shape. The poem's action can be summed up in an infinitive phrase: "to avenge Roland" (or perhaps more broadly, "to free Spain from the infidel" or "to vindicate Christendom"). The major conflicts that drive this action are not only, on an individual level, Roland against Ganelon, or Roland against Oliver, but also more broadly the hero versus the king,[16] or the Cross versus the Crescent, and most significantly the varieties of feudalism competing for the characters' allegiance. It is among these competing varieties of feudalism that disjunctions occur that reveal an aporia at the heart of early twelfth-century culture—the question of where faith should be placed and how it should be held. The double formula *par amur et par feid*, both legal in respect to the oath of fealty and stylistic in respect to the jongleur's craft of oral-formulaic composition, in its repetitions and numerous variations becomes a motif expressing the major theme of the poem, keeping faith. An inspection of the poem's imagery, too—the many instances of hand(s), glove, baton, bow, horn, sword, the various nearly heraldic animals (boar, bear, lion, leopard, dog, dragon), and the leitmotif of atmospheric descriptions ("Halt sunt le pui e li val tenebrus," first at line 814 and many times thereafter)—would show most images implicated in questions of faith-keeping or faith-breaking. Each of the prevalent expositors' choices for the basic structure of the poem—two-, three-, four-, or five-part—could be supported by arguments connecting them to conflicts that arise in the working out of relationships between varieties of feudalism.[17]

The most severe of the conflicts is that between feudalism and the ethos of the honor/shame culture in which it was embedded. Both of these ways show elements of the individualistic, with an emphasis on the singular hero's honor or shame, and of the communalistic, since only the community has the power to *grant* honor or shame. In either respect, it is an "other-directed" ethic, and yet not necessarily a highly social one, for the excesses of the individual may prove destructive to his society as well as himself. As the frequently recurring motif "let no bad songs be sung about us" (vv. 788, 1014, 1016, 1466, 1517) reveals, such an ethic finds its appropriate reflection in the self-reflexive nature of primary epic, which is aware of its own meaning and weight as a cultural vehicle.

It is appropriate to speak of a "culture" of feudalism, rather than just "feudal society," because feudal practices go beyond the merely political (achieving mutual security, holding off the barbarians, limiting chaos), the economic (determining who will own land, who hold it, and who work it), and the social (creating a stratified class of fighters-owners-governors), to create a cultural gestalt inescapable for the people of that time and place. Under the sway of this mind-set all other aspects of life are seen and lived *sub species feudalitatis.* Every other relationship that an individual in the world of the poem experiences becomes influenced by the feudal relationship; thus each other relationship becomes in essence some *version* of the feudal relationship. This is especially true of religion: God becomes a feudal seigneur to whom the mortal Christian is a worthy or unworthy vassal. Concomitantly, every other relationship exists *in competition with* the feudal one, striving for the person's allegiance or faith—as is the case, for instance, with family relationships, peer relationships, and any broader community relationships that are not in themselves specifically feudal. The poem itself knows and explicitly names two of these rival focuses of faith, the *lei de chevalers* (vv. 752, 1143) and the *lei de chrestiens* (vv. 38, 471, 2683). But through its characters' actions and implicitly their thoughts, the poem shows a third, the *lei de féodalité.* To speak of a third *"lei"* in *Roland* is misleading, though, because the feudal relationship per se was somewhat equivocal in its meaning and in its application to people's living, by the time of the *chanson's* composition. The vassal has divided calls upon his allegiance because of layers of feudal obligation to seigneur or to *liege* lord, and at least some of this complexity is reflected in the poem. When the *suzerain* is also a monarch, the relationship with him becomes further entwined in a relationship with his people (*li Franceis*) or nation (*dulce France*) or empire (*Tere Majur*), which in this case is more or less coextensive with Christendom itself.

The bond essential to holding together each of these relationships is that prime feudal virtue, fidelity. Keeping the faith means making an oral promise (in effect, a legal contract) and then keeping the promise by living up to it, or if necessary, dying for it. The obligation is symbolized first and most centrally by the ceremony of homage, and immediately thereafter by the oath of fealty, which is the verbal sign of the obligation. Taken at its broadest signification, keeping faith can be seen as an activity with many expressions. The person or literary character, first of all, keeps faith with himself by creating an appropriate self-image and then fulfilling it through a series of life choices (to blow or not to blow the horn). Lest this seem exclusively a concern of our own culture of narcissism, consider how important it would also be in an honor/shame culture. Who is Roland, the poem asks, and how can he best know and be himself? He is a *baron*, which is to say a worthy fighting man who is courageous, true, and faithful; among *barons* he is a *per*, one of the highest rank singled out for his service to the emperor; as a *baron* he is *proz* (but less notably *sage*); he is stepson (*filastre*) of Guenes and relative to his other *parenz*; he is nephew (*niez*) of his maternal uncle, Carles; at the same time, though, he is vassal of Carles (an explicitly feudal relationship) and a subject of the *reis magnes* and *emperere* (a political relationship that is not explicitly feudal); he is himself feudal seigneur of some of the members of his rear guard and certainly their military leader, thus on two counts owing them protection or *guarant*; and in a different respect he is a son of God who is shown as God's vassal, in the climactic scene.

Appearing throughout the poem is a conflict within Roland's character indicated by the vastly different public faces he turns toward enemies and friends: can one person really exist in such antithetical modes, hateful and loving? Roland's death scene is a tour de force in which almost every variety of feudalism is played upon or alluded to as Roland reviews his life, reminiscing over the many victories he has won for Carles—to his own fame and that of his *lignage*—attempting to prevent Durendal from falling into unworthy hands, and then making peace with God.

Thus to the competing ways of life named in the text, the heroic *lei de chevalers* and the religious *lei de chrestiens*, has been added a third law very broadly shown by the poem, the social *lei de féodalité*. As the *Song of Roland* demonstrates, whichever of these laws may be uppermost, each depends on the essential act of keeping faith, *par amur et par feid*.

Notes

1. Citations of the poem are taken from Gerard J. Brault's paperback one-volume student edition with facing translation: *"La Chanson de Roland": Student Edition— Oxford Text and English Translation* (University Park: Pennsylvania State University Press, 1984), by *laisse* (given as L. or LL. in absence of line/verse number) and/or verse number.

2. It would be attractive but fanciful to trace the etymology of *feudal* (*féodale*) and *faithful* (*féauté, fidelitas*) to the same Indo-European root. *Feudal*, which did not come into use in English until the seventeenth century, derives from **pekll*, a woolly animal, sheep used for barter. According to Joseph T. Shipley, "When cattle came to be considered private property, thus could be bartered, via Germanic (in which *p* changed to *f*) came *fee, fief, feu*, and the *feudal* system. The *d* in *feud* was added by association with Late Latin *alodis*: freehold land." The words for faith can be traced to Indo-European **bheidh*, trust, faith, via Latin *fidere* and French *feau(l)te, fealte*. (See *The Origins of English Words: A Discursive Dictionary of Indo-European Roots* [Baltimore: Johns Hopkins University Press, 1984], 294, 31–32.) *The Oxford Dictionary of English Etymology*, ed. C. T. Onions et al. (New York: Oxford University Press, 1986), is much less definite about the etymology of *feudal*, claiming that medieval Latin *feudum, feodum* is "usually" taken to be of Germanic origin, but that no evidence can be adduced (s.v. *feud²*).

3. Numerous variants on *par amur et par feid* include "serez ses hom *par honur e par be*" (39), "si saluerent *par amur e par bien*" (121), "jointes ses mains tis hom / E tute Espaigne *tendrat par vostre dun*" (2223–24), "*Par amistiez*, bel sire, la vos duins" (622), "*Por lor parenz par coer e par amor*" (1447), "Respont Rollant: 'Ne poi *amer* les voz' " (1548), "E cil respundent dulcement, *par amur*" (2440), "*Par bel amur* malvais saluz li firent" (2710), "Cumunement l'en prametent lor *feiz*" (3416), "Pais ne *amor* ne dei a paien rendre" (3596), "Receif la lei . . . Chrestientet, e pui te *amerai* sempres" (3598; emphases added).

4. *The Ethos of the "Song of Roland"* (Baltimore, Md.: Johns Hopkins University Press, 1963). The two opening chapters of semantic analysis are solidly grounded and quite valuable (9–95); however, the book's theoretical basis in anthropology— used to support the thesis that the ethos of the poem is an explicitly heroic one

appropriate to an honor/shame culture—is minimal, depending on just three sources: Ruth Benedict's *Patterns of Culture* (Boston: Houghton Mifflin, 1934); her study of Japan, *The Chrysanthemum and the Sword* (Boston: Houghton Mifflin, 1946); and David Riesman's *The Lonely Crowd* (New Haven: Yale University Press, 1950). (A seminal study on the subject, *Honour and Shame: The Values of Mediterranean Society*, ed. J. G. Peristiany [London: Weidenfeld & Nicholson, 1966], did not come out until a few years after Jones's book.) The semantic analysis of the verb *aimer* and related forms begins chapter 2, pp. 36–45; see especially pp. 43–45 for *par feid et par amur* and its variants.

5. Jones, *Ethos*, 44. Other phrases from the poem that sound like and at least partially function as legal formulae include "par amur e par bien," "par honur e par ben," "e dreiture e honur," "perdre e del quir e del peil," "perdre del sanc e de la char" (these last two from Roland's credo of the *bon vassal*), "clame quite," and "plevir leial."

6. Jones, *Ethos*, 44.

7. Jones, *Ethos*, 38.

8. Jones, *Ethos*, 38–39.

9. Jones, *Ethos*, 40–42.

10. Jones, *Ethos*, 43.

11. To speak of the "feudalism" of *The Song of Roland* may be misleading. Actually, three aspects of the relationship of feudalism to the chanson must be distinguished. There are the historical conditions of Carolingian prefeudalism that pertained at the time of the events of the poem in the last quarter of the eighth century, the state of feudalism in the Capetian kingdom around the time of the first Crusade in the late eleventh or early twelfth century when the form of the originally oral poem was fixed by written transcription, and the idealized, much less historical "feudalism" of the narrative itself. All three aspects must be considered in complex relation to one another, in speaking of "the feudalism" of the poem. Sometimes one aspect is more prominent, or more pertinent to an understanding of the function of feudalism in the poem; sometimes another is.

12. This bifurcation of character amounts to a veritable *topos* of epic narrative, according to George F. Jones, "Grim to Your Foes and Kind to Your Friends," *Studia Neophilologia* 34 (1962):91–103. In *The Ethos of the "Song of Roland,"* he calls it a "classical commonplace" and notes that it can be found in the Icelandic *Njal's saga* as well as in the *Karlamagnus saga*, the Norse compilation of *chanson* materials (103 n. 17).

13. There are two characters named Tierri in the poem. The less important of the two, Tierri d'Argone, appears only in the Baligant episode, at lines 3083 and 3534, and is to be distinguished from the more important Tierri, brother of Gefrei d'Anjou, who fights Pinabel in the judicial combat over Guenes's guilt. Joseph J. Duggan uses this confusing duplication of characters' names as one of his evidences that the Baligant episode was a late addition (eleventh century?) to the plot of the poem; see chapter 3, "The Episode of Baligant: Theme and Technique," in his *"The Song of Roland": Formulaic Style and Poetic Craft* (Berkeley & Los Angeles: University of California Press, 1973), 80 n. 18. The more important of the two Tierris,

brother of Gefrei d'Anjou, is himself a very minor character in the poem before the
trial of Guenes (named at lines 3818–19: "Ais li devant uns chevalers, / Frere Gefrei,
a un duc angevin"; described in 3820–21; named again at 3843, 3850, 3871, 3892,
3896, 3899, 3916, 3934, and 3939).

14. The possible linkage between consecutive *laisses* is carefully worked out by
Jean Rhychner in *La Chanson de geste: essai sur l'art epique des jongleurs* (Geneva: Droz,
1955). In chapter 4, "La Structure strophique des chansons," Rhychner discusses
five distinct types of linkage: (1) *enchaînement* (concatenation), (2) *reprise bifurquée*,
(3) a second type of branching, (4) parallel laisses, and (5) *laisses similaires*. Of these,
the most significant and complex are parallel laisses (formulaic repetition of the
same type of action, such as the armed encounter between Frankish and Saracen
knights—such parallel laisses are not necessarily contiguous to one another) and
laisses similaires (the *same* action repeated once or twice for a total of two or three
successive laisses). There are nine such groupings in the poem, totaling twenty-five
laisses in all, including four double sets: laisses 40–42, 43–44, 83–85, 133–35, 136–
38, 171–73, 174–76, 206–7, 208–10. These are usually devoted to high points in the
action of the poem (Duggan, "*The Song of Roland*," 98–99).

15. Many of the critical problems relevant to the episode of Guenes' trial have
been thoroughly dealt with in Emmanuel J. Mickel's *Ganelon, Treason, and the "Chanson de Roland"* (University Park: Pennsylvania State University Press, 1989). Mickel
concludes that there is no conflict in the poem between feudal powers and the monarchy: "the vision of a *Roland* which presents tensions between centralized authority disappears" (162). But Mickel actually spends much of the book showing just
how those tensions are worked out.

16. Throughout his posthumously published study of mainly medieval epic, *The
Hero and the King: An Epic Theme* (New York: Columbia University Press, 1982),
W. T. H. Jackson consistently returns to Roland and Charlemagne as the paradigms
of younger hero and older king in competition with one another for domination
that he sees as a governing pattern in epic: "loyalty is not only an issue in all these
poems but perhaps the most important issue. In all the major epics, except for the
Odyssey, there is tension because of the relation between a ruler and a major figure
in the work. The tension may be discussed in terms of loyalty, and the formal situation in the epics is often such that loyalty to a ruler is demanded of a young and
ambitious warrior. Yet the true situation is not so simple. The conflict between the
ruler and hero is often as much a conflict of values as of personalities and seems to
be an essential theme of epic poetry" (4). Although this short book is not divided
into chapters, and the Roland-Charlemagne paradigm is found *passim*, there is a
section focusing on *Roland* (54–72; see especially 58–59, 71–72; other chansons de
geste, 72–78; and Jackson's central statement of thesis, 14–16).

17. Depending partly upon whether the Baligant episode is accepted as integral
to the action, three-, four-, and five-part structures have been proposed for *Roland*.
The most widely agreed upon is the four-part structure:

I. Lines 1–702 (c. 700 lines) The plotting of the treason
II. Lines 703–2608 (c. 1900 lines) The battle of Rencesvals (including Roland's

death and the pursuit of Marsile's forces)

III. Lines 2609–3704 (c. 1100 lines) The episode of Baligant

IV. Lines 3705–4002 (c. 300 lines) The trial of Guenes

The most notable exponent of a five-part structure is Fern Farnham, who "would set the death of Roland aside as a pivotal episode around which the other themes rest significantly" (Duggan, *"The Song of Roland,"* 168). See Farnham's article "Romanesque Design in the *Chanson de Roland"* (*Romance Philology* 18 [1964]:143–64) in which, according to Duggan's summary, she "imaginatively compares the poem's structure to the five-part recessed panel arrangement of the tympanum at Moissac and other similar Romanesque sculptural representations. The death of Roland holds the central position in her scheme, flanked symmetrically by, on the one hand, the battle of Roncevaux and Ganelon's plotting, and, on the other, 'Baligant' (including Charlemagne's initial defeat of Marsile's forces) and Ganelon's trial" (Duggan, *"The Song of Roland,"* 63).

KAREN S. NICHOLAS

8 When Feudal Ideals Failed

Conflicts Between Lords and Vassals
in the Low Countries, 1127–1296

⎯⎯⎯⎯⎯⎯⎯⎯⎯⎯⎯⎯⎯⎯⎯⎯⎯⎯⎯⎯⎯⎯ ✦

EUDAL IDEALS demanded of the vassal an unquestioning, unswerving loyalty to his lord, which could not be renounced unless the lord caused his vassal grievous personal harm. In the chanson de geste, Bernier, vassal of Raoul de Cambrai, suffers repeated mistreatment from his lord, but does not renounce his loyalty until Raoul strikes him.[1] In the *Roman de Gilles de Chin*, a summons from his lord arrives when the chivalric hero is in his bath. He rises at once, telling his wife that it would be villainy and felony not to obey immediately, even though he must depart only half-washed.[2] The extremities of vassalic devotion are expressed in the *Doon de Mayence:*

> If my lord is slain, I want to be killed,
> And if he is hanged, hang me with him.
> If he goes to the stake, I want to be burned,
> And if he is drowned, throw me in with him.[3]

This ethos of the warrior freely giving devoted loyalty and service to his chief emerged in an expanding Germanic society, in which the interests of chief and warriors generally coincided and a common front was needed against external foes. In the High Middle Ages, however, the interests of princes and their vassals often diverged. Indeed, it was largely at the expense of the nobility that kings and princes consolidated their power. Princes could make use of public authority and eventually of an emerging money economy more effectively than the nobles who were their vassals. Thus the balance of power was moving against the nobility, and it was inevitable that some of the most prominent nobles would try to fight back.

In the historical sources for the Low Countries in the High Middle Ages, ordinary deeds of loyalty generally go unrecorded, while extraordinary acts of treachery are denounced by chronicles that resonate with ecclesiastical and princely indignation. Consider, for example, the question that rings out from the pages of Walter of Thérouanne: "Whom did you slay, and why, and when, and where, and how, you most evil Borsiard?" Walter answers his own questions: "Your lord, because of his concern for justice, in Lent, in church, and in violation of the reverence due him."[4] Chronicles and charters show that Low Country vassals perpetrated disloyalty in various forms, treason, and even murder. This present inquiry is bounded by two murders of a prince by his vassals: the murder of Charles the Good, count of Flanders, in 1127, to which Walter of Thérouanne refers, and the murder of Count Floris V of Holland in 1296.

What conditions or situations created conflicts between lords and vassals in the Low Countries? The most frequent cause of such conflict was failure of the lord or vassal to fulfill the obligations imposed by the feudal relationship. Vassalic failures were often promoted by the existence of multiple homages, in which vassals owed fidelity and service to several lords, while their obligations to each lord, especially in cases of conflicts among the lords, were often not defined precisely enough. Some vassals who had several lords stipulated in a charter exactly how they would behave if their lords went to war against each other. Often they declared that they would remain neutral in any conflict among their lords, but occasionally they made other arrangements, such as sending a certain amount of knight-service to each lord or promising to aid each lord in defending his own lands against attack by any of the other lords.[5] Lords might not be willing to accept these limitations of vassalic service, however, so that many vassals whose lords came into conflict were unable to fulfill their obligations to all of their lords. The honorable course was for such vassals to resign the fiefs held of lords whom they were unable to support, as several French vassals of Guy of Dampierre, count of Flanders, did in

1296–97.[6] For vassals who did not wish to deprive themselves of a considerable portion of their livelihood, the only alternative was treason against any lord for whom the vassal could not perform the services owed.

Complications also arose when vassals sought to cover over their naked usurpations of their lords' lands by proclaiming that they held these lands in fief, or when lords sought to justify their illegal seizures of their vassals' lands by calling them escheats. It was possible, however, for vassal and lord to settle their differences within the framework of feudal law. Feudal custom provided a wide variety of legal sanctions to be used by lords against disobedient or disloyal vassals, while allowing vassals to seek redress for their lords' injuries by judicial process or by war.

A special situation arose when a vassal's fief lay along the border between two principalities. Border vassals might attempt to preserve their independence by playing their lords against each other, as the nobles of Zeeland did with the counts of Flanders and Holland. When a border vassal held the great majority of his fiefs from one prince rather than the other, there was generally less confusion about where his stronger loyalty should lie. For example, in 1184 Lord Raas of Gavere, whose most important fiefs were held of the count of Flanders, joined the Flemish army in invading the lands of the count of Hainaut, who was also his liege lord. Because the lord of Gavere was recognized as more a vassal of Flanders than of Hainaut, Count Baldwin V of Hainaut apparently did not punish him for his disloyalty.[7]

The counts of Hainaut were not as lenient, however, with border vassals clearly owing paramount loyalty to them, but trying to escape comital authority by obtaining the protection of other princes. During the reign of Count Baldwin IV (1125–1171), Hugh, lord of Enghien, a vassal whose lands lay along the border between Hainaut and Brabant, built a castle on land held in fief of Hainaut and brought it in *fief de reprise* to Godfrey, duke of Brabant. During the reign of Count Baldwin V (1171–1195), dukes Godfrey and Henry I frequently used the castle of Enghien to the detriment of the count of Hainaut. After an unsuccessful attempt to besiege the castle in 1191, Baldwin V finally captured and destroyed the castle of Enghien in 1194.[8]

Low Country princes tried to stabilize border areas when possible. In 1176 Baldwin V of Hainaut and his brother-in-law Philip, count of

Flanders, made a treaty specifying that neither prince would build fortifications in the border area (*marcha*) and that no other fortifications would be constructed without the consent of both princes. They promised not to retain each other's men or shelter each other's fugitives, and to allow no men of their land to attack the other prince.[9] Powerful princes such as the counts of Flanders and Hainaut could do much to stabilize their borders and to control their vassals. Often, however, a treaty or truce was not possible in a society in which war was the normal state of affairs.

Even the counts of Flanders had problems with border vassals. When Baldwin V of Hainaut succeeded his brother-in-law Philip as Count Baldwin VIII of Flanders in 1191, several nobles of maritime Flanders, encouraged by Count Dirk VII of Holland, rebelled against the new count of Flanders.[10] On the southern border of Flanders during the late thirteenth century, Lord John of Oudenaarde tried to use the protection of his lord, the count of Hainaut, to become more independent of his primary lord, the count of Flanders. In 1280, John brought to the count of Hainaut in fief de reprise the villages and castles of Flobecq and Lessines. Guy, count of Flanders, who was John's first and most important lord, contested the grant and declared war on John. Because John then needed the protection of the count of Hainaut in order to keep possession of Flobecq and Lessines, he secured this protection by ceding half of these lands to the count. Finally, in 1298 John resigned all of Flobecq and Lessines to the count of Hainaut in exchange for the fief of Feignies, which he had previously sold to the count.[11]

Just as the counts of Flanders had frequent difficulties in subduing the men of maritime Flanders, so the counts of Holland faced frequent rebellions from the men of Zeeland, on the southern (Flemish) border of their principality. The most noteworthy crisis between the counts of Holland and the men of Zeeland occurred in 1290, when the men of Zeeland objected strongly to some of the clauses in Count Floris V's ordinances for Zeeland, promulgated earlier that year, because they felt that their rights were being infringed upon. Consequently, about forty vassals from Zeeland, including the lords of Borselen, Brederode, Cruiningen, and Renesse, renounced their homages to Floris V and brought their lands in Zeeland in fief de reprise to Guy, count of Flanders. Guy awarded generous income fiefs to the lords of

Zeeland, probably partly in compensation for the temporary loss of most of their lands, which had been overrun by Floris V in retaliation for their defiance. Finally Floris agreed to allow Guy, with his son Robert and with John I of Brabant, to arbitrate between himself and the Zeelanders. The arbiters were able to reach an acceptable compromise over the controversial clauses and declared that all vassals in Zeeland should hold their fiefs under the same conditions as before the war.[12]

One of the most celebrated cases of Low Country border vassalage caused the War of the Cow of Ciney,[13] which broke out in 1275 between Jean d'Enghien, bishop of Liège, and Guy of Dampierre, count of Namur and Flanders, and his Luxembourg allies. The war received its picturesque name from contemporaries, who thought that it was caused by the theft of a cow, which was instead one of its first incidents. The real cause of the war was a disputed question of feudal law. In 1271, John, lord of Goesnes, a vassal of the bishop of Liège, brought the seigneurie of Goesnes in fief de reprise to Guy, count of Namur. Since the seigneurie of Goesnes was already a fief of the bishop of Liège, this act was of questionable legality, and indeed Bishop Jean d'Enghien later proclaimed it illegal. In addition, part of the seigneurie was assigned to John's wife as dowry, and John did not secure her permission for this new homage, as was necessary, before offering the land in fief de reprise.

When John died soon after in 1273, his brother Rigaud of Beaufort bought the seigneurie of Goesnes from John's testamentary executors. Rigaud did homage and received investiture of the fief first from the bishop of Liège and subsequently from the count of Namur. In the same year he ceded the land to his son Rigaud, who in turn ceded it to his brother Nicholas. Each in turn did homage to the count of Namur. Henry of Guelders, bishop of Liège, immediately protested the illegality of these homages to the count of Namur and proceeded to occupy the seigneurie of Goesnes. When Bishop Henry was deposed the next year, his vassals were able to return. They subsequently assaulted and killed the mayor and one of the échevins of Ciney. Fearing retaliation from the new bishop, Jean d'Enghien, they sought the protection of Guy, count of Namur. Although Guy sent them a few men, they were not able to prevent the bishop's marshal from seizing and burning the manor of Goesnes. Count Guy complained that these acts infringed upon his rights as feudal lord. Bishop Jean refused to make reparation and proposed arbitration instead; Guy of Namur refused.

The war took the form of sporadic violence and pillage, with Namur-Flanders in alliance with Luxembourg and occasionally Brabant against Liège. The war lasted for three years and wrought much destruction within the bishopric of Liège. In 1278 the princes submitted their differences to King Philip III of France, who helped Count Guy and Bishop Jean to choose five arbiters to resolve the conflict. There is no record of a final settlement, but it is likely that the decision favored Namur, for the seigneurie of Goesnes in the fourteenth century was considered a Namurois fief and part of the county of Namur.

Border vassalage was extremely troublesome for ecclesiastical princes, whose territory was acquired piecemeal, through grants and donations, and whose borders hence were not natural or easily defensible. Episcopal vassals took advantage of any momentary weakness: an interregnum, a disputed election, or an ailing or ineffectual bishop. During a long, disputed election at Cambrai in the early 1130s, certain knights and even some peasants occupied and held episcopal villages, woods, waters, and fields. Some even dared to sell the land which they had taken. For Bishop Burchard II to regain possession of these lands, lengthy lawsuits were often necessary.[14]

The baron Gerard Malfilastre was particularly well known for his rebellions against Bishops Liétard and Nicholas of Cambrai. He had a history of kidnapping the bishop's men and oppressing the peasants. In 1133 Gerard gathered an army of knights and took Château-Cambrésis by fire and force. Over one hundred people and five churches were burned in the siege. Gerard took possession of all goods attached to the castle. Bishop Liétard said that he would not absolve Gerard until he restored the five burned churches and paid a huge fine, assessed at five shillings per knight and twenty pence for each foot soldier who participated. Many offenders refused to pay, which made the citizens of Cambrai extremely angry at the bishop's inability to enforce his penalty.[15]

When Bishop Liétard died and Bishop Nicholas succeeded in 1135–36, Gerard, not wanting to do homage to the new bishop, tried to hold his land and castle as if they were allods and erected a tower on his house for defense against the bishop. He then proceeded to seize some of the bishop's men, animals, and revenues. The bishop was powerless to make reprisals until one day, by chance, he captured Gerard. Although the burghers of Cambrai clamored for Gerard's death, characterizing him as the worst possible felon, the bishop was much more merciful. He set Gerard free on condition that he return all goods stolen from the bishop, do liege homage, and deliver to the bishop many hostages.[16]

War broke out again in 1137 after members of Gerard's household stole four of the bishop's oxen. Gerard refused to pay for them or even to listen to the bishop's message. He threatened to capture Neufchâtel without a formal renunciation of homage (*diffidatio*) in advance, as was customary. The war involved much carnage and destruction of property on both sides. By chance Gerard fell into a trap laid for game outside Neufchâtel, an event which the bishop's chronicler regarded as an act of divine intervention, for the war ended with no further casualties or captures. The bishop's men, against their lord's wishes, hanged Gerard in the castle and threw stones at his body. The bishop returned the excommunicated corpse to Gerard's men, who "grieved greatly, wept, and glorified their lord." Bishop Nicholas personally regretted Gerard's death, as he would rather have kept Gerard alive as a captive and thus assured a continuing peace. Baldwin IV of Hainaut and other nobles complained to the bishop about Gerard's murder, but all of Gerard's supporters made peace with the bishop. Two of Gerard's vassals returned the castle of Saint-Aubert to Bishop Nicholas.[17]

Further conflict ensued when Bishop Nicholas promised to give the castle of Saint Aubert to Simon d'Oisy, castellan of Cambrai, the bishop's relative and vassal. The bishop's counselors advised against increasing the power of Simon, who already had control of five castles, and the townspeople of Cambrai agreed. Bishop Nicholas was uncertain of what to do: whether to break faith with Simon and offend God, or to offend the citizens of the city. In the end he gave the castle to Simon. Baldwin IV of Hainaut came to besiege it and allied with the townspeople, who burned Simon's house and caused the bishop to flee the city. At this point Philip of Alsace, count of Flanders, intervened at Bishop Nicholas's request to restore order and secure episcopal property. Bishop Nicholas was reluctant to proceed against Simon, even to restore order, but Count Philip occupied the castellany of Cambrai, including Oisy, and took a total of eight castles from the bishop's control. He restored Gerard's ancestral lands to Gerard's son and allowed Simon to hold Oisy and the castellany of Cambrai on condition that these become a Flemish fief and Simon a Flemish vassal. Thus Cambrésis effectively became a Flemish protectorate, and the bishop's vassals caused little further disturbance.[18]

The bishops with jurisdiction over Flemish territory could rely, in return for profitable privileges, on the support of the counts of Flanders against their turbulent vassals. In Lotharingia this protection was traditionally supplied by the German emperors. When after the Concordat of Worms the emperors could no longer control the nomination of bishops, they gradually withdrew the imperial mantle of protection from the bishoprics. This withdrawal of support was detrimental to the bishops of Liège, as can be seen in the War of the Cow of Ciney, but it was catastrophic for the bishops of Utrecht, who were weaker and less able than the bishops of Liège to prevent vassalic usurpations. The bishops of Utrecht were feudal lords of the princes whose lands lay on their borders. These princes, however, often succeeded in having one of their younger sons elected bishop of Utrecht. These cadets frequently favored their families at the expense of episcopal rights and property. The counts of Holland, according to the chronicler of the bishops of Utrecht, were like sties in the eyes and lances in the sides of the church of Utrecht. In the course of a war between Count Dirk VII of Holland and his brother William, the count captured Bishop Dirk of Utrecht, who later escaped. For this enormity the count came before the bishop barefoot and clad in a simple woolen garment and humiliated himself at the feet of the bishop, who granted him forgiveness.[19]

Powerful relatives of the bishops sometimes promoted conflicts with episcopal vassals. The brother of Bishop Baldwin of Utrecht, Otto, count of Bentheim, encroached upon Koevorden with exactions and eventually besieged the castle. The castellan of Koevorden had died, but his widow's stepfather Floris and her brother Volker vigorously defended the castle. The widow's brother Rudolf, however, blockaded Koevorden's supply lines, forcing Floris to surrender the castle and his stepson Volker to the bishop, who held the castle nine years and imprisoned Volker in chains in the castle at Horst. While in prison, Volker seduced and married the daughter of a rich knight, Albert Leo. Friends influenced the bishop to absolve him and allow him to return to his ancestral lands at Enschede. Since Bishop Baldwin refused to return the castle of Koevorden to the castellan's family, his relatives later made war against the episcopal castle at Groningen. Later there was also a conflict which escalated into war about the wardship of the heir of Rudolf, brother of the castellan's widow. Relatives wanted the wardship to go to Rudolf's brother Hecbert, but the bishop chose an unrelated man more loyal to him. The war caused the destruction of episcopal property throughout Drente.[20]

It was generally the most powerful nobles who were strong enough to dispute the might of a prince. The highest nobles especially resented princely consolidation and exercise of authority, which often occurred at their expense. An instructive example is the relationship during the twelfth century of the counts of Hainaut with their rebellious vassals, the Lords of Avesnes. The chronicler Gilbert of Mons, biographer and partisan of Baldwin V of Hainaut, describes the lords of Avesnes as *contrarii et rebelles* to the counts of Hainaut. In the early twelfth century Lord Gossuin d'Avesnes built a tower at Avesnes against the express prohibition of Count Baldwin III of Hainaut. Count Baldwin attacked Gossuin in battle, took him as a captive back to Mons, and ordered that his beard be cut off. This humiliation was apparently considered sufficient punishment, for Gossuin returned to the count's favor and was allowed to keep his tower.[21] A generation later, when Lord Gautier d'Avesnes and his men robbed and damaged the church at Liessies, Count Baldwin IV of Hainaut brought his men to protect the church and built a tower, which infuriated Gautier, who later tore it down. Then Gautier moved in earnest against the church, expelling its monks. Baldwin IV summoned Gautier to appear before the count at Mons and account for his misdeeds. The judgment went against Gautier, who indignantly claimed that his peers on the court were guilty of lies and false judgment. He withdrew angrily to another room, where he lay down and died of a stroke, presumably the result of rage. His son Nicholas refused to restore anything to the monks. Thus Gautier, in death, prevented a permanent resolution of the quarrel.[22]

It is Jacques d'Avesnes, son of Nicholas, whom the chronicler Gilbert of Mons castigates so severely for his many treasonable acts against Baldwin V of Hainaut. Gilbert relates that in 1173 Lord Jacques took advantage of the temporary absence of Count Baldwin to demand of Baldwin's regent, Countess Margaret, that the construction

FIGURE 9. Knights looting a house. B.L., MS Royal 20 c. VII, fol. 41v. Courtesy of the British Library.

of a comital castle at Beaufort be halted because it infringed upon his rights. When the countess asserted that building the castle was within the count's rights and that she would continue what her husband had begun, Jacques withdrew from her presence and renounced his homage to her. After the countess had gathered an army to proceed against the lord of Avesnes, Count Baldwin returned home unexpectedly early and hastened to lead the campaign, which caused Jacques to make his peace with him.[23]

The next year, while the bishop of Cambrai was traveling through Hainaut under Count Baldwin's safe-conduct, several of Jacques d'Avesnes's men murdered him at Condé. At this breach of safe-conduct and of the law of the land, Count Baldwin burned the village of Condé and took the castle there by siege, returning it on condition that Jacques would subsequently surrender the castle to the count on demand. Count Philip of Flanders, who was also Jacques's lord and a friend and patron of the murdered bishop, demanded that Jacques give back to him two castles. When in 1175 Count Baldwin asked Lord Jacques to hand over that castle of Condé according to their agreement, Jacques first tried various evasions and then refused to do so. When Baldwin marched against him with an army, Jacques sought the count's pardon and offered to render him the castle. Baldwin then destroyed the castle of Condé and proceeded to help Count Philip of Flanders gain possession of the two desired castles. Jacques, fearing reprisals against his other castles held in fief of Hainaut, astutely placed them under Baldwin's protection, for Count Baldwin as lord might do no harm to a vassal's fiefs committed to his care.[24]

In 1184 Lord Jacques acted against Count Baldwin's interests in promoting war between Hainaut and Flanders. Baldwin, seeking to prevent Jacques's defection in the coming war, demanded and received promises that Jacques would hand over to Baldwin all his castles held in fief of Hainaut and return his castles held of Flanders for the duration of the war. Within forty days Jacques had joined the Flemish army in an invasion of Hainaut. Instead of renouncing his homage to the count before proceeding against him, as was the custom, he invaded Hainaut by force of arms on the very same day that he proclaimed his diffidatio. After the invading army was forced to retreat because of famine, Baldwin marched upon the lands of Jacques d'Avesnes and burned seventy-two villages. Jacques offered to prove that he was justified in renouncing his homage to Baldwin by fighting in judicial duel any knight of Baldwin's choice. After many knights had volunteered to fight Jacques, and Baldwin was about to name a time and place for the duel, Jacques refused to fight and retreated under the protection of the count of Flanders. Baldwin retaliated by burning 110 villages on Jacques's lands and by devastating the seigneurie of Avesnes. With a final truce in 1185, all hostilities ceased.[25]

Gilbert of Mons, a strong partisan of Baldwin V, can scarcely find words of condemnation strong enough for the treachery of Jacques d'Avesnes. Throughout his long chronicle the only good words he has for Lord Jacques concern his ability as a knight and his meritorious death on the Third Crusade.[26] Gilbert's account, however, shows that Baldwin was a harsh master who rewarded infidelity with extreme severity. It is not entirely surprising that vassals who had committed acts of infidelity or treachery against him sought strong protection against his wrath. Our sources portray vividly the anger of Count Baldwin; we are left to imagine the indignation of lords like Jacques, whose privileges were being curtailed by the extension of the prince's justice and the prince's peace. The house of Avesnes would enjoy better fortune in the thirteenth century, when Bouchard d'Avesnes, as bailiff of Hainaut, received custody of Margaret, soon to inherit Hainaut, and married her, thus establishing a comital house of Avesnes in Hainaut.

Sometimes disputes between lords and vassals, arising either from conflicting multiple homages or from other causes, could not be settled peaceably, and resulted in the dissolution of the feudal relationship by the lord or the vassal. Throughout Western Europe, from about 1100, it was common for a lord or a vassal to dissolve the bond of homage between them by a formal act, called in the sources *exfestucatio* or *diffidatio*, in which the renunciation was symbolized by breaking or casting away a *festuca* (a rod, stalk, or wand). It was this act, rather than any preceding injury, denial of justice, or treasonable act, that dissolved the feudal relationship. Traditionally, the exfestucatio was a formal ceremony in which the lord and vassal confronted each other face to face. Actually, especially if war was impending, it was frequently impossible for such direct confrontation to take place. Sometimes the party wishing to dissolve the feudal bond performed the exfestucatio by proxy. Sometimes it was not performed at all. As the use of writing to commemorate all important acts became increasingly widespread, the formal ceremony of exfestucatio was abandoned in favor of written declarations of renunciation of homage. Consequently, Marc Bloch, who made a formal study of this ceremony, found no example of it after 1230.[27]

There is considerable evidence of the practice of exfestucatio or diffidatio in the Low Countries. Bloch cites the detailed descriptions of this ceremony given by Galbert of Bruges.[28] The first incident described by Galbert occurred when castellan Hacket, besieged in the castle of Bruges, offered with his relatives and vassals to prove their innocence in the murder of Count Charles the Good. Walter, one of the knights besieging the castle, replied that the besiegers owed nothing to the besieged, who had prevented proper burial of the count, had shared the count's treasure with the guilty, and were holding the castle unjustly; and as they had acted lawlessly and faithlessly, the besiegers renounced any faith or loyalty previously owed to them. "The whole crowd of the siege was present at this parley," Galbert relates, "and immediately after this reply, they seized rods and cast away their homage, breaking their faith and loyalty to the besieged."[29]

Later, after William Clito was chosen count, the townsmen of Ghent called Count William to a reckoning. Their spokesman Ivan of Aalst, a peer of Flanders, accused the count of breaking faith with the townsmen by not keeping the oaths that he swore to them, and of acting illegally and with hostility toward them. They asked the count to summon the court of the peers of Flanders to judge whether or not the count had acted lawlessly and faithlessly, and if so, William should resign the countship and allow the court to choose someone else as count. "Then," Galbert continues, "the count leapt forward and would have thrown back the festuca to Ivan, if he had dared to do so in the midst of the tumultuous crowd of citizens, and said: 'I wish, then, to make myself your equal by rejecting the homage you have done to me, and to challenge you without delay to combat, because as count I have thus far acted reasonably and rightly in every way.' But Ivan refused." They agreed instead to settle their differences peaceably at Ypres. Count William, however, filled the town in advance with mercenaries and knights, ready for fighting. When Ivan and Daniel of Dendermonde heard about this, they stopped at Roeselaere and sent messages to the count saying: " 'Lord Count! Because the day was fixed in the holy time of fasting, when you should have come reasonably, in peace, and not with evil intent, in arms, and you have not done so but on the contrary are getting ready to fight against your vassals, Ivan and Daniel and the men of Ghent send word to you that they will no longer delay in rejecting through us the homage, which they have up to now maintained inviolably towards you, because you now come craftily to kill them.' And the messengers proceeded to throw away the *festuca* in the name of their lords and departed." Six weeks later the knights from Oostkerke, inscribing their names on parchment, sent a message on behalf of themselves and many others to Count William, renouncing the fidelity and homage which they had once pledged to him.[30]

Although the exfestucatio of a lord by a vassal was much more common than that of a vassal by a lord, the chronicler Walter of Thérouanne, who like Galbert relates the events following the murder of Count Charles the Good, provides us with another example of a lord who delivered his diffidatio to a vassal. According to Walter's account, after the murder of the count, Bertulf, provost of Saint Donatien at Bruges and head conspirator, fled to the home of Alard of Waesten, vassal of William of Ypres. When William heard rumors of this, he went to Alard's house and searched for the provost. Not finding him, he became angry and burned down the house. Then William renounced Alard's homage, proclaimed his diffidatio, and proceeded to seize all of his fiefs.[31] Thus the lord, without absolute proof of his vassal's treason, committed violence against him, dissolved the feudal relationship between them, and confiscated his fiefs.

Lambert of Waterlos, the chronicler of twelfth-century Cambrésis, tells that in 1157 Thierry of Alsace, count of Flanders, called all his vassals and some other men to a council at Artois. Bishop Nicholas of Cambrai, however, did not attend. When Simon d'Oisy, castellan of Cambrai, was summoned, he refused to come, and breaking the treaty between the count and himself, renounced his homage to him. "Thus," declares the chronicler, "he revealed openly the evil in his heart." On the same day Gerard, provost of Douai, also renounced his homage to the count. Thierry sent his son Philip with some of his knights on an expedition against his two defiant vassals, but Philip's contingent, though perpetrating much destruction and pillage, accomplished no decisive results.[32]

Gilbert of Mons also sheds some light on the practice of diffidatio in the Low Countries. As discussed earlier in this chapter, Jacques d'Avesnes proclaimed his diffidatio twice, once in 1173, during the absence of the count, to Countess Margaret, and once in 1184, when he announced his diffidatio to Count Baldwin V and on the very same day proceeded to mount an armed invasion of the count's lands. Vanderkindere notes in connection with the latter incident that it was customary to allow at least a week or two to pass between announcement of the diffidatio and the opening of hostilities.[33]

In the late thirteenth century there were still many cases of renunciation of homage, although this act was ordinarily carried out in writing rather than by a formal ceremony of exfestucatio. In 1280 Arnold, lord of Ijsselstein, wrote to the advocates of the cathedral at Utrecht, declaring that as they had first announced their diffidatio to him and then entered his lands by force of arms and devastated them, he therefore resigned his fiefs held of the Utrecht cathedral chapter. In 1296, following the murder of Floris V of Holland by the lords of Amstel and Woerden, Giselbert of Ijsselstein (probably the son of Arnold above) sent his diffidatio as vassal to the lord of Amstel and requested his overlord, the new count of Holland, to protect him in the possession of his fiefs. The count of Cleves promised to intervene on his behalf and procure a letter (promising protection) from the count of Holland when he should arrive from England.[34]

Finally, a large number of renunciations of homage were provoked by the imminence of a French invasion of Flanders in 1296–1297. Guy of Dampierre, count of Flanders, had many French vassals, whom war between Flanders and France had placed in an impossible position, but who elected to resolve the problem honorably by renouncing their homage to Guy in advance. Among the vassals who chose this course were the count of Dreux and the lords of Cauny, Fontaines, Harcourt, Harnes, and Matringem.[35] In 1297 Guy himself sent his diffidatio to Philip the Fair, listing in detail his grievances against the king.[36]

Conflicts between lords and vassals could be settled by formal or informal arbitration, by legal judgment, or by war. Following a diffidatio by either lord or vassal, war was the usual result. Wars between lords and vassals might take the form of pitched battles or systematic sieges of the enemy's castles, but more often consisted of sporadic pillage and devastation of the enemy's lands. The medieval predilection for war was such that sometimes outsiders cheerfully entered the fray, either on behalf of one of the combatants or purely for their own advantage. For example, in 1178 Bishop Baldwin of Utrecht, feeling confident in the support of his brothers the counts of Holland and Bentheim and his brother-in-law the count of Cleves, seized the pretext that the count of Guelders had not received his fief formally and legally from the duke of Brabant (who in turn held it of the emperor) to declare that as a result, the position of lord of Veluwe was vacant. He then proceeded to devastate the area. Finally the emperor Frederick Barbarossa intervened and settled the quarrel by seeing that the duke and the count each in turn did homage and received proper investiture of the fief.[37]

Lords who overcame their vassals in battle usually meted out such punishments as confiscation of all or part of a vassal's fiefs, compulsory fief de reprise, payment of an indemnity, or homage of atonement. The homage of atonement imposed by a prince could be either a strengthening or amplification of a previously existing homage, or the creation of a new feudal relationship. As an example of the latter, around 1198 John archbishop of Trier conquered the castles of Starkenburg and Ham from the count of Sponheim and the castles of Dollendorf and Gerland from the count of Vianden, and returned the castles to the counts on the condition that they hold them in fief.[38] In 1298 Henry "the Pirate," castellan of Montfoort (and former bishop of Liège), when captured in battle by John I of Brabant, became reconciled to him and became his vassal on the very field where he was taken. He promised to give advice and perform military service against all but the bishop of Utrecht, on pain of forfeiture of all his property.[39]

The cases of strengthening a previously existing homage by homage of atonement are legion. In 1202 Duke Henry I of Brabant captured the counts of Holland and Guelders in battle. As the duke had gone to war originally because Count Otto of Guelders had not performed the military service he owed the duke as liegeman, Duke John agreed to peace on condition that Otto pay an indemnity of 2,050 marks and that if he did not fulfill his feudal obligation, he must freely resign his fiefs to the duke. Otto promised further to serve the duke faithfully as his liegeman and to see that the count of Holland did no further damage to the duke. Otto did not keep his promise, for some of his own vassals, with the count of Holland, burned Tiel and Orten and captured some of the duke's men. As a result, his peers as vassals of Brabant sentenced him to forfeiture of his fiefs. Otto, however, made good the duke's losses, and Henry restored to him his fiefs.[40]

Finally, in 1298 Otto, lord of Buren, and his son Alard, because of excesses previously committed against Count Renaud of Guelders, did homage to him and brought in fief de reprise their castle at Buren. The castle was to be an open house for the count of Guelders in war, for his use and protection. If the count did not want to occupy the castle in war, the lord of Buren must serve him with it at his own expense.[41]

There were also many cases in which Low Country lords confiscated their vassals' fiefs. In 1198, Dirk VII of Holland made donation of land near Maelwijk, which he had confiscated from John Nagel.[42] In 1213 Henry I of Brabant enfeoffed Godfrey lord of Breda with half of the toll rights on the Scheldt and one of its tributaries. These toll rights had previously been confiscated from the vassals who held them, by judgment of their peers, "because of the insolence and violence which they inflicted upon passersby." Similarly, Henry enfeoffed Godfrey with Schakerslo, which other vassals had forfeited "because of the injuries and violence which they had inflicted upon men, on land and sea."[43]

In 1244 the count and countess of Flanders confiscated the lands of Crèvecoeur and Arleux, because of Matthew of Montmirail's damages to them.[44] In 1265 Countess Margaret, who had seized goods which Henry, count of Luxembourg, held in fief of Flanders, because of rights claimed to them by Waleran, lord of Montjoie and Marville, restored them to Count Henry.[45] Also within the county of Flanders, in 1277 the lady Mainses de Makembiecke complained to the executors of Roger of Mortagne that when her relatives killed one of their enemies, breaking a truce, she was called into the court of the lady of Courtrai. Finding no one to defend her, she was condemned and banished, and her fief of three *bonniers* held of Roger of Mortagne was seized, including her barn with the wheat inside. She demanded justice, as Roger had confiscated her fief without a court decision declaring it forfeit.[46] Unfortunately, there is no record of the final result of this complaint.

There are three interesting sentences promulgated by Low Country lords on the subject of confiscation. In 1281, Floris V of Holland confirmed the sentence of Hemerand of Riderweert (who was presumably his vassal) that if anyone abandoned the dikes when they ought to work on them, those dikes should henceforth belong to the lord from whom they were originally held.[47] This judgment undoubtedly improved the maintenance of the dikes, which was of vital importance in the county of Holland, but also reinforced seigneurial and princely authority. In 1295, Adolf of Nassau, king of the Romans, promulgated a sentence that if a vassal used armed force against his lord, he had to submit to the sentence of his peers against him.[48] King Adolf, of course, was powerless to enforce submission to his decree throughout the Low Countries. His sentence, however, is interesting as a reflection of princely attitudes toward miscreant vassals. The sentence of a court of peers against such a vassal would probably be forfeiture of fiefs. In the same year Herman, lord of Woerden, asserted as part of a legal judgment that the right of a vassal, who occupies his land and has undisputed title over it, to keep his land takes precedence over the right of the lord of the land to dispossess his vassal with his own men.[49] That is to say, in legal terminology, that vassalic tenure takes precedence over eminent domain. As we have seen, this did not always occur in practice, although occupation of the land gave the tenant a definite strategic advantage.

A case from the county of Holland shows an unusual sanction which might be applied to a disobedient vassal. In 1290, William, lord of Strijen, promised to serve the count of Holland in all ways that the lords of Borselen and Arkel had to serve the count, on penalty of £1,000. The charter stipulated that the count had the right to seize William's lands, if he failed to fulfill his obligations, until he collected £1,000 in revenues from them.[50] This is the first time in the Low Countries that distraint of land is prescribed by charter as a legal sanction against a disloyal vassal.

Vassals and lords might settle their differences not only by war, but also by legal judgment or by formal or informal arbitration. Many quarrels were settled by arbitration, including such important issues as the struggle between Avesnes and Dampierre, which divided Hainaut from Flanders and which was settled by the judgment of Louis IX of France in 1246.[51] Many other quarrels between lords and vassals were settled by legal judgment. The *Gesta Abbatum Trudonensium* lists literally dozens of usurpations by vassals of monastic lands and revenues, which were restored to the monastery of Saint Trond during the twelfth century by judgment of the court of peers of the monastery.[52]

Vassals who felt that they had been wronged by their lords might appeal to their overlords or to someone else of great prestige or authority. In 1287, Gerard of Oudenaarde, clerk of Guy of Dampierre, declared that the emperor Rudolf had confiscated Guy's imperial fiefs of Aalst, Waas, Grammont, and the *Quatre Métiers* and had proscribed the barons, nobles, other vassals, échevins, and mayors who took the count's part in these places. As the count had not been warned in advance, Guy declared the judgment unjust, and thus null and void. He appealed to the pope, sending Gerard to plead his case.[53]

Sometimes vassals entered into the homage of their overlords, either to escape the authority of their immediate lord, or because treason or injury by their immediate lord nullified their homage to him. We have seen examples of this already, as when the nobles of Zeeland renounced their homage to Floris V of Holland and did homage to Guy of Dampierre in 1290, and when the lord of Ijsselstein renounced his homage to the lord of Amstel as murderer of Floris V, and became a direct vassal of the new count of Holland.[54] Sometimes lords, wishing to ensure the loyalty of their vassals, demanded oaths of their rearvassals that they would not support their lord in disloyalty to their overlord, should their lord prove disloyal. In 1283, several vassals of the lord of Vianden promised Henry III of Luxembourg that if Henry released the lord of Vianden from prison, they would act as sureties for his good behavior. If he should not fulfill his obligations to the count, they would henceforth hold their fiefs directly of the count.[55]

Princes often relied for assistance in consolidating power within their principalities not upon the highest nobles, but upon lesser nobles and persons of even lower status. Most notable in the Low Countries for elevating servants (*ministeriales*) were the dukes of Brabant. Between 1227 and 1254, the dukes introduced into a nobility of thirty-odd existing families seven new ministerial families, and promoted the new nobles at the expense of the old ones.[56]

The powerful counts of Flanders in the twelfth century relied primarily upon the numerous Flemish nobility for support, but depended upon lesser servants as well. These men might rise through knightly or administrative service. Count Charles the Good of

Flanders (1119–1127), who had grown up in Denmark as a stranger
to the Flemish nobles, was more comfortable in relying on lesser
men. This favor encouraged the Erembald clan, who had risen to
power in ministerial positions in Flanders, to aspire to high positions
within the nobility. This displacement alienated the Flemish nobles,
so that while they did not act directly against the count, their lack of
lamentation at his death was noticeable, as were their ties to the
conspirators.[57]

Count Charles the Good was a prince more respected than loved.
His dreams were not of conquest and glory, but of peace and justice.
He was uncompromising in his attempts to assert comital rights in relation to the peasantry, the townspeople, and the nobility. He was especially active in curtailing the depredations of noble advocates
against the churches that they were supposed to protect. He burned
down the house of Borsiard, one of the Erembald clan, in retaliation
for unrestrained private pillaging. He sought to lay hands on all comital serfs, and showed immediate interest when a litigant in a judicial case asserted the Erembald clan was unfree. The Erembalds
claimed, on the contrary, that they were noble vassals of the count.
Count Charles hoped to establish that they were bound to him by ties
much more strict than vassalage. Seeing the count's intent as a dire
threat to their security, the Erembalds laid their plans and succeeded
in murdering Count Charles. Their plans were countenanced by a
number of discontented vassals who hoped to act as prince-makers
and to profit thereafter. In the end, however, few would shelter the
murderers of a prince, who eventually suffered capital punishment.[58]

Less well known outside the Low Countries than the murder of
Charles the Good is the murder of Floris V, count of Holland, in 1296.
It is interesting that both counts were conspired against by ministerial
families whose pretensions the princes were trying to depress. The
conspirators in Holland were the lords of Amstel and Woerden, who
had a long history of quarrels with Floris V, and whose ancestors
quarreled both with the counts of Holland and with their primary
lords, the bishops of Utrecht. In 1159, the ministeriales of Utrecht, including the lords of Amstel and Woerden, formed a sworn association
to protect their rights. With the help of Henry count of Guelders, they
fought against the bishop of Utrecht and besieged him in his tower,
but he managed to escape. The allies fortified the castle of Woerden

and from there they devastated the surrounding countryside. Finally peace was secured through the mediation of the archbishop of Cologne and by order of the emperor Frederick Barbarossa.[59] In 1169, Bishop Godfrey of Utrecht became reconciled to Egbert of Amstel on condition that he return to the bishop the lands he had appropriated as fiefs and receive them back as ministerial goods.[60] Bishop Godfrey thus insisted that Egbert recognize publicly that he was not the bishop's vassal, but his servant.

In 1232, Gilbert lord of Amstel granted to Count Floris IV of Holland and received back in fief his stone house at Utrecht. The fief was to be hereditary, and the house was to be open to the count upon demand.[61] This was an obvious affront to Gilbert's primary lord, the bishop of Utrecht. In 1257, Lord Gilbert made reparation to the bishop by paying an indemnity of £1000 and by appearing (with five hundred others) barefoot before the bishop and asking for his mercy.[62]

The powerful Count Floris V of Holland was determined to subjugate definitively the Amstels and the Woerdens. In 1285, Floris V and John bishop of Utrecht forced the Amstel brothers to agree to the following terms: they must yield all their allodial lands to the count and receive them back in fief; they must obtain letters from the counts of Guelders and Cleves, the duke of Brabant, and the bishop of Utrecht that these princes would never support them against the count of Holland; and they must provide a double set of sureties, all of whom would forfeit all feudal and allodial lands to the count of Holland if the Amstels did not observe the agreement.[63] In 1288, Herman, lord of Woerden, who had entered with his kinsmen the Amstels into rebellion against Floris V, sought reconciliation with the count. Floris declared that Herman must forfeit all fiefs within the bishopric of Utrecht, and Floris himself would henceforth hold them in fief of the bishop. Herman then had to bring all his lands, feudal and allodial, in *fief de reprise* of Floris, and had to procure letters from the duke of Brabant, the bishop of Utrecht, and the counts of Guelders and Cleves, promising that they would not aid him or his descendants in a war with the count of Holland. Herman then had to promise not to marry off his daughters without the count's consent. He had to open his castle at Woerden to the count of Holland upon demand, for use against anyone. If he should ever break this treaty, he was to forfeit all of his lands to the count of Holland. He was forced to provide a long list of sureties, whose lands would also be forfeit if he should break the treaty, and who must serve the count of Holland against Herman at their own expense, on land or ship, with a certain number of men specified for each surety in the charter.[64] Of all cases before 1300 of nonviolent reprisals by Low Country lords against their disloyal vassals, this is by far the most punitive settlement. Thus the magnitude of the grievances harbored by the Amstels and the Woerdens against Floris V is apparent.

Not surprisingly, the Amstels and Woerdens later decided, with a few others, to capture and depose Floris V and to replace him with his son John, with whom they hoped to exercise greater influence. Floris was duly isolated and captured; but when he attempted to escape, one of the conspirators, fearing reprisals if the count returned to power, killed him on the spot. The judgment against the conspirators was confiscation of property and exile from Holland; against the murderer, Gerard of Velsen, the sentence was death.[65]

In the Low Countries, vassals who brooded upon the misdeeds of their lords might commit treason or even murder. Vassals also employed less drastic means of contesting the power of their lords. They might formally renounce their homage, whether symbolically by verbal defiance and physical breaking of a rod or wand symbolizing the fief, or later, by the thirteenth century, in writing. Conflicts might be avoided by the resignation of fiefs or settled by arbitration. Arbitration was successful if lord and vassal were willing to accept the judgment of the arbiters. Judgment by a court of the vassal's peers usually carried a certain degree of finality, but it could be ineffectual if the lord lacked the power to enforce the court's judgment. The ultimate sanction, of course, was war, involving at the individual level a judicial duel between the two parties or their champions, or at the collective level a full-scale battle between the feudal hosts of the two parties, each with his allies. The results of the judicial duel were clear and usually definitive. Following a full-scale battle, the vanquished— often killed, wounded, or led from the battlefield in chains—was usually in no position to dispute the result, at least for the time being. Arbiters often settled disputes on the basis of the results of war. In wars between lord and vassal, when the lord was a prince with territorial as well as feudal authority, he usually had superior financial and military resources with which he could overcome his vassal. Murderers of princes were usually executed. Conquered vassals might, depending upon the seriousness of their offenses, be exiled, imprisoned, or subjected to confiscation of fiefs, fines, compulsory fief de reprise, or homage of atonement. Thus, offenses against the property of a lord might prove occasionally profitable, but attacks upon the person of a lord resulted in extremely severe punishment.

Despite the many conflicts between lords and vassals in the Low Countries, the feudal ideal of a vassal's loyalty and devotion to his lord did not disappear during the twelfth and thirteenth centuries. Instead, the personal bonds between lord and vassal declined in favor of a relationship increasingly bound by a written contract which specified the obligations of both lord and vassal. The emphasis in the charters is less upon personal relationships than upon the transmission of property. Thus the obligations surrounding the fief gradually became more important than the personal relationship between lord and vassal. By the end of the Middle Ages the personal element in the feudal relationship would virtually vanish, and the fief would become essentially a particular kind of land tenure governed by special laws, rather than an award granted to facilitate a vassal's personal service to his lord. Thus the personal bonds of lord and vassal were gradually supplanted by contractual, cash-nexus relationships, like those of fifteenth-century English lords with their liveried retainers.

Notes

1. The story of Raoul de Cambrai is related in English in *The History of Feudalism*, ed. David Herlihy (Atlantic Highlands, N.J.: Humanities Press, 1979), 131–77. The bond of the vassal to his lord was originally unique and effective for life, but intolerable offenses by the lord could cause his vassal to defy him, and by 1100, formalities had been developed for the renunciation of homage.

2. Gilles de Chin is quoted in N. Didier, *Le Droit des fiefs dans la coutume de Hainaut au moyen âge* (Paris: A. & J. Picard, 1945), 69 n. 43.

3. The *Doon de Mayence* is quoted in Marc Bloch, *Feudal Society*, 2 vols., trans. L. A. Manyon (Chicago: University of Chicago Press, 1961), 1:231–32. The English translation is mine.

4. Walter of Thérouanne, *Vita Karoli*, in *Monumenta Germaniae Historica, Scriptores*, 32 vols. (Hannover: Impensis Bibliopolii Hahniani, 1826–1934), 12:549 [hereafter cited as *MGH*].

5. Karen S. Nicholas, "Feudal Relationships in the Low Countries: A Comparative Study of Nine Principalities, 1000–1300" (Ph.D. diss., Brown University, 1972), 202–3.

6. Nicholas, "Feudal Relationships," 252–53.

7. Nicholas, "Feudal Relationships," 269.

8. Gilbert of Mons, *Chronicon Hanoniense*, ed. Léon Vanderkindere (Brussels: Librairie Kiessling, 1904), 91–92, 265, 290.

9. *De oorkonden der graven van Vlaanderen*, eds. Thérèse de Hemptinne and Adriaan Verhulst #428. Forthcoming.

10. Gilbert of Mons, *Chronicon*, 289–90, 295–98.

11. J. de Saint Genois, *Monuments anciens* (Paris & Lille, 1782), 1:388–91.

12. *Oorkondenboek van Holland en Zeeland*, 5 vols., ed. L. Ph. C. van den Bergh (The Hague, 1866–1873), 2:306, 313, 314, 316–22 [hereafter cited as *OBHZ*].

13. The ensuing discussion of the War of the Cow of Ciney was derived largely from the definitive study of E. Poncelet, "La Guerre dite 'de la Vache de Ciney,' " *Bulletin de la Commission Royale d'Histoire*, 62 (1893):275–395. J. Balon also discusses this war in "l'organisation judiciaire des marches féodales," *Annales de la Société Archéologique de Namur* 46 (1951):5–72. Balon supports the Beauforts' claim that the seigneurie of Goesnes was an allod which they were free to grant in *fief de reprise;* if this were true, however, why did Rigaud of Beaufort do homage first to the bishop of Liège, and only subsequently to the count of Namur?

14. *Gestes des Evêques de Cambrai, de 1092 à 1138*, ed. Ch. de Smedt (Paris, 1880), 157.

15. De Smedt, 162–66.

16. De Smedt, 178–83.

17. De Smedt, 188–202.

18. *Gesta Episcoporum Cameracensium, Continuationes, MGH, SS*, 7:507–10; de Smedt, 203–40.

19. *Gesta Episcoporum Traiectensium, MGH, SS*, 23:408.

20. *Gesta Episcoporum Traiectensium*, 404–5.

21. Gilbert of Mons, *Chronicon*, 35–36, 75–77.

22. *Chronicon Laetiense, MGH, SS*, 14:500–1. See also *Herinanni Liber de Restauratione Monasterii Sancti Martini Tornacensis, MGH, SS*, 299–300.

23. Gilbert of Mons, *Chronicon*, 113–14.

24. Gilbert of Mons, *Chronicon*, 115–16, 119–21.

25. Gilbert of Mons, *Chronicon*, 153–54, 169–79, 181–85.

26. Gilbert of Mons, *Chronicon*, 78, 273–74.

27. Marc Bloch, "Les formes de la rupture de l'hommage dans l'ancien droit féodal," in *Mélanges Historiques*, 2 vols. (Paris: S.E.V.P.E.N., 1963), 1:189–209.

28. Bloch, "Les formes de la rupture de l'hommage," 1:190–92. See Galbert of Bruges, *The Murder of Charles the Good*, ed. and trans. James Bruce Ross (Toronto: University of Toronto Press, 1982), 170–71, 269–70, 273, 277–78.

29. Galbert of Bruges, *Murder of Charles the Good*, 170–71.

30. Galbert of Bruges, *Murder*, 267–70, 278.

31. Walter of Thérouanne, *Vita Karoli*, 554.

32. Lambert of Waterlos, *Annales Cameracenses, MGH, SS*, 16:530–32.

33. Gilbert of Mons, *Chronicon*, 170 n. 3.

34. Frans van Mieris, *Groot Charterboek der Graven van Holland van Zeeland, en Herren van Vriesland* (Leiden, 1753–1756), 1:409; Samuel Muller et al., eds., *Oorkonden-*

boek van het Sticht Utrecht tot *1301*, 5 vols. (Utrecht & the Hague: A. Oostheok, 1920–59), 5:279 [hereafter cited as *OBU*].

35. *Inventaire-Sommaire des Archives Départementales antérieurement à 1790. Nord; Archives Civils; Série B* (Lille, 1864), 64, 65, 66; J. de Saint Genois, *Inventaire analytique des chartes des comtes de Flandre* (Ghent, 1843–1846), 263.

36. For the political background of the French invasion, the grievances of the count of Flanders, and the results of the war, see Nicholas, "Feudal Relationships," 88–90.

37. L. A. J. W. Sloet, *Oorkondenboek der graafschappen Geire en Zutfen tot . . . 1288* (The Hague, 1872–1876), 347 [hereafter cited as OBGZ]; *Gesta Episcoporum Traiectensium*, 404.

38. Heinrich Camillus Wampach, *Urkunden- und Quellenbuch zur Geschichte der altluxemburgischen Territorien bis zur burgundischen Zeit*, 5 vols. (Luxembourg: Druck und Verlag der St. Paulus-Druckerei, 1935), 1:770–71.

39. Bergh, *OBHZ*, 2:469–70.

40. Sloet, *OBGZ*, 405–8.

41. Van Mieris, *Groot Charterboek*, 1:593.

42. Saint Genois, *Monuments anciens*, 432.

43. Bergh, *OBHZ*, 1:136.

44. *Inventaire-Sommaire, Nord*, 9.

45. *Inventaire-Sommaire, Nord*, 18.

46. V. Gaillard, *Inventaire analytique des chartes des comtes de Flandre* (Ghent, 1857), 105–6.

47. Saint Genois, *Monuments anciens*, 415.

48. Saint Genois, *Monuments anciens*, 333.

49. *Oorkondenboek van het Sticht Utrect tot 1301*, ed. S. Muller et al., 5:233.

50. Bergh, *OBHZ*, 2:348.

51. Nicholas, *Feudal Relationships*, 87–88.

52. *Gesta Abbatum Trudonensium*, MGH, SS, 10:281–91.

53. J. de Saint Genois, *Inventaire analytique des chartes des comtes de Flandre* (Ghent, 1843–1846), 132–33.

54. See the previous discussion of these events.

55. F. Z. Wurth-Paquet, *Table chronologique des chartes et diplomes relatifs à l'histoire de l'ancien Pays-Duché de Luxembourg et Comté de Chiny* (Luxembourg, 1858–1861), 16:58–59.

56. L. Genicot, *Études sur les principautés lotharingiennes* (Louvain: Bureau du recueil, Bibliothèque de l'Université, 1975), 57.

57. Galbert of Bruges, *Murder of Charles the Good*, 14–18. See also *Actes des comtes de Flandre, 1071–1128*, ed. F. Vercauteren (Brussels: Palais des académies, 1938), 241–43, 245–51, 255–57.

58. See Galbert of Bruges, *Murder of Charles the Good*, passim; *Walter of Thérouanne, Vita Karoli*, 537–61; and commentary in E. Warlop, *The Flemish Nobility Before 1300*, 2 vols. (Kortrijk: G. Desmet-Huysman, 1975), 1:55–104, 185–208.

59. *Annales Egmundiani*, MGH, SS, 16:461–62.

60. S. Muller et al., *OBU*, 1:413–14.

61. Bergh, *OBHZ*, 1:188.

62. S. Muller et al., *OBU,* 2:180–83.
63. Bergh, *OBHZ,* 2:249–51.
64. Bergh, *OBHZ,* 2:275–77.
65. Henri Obreen, *Floris V, Graaf van Holland en Zeeland, Heer van Friesland* (Ghent: E. van Goetham, 1907), 152–61.

Rejecting Chivalry

Reinscribing Feudal Ideals of Order

THE BRUTAL REALITY of many aspects of medieval life and warfare frequently challenged and proved inimical to feudal ideals of order and stability. Chivalric prowess, perhaps the most conspicuous way of demonstrating fidelity to one's lord, might quicken the step of even a reluctant follower or, in retrospect, become the stuff of legends. When evidenced within range of the deadly, accurate enemy crossbow, however, it often suddenly—and horribly—lost its significance. Such is the position John W. Schwetman takes in "Feudal Chivalry in Popular Medieval Battle Poems," a study of so-called medieval soldier and battle poems.

According to Schwetman, many of these works reveal that attempts to adjust the feudal ideal of order to accommodate the grim and brutal reality of medieval warfare frequently resulted in the undermining of the ideal itself or, in some instances, the outright expression of contempt for it. Following Johan Huizinga and others, Schwetman argues that the feudal ideal of chivalry is little more than literary affectation in many of these works, which can be organized into three general groups, the first consisting primarily of ballads treating Scottish border battles; the second, of soldiers' songs contained in collections such as those of Pierre de Langtoft, Robert de Mannying, and Laurence Minot; and the last, of longer narrative poems dealing with significant events, such as the Battle of Agincourt or the Siege of Rouen. Furthermore, Schwetman demonstrates that articulation of contempt for the feudal ideal is usually determined by a poem's implied or actual audience, a group usually consisting of ordinary soldiers or even mercenaries to whom the actual features of warfare—namely, brutality, deprivation, and suffering—were very real.

Responding to feudal ideals of chivalry and order with a contemptuous disregard for their practicality is one way of depreciating their value. Another is to reveal the patent absurdity of those and related ideals. Such is the object of Ross G. Arthur's "The *Roman de Jaufre* and the Illusions of Romance." This romance, Arthur argues, displaces chivalric ideals in such a way that the hero has to give up lofty notions of prowess, courage, and so forth just to survive. The constant tension in the poem resulting from challenges to the ideal by features of an ever-present, intrusive reality creates many humorous moments, which both uphold and frustrate genre expectations. In the end, Arthur concludes, the "broad rhetorical structures of the genre are triumphant" as the hero marries Lady Brunissen at Arthur's court, dispenses wealth, and secures the realm. These developments occur, however, only after the poet has convincingly shown how actual circumstances often have a deleterious effect on ideals even when the latter have been pragmatically adjusted to accommodate them.

JOHN W. SCHWETMAN

9 Feudal Chivalry in Popular Medieval Battle Poems

─── ✿

N THE Epilogue to his translation of Ramon Lull's *The Book of the Ordre of Chyvalry,* William Caxton wrote, "O ye knyghtes of Englond where is the custome and vsage of noble chyualry that was vsed in tho dayes."[1] He then urges the knights of his time to read of "lancelot of galaad of Trystram" and others among Arthur's knights and advises that they pay heed to the deeds of Richard Coeur de Lion, Edward I, Edward III, and other kings and knights, including "that vyctoryous and noble kynge Harry the fyfthe and the capytayns vnder hym his noble bretheren."[2] Among the exemplars Caxton mentions, both Edward III and Henry V figured large in a sizable number of fourteenth- and fifteenth-century poems in Middle English devoted to historic events, several specifically to decisive battles. These poems treating events in the reign of these two successful warrior kings are examples of the fifty or so poems in Middle English devoted to battles. Caxton wrote that these two kings exemplified chivalric virtues, and, one could assume, other English kings of this time might also personify the high standards of this style of action; however, contemporary poems about contemporary events give a somewhat different interpretation of these and other English figures involved in battles and campaigns. While the poets occasionally seem aware of chivalric virtues to some degree, these popular poems suggest that the historic events ultimately were conducted with little regard to these refined codes of behavior.

The general question raised by this collection of essays is how closely actual feudal realities in medieval England or Europe approximated feudal ideals of order; the specific question I wish to treat is how the ideal of feudal chivalry influenced conduct in real courts and on real battlefields, as seen in the popular battle poems in Middle English. The general question has had particular pertinence since the appearance of Maurice Keen's *Chivalry* in 1984.[3] There, Keen disputes the contention of Johan Huizinga's highly influential work, *The Waning of the Middle Ages*,[4] that at least by the later Middle Ages, chivalry had decayed as a code of behavior (a view much like that of Caxton, as discussed earlier), and was honored in the literature of romance if it was honored at all; that in the real world chivalry was little more than a literary affectation, given lavish display in self-consciously artificial tournaments and related spectacles. Making extensive use of contemporary sources, Keen argues that instead of decaying, the chivalric code remained as real a force in governing behavior in the late medieval period as it had been earlier.

Keen's interpretations have greatly influenced contemporary discussions, as is evident from the contributions to the recently published collection *The Study of Chivalry*.[5] The reality of the code has been debated. One source of evidence little used in this debate consists of a fairly sizable number of Middle English poems arising from battles involving English kings and English forces. The evidence from these poems, though not unequivocal, offers some intriguing hints about the conduct and interests of real warriors in real warfare, or at least of how the poets and singers perceived these figures and their actions. It does suggest that, at least in soldiers' songs and in popular ballads, the chivalric ideal was not a fundamental factor; in the longer narrative poems depicting battles, chivalry may be seen as a part of courtly tradition, yet it seemed to exert little influence on actual practice in the field of battle.

Poets of almost all ages have looked to warfare as an important source of material; indeed, military exploits have at times seemed the principal inspiration for the poetic muse. Jon Stallworthy, in preparing *The Oxford Book of War Poetry*, starts with Homer and the Book of Exodus and sweeps on into the mid-twentieth century with poets like

FIGURE 10. Cavalry melee. Pierpont Morgan, MS 638, fol. 10, detail. Courtesy of the Pierpont Morgan Library.

Robert Lowell, Galway Kinnell, and Seamus Heaney in gathering his examples of poems about war.[6]

Poets writing in Middle English add to this long-standing tradition of poetry about battles. I have located fifty-one of these Middle English poems in various sources, mostly in the manuscript collections in libraries in London, Oxford, Cambridge, and Dublin. None of these, I think, is as well known as the Old English battle poems *The Battle of Maldon* and *The Battle of Brunanburh*, and most are probably not as familiar as Renaissance battle poems like Michael Drayton's "To the Cambro-Britons, and their harp, his Ballad of Agincourt" or his epic on Agincourt. The Middle English battle poems show a good bit of variety in form and admittedly in literary quality; I would like to discuss three broad classes of the poems that allow observations about what we can call *chivalry*, conduct that reflects such things as honor among combatants, mercy toward the weak, and devotion to an ideal of behavior that sets battle apart from mere bloodletting and slaughter.[7]

The first group of poems consists of ballads depicting battles, for the most part along the Scottish borders. Of these poems, the best known is probably *The Hunting of the Cheviot* (MS Bodleian 6933), and the somewhat different ballad depicting the same conflict, *Chevy Chase*

(MS BM Addit 27879, the Percy MS).[8] The chivalric nature of these poems is strongly suggested by what Sir Philip Sidney said in a passage in *The Defense of Poetry:* "I never heard the olde song of Percy and Duglas that I found not my heart mooved more then with a trumpet; and yet is it sung so evill apparrelled in the dust and cobwebbes of that uncivil age, what would it worke trymmed in the gorgeous eloquence of Pindar!"[9] Though the quotation could refer to either of the poems about the border conflicts involving Douglas and Percy, Francis James Child assumes that Sidney was speaking of *The Hunting of the Cheviot.*[10] Of *The Hunting of the Cheviot,* F. J. Furnivall and J. W. Hales add that the work is "historically highly valuable for the picture it gives of border warfare in its more chivalrous days, when ennobled by generosity and honor."[11] These later commentators must have seen a chivalric code, in effect, primarily in the relationship between Henry Percy and Lord Douglas, in their treatment of each other as fellow warriors worthy of respect.

The poem depicts a raid by Henry Percy of Northumberland into the Scottish territory of Lord Douglas in 1436, avowedly to pursue, unauthorized, the game in Douglas's lands, a raid that is senseless and therefore appropriate to rash and impulsive knights. Learning of the incursion, Douglas raises a force to oppose this violation of his territory. When the two forces confront each other, hostilities are inevitable; but in actions leading some critics to view the poem as expressing the highest chivalric idealism, the leaders treat each other as equals under the code of honor. First, Douglas says that it would be a "great pitte" to kill the gathered forces (apparently meaning Percy's) and proposes single combat. Percy, of course, agrees, saying

> Nethar in Ynglonde, Skottlonde, nar France,
>   nor for no man of woman born,
> Bot and fortune be my chance
> I dar met him on man for on. [st. 21]

The warriors on both sides, however, epitomized in this case by "Richard Wytharyngton . . . off Northombarlonde," desire so to fight and protect their lords that general combat becomes inevitable. The resulting conflict is carried out with a mixture of honor and barbarity. When Percy sees Douglas struck down by an arrow, he takes the dying man's hand and says, "Wo ys me for the!" (st. 38), adding:

To haue savyde thy lyffe, I wolde haue partyde wiþ
   my landes for years thre
For a better man, of hart nare of hande,
   was nat in all þe north contre. [st. 39]

Though the poet ascribes noble sympathy and respect among fellow knights to the participants, the battle is fierce and bloody; according to the poet, of the fifteen hundred English archers who enter the
battle, only seventy-three leave it alive. And when a nobleman has
both his legs hewed in two, he "knyled and fought on hys kny" (st.
54). In spite of a nod toward sentiment to soften the harsh bloodiness
of war, the poem works to its bloody end, with nearly all participants
slain, including both Douglas and Percy. What elements of chivalry
appear in the poem seem part of the general hyperbolic tone of the
poem, a degree of unreality that makes the events seem distant in
time; though we cannot know when the poem was composed, the
manuscript containing the description of this early fifteenth-century
battle is of late sixteenth-century origin.[12] The event seems a part of a
misty, romantic past.

Other ballads depict these border wars; one, probably fairly well
known, is *The Battle of Otterburn* (MS Cotton Cleopatra C.iv., and MS
Harley 293). Also arising from the English-Scots border wars are
Durham Field (MS BL Addit 28789, the Bishop Percy MS) and *The Battle
of Harlow* (no extant MS). They, too, generally draw an idealized image
of a chivalric past; the tone in each is not totally removed from the idealized view of the outlaw seen in the myriad visions of Robin Hood
as hero in a different idealized ballad motif. These ballads arising
from battles are generally not as aesthetically sophisticated as the
poem discussed above, and pay only scant attention to chivalric deeds
and attitudes.

A second group of poems, notable for their impression of immedi-
acy, the sense of being composed almost in the heat of battle, recount
battles from several times and places; they might be loosely labeled
soldiers' songs, for lack of a better designation. This group consists of
battle poems and fragments of poems from relatively early in the Middle English period. For example, in his poetic Anglo-Norman chronicle, which survives in at least thirteen manuscripts, Pierre de
Langtoft presents segments of poems he describes as having been

composed by English soldiers during the campaigns against the Scots. Robert de Mannying included several of these poems in his chronicle, which derives from Pierre de Langtoft.[13] The contemptuous tone of these poems is their most distinguishing feature, and a similar tone is found in the eleven poems of Laurence Minot, in a poem written on *The Flemish Insurrection* against the French in 1302, and in the English version of the well-known *Song of Lewes* or *The Song Against the King of Almaigne*. As might be expected from the above description, the tenor of these poems is not chivalric.

The soldiers' songs that Manning gives in his *Chronicle* are rough, both in form and in their treatment of the Scots:

> The Scottis had no grace
> To spede in ther space
> For to mend ther nisse
> Thei filed ther face
> That died in that place;
> The Inglis rymed this.

In an article entitled "Politics and Poetry in the Early Fourteenth Century: The Case of Robert Manning's *Chronicle*," Thorlac Turville-Petre says that for Manning "the treachery of the Scots was one of the chief lessons of history," and that Manning was, for all practical purposes, writing propaganda for Edward III, whom Turville-Petre describes as "well aware of the value of propaganda" emphasizing the guile of the Scots and the justice of his claim to Scotland.[14] In such documents, one would not expect a chivalric view of warfare and the enemy.

Laurence Minot, a poet in the service of Edward III who also wrote highly partisan verse, composed eleven poems on the military exploits of Edward that survive in MS Cotton Galba E.ix. Minot's poems are a cut above those attributed to the English soldiers by Manning, but to a large extent, their tone is the same. There is much talk of the falseness of the enemy, be they Scots or French, and frequent reference to cracking of the crowns of, for example, "wild Scottes and alls of tame" (fol. 52a). The weapons of choice are "brade ax and bowes bent" (fol. 55a), more often than they are the "spere and schelde and helmis schene" of Edward (fol. 55a). These poems, too, seem addressed to the foot soldier or perhaps written by one closely allied with these common soldiers. Occasionally the poems suggest an

FIGURE 11. *Le Massacre des Innocents*, 1863. From the atelier de Jean de
Brecquessent. Marble, h. 38, l. 17, w. 8. Abbaye de Hautecombe. Courtesy
of the Musée de Chambéry, Savoy.

awareness of a higher code of conduct, one perhaps demanded, at least in theory, of the noble class. The feudal responsibilities of a vassal are depicted in an elaborate swearing of feudal service by "the kayser lowis of bauere" (fol. 52), and the king is aware of the suffering of his subjects before the onslaught of the enemy and his duty to protect them (fol. 52b). Though the poet seems aware of how a noble enemy should behave when he describes "William þe Dowglas with men of honorwe" (fol. 56b1) and says of Philip of France, "Vnkind he was and vncurtayse" (fol. 55b1), Minot sees the enemy as rough, crude, false, and villainous, suggesting that galleymen came to England near Northampton

> for no thing spare
> Bot brin and sla both man and wife
> And childe, þat none suld pas with life. [fol. 52b2]

Occasionally the poet sees the suffering of those involved in battle, combatants and noncombatants alike, when, for example, he describes citizens of Calais under the hard confines of siege, speaking of their hunger:

> Oure horses that war faire and fat
> Er etin vp ilkonebidene
> Haue we nowþer conig ne cat
> Þat þai ne er etin and hundes kene
> All er etin vp ful clene
> Es noþer leuid biche ne whelp
> Þat es wele on oure sembland sene
> And þai er fled þat suld vs help. [fol. 56a¹]

At another point, the corpses on the field after the French attacked Southampton in 1338 are depicted by Minot with little of the usual mocking tone as they "lay stareand on the sternes" (fol. 53a). These examples of concern seem, however, to be expressions as much of simple human sympathy as of chivalry; for Minot, chivalry is simply not an issue, as far as I can see. Minot's attitudes are more representatively seen in passages like the following:

> Whare er 3e skottes of saint iohnes toune
> Þe boste of 3owre baner es betin all doune

> When ȝe bosting will bede sir Edward es boune
> Forto kindel ȝowre croune and crak ȝowre crowne
>> He has crakked ȝowre croune wele worth þe while
>> Schame bityde þe Skottes for þai er full of gile [fol. 52b¹]

An even more antichivalric attitude is seen in *The Song of Lewes* or, as it is often labeled, *The Song Against the King of Almaigne*, from MS Harley 2253. This poem, obviously composed by a supporter of Simon de Montfort and the barons allied with him, depicts their battle at Lewes against Henry III and other nobles, including Henry's brother Richard, Earl of Cornwall and King of Germany in 1264. (Robbins dates the poem from almost immediately after the battle and Nel Ker dates the manuscript from the first half of the fourteenth century, so the poem is early.)[15] The poem denies the possibility of chivalry. The King's brother Richard of Almaigne demands thirty thousand pounds to stand beside his brother; Richard has spent all of his money on "swyvyng"; in his retreat he mistakes a windmill for a castle and the sails of the mill for a catapult:

> Þe kyng of alemaigne wende do ful wel
> he seised þe mulne for a castel
> wiþ hare sharp swerdes he grounde þe stel
> he wende þt þe sayles were mangonel. [fol. 58b]

Here we seem to have a lecherous Don Quixote who mistakes windmills for something else and will not fight without first being paid in gold and in silver also. Throughout, the poet repeats the scurrilous refrain, "Richard þah þou be ever trichard / trichen shalt þou nevermore." Obviously, no brotherhood of knights is possible when the enemy is of such low character.

Thus many poems in Middle English dealing with contemporary battles treat chivalry as something distant from the poet and his audience. The ballads allow chivalric action, but see it in a nostalgic and unreal glow of the past. The soldier poems and those like them display little interest in the niceties of chivalry or are even antichivalric. Poems in a third group, longer narratives of significant battles, treat battles with greater attention to detail and to the actions of individuals; in their greater sophistication, these poems suggest an audience that subscribed to the virtues of chivalry, and the poets do talk a good bit

FIGURE 12. Prisoners in front of army. B.L., MS Egerton 1894, fol. 8v, detail. Courtesy of the British Library.

about the participants' nobility and chivalric reputations, yet, in the end, the details do not support an argument that chivalry provided a guide for action in the conduct of warfare. Many of these poems are to be found in association with the prose chronicles, and in at least one case, a poem on the Battle of Halidon Hill of 1333, in MS Harley 4690, the writer paraphrases a poem, obviously his source, in prose until the poetry simply takes him over and he presents the material displayed as poetry. The most interesting of these poems are several longer narrative poems arising from battles of the early fifteenth century: from the reign of Henry VI, two on the Siege of Calais in 1436;

and from the reign of Henry V, several on Agincourt in 1415, and one on the Siege of Rouen in 1419.

One of the poems on the Siege of Calais, found in MS Cotton Galba E.ix, is a rather interesting, if a bit odd, battle poem of 168 lines.[16] It opens with a conventional nature gambit—conventional in love lyrics and the like but not in battle poems. July, the time when the flowers of April have begun to fade, it turns out, is an ideal time to win renown in war:

> Than comyth tyme off labowr,
> To profit and to wirschip wyne
> In armes so ther be no treson inn
> Untruth, ne fals colowr. [fol. 113b]

Such chivalric ideals, however, are not generally the subject treated in the poem, as the Duke of Burgundy has assembled one hundred fifty thousand knights in "chevalry" to win Calais from the English and to make die "Both man, woman, and chyld." The poet takes some interest in the pomp and panoply of the Duke's assembly before the town, but he seems at least as impressed by the nine thousand cocks the French have brought to crow all night as by the flower of knighthood spread out before the town. The English nobles within the town are quietly assured (they never close the gates of the city during the whole siege) and they express concern for the weak—the men, women, and children threatened by the bombardment of the Duke's cannon—as good knights should. Yet in an engagement marked by skirmishes but little actual fighting and ended by the besiegers' fleeing at the rumor of approaching reinforcements, a few comic details seem more noteworthy than do any deeds of arms: the poet spends much time describing the Irishman who rides his hobby back and forth before the French horde, shouting curses and shaking his darts, and the water baily's dog that snaps at the heels of horses and men alike. While the poet acknowledges in the beginning the desire to seek fame in deeds of arms conducted honorably and depicts the English as noble and concerned with behaving in a fashion befitting knights, the poem disintegrates into something approaching farce.

When poets turn to that heroic figure Henry V, the favorite of historian and playwright alike, they seem to find a man to be taken seriously as warrior and leader, a figure pious and stern, concerned with honor and glory and the welfare of the unfortunate—in other words, the epitome of chivalry. At least six battle poems survive in Middle English in which Henry is the central figure, among them two that are among the longest and best poems in the corpus under review. Both of the poems depict a ruler and his noble followers who pursue a chivalric code of conduct, at least superficially.

A long poem on the Battle of Agincourt survives in three versions, MS Bodleian 11951 (formerly Rawlinson C.86), MS Cotton Vitellius D.xii (one of the manuscripts that burned in 1731, but not before a version had been transcribed and published), and MS Harley 565. The poem contains three actions and is, in fact, divided into three sections or *Passus* in the Harley MS, the source of quotations in the following comments. In the first action, the King decides to collect tribute due him by the King of France, and when the tribute is refused, he mounts an expedition, which lays siege to Honfleur and wins the city; in the second, he meets and defeats the French at Agincourt; in the third, he and his army return in triumph to England and are feted by the population upon their entrance into London. The French are contemptuous of the English king and the English fighting men; the contempt is most apparent in the oft-recounted gesture of the tennis balls sent to Henry by the Dauphin, but it is seen as well on the eve of battle when the French complain that there are so few Englishmen that ransoms will be hard to win:

> Ther be so fewe of thise Inglyssh men
>
> . . . . .
> XXti of us it will be falle
> Of hem haue on prinsonere [fol. 108b–109a]

They say that they will play dice with the lords of England and that the archers will be sold:

> Her archers be sold full fayr plente
> And alle þe beste bowemen ich on
> All for a blank of oure mone [fol. 109a]

On the other side, the English behave with courtesy—except for the English guns: at the siege of Harfleet, the English guns (named "London," "Messagere," and "the Kynges doughter") cast their balls or gun-stones at the city, contemptuously calling out the score: "Fyftene before seyd london tho," as its cannonballs struck the steeple of Har-fleet (fol. 105b). The other guns respond with similar comments until all of the King's engines are raining destruction on the city. The hu-man actors on the English side deport themselves in more seemly fashion. The king grants the besieged a truce while they send for aid to lift the siege; when the aid is not forthcoming, the King seizes the city as his own. Then, before Agincourt, the Duke of York falls on his knee before the king and asks as a boon that he be granted the forward position, and the King grants the boon, an exchange found also in later battle poems, including one on Bosworth Field included in the Bishop Percy MS. The nobles piously prepare themselves for battle, calling on Mary and Saint George for protection. The king himself fights as a true knight and leads his prisoners away after the battle. Interestingly, in this version of the story, nothing is said of the order to kill all prisoners in response to the fear of a new attack, an event fairly generally attested to in accounts of the battle.[17] The final section of the poem presents the triumphant entry into London. The poem stresses the valor of the king, his dignity, and his piety; the English generally are more humble and more courteous than their French counterparts. The poem does not focus on chivalry; although the poet says that the English nobles show virtues of chivalric knights, more is said than is actually demonstrated in the account of their actions.

Henry V is also at the center of what is an interesting, if somewhat repetitious, battle poem, *The Siege of Rouen*, usually attributed to John Page. This poem survived into the twentieth century in seventeen manuscripts, though the location of six of those manuscripts is no longer known.[18] Obviously, the survival rate of a poem cannot tell us how popular it was in the Middle Ages, but no other of the battle po-ems survives in more than three manuscripts, and many, including the eleven poems of Laurence Minot, survive in unique copies. *The Siege of Rouen* is often incorporated into the prose *Brut*. The most com-plete version is in MS Egerton 1995. Robbins says of the poem, "This account, though simple and unpretentious yet possessed of a vivid narrative and genuine pathos, colored all later chronicles, including, for example, Titus Livius, the pseudo-Elmham, and Hall, Stow, and Holinshed."[19] In the beginning of the poem, the poet tells us that many accounts of sieges exist, "Both in romans and in ryme" (fol. 87a), and that he plans to tell of one of the greatest, that of Henry V at

Rouen. The narrative is fairly direct; it begins with the setting of the siege, with a good bit of detail given to technical matters; it moves to an account of sorties and skirmishes; but eventually it focuses more and more on the suffering of the besieged, particularly the common people. Throughout the poem, the poet stresses the chivalric virtues of the English nobles and particularly of the English King. Even the fighting men of Rouen come in for praise, as the poet describes them as men both hardy and proud, "And poyntes of warre many one dyd showe / Whenne they yssuyd owt most comynly" (fol. 93a). As the hardship of the citizens increases, they call to the English from the various gates of the city until one responds— Umfraville, a knight of the old blood of Normandy. They praise his graciousness and ask him to intercede with the King. He gains the support of Clarence, Exeter, and Gloucester, all of whom the poet describes in terms of their chivalric qualities: "Loo! thes gret men of chyvalrye / Soo sone were in charyte" (fol. 98a). When the King agrees to see representatives of the city, the poet says of him: "Lo! that prynce pryncypalle / Of worthynys he passythe alle" (fol. 98b) and describes him as both manful and merciful. Yet the townspeople had to call on many of the British nobles before they could find one willing to intercede for them, and the King was certainly mindful of the plight of the poor, since they were huddled in the moat between the English lines and the city. I will not belabor the point with further representations of what the poet says of the gentle yet manly qualities of the King as he is presented in the poem, but the details abound. However, one of the strongest features of the poem is the depiction of the suffering of the besieged, particularly the poor, and the pity the English feel for them; the poet gives many specific details of that suffering, of the cost of a cat or a mouse as the supply of meat ran low, of family members suffering and dying after they have been put out of the city by the more wealthy townsmen. Henry feeds the poor on feast days and is said to be acutely aware of their suffering, but when the burghers call on him to pity the poor, he sternly asks who put them in the moat in the first place. A stern king, a pious king, but a mighty warrior, Henry seems to be, but a knight desirous of protecting the meek and the helpless whose plight is visible to him, he does not truly seem to be, as he seeks to conclude the siege. *The Siege of Rouen* goes on to present in detail negotiations—commenced, broken, and resumed—and the fail-

ure of the French king to come to the aid of the besieged. Without succor, the city surrenders, and Henry enters the city, which he
considers rightfully his, though denied him for so long by the city
leaders. Only then are the poor fed. In maintaining his rights, Henry
has allowed the poor to suffer; he has denied protection to the weak,
something demanded of him by the code of chivalry. Though the poet
insists that Henry is the epitome of the chivalric warrior, his actions
are at odds with that judgment.

Do the battle poems suggest that Caxton's catalogue of chivalric exemplars was widely accepted by poets of preceding generations? That
poets saw the knights and kings around them in chivalric terms? If the
Middle English battle poems provide a partial answer to those questions, that answer would seem to be that chivalry was not very important in the heat of actual battle. The sampling of ballads devoted to
battles suggests that chivalry was admired, but the context suggests
that such a code of behavior was part of a hyperbolic, fantasized
world. The soldiers' songs display no interest in the question. The
long narrative poems, poems often associated with chronicles, speak
of the noble heroes as true sons of chivalry, but these poems are little
concerned with the chivalric code in fact. These last poems suggest an
awareness of a tradition of a code of chivalry, perhaps acquired
through the romances. The poets seem to know how knights were
supposed to behave, and they speak of chivalric ideals. Seldom, however, do the poems provide any convincing evidence that the code influenced action on the real battlefields of real wars.

Notes

1. *The Book of the Ordre of Chyvalry,* translated from Ramon Lull's *Libre del ordre de
cauayleria* and printed by William Caxton, ed. A.T.P. Byles, EETS, o.s., 168 (London,
1926; rpt. New York: Kraus, 1971), 122.

2. Caxton, *Book of the Ordre of Chyvalry,* 122–23.

3. Maurice Keen, *Chivalry* (New Haven and London: Yale University Press,
1984).

4. *The Waning of the Middle Ages: A Study of the Forms of Life, Thought and Art in
France and the Netherlands in the* xivth *and* xvth *Centuries* (London: Edward Arnold,
1924).

5. *The Study of Chivalry: Resources and Approaches,* ed. Howell Chickering and
Thomas H. Seiler (Kalamazoo, Mich.: Medieval Institute Publications, 1988).

6. *The Oxford Book of War Poetry,* ed. Jon Stallworthy (Oxford & New York: Oxford University Press, 1984).

7. Definitions of the term *chivalry* are generally impressionistic and dependent on sources and context, as Maurice Keen suggests. He adds, "One can define within reasonably close limits what is meant by the word knight, the French *chevalier*: it denotes a man of aristocratic standing and probably of noble ancestry, who is capable, if called upon, of equipping himself with a war horse and the arms of a heavy cavalryman, and who has been through certain rituals that make him what he is—who has been 'dubbed' a knight" (1–2). Keen goes on to say: "From a very early stage we find the romantic authors habitually associating together certain qualities which they clearly regarded as the classic virtues of good knighthood: prouesse, loyauté, largesse (generosity), courtoisie, and fraunchise (the free and frank bearing that is visible testimony to the combination of good birth with virtue)" (*Chivalry*, 2).

8. For these and all of the other poems cited in this paper, I have consulted the manuscripts containing the poems and have given my best reading of the MSS. Throughout I will cite sources where the poems have been printed, though not all of these sources are widely available.

Texts of "The Hunting of the Cheviot" and "Chevy Chase" are found in *The English and Scottish Popular Ballads*, 5 vols., ed. Francis James Child (New York: Houghton Mifflin, 1882–98; rpt. New York: Dover, 1965), vol. 3. Quotations in my text are based on the MS.

9. *The Defense of Poetry*, in *Miscellaneous Prose of Sir Philip Sidney*, ed. Katherine Duncan-Jones and Jan Van Dorsten (London: Oxford University Press, 1973), 97.

10. *Ballads*, 3:295.

11. *The Percy Folio MS*, 4 vols., ed. F. J. Furnivall and J. W. Hales (London, 1867–69); the quotation is cited by Rossell Hope Robbins, "xiii. Poems Dealing with Contemporary Conditions," in *A Manual of the Writings in Middle English: 1050–1500*, ed. Albert E. Hartung (New Haven: Connecticut Academy of Arts and Sciences, 1975), 1423. (Part 13 is in volume 5 of this yet-unfinished seven-volume work.)

12. See Robbins, though he incorrectly labels the MS "Bodl 6333," instead of Bodl "6933" ("Poems Dealing with Contemporary Conditions," 1663).

13. Robbins cites eleven MSS for Langtoft and three for Mannyng ("Poems," 1648).

14. *The Review of English Studies* 39 (1988):9, 12.

15. Robbins, "Poems," 1404; N. R. Ker, *Facsimile of British Museum MS Harley 2253*, EETS, 255 (London, 1964).

16. The poem is also in a manuscript in Rome, Venerable Eng Coll 1306, which I have not yet been able to examine.

17. See, for example, John Keegan, *The Face of Battle* (New York: Viking Penguin, 1978), 108–12.

18. Robbins, "Poems," 1665. MS Egerton 1995 is the source of quotations in my text.

19. Robbins, "Poems," 1428.

10 The *Roman de Jaufre* and the Illusions of Romance

NE OF THE chief tasks facing the author of a medieval adventure romance is to reconcile the young men in his audience to their paradoxical social situation as members of a twelfth- or thirteenth-century court. These men are in service to a lord because of economic necessity, but they are told that their service has self-development as its purpose. They are likely to remain in service into their thirties or forties, if they survive that long, living in hope of a permanent escape from military service through marriage to a woman with a large dowry. As that reward is delayed, they are encouraged to persevere, both by temporary material pleasures and by literary assurances that their duties are proving grounds for individual worth. They hear stories about young men much like themselves, acting under the guidance of a benevolent leader—usually a king called "Arthur"—and following the code of conduct of a group of established knights; these fictional knights are invariably rewarded for following the socially acceptable path. The young men in the audience are promised, repeatedly, that a reward will come to them too, magically, and that it will be of a magnitude beyond their most extravagant dreams.

As poets attempt to gloss over the contradictions between the fictional world of their heroes and the concrete environment of their audiences, gaps appear in their poems into which evidence of that

audience's insoluble social problems can slip. Much recent scholarship has been devoted to such aspects of the works of Chrétien de
Troyes, stripping away the vestiges of a nineteenth-century romanti-
cism that located his poems in a timeless literary tradition ("mythical"
in two senses of the word) stretching back into Celtic prehistory. Such
studies have done a great deal to show us precisely how much the
modern critical evaluation of such canonized texts depends on
nineteenth-century attitudes and, conversely, how wasteful it has
been to exclude a larger number of medieval poems that perhaps reveal even more about the societies that produced them.

For all its uniqueness—it is the only surviving Arthurian romance
in Provençal[1]—*Jaufre*[2] is not as well known as it ought to be, in part
because the conditions under which it was composed led its author to
treat the conventions of courtly and feudal life in a manner not pleasing to the scholars who established the romance canon. *Jaufre* offers an
interesting set of contrasts with the general romance background in at
least three important areas: its treatment of ideals surrounding King
and Court; its attitude toward chivalry as an ordo; and its presentation
of individual prowess in the context of a world moving toward warfare
based on collective action. In each of these areas, the text's implied
judgments may be related to the particular historical situation prevail-
ing in Aragon-Catalonia at the time of the poem's composition.

The King and the Court

Jaufre is dedicated to a king, Jaume el Conqueridor of Aragon-
Catalonia; at the time when it was composed, however, Jaume was not
yet a conqueror and barely a king. If the poem was written before
Jaume's stunning conquest of Mallorca in 1228–29, which seems
likely,[3] he would not have been out of his teens when the poet's
praises of his nobility and generosity were first uttered. Despite this
royal dedication, however, *Jaufre* does not seem to be an overtly mon-
archist poem. In fact, a reading of the first episode leaves many readers feeling that the poet must have felt nothing but contempt for kings
and their immediate retinues, since he starts with a preliminary "fake
adventure"[4] in which Arthur and all of the knights of the Round Table
are thoroughly mocked and degraded.

The poem opens with Arthur and his courtiers assembled at the traditional Pentecost feast, unable to begin eating until an adventure has

come. In other examples of this "dinner delayed" motif an adventure comes almost immediately,[5] but this time the courtiers have to wait all afternoon; Arthur finally decides that they will have to go out and hunt one down, ignoring both the spirit and the etymology of "adventure."[6] Once they are out in Brocéliande, they hear the cries of a woman in distress. Despite offers of assistance from Gawain, Arthur insists, impetuously and imperiously, that the adventure belongs to him alone. He finds that a strange beast has come down from the mountains to the woman's mill, and is busy gobbling up all her grain. When the beast pays no attention to Arthur's armed threats, he grabs it by the horns and tries to wrestle it to the ground. When his strength proves insufficient, he decides to punch it in the head, but his hands are glued fast to its horns. It lumbers off and goes up to the top of a cliff, dangling Arthur precariously over the edge. For safety's sake, the knights decide to make a pile of all their clothing so that Arthur will have something soft to land on. As they stand below, naked and distraught, the beast leaps from the cliff—and then transforms itself back into one of Arthur's knights. He has mastered all the liberal arts (including magic), and has earlier made a bet with the king that he could enchant him on a high feast day. The reward for his success is to be a gold cup, a fine horse, and a kiss from the most beautiful woman at court. Now that they have found an adventure, he explains, the king and his knights may begin the feast. After a scramble for clothing, everyone returns to the palace to eat (95–484).

Almost every surface detail of this episode promises successful adventure of the sort a romance audience would expect, but in every case the encounters lead to failure. Brocéliande is not the miraculous locale of the fountain of Calogrenant and Yvain (374–469, 800–811), the allegorical combat between good and evil of *Le Torneiement Anticrist*,[7] or the enchanted prison of *Claris et Laris*.[8] It is not a trackless wilderness dotted with magical chapels and inhabited only by hermits, but a rather ordinary region, close enough to civilization to have a mill. There is nothing mysterious about either the miller or the mill: both are simple participants in the ordinary economy of medieval society. The gigantic monster, in itself, resembles the ten-horned beast of Apocalypse 13:1 or the monstrous animal raised by Mohammed,[9] but the confrontation which follows forestalls any such associations. This animal does not humble itself before a king, like Bucephalus before Alexander;[10] it is not subdued by knightly weapons, like those wielded by Richier in *Aspremont;*[11] it cannot be tamed by brute physical force, like the bulls that yield to the herdsman in *Yvain* (341–55). Arthur fails, his failure is observed by the knights of the Round Table, and his powerlessness quickly spreads through the ranks. Because of the circumstances, the knights are unable to do anything as knights to save their lord, despite their assertions that it is their duty to do so (286–92). Gawain throws away his lance and shield (321–22), and they all start lamenting, shredding their clothes and tearing their hair (350–68). The knights' decision to pile up their clothing puts them in a ludicrous position, especially since the beast's transformation, immediately afterwards, shows that the disrobing was unnecessary; in the context of the tradition, it must be seen as ridiculous.[12] The enchanter in *Jaufre* is no Merlin,[13] but an ordinary courtier, fully integrated into Arthurian society, who has learned magic as if it were little more than the eighth liberal art;[14] he does nothing but play games with his power, and his only purpose is to win a bet, for a reward which, on the practical level at least, seems quite trivial.

Shortly before the end of the poem, the poet takes the opportunity to show that this deficiency of the court is not a transitory situation. Arthur and his knights become involved in another marvelous adventure, during the wedding feast for Jaufre and Brunissen. A squire rushes in, interrupting the entertainment, and announces that he has been attacked by a huge bird, with a head as big as a barrel, feet as big as a door, and eyes which flash like carbuncles (9830–50). As before, Arthur takes up the challenge and, rejecting the aid of Gawain, Melian, and Jaufre, goes out alone to face the beast, just as impetuous and imperious as he was more than nine thousand lines before. He advances carefully with his sword and shield, but he simply angers the bird, which disarms him and carries him off into the sky (9885–904).

Arthur's followers fall into despair and lamentation, just as they have done in the Brocéliande episode. Finally, someone suggests that the mourners *do* something instead of just lamenting. A nameless count advises them to slaughter some cattle so that the bird will come down to eat them. This is done, in haste, but then the carcasses have to be dragged the distance of a good bowshot, for they have neglected to lead the cows to the field where the bird is circling about. None of this matters very much, of course, for the bird simply flies off, carrying the hapless king. The marvelous bird turns out, once again, to be the court enchanter, and Arthur is released unharmed. He then turns his attention to the state of his knights' clothing. In Brocéliande the courtiers all disrobed; this time, they have ripped all their fine apparel into shreds. Arthur summons merchants from the town, and the next thirty-five lines are devoted to talk of fine furs and costly material, as if proper clothing were the major state issue of the day. Any reader who finds this all rather ridiculous will be thankful to the poet for cutting off his description of the couturiers plying their trade for the thousands of lords and ladies because "it would be tedious to hear" (10107); the poet's more general attitude toward fine clothing is apparent from the earlier address to the audience in which he compares worthless men in rich clothes to worm-eaten wooden vessels covered with costly paint (2599–602).

Arthur's adventures with the mutant bull and the giant bird are temporary affairs, games with fixed beginnings and ends that take place outside everyday life. A more serious episode of deficiency of the established court occurs at the one point in the narrative when the Round Table knights are challenged to put into practice their much-vaunted willingness (compare lines 24–52) to aid the oppressed. Fada de Gibel (her name is not revealed until much later) comes to Arthur to ask for a champion to aid her against the aptly named villain Fellon d'Albarua. He has taken all her lands except one small castle, and she has only a week to find a defender or she will have to surrender even that to him. Arthur is sympathetic and declares that anyone who helped such a maiden would win great honor, but the poet conveniently arranges to have the most suitable candidates absent from court. Gawain, or Yvain, or Jaufre could certainly help, says Arthur, but none of them is present. The lady's plea to the court's remaining knights falls on deaf ears:

> Et anc negunz non sonet motz.
> E la piusela, auzent totz,
> Escrida: "Cavalliers, non sia!
> Per Dieu, no m'en torn a fadia!

Non sia esta cortz desmentida,
C'om diga qu'ieu m'en tor fallida!"
E negunz non a mut sonnat. [6329–335]

[But no one said a word. The maiden cried out so that all could hear,
"Knights, it must not be! By God, do not let me return with a refusal!
Do not let this court be defamed, don't let it be said that I left it dis-
appointed!" But no one said a word.]

Fada de Gibel does not so much leave the court as vanish, in the space
between two halves of a rhyming couplet. Her pleas are interrupted
when a crowd of people arrives, bringing news of Jaufre's spectacular
successes, and the court's attention turns instantly to them. All the
lords and ladies of Cardueil listen intently to the tale of battle and the
life histories of the defeated villain and his freed captive, but the one
damsel in distress who comes to Cardueil in the whole course of
the poem does not find a champion. In the "adventure" in Brocéliande, a story of an ersatz adventure was treated as if it were an adventure itself; here a story of an adventure is preferred to the
challenge of a real adventure.

The *Jaufre*-Poet is making use of contrasts with the general set of romance norms to reveal systemic flaws in this court. In an insightful
study of the decision-making process of a variety of courts in Arthurian romances, Dominique Boutet[15] has distinguished three stages
through which an ideal Arthurian-romance group proceeds in order
to determine an effective course of action. The primary raison d'être of
Arthurian society is to maintain order in the world, and the duty to
rectify disorder is incumbent on all its members, the king as well as
his entourage. The king is not an absolute monarch whose will is law,
for his actions are governed by the *mos majorum*; nor is he simply pri-
mus inter pares since the initial stage is his personal and particular
duty to perceive the disorder in the social situation and to decide to
remedy the problem. The second stage requires consultation between
king and council; the group as a whole is involved in strategic decisions concerning the sort of action to be taken, including, in the case
of warfare, the size of the army to be sent out. The third and most
concrete stage is dependent on the king alone, since he must make
executive decisions and announces particular decrees; he chooses, for
example, the individuals who will make up an expeditionary party.

In the court scenes of *Jaufre*, this orderly, sequential decision-making process is consistently short-circuited. At the Pentecost feast, Arthur decides, according to his own individual will, to breach the custom of his court. He takes no advice from his council concerning the choice to enter Brocéliande; when they hear the cry of the distraught woman, he decides simultaneously on the general strategy (one man will respond) and on the particular details (he will be that man). Once the king is out of commission, the role of counsel-initiator falls to Gawain, but in place of a reasoned group discussion and analysis, there is only one rather farfetched idea, which passes from knight to knight and wins general acceptance rather than rational assent. The response to the threat to order occasioned by the enchanter-as-bird follows a similar pattern, and results in a similar loss of dignity for the whole Round Table. The court, then, in this poem, does not function as the true home of the values to be acquired by the young knight who dominates the poem; on the contrary, a major portion of the poem's action is devoted to arranging his escape from the attitudes and behavior patterns of the court.

In order to effect this escape, the poet carefully establishes considerable distance between his hero and any person or group that might be seen as representing the past or the established social elite. Jaufre is nobly born, of course, as all romance heroes should be, but any possibility of paternal influence on the young man's career is systematically excluded. His father Dozon, otherwise completely unknown, is not mentioned until after Jaufre has been knighted. Despite the fact that Dozon is praised as a worthy member of the Round Table, the only thing we learn about him when he is first mentioned is the fact that he died not in proper chivalric combat but as a result of a wound from a crossbow during a siege. Later in the poem, his memory is invoked by Augier, one of his old companions in arms, as part of an attempt to induce Jaufre to give up his quest and settle down, as lord of a small castle, with his father's friend's daughter; politely but firmly, Jaufre refuses to be bound by the aspirations of the previous generation (4527–644). This rupture of the expected genetic continuity is matched in the poet's praise of the king to whom the poem is dedicated, for he is removed from his physical lineage and placed instead in a genealogy of virtues: he is the "father of Worth, the son of Generosity, the lord of Good Adventure" (62–63).

Viewed in the light of other contemporary materials from Catalonia, this tendency to erase the effects and diminish the power of preceding generations appears to be part of a widespread attempt to create a sharp break between the society of the past and the new regime inaugurated by Jaume I. This is especially evident in the Catalan chronicles in the sections dealing with King Jaume's father, Pere el Catòlic, and with the influence of older nobles on the young king's life. Pere died in the Battle of Muret, fighting against the Albigensian Crusaders under Simon de Montfort. He was engaged in a war to assist his own beleaguered and mistreated vassals, but his defeat and the fact that he was fighting against forces that had papal approval for their actions were both problems and embarrassments for later Catalan writers. His support for the "enemies of the faith" was variously explained as a result of family loyalty to his sisters, who were married to the lords of Toulouse[16] and blamed on Occitan nobles who seduced him by offering him their beautiful wives and daughters.[17] His defeat was attributed either to a lack of organization of his troops, or to the fact that he had spent the previous night carousing with loose women,[18] or to his refusal to wait for reinforcements and his impetuous charge into the enemy forces without heed for basic survival tactics.[19] When his son Jaume became king, without ever having known his father and after being raised by the Knights Templar, who were hostile to his father's projects, the simplest strategy for dealing with Pere was to reduce him to the status of an unfortunate detour in the glorious history of the lineage. While his father was alive, Jaume was called "Petrus" in court documents, after his father, or "Petrus Jacobi,"[20] but after his father's death he is called by the name his mother gave him as a result, we are told, of divine intervention.[21] Within a few years, Jaume's conception was turned into a poetic story modeled on the conception of Galahad by the lascivious Lancelot: Jaume's mother, the saintly Maria of Montpelier, was introduced secretly into Pere's bed, we are told, when he was expecting to sleep with a young lady of the town who had caught his eye.[22] Jaume's birth is presented as part of a long-term divine plan stretching back to the time of his grandparents, only incidentally involving the unlucky Pere.[23] Jaume's own decrees pointedly refer to his reaffirmation of the customs of "our ancestors," not "our father,"[24] and when later nationalist chroniclers wanted to assert the glory of the lineage of the Kings of Aragon, they harked back to legendary stories of much earlier kings.[25] Jaume's relations with the surviving members of his father's retinue and family were constantly troubled, according to his autobiography, by their unbridled ambition and propensity for treachery; whenever one of them tries to play on family loyalty, the young king ultimately suffers for it.[26]

The Chivalric Ordo

Romances played no small part in the propagation of the idea that warriors on horseback were, as members of an "order," different from other human beings. The Latin word *miles*, which had meant simply "soldier," and the French word *chevalier* and its cognates in other Romance languages, which had meant simply "horseman," had come by the early thirteenth century to designate a noble man who had been ritually inducted into a group of people following a code of behavior, with rules to govern every facet of life. The French verb *adouber* and its cognates had originally meant simply "to give someone some armor," but by the period in question it had come to mean "to make someone a knight."[27] Giving a man his spurs, that is, had come to mean "giving a man his spurs." Each action in the dubbing ritual and each piece of equipment had been invested with symbolic significance, spelled out in detail by various writers of treatises on chivalry. The candidate is bathed to remind him of baptism and put in a comfortable bed to remind him of paradise. He is dressed in a white robe for purity and a scarlet cloak for the blood he is willing to sacrifice. The two edges of his sword stand for justice and loyalty, or, alternatively, for defending the poor and attacking the oppressor. Brown stockings are for the earth where his body will ultimately lie, and a white sash at his waist is for restraining his lust. The helmet signifies a sense of shame, and his spurs tell him to be as responsive to God's commands as a charger is to the prick of a spur. The kiss from the officiant is a sign of faith and peace.[28]

   Let us now examine how these ceremonial concerns are treated in *Jaufre*. Just after Jaufre arrives at Arthur's court, the villain Taulat rides in, kills an unarmed knight, and leaves, threatening to shame the king in this same way every year on the same day. Jaufre is given permission to avenge this insult; since he is only a squire, he must be properly knighted before he can undertake the task. He gets a

FIGURE 13. Knight struggling with heavy mail. Pierpont Morgan, MS 638, fol. 28, detail. Courtesy of the Pierpont Morgan Library.

condensed version of the ceremony, with no nightlong vigil, no bath, and no bed, but he gets the armor piece by piece, and the ceremony ends with King Arthur attaching the right spur and the sword and giving him the symbolic kiss. He goes outside and asks two handy by-standers where Taulat is, only to be told that he has waited around inside too long, and the villain is long gone (724–27). Because of the delay for the ritual, he takes another five thousand lines to catch up with him. This is only the first of several indications that the poet sees some serious problems with the discrepancies between the ceremonial view of knighthood and the practical demands placed on a warrior in a violent society.

As he is riding along in pursuit of one villain, Jaufre meets another, a castellan named Estout de Vertfueil. Estout demands that he surrender his shield, his hauberk, his sword, and his horse. Jaufre refuses, saying, "I will not, because the good king gave them to me when he dubbed me a knight" (1044). He would rather fight to the death than give up the symbols of his newly won status as a Knight of the Round Table. In addition to being ceremonial tokens, however, these weapons are also physical objects, tools of the trade. Whatever their symbolic value, in combat the important thing is how well they function. Here, too, plot events, in the form of an apparently traditional combat scene, undercut the idealized view of the adventure romance hero. Jaufre slashes away at Estout with all his might, but he cannot pierce his armor. Estout seems to lack the sense of shame it is supposed to symbolize, but still his helmet resists numerous direct blows. On the other hand, Jaufre's shield is first pierced by Estout's lance and then sliced away bit by bit by Estout's sword. His hauberk is ripped, his helmet is shattered, a glancing blow shears off his spur, and his sword breaks in half (1055–1123). The ceremonial armor is useless, or rather worse than useless since it inspires false confidence. When it is all over, Jaufre prudently rearms himself in the weapons of the villain: a helmet that cannot be cut, a shield that cannot be pierced, an irresistible sword—armor with no lofty symbolic value (1178–81).

The dubbing ceremony had, by the early thirteenth century, acquired a quasi-sacramental character throughout western Europe, but the Albigensian Crusaders, the opponents of the Catalans and Aragonese for whom the poet was writing, went further than anyone else. Simon de Montfort had his young son Amaury made a knight in a ritual presided over by the Bishop of Orléans.[29] In *Jaufre*, the plot makes it clear that the qualities esteemed by the knightly order—justice, loyalty, and the willingness to risk one's life to aid others—are not part of the genetic inheritance of every youth of noble birth and are not sacramentally transferable through the ceremony of dubbing. As the story proceeds, Jaufre will be put through a series of experiences that create in him a subtly modified version of those qualities, but the poet makes it clear that such a process can begin only after the hero has been "un-dubbed."

Modes of Combat

The most universal ploy for reconciling a romance audience to its social condition is the assumption—treated as axiomatic—that individual action, if it follows the rules and conventions of the ordo, leads to individual success and has a significant effect on the general well-being and harmony of the knight's own court and of the world beyond the walls. Once he sets forth from the court, the romance hero is free of the direct control of the lord, but he is now subject to a set of internalized norms of behavior. He is expected to use the weapons of his order according to a set of socially sanctioned military procedures in an attempt to live up to and enforce the moral values symbolized by those pieces of armor. Neither the battle rules nor the chivalric values are to be seen as an impediment to success, of course; rather, his proper use of his metal and moral equipment is shown leading directly to success, and temporary setbacks may be attributed to momentary lapses. He is stern in his opposition to wrongdoers but quick to grant mercy to the defeated; he devotes his energy not only to responding to the initial challenge to his court but also to rescuing the victims of subsidiary villains; he meets a rich and beautiful maiden, and, with the approval of the home office, marries her and lives out his life in honor, dispensing her wealth to her vassals to ensure their loyalty to him.

The new knight is expected to demonstrate his virtues in a series of proper chivalric combats with men of his own class who have gone slightly astray. The *Jaufre*-Poet, in contrast, sends his hero through a sequence of adventures with opponents who do not share the perspective of the chivalric order. Each separate encounter challenges the assumptions of the code, and the genre's characteristic episodic structure is used to show a progressive degradation of the ideal. Perhaps the most obvious sign of this descent may be seen in the social class of Jaufre's opponents: his first fight is with a castellan, the second with a knight, the third with a foot soldier, the fourth with a giant leper. In each encounter the mode of combat and the tactics needed for victory become less refined and more grossly physical.

If Jaufre had adhered to the code, he would have been killed or captured by line 1200. The battle with Estout begins properly enough, but after Jaufre's armor is shredded, he is victorious only because he stuns Estout and then squeezes him so hard that his ribs break—a most unchivalric maneuver. The combat with the Knight of the White Lance follows the appropriate path, but Jaufre ends it by denying mercy to his defeated opponent and hanging him on a nearby tree, where his own victims had formerly been displayed. The footsoldier attacks him not with lance and sword, but with a coward's weapons, darts and stones. He leaps on the back of Jaufre's horse, puts a knife to his neck, and forces him to ride toward a prison where he keeps his captives. Jaufre succeeds here again by adopting the tactics of a streetfighter: he waits for a moment of inattention, grabs the arm with the knife and twists it until it breaks, pulls off the soldier's left arm, and hurls him to the ground. Then, to ensure that no other travelers will be robbed, he cuts off the soldier's feet (1856–80). The last opponent in the sequence is the giant leper, who has bashed out an innocent knight's brains on a rock, is trying to rape a beautiful young damsel, and is systematically butchering babies to bathe in their blood and cure his disease. The giant's weapon is a club. When he connects, the blow sends Jaufre reeling; when he misses and strikes the floor or the columns of the house, the whole building shakes. The leper is so tall that Jaufre's sword can reach no higher than his hip; finally he is able to cut through his leg, and when the giant falls, Jaufre splits his skull. Still, the fight is not over. In a death spasm, the giant's remaining good leg kicks Jaufre in the groin and sends him flying across the room into a wall. He is so stunned that when the damsel in distress throws water in his face, he strikes out at her, thinking it is the giant. Fortunately, since he has dropped his sword, he simply knocks her down instead of decapitating her.

It may well be that all members of a warrior society realize, deep down, that human combat is brutal and brutish and that only a fool keeps to the rules: but there seems to be something quite appropriate in the fact that the poet's society was one that had just undergone a crushing defeat. The Albigensian Crusade was a notoriously barbarous affair, with acts of extreme cruelty on both sides earning astonishing praise from their respective propagandists. The winners, of course, were able to see glory in death, in the occasional reversal: they tell us that the body of Simon de Montfort, killed by a stone-throwing machine operated by the women of Toulouse, was pierced by five arrows in token of the wounds of Christ.[30] It was left to the vanquished to create a romance in which the first stage of the hero's education is the lesson that one must be willing to abandon lofty ideals about knightly weaponry and knightly behavior in order to survive.

In romances, and frequently in chansons de geste, single combat is the battle mode of choice. Two knights square off against each other, either on a crowded battlefield, or on a lonely forest path, or in an organized tournament observed by admiring noble damsels. They charge each other, with couched lances, and one or both fall to the ground. Vigorous swordplay follows, and continues until one of the warriors is defeated. In the chansons de geste he is generally killed; in the romances, he cries mercy and leaves the field in dishonor. The realities of early thirteenth-century warfare were quite different. Cities and castles were captured not because the chosen champion of one side defeated a hero from the other side, but because the besiegers broke through the wall with huge engines, or because the besieged succumbed to starvation or dysentery. Pere el Catòlic, Jaume's father, fighting against the Crusaders to protect his Occitan vassals, called out "I am the King" to rally his beleaguered troops—one thinks of Arthur's impatience as he claims the battle with the mutant bull or the giant bird—and was cut down by a crowd of mercenaries.

Romance that it is, *Jaufre* tends, as a whole, to support the dominant fantastic ideal of a world in which individual chivalric activity is successful in bringing about changes both to the knight's status and to the condition of the oppressed. The hero defeats Taulat and rescues Melian in a one-on-one joust, an action that contributes to his success in winning Brunissen. Jaufre's individual talent rescues Fada de Gibel from Fellon d'Albarua: such victories earn him honor from both the rescued victims and from the older established knights of the Round Table. There is one situation, however, when a contradiction in the narrative draws our attention to the fantastic nature of the romance portrayal of the solitary knight.

During the time that Melian has been kept captive by Taulat and, in complete violation of the chivalric code, tortured by being whipped up a mountain naked, once a month, until his wounds open again, five hundred of his vassals have set out, one by one, to defeat Taulat and rescue their lord. Each of them has been defeated, in sequence, and when the story opens, they are all camped around Taulat's castle, patiently waiting for a rescuer. Back in his own country, Melian's people display their love for him and their grief over his captivity by falling into extreme mourning and lamentation four times a day and by attacking anyone who asks them the reason for their strange behavior. Jaufre, who does not yet know about the captive Melian, is repeatedly pummeled with swords and sticks and, on one occasion, a small dog when he is foolish enough to ask why these people are tearing their hair, scratching their faces, and falling to the floor from their full height. A modern observer of such a situation, as ignorant of the rules regarding the willing suspension of disbelief as Jaufre is of the cause for this lamentation, might well ask different questions. Why, instead of lamenting their lord so pointlessly and self-destructively, do not these people *do* something about his wretched situation? Why, instead of fighting Taulat one at a time despite his obvious superiority in such a mode of combat, do they not attack him en masse, given that there are thousands of them in the castle of Monbrun, many more in other surrounding castles, and even five hundred ready to be a fifth column within Taulat's own domain?

This question really is impudent. It violates the rules of the genre and attacks the presuppositions of all adventure romances and most chansons de geste. To ask it, as a modern critic, may seem as irrelevant as for a biblical scholar to ask why, if an omnipotent God wants the Israelites in the Promised Land, he doesn't just pick them up and put them there instead of going through the whole rigmarole of hardening Pharaoh's heart, sending plagues, and parting the waters. A romance author who showed such a massed assault succeeding against a villain would explode the whole genre from the inside, and romance castles would now fall to mercenary armies and the ravages of dysentery, just like castles in the real world. The *Jaufre*-Poet cannot ask these questions and still remain a romance poet. He can, however, come close to suggesting that even the most basic principle of his genre is a sham.

Immediately after the episode with the lepers, Jaufre finds himself in a beautiful garden attached to the castle of Monbrun. Because he is there, the birds do not sing, and because they are not singing, Lady

Brunissen cannot sleep between her episodes of violent mourning for her imprisoned overlord. She sends out her seneschal to rectify the situation by killing or capturing the intruder. He awakens Jaufre, challenges him to a couched-lance horseback duel, and loses. A second Monbrun knight comes down, fights Jaufre, and loses. A third Monbrun knight comes down, fights Jaufre, and loses—although Jaufre is so exhausted that he thinks it is the same man coming back again and again. At this point, the seneschal says, "I advise you not to send a knight alone, or he will deal with each man of Monbrun in the same way" (3520), and Lady Brunissen replies, "I have plenty of worthless knights; fifty or a hundred or more if it's necessary, can go there, and I'll see if they can bring him back to me."

Other adventure romances raise the possibility of a collective expedition against the hero. In *Blandin de Cornoalha* (1166–248), ten knights bar Blandin's way into a palace where his Sleeping Beauty is imprisoned. He kills the first four, one at a time, including their leader. The other six are demoralized and surrender. In Chrétien's *Erec*, a lecherous count leads a hundred warriors against the hero to steal his beautiful wife. The count is wounded, sees the error of his ways, and calls off the attack (3592–3652). In *Jaufre*, there is no leader and no chance for one-on-one battles. A whole crowd of nameless knights runs down from the palace to the garden, and

> . . . qui pot avenir premers
> Qel pren, e aqo volenters.
> Qil pren per cambas, qi per bratz,
> Qi per cueisas, qi per costatz,
> Qi per espatlas, qi per testa. [3537–41]

[Whoever could get there first grabbed him, and willingly. One took his legs, another his arms, his thighs, his sides, his shoulders, his head.]

He is carted off unceremoniously into the palace, where he is totally at the mercy of the beautiful Brunissen.

The realities of nameless collective power are suppressed, however, almost as soon as they are recognized. Jaufre escapes and goes on to triumph in more crucial single battles. He wins Lady Brunissen's love, and after the detour in which he is forced to defend the damsel in distress, again in single combat, he marries his lady at an elaborate feast at Arthur's court. He returns to her castle to dispense her wealth to her followers and to win gratitude for himself and the same sort of social security with which traditional romance heroes are rewarded. This is, after all, a romance, and the broad rhetorical structures of the genre are ultimately triumphant.

If the Impudent Question had been asked, I do not believe that the poet would have been pummeled with swords and axes and small dogs, if only because the Court of Aragon had a long tradition of hospitality toward troubadours. But the question was not asked, and the implications of the episodes that might have provoked it were not carried through to their logical conclusions. The little surviving medieval evidence for the poem's reception shows the victory of the generic form. For Ramon Muntaner, a Catalan chronicler writing a hundred years later, Jaufre is no more than one of a list of heroes, including Lancelot and Roland, to be trotted out for comparison with his own real-life warrior heroes.[31] *Jaufre* was translated into Castilian prose,[32] leaving out all the episodes that bring discredit on Arthur's court or challenge dominant attitudes toward honor and individual valor. Although Catalonia and Provence did not become centers of romance production, French texts received enduring attention and admiration in the region even after they had gone out of fashion in the best circles in France and had lost their social relevance. Jaufre's exploits were made into painted decorations for the palace of a King of Aragon called Pere the Ceremonious; one of the manifestations of his ceremoniousness was a translation from Castilian into Catalan of Alfonso el Sabio's *Treatise on Chivalry*, complete with its emphasis on noble birth, on the rules of single combat, on the symbolic significance of ritual dubbing. This treatise informs us that *caballeros* are so named not because of anything so mundane as the fact that they ride around on *caballos*, but because knights are the most honorable of men just as horses are the most honorable of ridable animals.[33]

Notes

1. *Blandin de Cornoalha*, ed. C. H. M. Van Der Horst (The Hague: Mouton, 1974), follows much the same pattern as an Arthurian romance, but there is no mention of Arthur. Guilhem de Torroella's *La Faula*, ed. Pere Bohigas and Jaume Vidal Alcover (Tarragona: Edicions Tàrraco, 1984), has a great deal of Arthur but little of the structure of an adventure romance.

2. *Jaufré: Roman arthurien du* xiii*ᵉ siècle en vers provencaux*, ed. Clovis Brunel (Paris: Société des Anciens Textes Français, 1943). References in the text are to line numbers in this version.

3. There has been considerable debate, of course, over the year of the composition and over the identity of the King of Aragon mentioned in lines 58ff. For a full bibliography on the question, see Francois Pirot, *Recherches sur les connaissances littéraires des troubadours occitans et catalans des* xii*ᵉ et* xiii*ᴱ siècles* (Barcelona: Real Academia de Buenas Letras, 1972), 498–506; Pirot's conclusions, like those of Rita Lejeune and Marti de Riquer, that *Jaufre* as we have it—or at least a portion thereof—dates back to the third quarter of the twelfth century, have not met with widespread approval.

4. The Hunt for the White Stag in Chrétien's *Erec et Enide*, ed. Mario Roques (Paris: Honoré Champion, 1978), ll. 27–80, 279–341, 1733–84, and the adventure of Calogrenant in *Yvain*, ed. Mario Roques (Paris: Honoré Champion, 1978), ll. 142–580, perform similar functions.

5. In *La Queste del Saint Graal*, ed. Albert Pauphilet (Paris: Librairie Honoré Champion, 1975), 4–5, Kay intervenes after Arthur has forgotten not to eat; immediately afterward, it is reported that there is a stone floating on the water outside. In *Li Chevaliers as Deus Espees*, ed. Wendelin Foerster (Halle: Niemeyer, 1877; rpt. Amsterdam: Rodopi, 1966), ll. 157ff., Arthur does not feel like eating because no adventure has come, despite the fact that he is holding a magnificent feast; the problem is no sooner mentioned than a threatening messenger arrives from the King of Outre-Ombre. In *Sir Gawain and the Green Knight*, ed. J. R. R. Tolkien and E. V. Gordon, rev. N. O. Davis (Oxford: Oxford University Press, 1967), the custom is announced in lines 85–99, and then, following a list of those present at the feast and a brief reference to the food served to them (for here only Arthur must fast), the strange and ominous Green Knight arrives at line 136.

6. Jaufre is not the only example in which the anticipated adventure is slow in coming. In *La Vengeance de Raguidel*, in Raoul de Houdenc, *Sämtliche Werke*, vol. 2, ed. M. Friedwanger (Halle, 1909; rpt. Geneva: Slatkine, 1975), ll. 18ff., the narrator announces the custom and, immediately afterward, the lack of an appropriate adventure; Arthur is so upset that he goes off to his room and tosses and turns all night until he sees a marvelous ship, with only one passenger, a dead knight whose body has been pierced by a lance (ll. 105–29). Arthur is overjoyed that an adventure has finally come to his court, and not because it means that he can eat. Rather, the arrival of the ship is a sign of divine approval for his steadfast adherence to the custom (ll. 137–39). In *Le Haut Livre du Graal: Perlesvaus*, ed. W. A. Nitze and T. A. Jenkins (1932; rpt. New York: Phaeton, 1972), the lack of adventure can be rectified only when Arthur submits to the rules of a very well-defined adventure at the chapel of Saint Augustine in the White Forest: breaching the rules results in the death of one of his followers. In comparison, Arthur's personal decision in *Jaufre* to "get" an adventure on his own terms seems rather shocking.

7. Huon de Méri, *Le Torneiement Anticrist*, ed. M. O. Bender (University, Miss.: Romance Monographs, 1976).

8. *Claris et Laris*, ed. J. Alton, *Bibliothek des literarischen Vereins in Stuttgart* 169 (1884).

9. Embricon de Mayence, *Le Vie de Mahomet*, ed. Guy Cambrier (Brussels: Latomus, 1962), ll. 369–86.

10. See *The Medieval French Roman d'Alexandre*, vol. 2, *Version of Alexandre de Paris*, ed. E. C. Armstrong, D. L. Buffum, Bateman Edwards and L. F. H. Lowe (Princeton, N.J.: Princeton University Press, 1937), ll. 429–33 and 461–63.

11. *La Chanson d'Aspremont*, ed. Louis Brandin (Paris: Honoré Champion, 1919–20), ll. 1822–34.

12. In her survey of all the examples of nudity in the romance corpus (except, of course, the "anomalous" *Jaufre*), Danielle Regnier-Bohler, "Le corps mis à nu: Perception et valeur symbolique de la nudité dans les récits du Moyen Âge," *Europe*, no. 654 (October 1983):51–62, has shown that male nudity always represents a state of transition: the disrobing is a sign of segregation, exile from collective life, to be followed by a ritual reintegration into society through a formalized reinvestment with the visible signs of one's place in society. The best-known example, Yvain's mad disrobing after he has violated his covenant with Laudine (ll. 2776ff.), is in many ways the most typical. The knights in *Jaufre*, however, make a rational and social choice to remove their clothes, and do not go through any kind of purgative regression to a state of nature. When they get dressed again, "negus anc noi a triat, / Qui pren capa, qui pren mantel" (no one was too choosy about who took whose cape or mantle) (ll. 476–77); the re-clothing is not a sign of the reestablishment of individual identity, but reveals the courtiers as an undifferentiated crowd.

13. William Calin, "Toward a New Reading of *Jaufre*: A Dialogue with Marc-René Jung," in *Studia Occitanica in Memoriam Paul Remy*, 2 vols., ed. Hans-Erich Keller (Kalamazoo, Mich.: Medieval Institute Publications, Western Michigan University, 1986), vol. 2, *The Narrative-Philology*, calls him "a Merlin-figure" (14); in the same volume, Ann Tukey Harrison, "Arthurian Women in *Jaufre*," goes so far as to declare that he is "Merlin in disguise" (66); and Jean-Charles Huchet, "Le roman à nu: *Jaufre*," *Littérature* 74 (1989), calls him "Celui qui ici occupe la place de Merlin" (93). There are similarities, to be sure, but in my view they are more than outweighed by the differences.

14. As Yves Lefevre notes, in "Partenopeus de Blois," in *Grundriss der Romanischen Literaturen des Mittelalters*, IV/1, ed. Jean Frappier and Reinhold R. Grimm (Heidelberg: Carl Winter, 1984), a comparable revelation that the magic of Melior in *Partenopeus* is the product of education "ôte en une certaine mesure tout caractère surnaturel au merveilleux qui pénètre jusque-là le roman" (275).

15. Dominique Boutet, "Carrefours idéologiques de la royauté arthurienne," *Cahiers de Civilisation Médiévale* 28 (1985):3–17.

16. *Gesta Comitum Barcinonensium: Textos Llatí i Català*, ed. L. Barrau Dihigo and J. Massó Torrents (Barcelona: Institut d'Estudis Catalans, 1925), 18, 53, 140–41.

17. Jaume I, *Crònica, o Llibre dels Feits*, pp. 1–402 of *Les Quatre Grans Cròniques*, ed. Ferran Soldevila (Barcelona: Editorial Selecta, 1971), chap. 8.

18. *Llibre dels Feits*, chap. 9.

19. Bernat Desclot, *Llibre del Rei En Pere*, pp. 405–664 of Soldevila, *Les Quatre Grans Cròniques*, chap. 6.

20. Ferran Soldevila, *Els Primers Temps de Jaume I* (Barcelona: Institut d'Estudis Catalans, 1968), 12, 24.

21. *Llibre dels Feits*, chap. 5.

22. Bernat Desclot, *Llibre del Rei En Pere*, chap. 4, and Ramon Muntaner, *Crònica*, pp. 667–1000 of Soldevila, *Les Quatre Grans Cròniques*, chaps. 3–6. Although written considerably later than the events, these chronicles contain prosified versions of near-contemporary popular poems on the subject. See Soldevila's notes and Beatrice Concheff, "The Hypothetical Epic Narrative Sources for the Catalan Chronicles of Jaume I, Desclot and Muntaner" (Ph.D. thesis, University of Wisconsin, 1976).

23. According to the story, Jaume's paternal grandfather was supposed to marry his maternal grandmother, but the marriage never took place. Still, by the grace of God, the bloodlines were united in the next generation: "E Nostre Senyor volc per aquella promesa que el rei havia feta primerament, co és a saber, que seria sa muller la filla de l'emperador Manuel, que aquella tornàs en son lloc: e par-ho en açò que la neta de l'emperador Manuel fo puis muller de nostre pare on nós venim. E per açò és obra de Déu que aquella convinença que no es complí en aquell temps, se complí depuis quan nostre pare pres per muller la néta de l'Emperador" (*Llibre dels Feits*, chap. 7). The whole story is a romanticization of a rather more sordid affair with a rather different cast of characters than Jaume believed; see Winfried Hecht, "Zur Geschichte der 'Kaiserin' von Montpellier, Eudoxia Comnena" *Revue des Études Byzantines* 26 (1968):161–69.

24. See, for example, Jaume's charter reestablishing the constitution of the Peace of God on December 21, 1288: "volentes antecessorum nostrorum sequi vestigia et exempla"; quoted in Gener Gonzalo i Bou, *La Pau i la Treva a Catalunya: Origen de les Corts Catalans* (Barcelona: Edicions de la Magrana, 1986), 132.

25. Immediately after his description of the death of Pere el Catòlic, Bernat Desclot, *Llibre del Rei En Pere*, proceeds (chaps. 7–10) to a lengthy retelling of the legendary tale of the Earl of Toulouse and the Empress of Alemaine, with either Ramon Berengar III or Ramon Berengar IV playing the lead role. This story serves to justify Catalan claims on Provence, as Soldevila notes (600); but Desclot avoids a reference to the rights of Pere el Catòlic, and turns instead to those of a Catalan monarch perhaps as much as a hundred years earlier.

26. The earlier chapters of the *Llibre dels Feits* are devoted to Jaume's descriptions of his difficult relations with the nobles of the previous generation; see especially chaps. 20 and 21.

27. See Jean Flori, *L'Idéologie du glaive: Préhistoire de la chevalerie* (Geneva: Droz, 1983) and *L'Essor de la chevalerie: XIe-XIIe siècles* (Geneva: Droz, 1986), subject to the criticisms of Michel Stanesco, *Jeux d'errance du chevalier médiéval* (Leiden: Brill, 1988), 45–49.

28. See the various versions of these clerical decodings of the dubbing ceremony in the *Ordene de Chevalerie*, in Keith Busby, *Raoul de Houdenc: Le Roman des Eles, and The Anonymous Ordene de Chevalerie* (Amsterdam: John Benjamins, 1983),

and Ramon Llull, *Llibre de l'Orde de Cavalleria*, ed. Marina Gustà (Barcelona: Edicions 62, 1980).

29. Maurice Keen, *Chivalry* (New Haven & London: Yale University Press, 1984), 75.

30. Pierre de Vaulx-Cernay, *Histoire de la guerre des Albigeois*, in *Collection des memoires relatifs à l'histoire de France*, 31 vols., ed. F. Guizot (Paris: J.-L.-J. Brière, 1824), 14:343.

31. *Crònica*, chaps. 116 and 148; compare chaps. 51, 128, and 134.

32. *Crònica de los Muy Notables Caualleros Tablante de Ricamonte y de Jofre, Hijo del Conde Don Ason*, in *Libros de Caballerias*, pt. 1, ed. Adolfo Bonilla y San Martin (Madrid: Bailly-Baillére é Hijos, 1907).

33. "Mas en Espanya apellem 'cavalleria' no per ço com van encavalgats en cavalls, mas per tal com, bé així com los que van en cavalls van plus honradament que en altra bestia, axi meseix los que són elets a ésser cavallers són plus honrats que tots los altres defensors" (Pere III, *Tractat de Cavalleria*, ed. Pere Bohigas [Barcelona: Barcino, 1947], 112–13).

Surveying Ruins

Considering the Absence of Feudal Ideals of Order

———————————————————————————— ❦

THE FINAL TWO essays in this collection introduce a perspective on the decline of the feudal ideal of order that concludes the present investigation. Perhaps the most difficult to define of all, this perspective treats the idea of decline in terms of the absence of the feudal ideal. Much about the nature of any decline can be learned from careful examination of what is left in its place—from careful examination, in other words, of ruins, leading particularly to an understanding of the decline's cause or causes. This is the purpose of Lois Roney's "Chaucer Subjectivizes the Oath: Depicting the Fall from Feudalism into Individualism in the *Canterbury Tales*."

Examining the three feudal motifs of fidelity, long-lasting service, and reciprocity as expressed in oaths in the so-called postfeudal age, Roney finds that adherence to the ideal usually gives way to expediency. This "fall," however, is fortunate and necessary because it enables Chaucer to reveal the inner workings of mind or subjectivity in action. The oaths between Palamon and Arcite fail, for example, not because Palamon and Arcite are unworthy, but rather because of the difference between the underlying belief systems they represent. Absolute obedience in the *Clerk's Tale*, likewise, is challenged by day-to-day realities and the autonomy of the individual. The causes for this and similar changes, according to Roney, can be located in new religious practice, the new logic of Scholasticism, and the economic renaissance.

Another result from the careful study of ruins is often a factual rather than a speculative appreciation for the former reality of things. The very notion of the feudal ideal of order, as the previous essays have attempted to show, may in fact be more of a historical construct than a medieval reality. What is more, the very idea of an age with which we associate the ideal of feudal order may not be historically accurate. Amos Lee Laine's "John Rastell and the Norman Conquest: Tudor Theories about the Feudal Age," the collection's final essay, addresses this issue and thus offers not only another perspective on the absence of the feudal ideal but also a corrective to potentially distortive historical thinking by demonstrating that even an early Renaissance humanist like John Rastell found it difficult to conceive of a feudal age, let alone feudal ideals. That Rastell, despite being a legalist and writer, could not understand how the fief and tenure problem resulting from the Norman invasion meant anything significant, Laine reminds us, should be weighed carefully in any consideration of the feudal age and its ideals.

11 Chaucer Subjectivizes the Oath

Depicting the Fall from Feudalism into
Individualism in the *Canterbury Tales*

EUDALISM WAS GONE in England long before Geoffrey
Chaucer began to write the *Canterbury Tales*. Like the voluminous fortress-churches it built and the monastic renewals it
sponsored, feudalism had faded into other social and political forms. K. B. McFarlane has traced the replacement, during the
fourteenth century, of the spoken tenurial bond between lord and vassal by the written contractual indenture between master and man. The
last summoning of the English feudal host was in 1327; feudal service
of all kinds and on all levels was now being regularly commuted into
money payments.[1] Richard W. Kaeuper has paralleled the growth of
large-scale direct taxation on personal property in the later thirteenth
and early fourteenth centuries with the growth of ever grander concepts of warfare, and has shown that once the Hundred Years War began, its persistent demand for money virtually ensured the growth of
Parliamentary control over most forms of taxation.[2] And Paul Strohm
has detailed the complex social groupings, some hierarchal, some
based on common interests and types of expertise, of the Londoners
among whom Chaucer lived and worked. Loyalties now were more often temporary than lifelong; knights were grouped with gentles rather
than barony; gentility was possible through household or military service; and important nongentles, such as merchants and aldermen,
were being ranked as equals of gentles in "honor" or in "importance

to the well-being of the realm."[3] Clearly, feudalism was gone. A society of written contracts, of money payments for service, of direct taxation on personal property, of tradespeople ranking alongside knights, of short-term loyalties and rival interest groups, is no longer a feudal society.

However, feudalism had left behind at least three of its great behavioral ideals—the importance of fidelity to one's oath, the value of long-standing service, and the mutuality of obligation between the more powerful and the less.[4] These three behavioral ideals are developed, debated, and sometimes shown debased throughout Chaucer's works. Indeed, they remain today among the treasured icons of "the good old days" of their youth that, for hundreds of years, people of Western European culture have fondly recalled. The fact is, even in Chaucer's day, the three had already begun to decline. In this study, I will look closely at Chaucer's depiction of the decline of the first, the oath, since the oath was the centerpiece of the earliest, most constant, and most characteristic institution of medieval feudalism, the vassalage ceremony.

First, by way of definition, the earliest signification for the word "oath" is given by the OED as follows:

> 1. A solemn or formal appeal to God (or to a deity or something held in reverence or regard), in witness of the truth of a statement, or the binding character of a promise or undertaking; an act of swearing; a statement or promise corroborated by such an appeal, or the form of words in which such a statement or promise is made.[5]

In its mature, twelfth-century form, the vassalage ceremony had three parts, all three symbolic: the enclosing of hands, the kiss of peace, and the oath. Marc Bloch speculated that the origins of the first part, homage, the symbolic enclosing of hands by which the man "wishing to serve" placed his hands inside the hands of another man "willing or anxious to be served" and became his "man" (homo), lay deep in the remote Germanic past, and that the oath of fealty was attached to it during Carolingian times.[6] The earliest known reference to an actual oath of vassalage, from the Annales regni Francorum of 757, is translated by David Herlihy as follows:

> [Year 757], King Pepin held his assembly in Compiegne with the Franks. Tassilo, the duke of the Bavarians, came there, and com-

mended himself with his hands to vassalage. He swore many, innumerable oaths, placing his hands upon the relics of the saints. He promised fidelity to King Pepin and to his sons mentioned above, the lord Charles and Carloman, as a vassal, with right mind and firm devotion, ought in justice to do to his lords.[7]

The earliest known description of the ceremony performed in conjunction with the granting of a fief (investiture) is from Galbert of Bruges' *Histoire du meurtre de Charles le Bon comte de Flandre (1127–1128)*, again translated by Herlihy, as follows:

> On Thursday, the seventh of the ides of April [April 7, 1127], acts of homage were again made to the count, which were brought to a conclusion through this method of giving faith and assurance. First, they performed homage in this fashion: the count inquired if [the prospective vassal] wished completely to become his man. He replied, "I do wish it," and with his hands joined and covered by the hands of the count, the two were united by a kiss. Second, he who had done the homage gave faith to the representative of the count in these words: "I promise in my faith that I shall henceforth be faithful to Count William, and I shall fully observe the homage owed him against all men, in good faith and without deceit." Third, he took an oath on the relics of saints. Then the count, with the rod which he had in his hand, gave investiture to all those who by this promise had given assurance and due homage to the count, and had taken the oath.[8]

Feudal oath making, from the ninth through the twelfth centuries, was practical, political, and public. The oaths themselves do not seem to have been problematic. Promising to become someone's man was a traditional commitment made at a public ceremony and interpreted if need be according to customary law. No doubt sometimes there was a gap between the tradition and the reality. No doubt there were abuses, resentments, and deep infidelities. Yet the public feudal oath worked as the shaper, maintainer, and enforcer of the political/ military system of most of Western Europe for over four hundred years, during which time European civilization rose from the chaos of the "Dark Ages" to become a well-organized, highly sophisticated culture.

The feudal system died out not only as personal service obligations and aids were converted to indentures, money payments, and taxes,

and as undifferentiated traditional knowledge and prowess were supplanted in the household and on the battlefield by specialized expertise. It died out also as people changed. A sense of the autonomy of
the individual was developing. The subjectivities of individual human
beings were no longer totally merged into their various social groups.
R. W. Southern,[9] Walter Ullmann,[10] Colin Morris,[11] and Robert W.
Hanning[12] have all written on different facets of the gradual separation of the individual from his or her communal background during
the period 1050–1250.[13] In the twelfth century, one can see this separation process already under way in Chrétien, whose characters sometimes soliloquize about their conflicting desires (that is, which group's
norm to follow, or which need to satisfy) and argue at length about the
priority of competing behaviors.[14]

The causes of this developing sense of the individual have been located in changes of religious practice and emphases, in legal practice,
in the new logic and Scholasticism, and in the economic renaissance.[15]
By the later fourteenth century, judging from the pilgrims of the *Canterbury Tales,* in urban Western Europe this psychological separation
had been fairly well completed. Individuals now chose when to merge
their thoughts and actions with those of their particular groups and
when to differ. Evaluated by this yardstick, some of Chaucer's pilgrims are strikingly individualized. The personal thoughts and moti-
vations and loyalties—that is to say, the individual subjectivities—of
Reeve, Pardoner, Wife of Bath, Prioress, Miller, Monk, Friar, and even
the Second Nun, cannot be predicted simply by identifying the social
groups to which they each belong (their estates, occupations, orders,
genders, and so on). Individual, rather than only group or universal,
psychologies are thus among the most interesting subjects of the *Canterbury Tales.* Not only among the pilgrims, but also among the characters in some of their tales, can be seen this postfeudal separation of
the individual subjectivity from its groups, this personal unpredict-
ability of particular individual minds—actively thinking, reacting,
speaking, and behaving on bases other than those of their various social affiliations.

The problem is, as individuals separate, interpretations begin to differ. Expectations begin to change. Memories grow fuzzy. In short,
trouthe—arguably Chaucer's highest value—will become problematic. And so, too, will the ancient feudal ideal of perfect fidelity to
one's oath.

Whereas the feudal system, at least in principle, had relied on the belief that oaths could be made verbally and understood by both parties objectively, Chaucer suggests that now, in the later fourteenth century, things have changed. Oaths have become uncertain. The specifics of intending, interpreting, remembering, and fulfilling any oath, even one with traditional content and made in good faith, now can depend greatly not only on the words of the oath itself, but also on the individual subjectivities of the persons who make it. In the *Canterbury Tales* as a whole, Chaucer presents for his reader a complete spectrum of oaths, vows, promises, pledges, expletives, and curses, ranging in intent from solemn to lighthearted to thoughtless to blasphemous to broken. In fact, oath making could easily be seen as *a* (but not *the*) totalizing concept for the whole *Canterbury Tales*. The pilgrims are all on the road to Canterbury, the holiest shrine in England, some of them presumably fulfilling vows (I.15–18).[16] Based on what we are told, all of them, except possibly the Shipman and the Cook, would have made professional, vocational, and/or marital oaths; and in some cases how well they are fulfilling their oaths is openly questioned from the start in their General Prologue portraits (Monk, Friar, Man of Law, Physician, Wife of Bath, Miller, Manciple, Reeve, Summoner, Pardoner), whereas in others it becomes questioned through their particular tales or links (Prioress, Clerk, Host, and, depending on interpretations, others). In fact, oaths were so prevalent in Chaucer's culture that it is difficult to know whether he had their fulfillment explicitly in mind as a continuing theme or whether he simply took them for granted as part of the ordinary conduct of human affairs.[17] Further, in addition to the oaths of the individual pilgrims, at the conclusion of the *Tales* (X.586–606), the Parson presents us with an almost scholastic analysis (that is, according to efficient, material, formal, and final causes) of the whole subject:

Swearing
> Causes (in the modern sense): anger, envy, gain, lawful
> compulsion
> Subject terms: God's name, throne, creation, city; Christ's
> body parts
> Lawful: truth; in a court; to honor God or to help one's fellow
> Christian
> False and needless: to impress others, out of habit, for magic
> and divination

In fact, swearing of one kind or another, which oftentimes is crucial to the action, turns up explicitly at least once in every tale except that of the Prioress. In her case we are told instead in the General Prologue that her greatest oath was "but by Seint Loy" (I.120).[18] Further, the Tatlock-Kennedy *Concordance* lists, for the *Canterbury Tales*, eight and one half columns (at approximately 100 lines per column) of uses of the word *God ('s)*, six columns for *true (-er, -est, truly, truth)*, two columns for *swear (-er, -eth, -ing, swore, sworn)*, one half column for the word *oath(s)* itself, one third column on *vouch* and *vouchsafe*, and one use of the word *vow*.[19] Clearly, oath making is an action to which Chaucer returns over and over again in the *Tales*.

Whereas the feudal use of oath-making seems to have been clear, customary, and nonproblematic, however, Chaucer, writing in the later fourteenth century, long after feudalism had degenerated into money payments and nationalisms, seems mainly interested in its psychology. Who swears, and why; who fails his vow, and why; who reinterprets or reneges—these are Chaucer's focus. The oaths of his characters sometimes are, sometimes are not, essential to their particular plot actions; but I doubt they are ever simply filler. Too many other kinds of words and phrases were available for filling out a line. In fact, all oaths are choices. Habitual oaths are merely reaffirmations of earlier choices. In Chaucer, it seems safe to say, oaths are always characterizing. Even in his three most noble, most feudal tales (the Knight's, the Franklin's, and the Clerk's), the characters' oaths are opaque rather than transparent. Their meanings are subjectively conditioned by their makers rather than intrinsically clear from their words.

One would not expect two young knights of exactly the same royal blood, family, upbringing, and city-state culture to interpret a traditional oath in radically opposing ways, but they do in the *Knight's Tale*. In this tale Chaucer raises explicitly the issue of *interpretation*: one oath, two conflicting interpretations, both valid. Similarly, one would not expect a noble and virtuous wife to swear an oath of infidelity to the husband she dearly loves, but she seems to think she has done so in the *Franklin's Tale*. In this tale Chaucer raises the issue of *intention*: at the time the oath was made, her intent never to fulfill it was perfectly clear, both to herself and to the man to whom she made it. She merely spoke the words. But later, when the demand for fulfillment is made, her intent is neither recalled nor considered, not by the narrator, not by herself. Likewise, one would not expect a peasant woman of the lowest status to make and fulfill that most difficult of all oaths, total annihilation of the will, but so she does in the *Clerk's Tale*. In this tale Chaucer raises the issue of *fulfillment*: when the expectations according to which an oath was made are unilaterally escalated from normal to criminal, what should one do? Oppose the unforeseen evil, or widen and reaffirm the oath? Thus, in all three of these, Chaucer's most feudal tales, the oaths have been subjectivized. When push comes to shove, the characters who made them reinterpret them in unexpected, individualized ways. Indeed, in all three tales, it is the subjectivization of the oaths—conflicting interpretations in the *Knight's Tale*, unremembered intentions in the *Franklin's Tale*, and escalated fulfillment in the *Clerk's Tale*—that drives the narrative action.

Interpretation—The *Knight's Tale* "Brotherhood Oath"

Interpretation is always an issue in Chaucer criticism, more so perhaps than with many other major writers, but here in the *Knight's Tale* Chaucer himself raises the issue explicitly and in its strongest form: one brotherhood oath, two conflicting interpretations, both of them valid.[20] In this tale, two young knights, cousins and sworn brothers, fall in love with the same fair lady. One insists he alone has the right to love her because he saw her first and the other has sworn to aid him in matters of love. The other insists he, too, has the right to love her because love is naturally irresistible and therefore first-finder's rights and positive oaths are irrelevant. In fact, the two are psychological opposites. Throughout the tale, their subjective reactions are repeatedly opposed, for example, to freedom from prison (1223–33, 1282–94), to the nature of the gods (1251–67, 1303–24), and to prayer (2221–50, 2373–420).[21] In pre-Renaissance literature such psychological oppositions are most unusual. In Virgil and Ovid, by way of contrast, characters constantly have to interpret prophecies and omens but only rarely other people; and conflict of equally valid viewpoints, as far as I can recall, does not occur. Interpretation of other people in Dante, Langland, and the *Pearl*-Poet is ordinarily a question of increasing one's knowledge (whether a character's or the reader's) rather than of balancing two equally valid views. My point is that the way Chaucer raises the interpretation issue here in the *Knight's Tale* is unusual. As far as I know, the contrast of two opposing but equally valid interpretations of essentially the same subject matter is a major technique only in some of the medieval literary debates (of water and wine but both liquids, of lily and rose but both flowers, of winter and summer but both seasons, and so on). In the *Knight's Tale*, the oath of brotherhood between Palamon and Arcite is a case in which the terms, the symbolism, and the intent of the oath are traditional and clear, and where both parties act in good faith. Yet the oath fails to keep the peace because the two parties interpret it in different but equally valid ways, as a result of different but equally valid belief systems. Palamon insists that positive law (the oath) must be honored, whereas Arcite insists that love is prior to the oath because love is irresistible, a law of human nature.

The opposition between positive and natural law is traditional. Positive law is law that has been positively enacted, decreed, or made known by open declaration. Natural law, on the other hand, is part of one's own nature as a human being. For example, in the Bible, the opposition of positive and natural law constitutes the primal conflict. The law of nature (natural appetite) in the garden of Eden would have told Adam and Eve to eat anything they wanted. God, on the other hand, told Adam explicitly (positive law) not to eat the fruit of that tree. Adam obeyed nature, disobeying positive law, and we all fell.[22] The conceptual opposition between the two kinds of law is absolute: something formally decreed, enacted, or made known (positive) versus something inscribed into one's created nature and instinctively felt to be right (natural; written on the heart and in the conscience, according to Paul [Romans 2:14–15]; written in the law of reason according to Albert the Great). The OED definitions speak of "positive" as a statement "formally laid down or imposed; arbitrarily or artificially instituted, proceeding from enactment or custom," and oppose it to "natural" as "based upon the innate moral feeling of mankind; instinctively felt to be right or fair." Philosophers from scholastic to modern have differently defined what is "natural" to human nature and therefore what is "natural" to law, but the distinction between the two kinds of law is clear and absolute: on the one hand, something imposed from outside; on the other, something arising from within.[23] Now, given the two kinds of law, a second question arises with regard to the natural: is it irresistible or is one free to choose whether or not to obey it? For example, given that one is hungry (a natural appetite), then, given the sight of an apple, is one compelled to eat it? Or, given that one falls in love with a woman (a natural appetite), is one compelled to pursue her? Is pursuing this particular woman totally beyond one's control? In the *Knight's Tale*, Arcite argues that his love for Emelye is irresistible, a "gretter lawe," and therefore exempt from the provisions of the oath of brotherhood. Palamon, on the other hand, argues that love is not irresistible: it is by free choice; and he demands that Arcite live up to his oath and simply stop loving her.

In the tale, the oath of brotherhood is not itself an issue. The issue is its scope. In Part I, when Palamon recounts its terms (1128–51), Arcite does not dispute them. Instead, defending his right to love Emelye in spite of Palamon's seeing her first and in spite of the oath, he offers a three-point argument: First, as to first-finder's rights, he was the first to discern her human nature (1155–61). Second, as to the brotherhood oath, it does not apply, and he cites both authority (1163–66, Boethius III, m.12) and experience (1167–71) to the effect that love is the "gretter lawe" since positive laws are broken for love every day. Third as to the realistic possibility of either knight's winning her, he points out initially that they are permanently in prison, and further that they two cannot determine who will win her because, in the court of the king (of love? of destiny?), each man receives whatever the king decides (1172–86). But Palamon is not persuaded, the strife continues, and in the grove in Part II Palamon again demands that Arcite live up to his positive oath and simply stop loving her.

"I drede noght that outher thow shalt dye,
Or thow ne shalt nat loven Emelye.
Chees which thou wolt, or thou shalt nat asterte!" [1580–95]

In response, Arcite repeats again that love is by natural necessity.

". . . I defye the seurete and the bond
Which that thou seiest that I have maad to thee.
What, verray fool, thynk wel that love is free,
And I wol love hire mawgree all thy myght!" [1599–1607]

The opposition between the two knights' beliefs about the oath—Palamon's that the positive oath between them must be kept and Arcite's that the natural law of love is greater than any oath—is resolved through their oaths of submission to Theseus and acceptance of his terms for winning Emelye (1827, 1870–77). As a result, the confict of positive and natural law is not mentioned again in the tale.

In this part of the overall rivalry between Palamon and Arcite, Chaucer has presented us with an example of an oath that failed even though the terms were well understood and traditional and both parties were acting in good faith. It failed because of differences in their underlying belief systems, differences so primal that between men of good faith and similar background they are rarely discussed, even in real life, unless conflict breaks out.

Much has been made by Chaucerians of this oath's failure. It is ordinarily treated as an exemplum of the power of passionate love over male friendship. My point instead is that, in this first of the *Canterbury Tales*, with the failure of the oath, Chaucer has deliberately posed for his reader the philosophically hard case of conflicting, equally valid interpretations. Further, Chaucer's remarkably even-handed presentation of the struggle between the two competing knights encourages his reader to try to compare them, and what is comparison but further interpretation? In addition, by way of outside evidence, both the oath and this first falling out between the two young knights over who has the right to love Emelye are Chaucer's additions to Boccaccio's story. None of this occurs in the *Teseide*. Moreover, at the beginning of the tale and before the conflict begins, Chaucer is at pains to establish the two knights' similarity: they are found in the same heap of bodies, wearing the same arms and coat-of-arms, in the same half-alive state, and sentenced to the same tower under the same conditions (1009–19, 1030–32). Furthermore the two belong to all the same background and kinship groups. As a result, since their nature/nurture backgrounds are the same, one would expect their thinking to be much the same, especially with regard to fundamental values. Yet, on this most primal, most fundamental issue of the relative priority of natural and positive law, they are totally opposed. What better demonstration could there be that the human mind has become separated from its social groups, that an individual's values are no longer to be inferred simply from his or her estate, family, profession, order, gender, or other such affiliations? that a person's *trouthe* has become subjective and therefore any person's perception of truth itself problematic?

Further, Chaucer has coupled the *Knight's Tale* with that of the Miller, provoking some surprising parallels and interpretive comparisons, and has then followed these two tales with that of the Reeve, provoking yet further parallels and comparisons and complex interpretations. In short, *interpretation* can be *a* (not *the*) totalizing concept for the *Knight's Tale* and Fragment I.

Intention—The *Franklin's Tale* "Rash Promise Oath"

The notion that intent is a major issue in the Franklin's Tale is clear not only from the tale itself but also from the changes Chaucer made in Boccaccio's story. Further, it is the issue that has drawn the most critical attention. In the tale, Dorigen actually swears two oaths to Aurelius, one serious, the other playful. The second oath is her "rash promise," made "in pley," to love him "best of any man" if he will remove from the coast the terrible rocks that she believes threaten her husband. This is the oath which Aurelius tries to hold her to. At the time she made it, however, her innocent intent was abundantly clear to both of them. The rash-promise oath is actually sandwiched between two flat, unequivocal rejections, the first a strong oath never to be an "untrewe wyf" and the second a blunt comment on the "folie" of men who pursue other men's wives. In addition, she immediately follows the rash-promise oath with a remark characterizing its performance as impossible, a judgment with which Aurelius immediately and explicitly concurs. Yet, several years later, when Aurelius suddenly shows up to claim that the rocks are now "aweye" and that she must fulfill the oath, the issue of her intent, which was so clear at the time she made the oath, is never raised. Has she forgotten that she swore it "in pley"? The reader is not told. Does she later tell her husband of her innocent intent in swearing it? The reader is not told. At the end Aurelius admits he knew she "swoor thurgh innocence," but does he realize this at the time of his demand, or only after he has released her from it? The reader is not told. Further, her marriage vow (758–59) would have invalidated her rash-promise oath under any circumstances, but does anyone in the tale consider this? The reader is not told. Instead, what the reader is not only told but shown is the contradiction between the innocence of her original intent versus the literal strength of her rash-promise oath:

Here is Dorigen's intent, stated twice, to rebuff Aurelius unequivocally:

"But now, Aurelie, . . .
By thilke God that yaf me soule and lyf
Ne shal I nevere been untrewe wyf
In word ne werk, as fer as I have wit.
I wol been his to whom that I am knyt.
Taak this for fynal answere as of me." [982–87]

and, after her rash promise,

". . . wel I woot that it [removal of the rocks] shal nevere bityde.
Lat swiche folies out of youre herte slyde.
What deyntee sholde a man han in his lyf
For to go love another mannes wyf,
That hath hir body whan so that hym liketh?" [1001–5]

On the other hand, here are the actual words of her rash-promise oath:

"Aurelie," quod she, "by heighe God above,
Yet wolde I graunte yow to been youre love,
Syn I yow se so pitously complayne,
Looke what day that endelong Britayne
Ye remoeve alle the rokkes, stoon by stoon,
That they ne lette ship ne boot to goon—
I seye, whan ye han maad the coost so clene
Of rokkes that ther nys no stoon ysene,
Thanne wol I love yow best of any man.
Have heer my trouthe in al that evere I kan." [989–98]

Since more than two years later, when Aurelius tries to hold her to this promise, she does not remind him that it was made playfully as an impossible, and that he had explicitly recognized it as such ("Madam," quod he, "this were an inpossible," [1009]), Chaucer critics have focused strongly on trying to resolve the problematics of her intent.

Their judgments vary widely. D. W. Robertson has argued that the second promise "so far as 'entente' is concerned is merely a repetition of the first vow to be true to her husband, since it demands an impossible task"; Dorigen is "downright silly" to take it seriously later.[24] Morton Bloomfield, however, has suggested that the second oath is only half playful, that Dorigen wishes the rocks removed "so much that she is willing to hazard her own love for and loyalty to him to get Arveragus back."[25] Anne Thompson Lee, on the other hand, has concluded that Dorigen's second promise is an unsuccessful attempt to "dally" with words in the courtly manner, that what she really means is that if Aurelius could get rid of those rocks for her, "she really would love him best of any man in a very pure and simple sense."[26] On the other hand, Wolfgang Rudat has pointed out that Dorigen's second oath does renege on her first; "she is *in word* being unfaithful to her husband," a "silly mistake," but also the beginning of an unattractive "domination game."[27] Derek Pearsall, however, suggests she makes the second promise in the kind of playfulness with "which we [all] find some release for our deepest anxieties."[28] Gerald Morgan has argued that in fact the second promise is understood by both to be an impossible: "there is never any doubt as to Dorigen's true intention . . . she wants the rocks off the coast of Britany [because] they imperil the return of her husband."[29] Douglas J. Wurtele likewise regards the second oath as a "non-serious promise." Further, a number of these critics cite medieval *auctoritees* on the whole issue of intention—Wurtele, especially, cites John of Salisbury, Theodore of Canterbury (a seventh-century archbishop), Thomas Aquinas, Peter Lombard, Robert of Brunne, John Bromyard, Robert of Flamborough, John Myrc, Saint Ambrose, Nicolas of Lyra, and Isidore of Seville, not to mention Chaucer's own Pardoner. These citations make it abundantly clear that the intention underlying the making of an oath was an important subject of medieval speculation. Further, they show that by late medieval times the conclusion had become a commonplace that, as Wurtele phrases it, "to break a mistaken oath is better than to keep it."[30] As a result, we readers of the *Franklin's Tale* know that Dorigen does not have to keep her rash-promise oath. She could refuse on grounds of underlying intent, on grounds of her immediately prior oath to Aurelius never to be an untrue wife, on grounds of her marital oath to Arveragus, and also on grounds that the rocks have not been removed (no one ever checks, and Chaucer has made it clear that the Clerk specializes in illusions). In short, *we* know she doesn't have to keep her oath, but *she* doesn't, nor does her husband.

Therefore, in interpreting the tale as Chaucer tells it, the clash between innocent intent and damaging oath is not to be resolved by simply reasoning Dorigen's way out of the oath that she did, literally, swear.[31]

Further, Chaucer added this clash between innocent intent and adulterous oath to the story he found in Boccaccio. In the *Filocolo*, by way of contrast, intentions are clear and the magic is real.[32] The wife wants to be rid of an unwelcome suitor and decides to get rid of him by setting him an impossible task. Much of Boccaccio's focus is on magically producing the real garden. Chaucer, however, shifts the focus of the story from the production of outward tangibles to the inward workings of Dorigen's mind. Instead of asking for a winter garden to get rid of the unwelcome suitor, Dorigen's impossible is the disappearance of the rocks that threaten her husband and so weigh heavily upon her thoughts. Instead of the impossible being deliberately thought up ahead of time, Dorigen is caught off guard, surprised by Aurelius's plea into a rejection so blunt that in courtly circumstances it would have seemed extremely rude, and as a result, apparently to save his feelings, she makes her playful impossible promise. Instead of real magic (in Boccaccio's garden the flowers can be picked and the fruits are eaten), the rocks in the *Franklin's Tale* are merely reported to seem to be away (1295–96). And instead of carefully verifying the garden's existence, Dorigen naively accepts Aurelius's word that the rocks are gone. Boccaccio's wife is close to the stock sharp-witted fabliau stereotype. Chaucer's Dorigen, on the other hand, is much more human, much more subjectivized. She is not particularly bright or imaginative, but she is capable of great confusion, anxiety, and suffering.

By characterizing Dorigen with these inward, subjective qualities, Chaucer has made her seem so "real" that by the end of the tale the reader has no fear she will ever again fall into making a playful oath. Although not individualized in the modern sense, what Dorigen says and what she does are not predictable from the norms of the various groups to which she belongs. No courtly married woman of the higher nobility, for example, would be expected to reject a suitor with the astonishing words Dorigen uses: "What deyntee sholde a man han in his lyf / For to go love another mannes wyf, / That hath hir body whan so that hym liketh?" (1003–5). Among other things, this remark-

ably candid rhetorical question demonstrates the extraordinary innocence of her intentions throughout this whole conversation. Yet, at
the same time, Chaucer makes her playful oath a serious business. In
life, after a time, intentions become hazy, ephemeral, difficult to recall
exactly; and they often surface only after the fact. Spoken oaths, on the
other hand, are—or should be—unequivocal, unchanging, and life-
long, as once upon a time they were.

In fact, the problematics of intention are a major Chaucerian motif
throughout the *Franklin's Tale*. On one level, in addition to the oaths
just discussed, Chaucer dwells on intentions, as well as accord, in the
marriage oaths (744–60, 791–98). And on a higher level, he raises
throughout the tale the question of God's intentions in allowing the
existence of so many kinds of dangers to trap us in this fallen world—
dangers presented by grisly rocks (865–92); by natural influences
(1031–35, 1049–54); by scientific calculations (1270–91); by unwelcome
suitors (925–59 and passim); by unreliable auctoritees (1367–1456); by
overwrought husbands (1472–85); and by magic and illusions in general. All of these pose serious pitfalls for innocents like Dorigen. What
could possibly be God's intent in allowing them to surround all of us
in this world? What could he have in mind?

In addition, Chaucer has linked this story with that of the Squire,
the last half of which consists almost totally of the falcon's complaint
to Canacee about the tigerish intentions of her tercelet mate, intentions that lurked, apparently for many years (524, 574), beneath his
obedient "humble cheere" (507). In short, just as *interpretation* can be
a (not *the*) totalizing concept for the *Knight's Tale* and Fragment I, so
can *intent* be *a* (not *the*) totalizing concept for the *Franklin's Tale* and
Fragment V.

Fulfillment—The *Clerk's Tale* "Obedience Oath"

Fulfilling one's oath is the central action in the *Clerk's Tale*. In this tale,
a peasant woman of supernal intelligence, beauty, and virtue stead-
fastly maintains her oath of marital compliance at enormous psychological cost, including assenting without protest to the murder of
her two beloved children. What meaning can one possibly make of
such a story? In the fourteenth century, although the meanings attached to it varied from the start, the Griselda story was immediately
popular. In Boccaccio it was ostensibly told "to illuminate the theme of

munificence—Walter's, in restoring Griselda as his wife," although Walter's "insane cruelty" is mentioned and the fictional audience discusses it at length. In Petrarch's Latin retelling (one of Chaucer's sources), the focus is on Griselda's virtue as "applicable to all Christians in their response to God." In the French translations (another of Chaucer's sources), Griselda is held out instead as an example for wives to emulate.[33] In the Clerk's retelling, although Chaucer has him repeatedly point out and condemn Walter's cruelty, at the end Chaucer surprisingly gives him only the same two morals as occur in the sources. The Clerk's first moral is stated literally and is Petrarch's, that every wight should emulate Griselda's virtuous "suffraunce" of whatever God sends (1142–62). His second moral is stated ironically in two different ways and is the French: on the one hand, the Clerk says today's women cannot live up to the testing that Griselda did, implying that at one time women could and so still should (1163–69); and on the other, the Clerk says noble wives should go forth into marriage as if into battle, implying that Griselda-type wives are really necessary for peaceful marriages (1183–1212). The question is, are these two morals—the one for Christians vis-à-vis God, the other for wives vis-à-vis husbands—really adequate? Although they are in his sources, would these be Chaucer's meanings as well?[34] One doubts it. Chaucer's endings rarely wrap up his tales. The Prioress ends her tale with an unmerciful prayer for mercy; the Physician ends his tale with inexplicable judgments and a strange non sequitur about forsaking sin; and the Pardoner ends his tale with an absolution offer that is insultingly audacious. It seems likely, therefore, that Chaucer did not intend the Clerk (or even Harry Bailly) to have the final say about the meanings in the *Clerk's Tale*.

The fact is, when reading the *Clerk's Tale*, no matter how much one tries to rationalize what happens, no matter how often one is assured by the text both explicitly and allusively that Griselda is a totally good woman, it is difficult to overlook the fact that she gives up without protest her two small children to be murdered.[35] Indeed, Chaucer was apparently at pains to increase this difficulty for the reader. Recent criticism has been helpfully abstracted by Bernard S. Levy.[36] Current interpretations tend to combine two or three of the following positions: Literally, the tale sets forth the Clerk's demonstration that obedience/patience is the virtuous road for wives or, conversely, that domination in marriage is evil; in either case the Clerk is responding directly to the Wife of Bath. Figuratively, it sets forth an emblem/ exemplum/allegory of the wise man's sovereignty over himself[37] or the virtuous soul's proper response to the worldly suffering by which it is being providentially tested/made strong. In this case Walter is sometimes read as a rather nominalistic God-figure[38] or, conversely, Griselda as a Mary- or Christ-figure.[39]

Looked at from the point of view of Scholastic logic, however, what has happened is that, in the Clerk's retelling, Chaucer has turned the Griselda story into a moral insoluble. On the one hand, Griselda is a paragon of every virtue; on the other, she assents to two murders. If either of these statements is true, then the other must be false.[40] Yet Chaucer's telling of the tale emphatically asserts both statements as true. Biblical allusions are constantly attached to Griselda, suggesting that the reader interpret her figuratively. Yet at the same time the psychological realism of her suffering is intensified, suggesting that the reader interpret her realistically. This conflict of reading conventions was first brought out by James Sledd[41] and Elizabeth Salter.[42] More recently, taking the allegorical/figurative side, Charlotte Morse has argued that the tale is an exemplum of the wise man's self-sovereignty, and Dolores Warwick Freese has highlighted Chaucer's repeated allusions to the spiritual life of the vowed religious.[43] Taking the side of psychological realism, however, Thomas H. Bestul has demonstrated from both patristic and physiognomic sources that Chaucer's additions deliberately intensify the tale's emotional realism.[44] Both sides are persuasive. The result is, one has to agree with both sides and therefore conclude that Chaucer has markedly heightened the insolubility of the Griselda story he found in his sources.

One aspect of this heightening is the fact that Griselda progressively strengthens the oath of acquiescence that Walter asks her to make before their marriage. First, she converts it from acquiescence into obedience and includes thoughts as well as deeds, and then she strengthens it again each time she agrees to give up a child. Originally, Walter just asks her to accept his desires and his freedom to do as he pleases, and neither to "grucche" about it nor to counter him in word or facial expression (351–57). But, possibly out of wonder, possibly out of fear (358), she immediately raises the ante:

". . . as ye wole yourself, right so wol I.
And heere I swere that nevere willyngly
In werk ne *thoght* I nyl yow disobeye." [361–63; emphasis added]

Where he has asked only for outward compliance, she has sworn inward obedience as well. Not even in her thoughts will she disobey him. Next, during the first test, when Walter is taking her daughter, she expands the terms from total obedience to total approval as well.

"Ther may nothyng, God so my soule save,
Liken to yow that may *displese me;*
Ne I desire nothyng for to have,
Ne drede for to leese, save only yee.
This wyl is in myn herte and ay shal be." [505–9; emphasis added]

Next, during the second test, when Walter is taking her son, she ups the ante again, from total approval to total conformity to him and prior approval of him, if such a thing is possible.

"I wol no thyng, ne nyl no thyng, certayn,
But as yow list . . .
For as I lefte at hoom al my clothyng,
Whan I first cam to yow, right so . . .
Lefte I my wyl and al my libertee . . .
And certes, if I *hadde prescience*
Youre wyl to knowe er ye youre lust me tolde,
I wolde it doon withouten necligence." [646–61; emphasis added]

Whereas all Walter asks for in the beginning is total outward compliance, Griselda has enlarged her oath first to inward obedience, then to absolute approval, then to total conformity of her will to his, including prevenient conformity to his will if she were able to know it. The issue she has been coping with all along is, what does one do when one's oath suddenly and unexpectedly is criminalized?

There is no way Griselda could have foreseen that her husband would ever ask the death of his own children. Indeed, the Clerk says that although Walter had earlier tested her and always found her true

(456–58), after the birth of their daughter he was overcome with this "merveillous desir" not only to "assaye" his wife but also to "affraye" her. In his telling, the Clerk dwells on the compulsive subjective processes going on in Walter's mind. Yet one cannot help wondering, is there not something compulsive about Griselda's responses to him? Like her husband, she too is given subjectivity—we pity her especially as she gives up each child to the cruel sergeant, each time kissing it, blessing it, begging the sergeant to bury its little body. Yet why, we wonder, doesn't she simply seize the opportunity she is given, both times, to just take the child and leave? It is one thing to assent to one's own death or dismissal or humiliation, as Griselda does in the third and fourth tests. But it is quite another to assent to someone else's death, as Griselda does in the first and second tests. Why would a supernally good woman do this? Indeed, how could she? Further, Chaucer specifies to the reader the fact that such behavior is not locally acceptable; among Walter's people the disappearance of the two children becomes a scandal (722–32). That the two children are not in fact killed is beside the point as far as Griselda's intent is concerned. In her mind and in the reader's, she has allowed them to be killed. Moreover, in Christian terms, one must wonder what will happen to such a woman on Judgment Day? She has assented to two murders. Can such a woman say, "I was only following orders," and expect such crimes to be erased?

Again, the issue here is fulfillment of a solemn oath when the terms of the oath are suddenly, unilaterally, criminalized. Ought one merely to reaffirm it and strengthen it to meet the new demands, as Griselda does, twice? Or ought one rather to repudiate it as now invalid because the evil new terms violate a prior, more compelling law, whether legal or moral (that is, natural)? When the Clerk's Tale was written, during the explosive days of the reign of Richard II, these must have been explosive questions.[45]

In any event, once people start thinking for themselves, subjectively, rather than automatically following the customary norms of the various groups to which they belong, verbal oaths, no matter how serious, can no longer reliably serve to predict future behavior. In the Clerk's Tale, fulfillment of what seemed to be a traditional oath turned out to be as unpredictable as interpretation of a different but equally traditional oath in the Knight's Tale. And in the Franklin's Tale, of course, an oath playfully made and apparently trivial under the circumstances turned out later to have serious consequences.

Earlier I suggested that *interpretation* could be *a* (not *the*) totalizing concept for the *Knight's Tale* and Fragment I, and that *intent* could be *a* (not *the*) totalizing concept for the *Franklin's Tale* and Fragment V. *Oath-fulfillment*, likewise, could be a totalizing concept for Fragment IV. The Walter/Griselda and January/May marriages seem paralleled in a surprising number of thought-provoking ways, oath making and oath fulfilling not the least of them.

Two Incompatible Goods

Is the ideal of perfect fidelity to one's oath incompatible with the existence of moral subjectivity? In the *Canterbury Tales* Chaucer seems to think so. In the *Knight's Tale*, Palamon regards Arcite's insistence on loving Emelye as a moral transgression. For him Arcite has become a "false traytour wikke" (1580). In the *Franklin's Tale*, Aurelius covers his adulterous demand with a moral cloak: sleeping with him is a question of Dorigen's "honour" (1331), he tells her; otherwise she will be breaking her "trouthe" (1320), a moral claim with which her husband apparently agrees. And in the *Clerk's Tale*, Griselda heightens her acquiescence oath rather than break it, increasingly resigning her will to Walter and thereby resigning to him (perhaps) her own moral responsibility for the fates of her children.

In Chaucer, one's *trouthe* is not simply the conformity of what one says with verifiable fact. One's *trouthe* is one's essential moral quality, one's very principle of being. In Chaucer, when a person is accorded love of "trouthe," as is the Knight (I.46), or swears by his "trouthe," as does the Friar's summoner (III.1525, 1527), the referent is the overall disposition of his moral character, in action and being as well as in speech, not simply his verbal veracity. For example, when the Monk (apparently) asks, "How shal the world be served?" and answers himself (apparently) with "Lat Austyn have his swynk to him reserved" (I.187–88), the reader takes this as a sign of an accommodating moral character because it indicates an accommodating way of fulfilling a sacred vow. In Chaucer, one's oath is always, I think, an indication of one's *trouthe* in this older, principled, essentialist sense of the word. Here is the primary OED entry for the word's first four usages. Notice how broad these older meanings are, and notice also that the first three of these four usages are now labeled rare or obsolete except in the context of a wedding; and even the fourth is unusual.

I. The quality of being true (and allied senses).
   1. The character of being, or disposition to be, true to a person, principle, cause, etc.; faithfulness, fidelity, loyalty, constancy, steadfast allegiance. (See also TROTH 1.) Now *rare* or *arch.*

(Citations run from the ninth through the nineteenth centuries.)

   2. One's faith or loyalty as pledged in a promise or agreement; a solemn engagement or promise, a covenant; = TROTH 2. *Obs.*

(Citations are drawn from the eleventh century through the fifteenth.)

   3. a. Faith, trust, confidence. (Cf. TROTH 3a.) *Obs.*
      b. Belief; a formula of belief, a creed. (Cf. TROTH 3b.) *Obs.*

(Citations run from the fourteenth through the seventeenth centuries.)

   4. Disposition to speak or act truly or without deceit; truthfulness, veracity, sincerity; formerly sometimes in wider sense: Honesty, uprightness, righteousness, virtue, integrity.

(Citations are from the thirteenth through nineteenth centuries.)

These older, broader meanings of the word *trouthe* preserve the ideal. By Chaucer's time, however, the reality of the word had apparently declined to the much slenderer state of being we readily recognize in the *Canterbury Tales'* oaths because we find that same lesser reality all around us today: "truth" now refers usually just to verbal truth, as "oath" now more often indicates just an expletive. The ideal of perfect fidelity to one's oath remains strong, as Chaucer shows in the *Knight's, Franklin's,* and *Clerk's Tales;* but, given the disappearance of the feudal groups in which the ideal developed, the possibility of attaining it seems also beyond recovering.

It has become traditional to find in feudal custom as it developed in England the roots of the Anglo-American system of law, and in feudal respect for law and the feudal principle of mutual obligation between higher and lower, the foundation of Anglo-American constitutional government. I want to suggest the additional possibility that the roots of modern Western self-assertive individualism may also be found in the feudal way of life. It seems likely that at least some of the pressures that drove individual subjectivities to develop and then to separate from the norms of their various groups during the High Middle Ages derived from circumstances peculiar to Western European feudalism, in particular to its unusual combination of economic localism with cultural internationalism.

The early chansons and the romances up through Malory and beyond have fostered in some of us specializing in literary studies a rather unrealistic picture of how feudal aristocrats spent their thoughts, energies, and time. In these stories, the nobles' estates seem to run themselves. Various foods appear on the tables, but their provenance is ordinarily unspecified. Who planned the crops, planted the fields, harvested, stored, and distributed the produce; who hunted and killed the game, who dressed the carcasses, who did the planning, organizing, and cooking—all this is unspecified. Noble men and women wear beautiful fur-trimmed garments, vassals have serviceable and often magnificent armor, but where it comes from, who designed and made it, how it was paid for, are again unspecified. Towns grew and trade resumed; crafts developed, roads and bridges were built; but again, who planned, organized, financed, and effected all this is ordinarily unspecified in the chansons and romances.

David Herlihy has described more realistically the horizontal sharing of power amongst the privileged. Feudal kings shared jurisdiction and authority with their great vassals, with the church and the clergy and the various orders, and with the towns and their guilds and governance bodies: ". . . . the principle that power should be shared and decisions based on consultation among those who held it [was] central to feudal government."[46] "What affects all, by all should be approved" was a feudal commonplace. What this meant in practice was that, because economic localism was the feudal norm, a lot of individual lords and vassals had to do a lot of thinking and planning and decision making on their own. It meant, further, that this responsibility for thinking about and making choices between alternative courses of practical action was passed down vertically, by reason of the principle of mutual obligation, to ever-widening layers of those lower on the social pyramid. The importance of any particular decision is not what matters here; what matters is that many people were having to evaluate, on their own, alternative possible courses of action. This process makes people become conscious of themselves as individuals and, especially as differences of opinion arise, as potentially separate from their various social groups.

Among other things, a vassal was obligated to give his lord "counsel," by which was meant, as Friedrich Heer explains,

> . . . the duty of supporting the lord in all his business and in his numerous lawsuits and disputes with his equals and with other vassals. If the king was his immediate overlord, the vassal was bound to advise him on matters of internal and external policy and medieval kings, even the greatest of them, however impetuous they were by nature, were often scrupulous in taking counsel from their most important vassals.[47]

Moreover, each vassal had to manage his fief well enough to support whatever knight-service was required of him, to pay his lord the customary aids, and to support his household. Among other things, he had to be able to calculate the value of this possible wardship or that possible son-in-law. He had to hold his own court and see to justice and order on his lands. Heer's description of these feudal lords fleshes out more realistically what must have been the real-life capabilities of real-life Ywains, Ottos, Gawains, and Ekkehards.

> The baronage who made history in the twelfth century and the later Middle Ages were energetic men; and kings who lived their lives in the saddle, like Henry II of England and the Emperior Frederick II, were themselves supreme examples of the type. Their very physiognomy was watchful and predatory, hawk-like. Their life was one of immense, strenuous activity, passed in conflict, hunting and pilgrimage. Cool-headed, stern to the point of harshness, they had their wits about them and knew how to crack a joke with their subordinates; they were quick on the draw and ready with their tongues, their talk and songs full of the joys of battle. They could be brutal, even in dealings with their women: a man "took" a wife, calculating her value as an object for political and economic ends. Questions of close calculation, indeed, absorbed much of their attention. How many men could such and such a fief support? How strong was this or that rival? What opposition was to be expected from the armies of the king of France or the Pope in Rome in such and such a conflict? Educated in the manners and habits of their own rank and people,

they were steeped in a culture which revered the customs sanctified by ancient usage, venerable and sacrosanct law. In fact they were very well versed in law, thoroughly competent in the feudal and territorial laws of their sometimes very mixed bag of subjects, all living under their own laws, territorial, municipal or customary.[48]

From the highest vassals all the way down the feudal pyramid to the pettiest knight and the smallest monastery, these people had to pay attention—to the price of wheat, the cost of a sheep, when to plow, how often to marl or compost. They had to attend someone's court and offer counsel, elect the king's sheriff, and help administer justice when necessary. They had to oversee their mills and ovens and forests and fisheries, to arrange for shipping their produce. In the towns, as trade and manufacturing grew, the burgesses sought and secured rights to elect their own sheriffs and other officials, to establish guilds that then set tolls and regulations, and to collect their own taxes. Since the local unit was the focal point of feudal society, although no doubt the final decisions reached by many different local groups were often the same, the fact remains that those local decisions were first made separately by individuals thinking practically and empirically for themselves before bringing their ideas to the particular groups to which they were obliged to offer counsel.

At the same time, the internationalism of the church and the higher nobility kept bringing in new ideas and interests. Between 1086 and 1300, the population of England doubled—from around two million to around five million is a good guess—due apparently to an absence of epidemics and improved agricultural planning and technology, including the three-field system, reclamation of wasteland, the introduction of the vertical watermill (by 1100, there were over five thousand of them in England),[49] the introduction of the windmill (apparently a Persian invention), and the introduction of the horseshoe and horse collar. In all of this, individuals on every level of society must have been thinking for themselves. They must have been learning from their own experiences, evaluating alternatives, planning for their own futures. Feudal localism, with its pressure for self-sufficiency and shared responsibility for decision making, and feudal internationalism, with its continual importation of new ideas and ways of doing things, together meant that large numbers of people had no choice but to think through all the conditions of their daily lives; and what is thinking something through but subjectivity in action?

Once individual subjectivities began developing, with their conflicts of interpretation, intent, and standards of fulfillment, as a practical reality the feudal oath was doomed to disappear. Its basis lay in unspoken group understandings, in group traditions and norms. The ideal of perfect fidelity to one's oath could remain golden, as it still does for many of us today, but the real-life decline in the solemn value of oaths, and their replacement by written articled contracts, was inevitable. The decline of the feudal oath must be blamed, therefore, at least in part, on the rise of individual subjectivities caused by the very conditions of feudal life.

Chaucer illumines the process of this decline in his three most feudal *Canterbury* tales. In Palamon's and Arcite's opposing interpretations of the oath of brotherhood they swore together "ful depe," in Dorigen's innocent intent of making "in pley" that second oath to Aurelius, and in Griselda's continuing choices to reaffirm and enlarge her oath—in all three cases, one can see evidence of individual minds that are separate and distinct from those around them. None of these four characters is as fully separated from his or her group mentalities as are some of the *Canterbury* pilgrims, for example, the Host, the Wife of Bath, and the Monk. The length of Dorigen's complaint and the woodenness of Palamon and Arcite have been especially criticized. Yet all four characters are clearly subjectivized; all four react unpredictably. In so doing, each of the four exhibits his or her own *trouthe*, in each case a *trouthe* that readers and critics have consistently found problematic rather than clear. The feudal ideal of perfect fidelity to one's oath was still very much alive in Chaucer's time, as it is in our own. But the reality was that for Chaucer, as for us, the intent, interpretation, and fulfillment of any oath are going to be more subjective than traditional, more problematic than pure.

Notes

1. K. B. McFarlane, "Bastard Feudalism," *Bulletin of the Institute of Historical Research* 20 (1945):161–80. Richard II's summons of the feudal levy in June 1385, ultimately withdrawn, seems to have been an unsuccessful attempt to collect a general scutage; see J. J. N. Palmer, "The Last Summons of the Feudal Army in England (1385)," *English Historical Review* 83 (1968):771–75.

2. Richard W. Kaeuper, *War, Justice, and Public Order: England and France in the Later Middle Ages* (Oxford: Clarendon Press, 1988), 34–36, 119.

3. Paul Strohm, *Social Chaucer* (Cambridge, Mass.: Harvard University Press, 1989), 1–21.

4. These three ideas are, of course, apparent in earlier literature, but they do not receive sufficient emphasis to be called motifs. For example, in the *Aeneid*, fidelity is important, but to one's father or purpose rather than to an oath. Achates seems to have accompanied Aeneas for years, but his length of service (if one can call it that) is not stressed, nor is he singled out over more recent companions. The general obligation of leader to people is apparent, of course, and Aeneas's men follow his orders, but there is nothing of the close personal military bonding or counseling that one associates with feudal leaders. Rash promises are a type of oath and a very ancient motif, but the literary focus is on reluctance to fulfill them rather than fidelity to them.

5. In this article I will use the terms *oath* and *vow* interchangeably. The former is Germanic, the latter Latinate; today their essential meanings substantially overlap. In actual use, the distinction seems to be that an oath calls upon the divine as witness to the truth of an affirmation or a promise, whereas a vow implies a consecration of some type to the divine as well.

6. Marc Bloch, *Feudal Society*, 2 vols., trans. L. A. Manyon (Chicago: University of Chicago Press, 1961), 1:145–46. David Herlihy comments that the mingling of hands "apparently set the model for the new posture of prayer which came to prevail in the Latin Church over the course of the Middle Ages. In the early Church, men had prayed with their arms outstretched, but in the feudal age they learned to pray with hands folded together. The image seems to have been that they were placing their hands within the hands of God. Thus, one who prays stands before God much as a vassal before his lord; he recognizes that he owes Him love and fidelity, and hopes in turn for His protection and support" (*The History of Feudalism*, ed. David Herlihy [New York: Harper & Row, 1970], xiii–xxvii).

7. *History of Feudalism*, 86.

8. *History of Feudalism*, 98.

9. R. W. Southern, *The Making of the Middle Ages* (New Haven, Conn.: Yale University Press, 1953).

10. Walter Ullmann, *The Individual and Society in the Middle Ages* (Baltimore, Md.: Johns Hopkins University Press, 1966).

11. Colin Morris, *The Discovery of the Individual, 1050–1200* (Toronto: University of Toronto Press, 1972).

12. Robert W. Hanning, *The Individual in Twelfth-Century Romance* (New Haven, Conn.: Yale University Press, 1977).

13. Ullmann's synthesis has been strongly attacked as oversimplified; for discussion of the positions, see Steven Ozment, *The Age of Reform, 1250–1550: An Intellectual and Religious History of Late Medieval and Reformation Europe* (New Haven, Conn.: Yale University Press, 1980), 135–37.

14. See, for example, *Yvain, The Knight of the Lion*, trans. Burton Raffel (New Haven, Conn.: Yale University Press, 1987), 122–23.

15. See nn. 9–13.

16. References to and quotations from the *Canterbury Tales* are from the Fisher 2d edition (*The Complete Poetry and Prose of Geoffrey Chaucer*, ed. John H. Fisher [New York: Holt, Rinehart & Winston, 1989]); fragment numbers, when obvious, are omitted.

17. For example, commenting on the "enormous amount of conventional perjury" that characterized all medieval university legislation, Hastings Rashdall speaks of the reform at the University of Paris in 1366, when some half-dozen of perhaps forty oaths required from inceptors were abolished, "probably those whose obligations were most systematically neglected—such as the duty of attending the funerals of scholars, of saying a 'whole Psalter' on the occasion of every death among the regents, of incepting in a 'new cope not borrowed or hired,' of lecturing for two years, and the requirement that each master should have a black cope of his own" (*The Universities of Europe in the Middle Ages* [Oxford: Clarendon Press, 1936], 1:446–47).

18. I.959, 3291–92, 4185–87; II.666–68; III.1009–13, 1403–5, 2137–39; IV. 504–6, 2162–64; V.528, 745–48, 758–59; VI.249–50, 699–701; VII.129–41, 873–74, 1827, 2595, 3424-25; VIII.149–50, 1044–46; IX.248; and the Parson's discussion in X.586–606.

19. John S. P. Tatlock and Arthur G. Kennedy, *A Concordance to the Complete Works of Geoffrey Chaucer* (Washington, D.C.: Carnegie Institute, 1927; rpt. Gloucester, Mass.: Peter Smith, 1963).

20. *Knight's Tale* criticism has made surprisingly little of the oath. Only a handful of scholars have even mentioned it, usually to Arcite's detriment. For comment, see (in chronological order), Charles Muscatine, "Form, Texture, and Meaning in Chaucer's *Knight's Tale*," *PMLA* 65 (1950):925; Joseph Westlund, "The *Knight's Tale* as an Impetus for Pilgrimage," *PQ* 43 (1964):528; Bernard F. Huppé, *A Reading of the Canterbury Tales* (Albany: State University of New York, 1964), 61; Robert S. Haller, "The *Knight's Tale* and the Epic Tradition," *ChauR* 1 (1966):69–70; Ronald B. Herzman, "The Paradox of Form: *The Knight's Tale* and Chaucerian Aesthetics," *PLL* 10 (1974):340–41; Peter Elbow, *Oppositions in Chaucer* (Middletown, Conn.: Wesleyan University Press, 1975), 75–77; A. J. Minnis, *Chaucer and Pagan Antiquity* (Cambridge: D. S. Brewer and Rowman & Littlefield, 1982), 111–12; Michael Stevens, "The Knight's Tale," in *Chaucer's Major Tales*, ed. Michael Hoy and Michael Stevens (New York: Schocken Books, 1983), 30; Helen Cooper, *The Structure of the Canterbury Tales* (Athens: University of Georgia Press, 1984), 96–97; Derek Pearsall, *The Canterbury Tales* (London: George Allen & Unwin, 1985), 133–34, 135, 335 n. 15. One has to go back to the days before Muscatine's paradigmatic interpretation (*Chaucer and the French Tradition: A Study in Style and Meaning* [Berkeley: University of California Press, 1957]), back when differentiation between the two young knights was considered the major critical issue, to find a thorough discussion. H. S. Wilson, "The *Knight's Tale* and the *Teseida* Again," *UTQ* 18 (1949): 141–43, provides possibly the best.

21. For discussion, see Lois Roney, *Chaucer's Knight's Tale and Theories of Scholastic Psychology* (Tampa: University of South Florida Press, 1990), 58–86.

22. In the *Parson's Tale*, Chaucer speaks of "mariage, that was establissed by God er that synne bigan, whan natureel lawe was in his right poynt in paradys" (920).

Since the Fall, of course, from this point of view, the struggle has been to subordinate human nature to its rightful position beneath this law.

23. For a summary article from Aristotle to Grotius, with detailed expositions of the positions of Aquinas and their enlargement by Suarez, see D. E. Luscombe, "Natural Morality and Natural Law," in *Cambridge History of Later Medieval Philosophy*, ed. Normann Kretzmann, Anthony Kenny, and Jan Pinborg (Cambridge: Cambridge University Press, 1982), 705–19. For a lengthy and highly enlightening explication of the extratheological implications of the concept of natural law and how it changed over time, see Joseph A. Schumpeter, *History of Economic Analysis* (New York: Oxford University Press, 1954), part 2, chap. 2, esp. pp. 107–15.

24. D. W. Robertson, Jr., "Chaucer's Franklin and His Tale," in *Essays in Medieval Culture* (Princeton, N.J.: Princeton University Press, 1980), 286.

25. Morton Bloomfield, "The Franklin's Tale: A Story of Unanswered Questions," in *Acts of Interpretation: The Text in Its Contexts, 700–1600*, ed. Mary J. Carruthers and Elizabeth D. Kirk (Norman, Okla.: Pilgrim Books, 1982), 190.

26. Anne Thompson Lee, " 'A Woman True and Fair': Chaucer's Portrayal of Dorigen in the *Franklin's Tale*," *ChauR* 19 (1984):173.

27. Wolfgang Rudat, "*Gentilesse* and the Marriage Debate in the *Franklin's Tale:* Chaucer's Squires and the Question of Nobility," *Neophilologus* 68 (1984):458, 460.

28. Derek Pearsall, *The Canterbury Tales*, 54.

29. Gerald Morgan, "Boccaccio's *Filocolo* and the Moral Argument of the *Franklin's Tale*," *ChauR* 20 (1986):295.

30. Douglas J. Wurtele, "Chaucer's Franklin and the Truth About 'Trouthe,' " *English Studies in Canada* 13 (1987):365.

31. Perhaps the most comprehensive discussion of the *Franklin's Tale* issues is that of Alan Gaylord, "The Promises in *The Franklin's Tale*," *ELH* 31 (1964): 331–65.

32. See W. F. Bryan and Germaine Dempster, *Sources and Analogues of Chaucer's Canterbury Tales* (1941; rpt. New York: Humanities Press, 1958), 378–83.

33. See Charlotte C. Morse, "The Exemplary Griselda," *SAC* 7 (1985):55.

34. The questions were suggested by William Kamowski, "Varieties of Response to *Melibee* and the *Clerk's Tale*," in *Chaucer in the Eighties*, ed. Julian N. Wasserman and Robert J. Blanch (Syracuse: Syracuse University Press, 1986), 199.

35. Thomas R. Lounsbury, *Studies in Chaucer*, vol. 3 (New York: Harper & Bros., 1892), 340–41, is the earliest critic usually cited for such objections. Marjorie E. Swann has attempted to incorporate the ugliness into her reading of the tale, in which the Clerk becomes convinced by his own telling: "He had confidently set out to controvert the Wife of Bath's heretical view of women's role in marriage but, instead, the Clerk has disabused himself of his original notions of proper wifely behaviour. As he told his story, the Clerk developed a new understanding of the injustice of husbandly domination: having empathized with Griselda, he can no longer idealize a relationship which would subject a wife to such trials. In Mary Carruthers' words, by the conclusion of his tale, the Clerk realizes that 'Griselda's virtue sets a standard not to be emulated but to be contemplated feelingly' " ("The Clerk's 'Gentile Tale' Heard Again," *English Studies in Canada* 13 [1987]:143–44). See

also Mary J. Carruthers, "The Lady, The Swineherd, and Chaucer's Clerk," *ChauR* 17 (1983): 221–34.

36. Bernard S. Levy, "The Meanings of the Clerk's Tale," in *Chaucer and the Craft of Fiction*, ed. Leigh A. Arrathoon (Rochester, Mich.: Solaris Press, 1986), 403–9.

37. Morse, "The Exemplary Griselda," 85.

38. Robert Stepsis, "*Potentia Absoluta* and the *Clerk's Tale*," *ChauR* 10 (1975):129–46; David C. Steinmetz, "Late Medieval Nominalism and the *Clerk's Tale*," *ChauR* 12 (1977):38–54.

39. Edward I. Condren, "The *Clerk's Tale* of Man Tempting God," *Criticism* 26 (1984):99–114.

40. Insolubles were among the scholastics' favorite genres. They were semantic paradoxes, statements of the type that, if they are false, they are true; and if they are true, they are false. For example, here is the famous Liar's Paradox: "What I am saying now is false." If that statement is false, then it is true, but if it is true, then it is false. See Paul Vincent Spade, "Insolubilia," in *Cambridge History of Later Medieval Philosophy*, 246–53.

41. James Sledd, "*The Clerk's Tale*: The Monsters and the Critics," in *Chaucer: Modern Essays in Criticism*, ed. Edward Wagenknecht (New York: Oxford University Press, 1959), 233.

42. Elizabeth Salter, *Chaucer: The Knight's Tale and the Clerk's Tale* (Great Neck, N.Y.: Barron's Educational Series, 1962).

43. Morse, "The Exemplary Griselda," 85; Dolores Warwick Frese, "Chaucer's *Clerk's Tale*: The Monsters and the Critics Reconsidered," *ChauR* 8 (1973):133–46. Several recent approaches have focused on Walter, on Griselda's curing his obsession for self-knowledge (Thomas A. Van, "Walter at the Stake: A Reading of Chaucer's *Clerk's Tale*," *ChauR* 22 [1988]:214–24), and on her helping him overcome his "vice of curiosity" (Kathryn L. Lynch, "Despoiling Griselda: Chaucer's Walter and the Problem of Knowledge in *The Clerk's Tale*," *SAC* 10 [1988]:41–70); and on Dantean political theory (Michaela Paasche Grudin, "Chaucer's *Clerk's Tale* as Political Paradox," *SAC* 11 [1989]:63–92). Alfred David has commented that, "if we can keep our attention firmly fixed on the *sentence* of the Clerk's Tale, it contains an eloquent lesson, but the Clerk has also contracted to tell a tale with human interest," and at times his "small additions," about Walter's cruelty for example, "far from coating the moral pill, tend to make us want to vomit it up" (*The Strumpet Muse: Art and Morals in Chaucer's Poetry* [Bloomington: Indiana University Press, 1976], 165–66).

44. Thomas H. Bestul, "True and False *Cheere* in Chaucer's *Clerk's Tale*," *JEGP* 82 (1983):514.

45. Clayton Roberts and David Roberts summarize Richard's final two years thus: "The King's conduct approached political madness. He pursued a fantastic design to gain the Imperial throne by bribing the Electors of Cologne and the Palatinate. He extorted large loans from the rich. He sought to exercise strict control over local government by influencing the election of sheriffs. He made use of courts of law that did not administer the Common law. He extorted from suspected persons sealed, blank charters which, if the givers offended him, he could later fill in

298   Lois Roney

as he wished" (*A History of England: Prehistory to 1714* [Englewood Cliffs, N.J.: Prentice-Hall, 1980], 186). See also Donald R. Howard's account, in *Chaucer: His Life, His Works, His World* (New York: Dutton, 1987), 383–89, 397–400, 450–54, 469–80.

46. Herlihy, *History of Feudalism*, 207.

47. Friedrich Heer, *The Medieval World: Europe, 1100–1350*, trans. Janet Sondheimer (New York: Mentor, 1961), 36.

48. Heer, *Medieval World*, 40.

49. Heer, *Medieval World*, 42.

12 John Rastell and the Norman Conquest

Tudor Theories about the Feudal Age

─── ❧

WHAT DID ARTICULATE Tudor citizens think about the effect of the Norman Conquest on the development of the society of England? Did they consider the civilization of the Anglo-Saxons to be sufficiently developed to withstand the harsh shocks of the Norman Conquest? Or did they trace all of the significant factors of the English society to the influence, however disruptive, of the effects of William the Conqueror? Remarking on the number of Englishmen of the sixteenth century interested in the past and its use for propagandistic purposes, David Douglas has noted that it is "surprising that a political crisis of the eleventh century should have led generations of statesmen and lawyers, pamphleteers and scribblers into a war of words about a subject which might well have been deemed to lie outside their interest. Here is a most curious phenomenon of British scholarship."[1] Interestingly enough, Douglas cites John Rastell as the early Tudor writer who foreshadowed the polemics of the seventeenth-century Parliamentarians' use of the Norman Conquest even though he did not, for obvious reasons, see the event in quite the same light.[2]

John Rastell (1475–1536),[3] a lawyer and a writer of a history of England, would never have used the word 'feudalism,' a concept invented a century later. Yet in the seventeenth century, Stuart Englishmen looked back with an attitude toward English history that possibly may have been held by such early Tudor humanists as Rastell or even his brother-in-law, Thomas More. But can these attitudes be discovered? Aware of the precarious venture involved in determining what people thought about any idea, even one as clouded by controversy as feudalism, one finds guidance to the discovery of the thought of a Tudor personality like Rastell in Arthur B. Ferguson's *Clio Unbound: Perception of the Social and Cultural Past in Renaissance England:*

> To recognize that medieval society was different in its basic structure from what went before and came after required two major adjustments in historical assumptions, both related to the myth of the immemorial antiquity of English law and, as a corollary, to the unbroken continuity of its history: first, the Norman Conquest had to be recognized as a break in that continuity, or at the very least a significant interruption; and, second, feudal law had to be seen as involving conditions of tenure different in certain essentials from those which had existed in Saxon times.
>
> The more sophisticated conclusion of present-day historians should not obscure the significance of these achievements in the early growth of historical understanding. It is all well and good for the modern medievalist to insist on the elements of continuity, long overlooked, linking Norman to Saxon society, and even to question the validity of so broad a general concept as feudalism. But he must bear in mind that the ability to recognize the distinctive character of periods and to create a model of social organization, however inadequate or artificial it may have been, was what gave structure to historical thought where little had existed, and what provided a necessary point of departure for the more mature researches of later historians.[4]

John Rastell presents the intriguing example of an Englishman whose life can be seen as the attempt to be accepted into intellectual circles for which he was not really qualified. He never achieved the high status that he so eagerly desired, yet he observed carefully the world in which he sought even a modicum of success. He wrote and printed a history, law books, essays, pamphlets, and interludes, and he even attempted to colonize the New World in 1517. And finally, as a publisher and propagandist embroiled in the religious and political crises of the Henrician Revolution, Rastell ended his long career of frustrated efforts confined in the Tower, from which death was to be the only release. His career chronicles the restless and inquisitive nature of early Tudor England.

Obviously, to use the word feudalism in connection with such a Tudor writer is not accurate, unless aspects of the concept can be discerned in writings of Tudor men who might have understood the ideas that only later would be called feudalism. These ideas were introduced in John Haywood's first textbook on the subject, *The Lives of the Three Norman Kings of England* (1613), John Selden's *Historia Novorum* (1623), and Henry Spelman's *Feuds and Tenures of Knight Service* (1629). Spelman, although he is not the sole discoverer of feudalism,[5] fits the formula set by Ferguson in his admission that the Normans, while adopting the laws of Edward the Confessor, nevertheless brought over the concept of feudal law based on the contractual exchange of land; as Ferguson says, "he advanced the unequivocal thesis that the hereditary aspect of the *feudum* was indeed a Norman importation."[6]

The problem of determining what Tudor intellectuals thought about how foreigners—and in this case, foreign-Norman-French—had affected the development of the English nation is further complicated by the growing sense of nationalism, or patriotism, among writers and others around the Tudor throne. After the Hundred Years' War, it is difficult to find an objective English viewpoint about contributions of the Normans to the elements of English society thought to be unique. What is evident, as Ferguson describes, is the emotional as well as historical problem created by the Norman Conquest for Englishmen of the sixteenth and early seventeenth centuries.[7]

It is at this point in the confusion of determining how to approach the problem of discovering Rastell's ideas about the feudal past that, unexpectedly, the work of Christopher Hill offers a way to tie together several approaches. Hill's essay "The Norman Yoke" presents the history of the myth of what the Normans did to the noble Saxon peoples. Hill contends that this myth, the "Norman Yoke,"[8] appears in a chronological tracing of writers from the fifteenth to the twentieth centuries who repeat a common strain of regret about what supposedly happened in 1066. All of the writers Hill surveys believe that the Saxons had progressed in developing a civilization of some worth only to have it disrupted and, in some cases, destroyed by the harsh treatment of the more brutal Norman conquerors. Thereafter, the history of England was the attempt of the Saxon lower classes to recover what remained of the pre-1066 society forever tyrannized by "the Norman Yoke."[9]

Hill finds three areas in which the writers he discusses show their anti-Norman feelings. The first is the effort to demonstrate that English common law existed before 1066, as did that other English institution, Parliament. Sir John Fortescue, in the fifteenth century, foreshadowed what Sir Edward Coke was to tell his Queen about the greatness of the structure of English law: "The Common Law of England has been time out of mind before the Conquest, and was not altered or changed by the Conqueror." Hill does admit that others like Reginald Pole felt that it was a "great shame . . . to be governed by the laws given to us of such a barbarous nation as the Normans be." Whether believers in the continuity or the break in English law, Englishmen saw the Conquest as an event of enormous importance.[10]

A second concern cited by Hill was to prove that the English church before 1066 was the true church but was forced by the Conqueror (with Papal approval) to undergo Roman influence until the Reformation of the 1530s could once more restore the true church of Saxons. Hill cites the radical group of intellectuals around Thomas Cromwell who propagandized this idea, though it was under Elizabeth's prelates that the full version of the uniqueness of the English church developed.[11]

And the final area of anti-Norman feeling Hill elucidates is the attack on the Arthurian legend as a result of the revival of interest in the Saxons. Arthur, according to Hill, was seen not so much as the Saxon hero as the symbol in medieval England of the upper-class ideal of "chivalry" at the expense of the other Englishmen. As Hill says, "The discrediting of the royal Arthurian legend, and its replacement by that of free Anglo-Saxon institutions, was thus of direct importance in the battle of ideas which preceded the civil war."[12]

Thus, Hill's thesis combined with Ferguson's definition of those who understand feudalism offers a formula to be applied in examining Rastell's works to discover what he thought about the feudal age. If he realized that a real break had occurred in 1066, what did he consider to have been the result of the Conquest's influence on the religion, laws, and social structure of England? More specifically, did Rastell recognize that conditions of tenure were affected by 1066?

If one applies this contrived but convenient method of investigation to John Rastell, the resulting match is much closer than might be anticipated. Concerning the attempt to prove the uniqueness of the Saxon Church, Rastell can be seen as an early supporter of this theory. He was, indeed, one of Cromwell's men who propagandized about the need to purge the Church of papal corruption.[13] Rastell even wrote and published an attack on the papal theory of purgatory that added fuel to the growing fires of discontent with the religious leadership in England. His work, *Boke of Purgatory,*[14] presents arguments to prove rationally and scripturally that the doctrine was invented by the hierarchy of the church. Rastell, in fact, became so radically Lutheran that he incurred the displeasure of Cromwell, and eventually Cranmer; thus, Rastell ended his life in the Tower as a religious fanatic.[15] This stand of such vehement support for the actions of the King against the Bishop of Rome has earned Rastell the epithet "bizarre and unstable."[16] Certainly, as a supporter of the authenticity of the English church before it was corrupted by the Norman Conquest, Rastell is an excellent example of one of Cromwell's men whose zealous drive to serve Cromwell and the commonwealth ultimately led to his death.[17]

There is little question that Rastell also qualifies as an advocate for the uniqueness of English common law. A lawyer by profession, Rastell printed not only laws but also books about the law.[18] Much of his career as a printer was devoted to the publishing of the medieval laws of England in order that, besides lawyers, the growing English reading public could become aware of the supremacy of their laws over other legal courts, especially those of other countries.[19] In this venture, Rastell can be seen as a transitional figure between Fortescue and Coke.

In printing law books, Rastell revealed patriotic tendencies understandable in one of his generation and career endeavors. Anti-French in all that he did, he was at the same time intensely convinced of the special quality of English life, English laws, and English institutions. He had argued that English colonies should be in the New World and even set out to do so but met with failure.[20] The result of this was an interlude, *A New Interlude and a Mery, of The Nature Of The Four Elementis*, dedicated to convincing Englishmen to plant colonies in the New World.[21]

Further evidence of Rastell's growing sense of patriotism is found in the introduction to a book of abridgments called the *Great Boke*,[22] in which he explains why he published English laws and why he did so in English. This combination of pride in English laws and in the ability of the English language to do what the Normans had prevented is remarkable proof of Rastell's understanding of what Hill calls the "Norman Yoke" and the disruptive effects of 1066 on Saxon civilization:

> But the very cause why the said laws of England were written in the French tongue, should seem to be this: first, it was not unknown, that when William, duke of Normandy, came into this land, and slew king Harold, and conquered the whole realm, there was a great number of people, as well gentlemen as other, that came with him, which understood not the vulgar tongue, that was at that time used in this realm, but only the French tongue: as also, because, the said king, and other great wise men of his counsel, perceived and supposed that the vulgar tongue, which was then used in this realm was, in a manner, but homely and rude, nor had not so great copy and abundance of words as the French tongue then had, nor that vulgar tongue was not of itself sufficient to expound and to declare the matter of such laws and ordinances, as they had determined to be made for the good governance of the people so effectually, and so substantially, as they could indite them in the French tongue, therefore they ordered, wrote, and indited the said laws, that they made in the French tongue. . . .
>
> But yet, beside this now of late days, the most noble prince, our late sovereign lord, king Henry VII . . . considering and well perceiving that our vulgar English tongue was marvelously amended and augmented, by reason that divers famous clerks and learned men had translated, and made many noble works into our English tongue, whereby there was much more plenty and abundance of English used, than there was in times past; and by reason thereof our vulgar tongue, so amplified and sufficient of itself to expound any laws and ordinances, which was needful to be made for the order of their realm; and also the same wise prince considering, that the uni-

versal people of this realm had great pleasure, and gave themselves greatly to the reading of the vulgar English tongue, ordained and caused, that all the statutes and ordinances, which were made for the commonwealth of this realm in his days, should be edited and written in the vulgar English tongue. . . . [23]

Rastell also championed English over Norman influences in the introduction to his publication of Chaucer's *The parlyment of fowles* in 1525. Here he proves his dedication to the use of the vernacular. Rastell compares Chaucer's works to Aurora, whose heralding of light dispels the blackness of night. Implied is an understanding of the transitional nature of Chaucer's works, though Rastell may not have meant that the dark should be interpreted as those ages called medieval. Yet with his reverence for noble verse, he cannot but realize the debt Englishmen of his day owed to Chaucer for their speech and linguistic style: ". . . his fayre eloquence and elygancy / shall see our tonge enlumyned so with his spech."[24]

Though Rastell may qualify as an Englishman who understands the effect of the Conquest on the religion, laws, and language of England, the final qualification for fitting the formula of Hill concerns Rastell's view of the Arthurian legend. In his history, *Pastyme of People*, Rastell does mention the Conquest but does not discuss directly the effect of the Conqueror.[25] Interesting woodcuts, done by Rastell, of the English kings from William to Richard III, provide some indication of what Rastell thought about the ruler. The woodcut of William depicts a strong conqueror with arrows in the background, a sign of war. William carries a sword in one hand, the orb of state in the other. His look is stern.[26] Much of Rastell's work obviously shows the influence of his sources, Fabyan and Polydore Vergil.[27] It is, however, in Rastell's treatment of the Arthurian myths that he demonstrates some daring originality and fits, therefore, into the formula of one who sees Arthur not as a benefit but a detriment to English history.

When first introducing Arthur into the narrative, Rastell follows Fabyan's example of questioning the fact that sources, like Bede, who should have known about Arthur, do not mention such a ruler. But Rastell goes a step further and introduces historical criticism of the authenticity of sources and material, as befits a legal antiquarian, a role ably fitting Rastell's abilities and temperament. Rastell chose as the crux of his investigation into the Arthurian problem an impression of Arthur's seal consisting of "red wax enclosed in crystal" with the legend, "Patricius Arthurus Britannie Gallie Germanie Dacie Imperator."[28] The impression was kept, in Rastell's day, at the shrine of the Confessor in Westminster Abbey. Rastell challenges the authenticity of this seal with three points derived from his interests as a legal antiquarian: first, though the monks at Westminster claimed that Arthur had used the seal in conveying a deed or some grant to the monastery, Arthur could not have given any gift to a house that was not founded until long after his death; second, no wax could have survived the span of almost a thousand years since Arthur lived; and third, seals of wax on important documents were not used until the time of William the Conqueror. By this last assertion, Rastell displays his research into the documents of the English political past as he describes how rulers of Arthur's day assigned their hands, not seals, to deeds.

There is, from the facts already presented, the temptation to fit Rastell into the formula that could prove that he, an early Tudor humanist, understood what later men would term feudalism. Such temptation should not force an investigator to jump to conclusions that cannot be demonstrated by more than instinct or wishful thinking. Clearly, Rastell understood that the Conquest was an event of enormous importance to the history of the society of England. As a lawyer, he did understand the history of the English common law and defended it against all other legal systems. He did proclaim the validity of English as a language for communication of ideas and not the vulgar tongue the Normans thought it to be. He did become involved in the religious controversy that sought to prove the English church superior to the Church of Rome that William had brought with him. And finally, Rastell did see the Arthurian legend as a harmless but ineffective way to explain England's past.

All of the above would seem to place Rastell securely in the Hill-Ferguson definition of someone who saw periodization in English history, even if he did not understand modern confusion about feudalism. But Rastell did not talk about tenures, and, according to Ferguson's two-part definition, for a Tudor historian to understand feudalism as a concept, there must be the realization that, with the Normans, changes had taken place regarding fief and tenure. Rastell, therefore, while recognizing the negative effects of the Normans (and this may be excused as nascent nationalism), in the final analysis, did not have the understanding of feudalism that his lawyer-parliamentarian descendants, such as Coke, had a century later in the controversy leading to the Civil War. Or at least, Rastell was not bothered enough by the fief and tenure problem to leave any discussion of it in either his writings or the products of his press. He does offer us, however, an example of a man of the English Renaissance who believed that the history of England was affected by the change wrought by the Normans in the distant past and that it was his duty, though self-imposed, as an articulate citizen to address ways to rectify the mistakes of the past in order to improve the Tudor commonwealth for future generations.

Notes

1. *The Norman Conquest and British Historians* (Glasgow: Jackson, Son & Co., 1946), 6. See also Peter Burke, *The Renaissance Sense of the Past* (London: Edward Arnold, 1969).

2. *English Scholars 1000–1730*, 2d rev. ed. (London: Eyre & Spottiswoode, 1951), 120. See also F. Smith Fussner, *Tudor History and the Historians* (New York: Basic Books, 1970).

3. For biographical information, see Albert J. Geritz and Amos Lee Laine, *John Rastell* (Boston: Twayne Publishers, 1983), 1–27.

4. (Durham, N.C: Duke University Press, 1979), 298–99.

5. J. G. A. Pocock, *The Ancient Constitution and the Feudal Law: English Historical Thought in the Seventeenth Century* (Cambridge: Cambridge University Press, 1957); see chap. 5.

6. *Clio Unbound*, 304.

7. *Clio Unbound*, 304.

8. In *Democracy and the Labour Movement: Essays in Honour of Dona Torr*, ed. John Saville (London: Lawrence & Wishart, 1954), 11.

9. For further discussion of changing perceptions of England after the Conquest, see Alan Macfarlane, *The Origins of English Individualism: The Family, Property, and Social Transition* (Cambridge: Cambridge University Press, 1979), chaps. 1 and 2.

10. Hill, "The Norman Yoke," 18.

11. Hill, "The Norman Yoke," 19.

12. Hill, "The Norman Yoke," 19.

13. Geritz and Laine, *John Rastell*, 20–21.

14. *A Critical Edition of John Rastell's The Pastyme of People and A New Boke of Purgatory*, ed. Albert J. Geritz and Stephen Orgel (New York: Garland Publishing, 1985), 403–92.

15. Geritz and Laine, *John Rastell*, 24–25.

16. Richard Marius, *Thomas More* (New York: Alfred A. Knopf, 1984), 7.

17. Arthur B. Ferguson, *The Articulate Citizen and the English Renaissance* (Durham, N.C: Duke University Press, 1965), 154.

18. *Liber assisarum* (STC 9599), Fitzherbert's *La Graunde Abbregement* (STC 10954) with his introduction, *Tabula prime partis* (STC 10955), and *An Abridgment of Statutes* (STC 9518).

19. Geritz and Laine, *John Rastell*, chap. 8. See also George W. Keeton, *The Norman Conquest and the Common Law* (London: Barnes & Noble, 1966).

20. Geritz and Laine, *John Rastell*, chap. 1.

21. John Rastell, *Three Rastell Plays*, ed. Richard Axton (Totowa, N.J.: Boydell & Brewer, 1979).

22. Howard Jay Graham, "*Our Tong Maternall Marvellously Augmentya:* The First Englishing and Printing of Medieval Statutes at Large, 1530–1533," *UCLA Law Review* 13 (1965):58–98.

23. Graham, "*Our Tong Maternall,*" 97–98.

24. Geritz and Laine, *John Rastell*, 11.

25. Geritz and Orgel, *Critical Edition*, 298–300.

26. Geritz and Orgel, *Critical Edition*, 123.

27. May McKisack, *Medieval History in the Tudor Age* (Oxford: Oxford University Press, 1971), 94. See also F. J. Levy, *Tudor Historical Thought* (San Marino: Huntington Library, 1967).

28. Geritz and Orgel, *Critical Edition*, 251.

Chivalry and the Other

S A METAPHOR for obligation within the social order, medieval chivalry becomes an elastic term whose meaning stretches to accommodate various historical changes. Clearly, in its origins chivalry, feudalism, or aristocratic heroism denoted a masculine and aristocratic code of behavior intended especially for the battlefield and only secondarily for the court. This denotation applies to whatever feudalism may have meant as a social and economic construct in the early Middle Ages, or whatever Germanic heroism may have meant as reflected in the literary portraits of success and failure ranging from *Beowulf* to the treachery and pride inherent in leadership in *Battle of Maldon,* just before the Norman Conquest of 1066. This restrictive chivalric ideal, however fabricated, provided a useful means of legitimizing monarchy, as we recall from Geoffrey of Monmouth's fictions of Arthurian genealogy in *History of the Kings of Britain* in his suggesting a tie between Arthur and Aeneas's grandson (or great-grandson) Brutus, eponymic founder of Britain, and his descendant Henry Plantagenet. Whatever its equivocations—as body of noble mounted warriors, as military expertise, as the class, as its code of values, or all of the above[1]—it developed in what is now France in the late tenth and early eleventh centuries, as a class identified by its omission in the prohibitions of various Church councils.[2] (The heroism of the Germanic comitatus, as J. R. R. Tolkien points out in his famous essay on "Ofermod" that follows his sequel to the "Battle of Maldon,"[3] in its communal structure of relational supports differed from the ideal of individual prowess that came to be identified with French romance and that was predicated most immorally on pride in ability, not on the subordinate's loyal service in battle to a brave chief.

In the Middle Ages, however, this feudal ideal proved most socially and politically useful—and its lapses most distressing—to the first estate, that of the clergy, whose members were for the most part drawn from the privileged, second estate, of aristocracy.[4] Originally chivalry was developed by the Church out of a lack of centralized secular power to keep rowdy armed laymen in line and to protect the clergy, women, children, the aged, and the unarmed on certain days and places, as attested by the Peace of God and the Truce of God (derived from Church councils in the late tenth and early eleventh century, in France),[5] or as a political means to gain military support for the Crusades initiated by Pope Urban II when he welded together Cross with Sword. This early affiliation perhaps explains why so many later commentators on chivalry were clerical, whether Gower, Ramon Lull, or Honoré Bonet, to list a few examples, even though in the twelfth and thirteenth century the Church banned tournaments.

The greatest problem with the feudal ideal is that knights were rarely chivalric in practice. Even in 1095, at the time of Urban's Proclamation, members of the highest secular classes seem not to have followed any code of idealized behavior. Pope Urban rallies "those who have been in the habit of wastefully waging private wars, even against believers," to "proceed against the infidel in worthy battle. . . . Now let those who formerly contended against brothers and kinsfolk rightly fight against the barbarians; now let those who were wont to be mercenaries for a small sum obtain eternal rewards!"[6] By the fourteenth and fifteenth centuries the ideal was assumed to be primarily a *literary* if also a moral and religious concept—John Gower's clerical misogyny in *Vox Clamantis* defines chivalry's greatest obstacle as lechery, noting that the knight's weapons are useless in this battle ("Neither the strength of Samson nor the sword of David nor the wisdom of Solomon is of any worth against her"); his honor dies from the wounding of spirit "with fiery darts" of lustful love, from this "womanish behavior," although Gower also names pride, avarice, and service to women.[7] Gower's central point is also Malory's in *Morte Darthure*, for the Order of the Round Table is destroyed by Lancelot's secret love for Guinevere, a threat both to society, to the marriage of Guinevere and Arthur; to the kingdom, in its treason to the king; and to the Church, in that Sir Galahad's chastity and spiritual weapon, that of faith, permit only to him the restorative vision of the Holy Grail—killing others, in individual combat, is not countenanced, even though Holy War may be. Once the knight is destroyed by love and spiritually consumed by that pride in his valor demanded of a Launcelot, the rest of society is undone—namely Church and commons—as to use Paul Strohm's phrase, the "vertical ties of domination and subordination" are loosened.[8]

In the later Middle Ages the usefulness of the chivalric metaphor for the third and fourth estates, for the "commons" and for women, would allow for the reconstruction of the ideal along democratic and humanist lines. As glosses on the meaning of feudalism and the aristocratized ideal of chivalry, two late medieval texts disturb our own modern pre- or misconceptions because they rearrange the social and political authority behind its long literary tradition. What do we make of a dissident cleric and a woman of the bourgeoisie penning two of the most powerful and important tracts on chivalry in fourteenth- and fifteenth-century France, those members of society excluded from bearing arms and usually from writing? Honoré Bonet wrote his *L'Arbre des batailles* in 1387 at the end of civil war in Provence; his "Arbre de deuil" (Tree of the devil) reveals bloody conflicts between Pope and Emperor, knights and serfs, and clearly is antiwar in many respects as well as sensitive to those Saracens and Jews intended as the Enemy. Lending weight to the authority behind his vision, Bonet dedicated his book to France's Charles VI and is depicted in a frontispiece presenting a copy to him (Brussels, MS Bibliothéque Royale, 9001–11, fol. 1). In *Les Faits d'armes et de cheualerie* (1410), Christine de Pizan, who spent much of her life as a writer and scholar decrying the courtly-love excesses of the *chevalier*, viewed Bonet as her master and in her book codified appropriate rules of warfare and behavior. A manuscript of this work was presented to another woman, Margaret of Anjou, as a wedding gift in 1445 by John Talbot, Earl of Shrewsbury, designated as Constable of France for accompanying her to England to marry Henry VI. Yet another manuscript of this popular work reveals

FIGURE 14. Poet Christine de Pizan presenting works to Isabelle, queen of France. B.L., MS Harley 4431. Courtesy of the British Library.

the code of arms of Marie of Hungary. It was translated into English and printed by William Caxton in the year 1490 at the request of Henry VII.

What place did women find in chivalry, other than as the *domina* or *midons* of troubadour and trouvère lyric who threatened to effeminize the chevalier—like the Enide of Chrétien de Troyes or the *Mabinogion*, who so softens Erec? For Christine, as she contemplated the model of Minerva, the Greek and Calabrian goddess of armor-making and wisdom, chivalry was a matter of universal moral and social concern because it involved law and order, the basis for both civil (internal) and also therefore international law. Christine, casting herself in the role of her Italian countryman Dante, envisioned the poet's role as both moral and social, to educate the monarch ruling the kingdom both in the flaws in society and in ways of mending them. Chivalry proclaimed that model, that moral code that knits together men like chain mail and, accordingly (as she implies in her use of the metaphor in her biography of Charles V), provides a bulwark against the assaults of sin—Original Sin—for our inner selves to create a social order. But for her, women in following Minerva make the armor through their (essentialized) role as nurturers, peacemakers, and creators. This idea may explain why the Earl of Shrewsbury made a gift of her book to Margaret of Anjou, or why Marie of Hungary would have owned a manuscript of the work.

In her attempt to disgender—or humanize—chivalry, Christine acknowledges its original existence in the *ordo* as a form of education for aristocratic children whose obligation was to govern society:

> The auncient noble men thenne that by haultnes of corage desyred al wayes that thexcersise of armes shuld be contynued to thende the comyn wele of theyre lordshipes and cytees shulde be the bettre amended and deffended made not theyre children to be norisshed in the kyngis & prynces courtes for to lerne pryde lechery nor to were wanton clothing But dide so by cause in tyme to come of theyre flowryng aage myght serue the prynce and the countrey in that offyce that apparteyneth to noble men.[9]

Only when good kings and knights served their country might the Commons be taken care of, the poor, the women, and the aged.

She also acknowledges her own foolish presumption in this enterprise, however, as a woman like others who "comynly do not entremete but to spynne on the distaf & ocupie theim in thynges of houshold" (1.1, p. 7) and justifies it, first, because of her contemplation of her countrywoman Minerva, goddess of armor making, and second, because of her "most plain and entendible langage" more readily accessible to those who have been "excersyng & experte in tharte of chyualrye" instead of the subtlety and polished words of the clerks. Education, after all, must be accessible if it is to be useful.

Her democratization of chivalry—from the wiser vantage point of the third and fourth estates, the Commons and women—is implied by the fact that she herself penned it and by that fact implies the possibility of the construction of a new social order. She expropriates the authority to write such a text about the second estate from that of the first estate, the clergy. Her interest in the structure of society has already been expressed in the *Le Livre du Trésor de la Cité des Dames* (*Treasure of the City of Ladies*, 1405), in which she addresses the members of the fourth estate, who by social classification belong to the other three. Breaking down the third estate into an increasingly greater number of subdivisions, she places value, both moral and social, on all classes, especially the lowest, as implied by her address at the very end to women beggars and prostitutes. The failure of the first two estates to end immoral war and destruction enables her to have a voice. Her speaking and writing are in fact demanded by the female personifications of Reason, Rectitude, and Justice in terms of appropriately gendered class metaphors of martial valor, bird catching, and clerical community:

> 'The knight who leaves the field of battle before the moment of victory is deeply shamed, for the laurel wreath belongs to those who persevere. Now stand up and make your hand ready.' . . . 'We hope that just as the wise birdcatcher readies his cage before he may take his birds, so, after the shelter of honoured ladies is made and prepared, devices and traps may be set with your help as before.' . . . 'Take your pen and write. . . . May all the feminine college and their devout community be apprised of the sermons and lessons of wisdom.'[10]

Chivalry is an outdoor activity, but Christine stays indoors, as the few manuscript illustrations for the *Faits* show, where she meditates on Minerva, while the soldiers outside attack each other (Paris, Ms. Bibliothèque Nationale, Paris 603 [formerly 7087], fol. 2; also fol. 49, in which Christine and Bonet stand on either side of a tree on which soldiers are fighting). She opens up chivalry for those marginalized, for those indoors, for those from the lower classes, just because she presumes it to be a rational and moral system of law and behavior within and outside nations. It is no accident that her pronouncements on the ethical basis of war (that is, against oppression or usurpation) and her rules for civilized warfare, which included the outlawing of the barbaric practice of plundering, excessive ransom, and the use of poisoned missiles, helped to form the concept of international law.[11]

As a footnote to this study of *The Rusted Hauberk*, Christine's texts and her appropriation of earlier Roman and French models freshly assert the chivalric model as feminized and feminizing, meaning *democ-*

ratized, socialized, culturally sensitive, and because so morally and socially available *humanized.* Put another way, as a coda to the history of a fictionalized masculine and aristocratic ideal behavior and social obligation, Christine's *Faits d'armes* by its very existence repudiates all those components: men, especially noblemen, do not usually behave nobly and certainly do not know how to wage war justly, nor have they for some time, nor can they be relied on to summon the wisdom to teach themselves how. And even Bonet, who ended his life as a Benedictine monk in exile satirizing the abuses of the Church, does not represent so much the viewpoint of the established Church as that of an outlaw who sees its failures too clearly.

If feudalism implies landholding, then this volume, in contrast, ends with bastard feudalism and a less rigid concept of service. If chivalry begins with the joust and individual combat, then here it ends with a vision of community and social order. The Truce and the Peace of God were initiated by the Church as a means of controlling the aristocracy and protecting the unarmed and weak, chiefly the other three estates; but by Christine's time the initiators are the un-armed and weak, the members of the other three estates, who are at-tempting to protect the aristocracy from itself. If the crossbow (along with the cannon and gunpowder, within the technology of chivalry, but also the devastating effects of civil and cross-channel wars and the Black Death) can be said to have ended chivalry as individual combat, then within the patriarchal text of history, chivalry ends with the real crusade of the commoner Jeanne d'Arc in the fifteenth century and a failure even of feminized and democratized chivalry.

During World War II the British novelist T. H. White rewrote the Arthurian legends in Malory's *Morte Darthure* to depict the chivalric ideal of the Arthurian Order of the Round Table as a Great Chain of Social Being whose goal was universal peace. The wizard Merlin teaches Wart—the young Arthur—the importance of transcending boundaries, and limitations, through his visionary transmogrification into paranoid and martial eagle, belligerent ant, building badger, and high-flying pacific wild goose. Moving away from the usual associa-tion of chivalry, or a feudal ideal, with a particular class, set of indi-viduals within that class, or even gender, White emphasizes egalitarian universal peace and harmony in analogue to pantheism and asserts true subordination of the subjective and personal to the greatest, most public good. Thus at the end, King Arthur, having failed because of his own weakness, remembers from Merlin's educational visions—his ordo—how the claiming of boundaries leads to war, but boundaries that are in fact imaginary. "It was geography which was the cause—political geography. . . . Countries would have to become counties—but counties which could keep their own culture and local laws. The imaginary lines on the earth's surface only needed to be unimagined." And so he imagines his own return, with "a new Round Table which had no corners, just as the world had none—a table without boundaries between the nations who would sit to feast there. The hope of making it would lie in culture. If people could be persuaded to read and write, not just to eat and make love, there was still a chance that they might come to reason."[12]

The dissociation of the chivalric ideal from wealth, class, birth, gender, and even religion and its reconstruction as an educational program is also remarked in the fourteenth century by Chaucer in his late ballade "Gentilesse" and in his tale of the Wife of Bath, when the Fairy Queen lectures to the rude and rapacious knight whom she has married and whose life she has saved about true gentility, whose model she takes as that of Christ. On the individual level, as in Chaucer, or on the social and world level, as in Malory, Christine, and even T. H. White, the re-creation of the chivalric and feudal ideal involves both gentleness and consideration for the Other, the breaking down of demarcation and intolerance for the greater good of peace and harmony. It is no accident that White ends his novel by inserting after the formulaic Caxton lines of "Explicit Liber Regis Quondam Regisque Futuri" the vernacular and modern note of hope signified by the phrase "The Beginning"—as, indeed, the chivalric metaphor in age after age has a habit of doing again and again.

Notes

1. Howell Chickering, "Introduction," *The Study of Chivalry: Resources and Approaches,* ed. Howell Chickering and Thomas H. Seiler (Consortium for the Teaching of the Middle Ages, Kalamazoo, Mich.: Medieval Institute Publications, 1988), 3.

2. See David Carlson, "Religious Writers and Church Councils on Chivalry," in Chickering and Seiler, *Study of Chivalry,* 141–71.

3. Part 3 of "The Homecoming of Beortnoth Beorthelm's Son," *Essays and Studies by Members of the English Association,* n.s. 6 (1953):1–18; rpt. in *The Tolkien Reader* (New York: Ballantine Books, 1975), 19–24.

4. Carlson, "Religious Writers," 144.

5. Carlson, "Religious Writers," 143; the relevant documents are appended to the end of the article, 148–66.

6. The Proclamation of the Crusade by Pope Urban II (1095), in *The Crusades: A Documentary Survey*, ed. James A. Brundage (Milwaukee, Wisc.: Marquette University Press, 1962), 17–21.

7. Cited in Robert P. Miller, *Chaucer: Sources and Background* (New York: Oxford University Press, 1977), 202, 199.

8. *Social Chaucer* (Cambridge, Mass.: Harvard University Press, 1989), 1.

9. *The Book of Fayttes of Armes and of Chyualrie, translated and printed by William Caxton from the French original by Christine de Pisan*, ed. A. T. P. Byles, EETS, 189 (London: Humphrey Milford/Oxford University Press, 1932), 28–29 (1.9).

10. See her Prologue to *The Treasure of the City of Ladies or The Book of the Three Virtues*, trans. Sarah Lawson (Harmondsworth: Penguin, 1985), 31–32.

11. See Charity Cannon Willard, *Christine de Pizan: Her Life and Works* (New York: Persea, 1984), 186.

12. *The Once and Future King* (1939; rpt. New York: Berkley Books, 1966–1984), 638–39.

CONTRIBUTORS

Ross G. Arthur, associate professor of humanities at York University in Toronto, is the translator of *Jaufre: An Occitan Arthurian Romance* (1992) and the author of *Medieval Sign Theory and* Sir Gawain (1987) as well as articles on a variety of medieval English and French topics, including "On Editing Sexually Offensive Old French Texts," in *The Politics of Editing Medieval Texts* (1993).

Jane Chance, professor of English at Rice University, is author, editor, coeditor, and translator of numerous articles and books, including *The Genius Figure in Antiquity and the Middle Ages, Tolkien's Art: A "Mythology for England," Woman as Hero in Old English Literature, Mapping the Cosmos, Approaches to Teaching Sir Gawain and the Green Knight,* Christine de Pizan's *Epistre Othea, The Mythographic Art,* and *The Mythographic Chaucer.*

William T. Cotton, associate professor of English at Loyola University in New Orleans, is the author of "Fidelity, Suffering, and Humor in *Paris and Vienne*," in *Chivalric Literature* (1980), and "Teaching the Motifs of Chivalric Biography," in *The Study of Chivalry: Resources and Approaches* (1988).

Cynthia Ho, assistant professor of English at the University of North Carolina at Asheville, has completed a study on Robert Mannying's *Handlyng Synne.* She has also published on T. S. Eliot.

Jean E. Jost, an associate professor of English at Bradley University who coedits *Chaucer Yearbook: A Journal of Late Medieval Studies,* is author of *Ten Middle English Arthurian Romances: A Reference Guide* (1986) and articles on Chaucer and Malory.

Amos Lee Laine is Trinkle Professor of History at Hampden-Sydney College, Virginia, and coauthor, with Albert J. Geritz, of *John Rastell*. He is currently working on Thomas More's rhetoric about women and family for a collection on the rhetoric of politics and Renaissance women.

Karen S. Nicholas is an associate professor of history at the State University of New York College at Oswego. She is currently working on studies of the Low Countries.

Patricia Orr, independent scholar and president of Ocean Tec in Houston, received the Clifford Lefton Lawrence award for excellence in the writing of British history for her Rice University dissertation. She is also the author of "Pallas Athena and the Threefold Choice in Chaucer's *Troilus and Criseyde,*" in *The Mythographic Art* (1990).

Daniel F. Pigg, assistant professor of English at the University of Tennessee at Martin, has published on *Beowulf, The Dream of the Rood,* Chaucer, and Malory. He is currently completing a study on the N-Town *Mary Play* and medieval sign theory.

Liam O. Purdon, professor of English at Doane College, has published on *Beowulf, The Owl and the Nightingale, King Horn, Havelok,* the *Pearl*-Poet, Chaucer, and Spenser. He is currently completing a study on the Wakefield Master and technology.

Lois Roney, associate professor of English at Saint Cloud State University, is the author of *Chaucer's Knight's Tale and Theories of Scholastic Psychology* (1990) and coeditor of *Sign, Sentence, Discourse* (1989). She has also published articles on the *Wakefield Shepherds' Plays* and the *Canterbury Tales*.

John W. Schwetman, professor of English at Sam Houston State University, has published on Old English metrics and on the language of Russell Hoban's novel *Riddley Walker.* He is currently working on an edition of *The Battle of Agincourt,* a fifteenth-century narrative poem.

Cindy L. Vitto, associate professor of English at Rowan College of New Jersey, is the author of *The Virtuous Pagan in Middle English Literature* (1989) and articles on Chaucer and Margery Kempe.

Julian N. Wasserman, professor of English at Loyola University in New Orleans, is the author and coauthor of numerous essays on a variety of medieval topics, editor of essay collections on Chaucer and Edward Albee, coeditor of essay collections on the *Pearl*-Poet and medieval language theory, and coauthor of book-length studies on Gottfried von Strassburg, Thomas Hardy, and the *Pearl*-Poet.

INDEX